LIBRARY LIT. 2 –
The Best of 1971

edited by

BILL KATZ

The Scarecrow Press, Inc.
Metuchen, N. J.   1972

ISBN 0-8108-0519-7

Library of Congress Catalog Card Number 78-154842

CONTENTS

iii

INTRODUCTION

Here is the result of the second annual excursion into the land of library literature. The 1971 trip follows the map first used in 1970 (i. e. <u>Library Lit. --The Best of 1970</u>). The jurors and I have selected 30 articles which we believe to be the best published in 1971.

Some 200 magazines were examined for the period from November 1970 to November 1971. In our lead article, Celeste West points out that there are "over 500 library and documentation journals currently at large and multiplying in the world." Still, it requires no great skill or knowledge of the field to realize that the vast majority of these mags simply aren't worth considering in a serious attempt to isolate the best of library literature. Within a rather arbitrary 200, which includes magazines other than those given over to librarians, there is more then enough material. The problem is not one of quantity, but of quality--and the quality of magazines in respect of intellectual rigors and imagination is not always impressive.

The hunt for genuine quality in our field is a difficult one. As there are more and more journals, there seem to be fewer and fewer really significant texts, certainly less substantial contributions. Many articles deal with such trivia that they can be easily dismissed. The contrasting notion that other fields offer more stimulating journals is often heard. It is part of the librarian's masochistic tendencies, not a real view of the real world. Library literature, after all, is not the only field in which questions of quality arise. The problems of research and expression are found in all areas. And the careful reader will find much to support a distinct feeling of wrong-headed writing in literature indexed in everything from <u>Index Medicus</u> to the <u>Readers' Guide to Periodical Literature</u>. Neither specialist nor generalist has a monopoly on poor writing, self deception, or downright bad research.

Of course, as Celeste West points out, "We print too damn much." In a disturbing number of cases, the litera-

ture supports her view. Still, knowledge of this fact is
almost institutionalized and I am afraid here is one case
where knowledge is of little use. I think one may assert
with some confidence that in the years to come there will
be more additions to library literature, not fewer. The
sharpness and meaning of the contributions begin to lose
their edge, but it is inconceivable to me that this will
change. The institution is too large, too stabilized in its
lack of perception to change.

Which leads me to the point of this anthology. The
simple yet appalling fact is that there is too much written,
and the only confident way of handling it is to cut it down to
a manageable size. Multiplication can be handled by judicious subtraction, and that's what this is pretty much all
about. As editor I searched the mags, came up with well
over a hundred selections. To these were added choices
made by students and suggestions sent in by contributing
librarians. By judicious reading and an effort to strike a
balance in various areas the number was reduced to 75.
Given 75 articles to consider, the jurors cut it back to the
magic 30--actually there were 33 but the extra three were a
safety. Some of the 30 failed to give permission to reprint,
or, in the case of this edition, simply did not reply to their
mail, publisher and author alike. So, three second choices
were picked up.

In terms of scope, this year's effort is much like
last year's. We intentionally have maintained the same subject areas and divisions. Interestingly enough, the part
given over to "The Social Prerogative" is smaller--which
seems to follow the general pattern of retrenchment or re-
grouping of the counter culture. Conversely, the sections on
"Libraries and Librarians" and "Technical Services" have
grown, while "Communication and Education" holds its own.
In terms of authors, there is only one second appearance--
David Peele, who in the 1970 anthology contributed an
article on performance ratings. The balance of journals
remains fairly much the same, although this year more
magazines are represented than last.

And while no first prizes are given, it should be
pointed out that the most frequently mentioned article was the
one by Ellsworth Mason on the computer (or "the great gas
bubble"). The jurors tried to find a suitable reply to
Mason's frontal attack on the hardware store, but nothing
quite came up to challenge his confident study. The general popularity of the findings, it seems to me, can be laid

to the fact that librarians simply don't trust the machine in their gardens, and when anyone comes along to give them a rationale for taking it apart they proclaim him hero. Of course, Mason is a villain in the mechanics' script, and perhaps sometime in 1972 one of them will pen an adequate reply for next year's anthology.

No one is going to agree with all of our choices, and this seems particularly true for the man or woman whose splendid notion of librarianship has never been committed to paper. I think Paul Dunkin, in his kind review of the first anthology, brought up this very point. The language of silence is an interesting idea. It's also a damn safe one which gives encouragement to egos, not to anthologies.

Neither the jurors nor I have proof that the 30 articles selected here are really the best. But a certain body of evidence, based upon experience and taste, indicates that in most cases we are at least close enough to the truth to warrant no apologies. Refined by the selection process, it seems to me the 30 entries are in the best tradition of library literature, and can be offered with confidence to the librarian and student. I hope this effort will encourage both readers and writers to follow a similar path.

Meanwhile, please send me candidates for next year. The reception of the first volume is good enough to warrant continuation of the series--a series which I and the jurors hope will encourage by subtraction, not multiplication, good library literature.

William A. Katz

Albany, New York
January 1972

ACKNOWLEDGMENTS

Jurors: The editor wishes to thank the jurors who carefully selected the 30 articles reprinted here: Patricia Schuman, associate editor, School Library Journal; Jane Stevens, editor, Library Literature, H. W. Wilson Co.; Robert Wedgeworth, editor, Library Resources & Technical Services; and Eric Moon, president, Scarecrow Press.

Consultants: The editor, also, wishes to thank those who so generously suggested entries for consideration: Jerry Shields, American Libraries; Katherine Eaton, Bureau of Government Research, University of Oregon; Sant Ram Bhatia, Indian Librarian; Rose Z. Sellers, Brooklyn College Library; Julie and Linda of the Liberated Librarians' Newsletter; Poul A. Christiansen, Restaurator Press; Janet Bailey, Special Libraries, Ervin Gaines, Minneapolis Public Library; Josef Stummvoll, National Library, Vienna; Lee Ash, American Notes & Queries; Jim Wells, Newberry Library Bulletin; Richard Dougherty, College & Research Libraries; Paul Murphy, Tennessee Librarian; Beryl E. Hoyt, Wisconsin Library Bulletin; Kathleen Imhoff, Horseshoe Bend Regional Library, Dadeville, Alabama; P. N. Kaula, Banaras Hindu University; Mary Frances Johnson, School Libraries; R. Luck, Berne, Switzerland; Perry Morrison, PNLA Quarterly; Martha Williams, Princeton Public Library; and a half dozen others whose names were not included (or clear) but whose suggestions were most helpful.

Editors and Authors: Finally a word of thanks to the editors of the magazines who were kind enough to allow reprinting; and to the authors whose works are honoring this anthology and the literature as a whole.

Prologue

STOP! THE PRINT IS KILLING ME!

by Celeste West

Reprinted by permission from Synergy (No. 33) Summer 1971, p. 2-5.

There are over 500 library and documentation journals currently at large and multiplying in the world. [1] Over 300 of them were gamely annotated by Winckler in 1967--descriptively, but not critically. [2] Therefore, all the annotations sound about the same; one can't quite separate the Tweedledee from the Tweedledum. Even the titles look so despairingly similar that Bookbird was almost refreshing, as was the candid elitism of the ALA Public Library Division's Just Between Ourselves. Bill Katz did have the temerity to critically rate 42 library periodicals. [3] There were only 13 above mediocre. Sic transit gloria.

I think a generous estimation would be that there are, in this country, about 20 library mags worth the paper. Eric Moon, previous editor of the venerable Lj, [4] is kinder. He says there are only three times too many American library periodicals. [5] Thus, every jackass article can be assured an outlet. Almost everything Moon rejected in nine years editorship was published in another journal. [6] Meanwhile, Library Literature is indexing fewer and fewer American titles! [7]

Why is it that we, ourselves on the front lines of the print explosion, so prodigiously feed the beast? The heavy-footed paragraphs above provide one answer. They pad a perfectly obvious point: WE PRINT TOO DAMN MUCH, with a supporting cast of previous commentary, familiar old props, and foreign phrases. Any dog's body can ferret out citations from "the literature." Of course, some are more dogged than others. I, for instance, lost all my footnotes and cannot therefore substantiate anything I have just said. Luckily, it was obvious. For the foot fetishists out there, in lieu of my own carelessness, may I recommend the January

1971 Journal of Library History (p. 41), with an article
which boasts (yes) 134 footnotes!

Alas, this sort of talk is NOT cheap. Simply consider the trees which perish that librarians might publish.
Or consider the time and anguish spent writing (and reading)
those articles which were birthed for cold professional ag-
grandizement, rather than from passion. Pages are expensive and time priceless. This page of Synergy, counting
material costs and salaries, is worth about 4¢. If you are
only getting 2¢ worth, write the editor (postage due) immediately, and tell her to stop wasting everyone's time,
money, and trees. Do this with every irrelevant library
publication you get. Make suggestions. Tell them if all
you want is a good reviewing service, what regular departments you need, etc. Give them a chance to change; cancel
if they don't.

Library literature has been a drag because librarians
passively take it. Bitch, baby. Bitch! Do you really enjoy the finely printed old quarterly your state library association puts out, or do you simply want a current newsletter of state activity? Do you find Bowker's Bedmates,
lively as they are, to be so full of advertising they should
be free to libraries like any publishers' catalogs? Couldn't
the Winsome Library Bulletin print up zonky center fold-outs
suitable for display? Have you asked the editor of American Libraries once, just once, to write up that official part
stoned? Couldn't there be some service started whereby
librarians could get reviews of the Great Unreviewed--those
60%-plus of all books published?

If all editors ignore you, and the plodders plod on,
there is only one thing to do. Get Kirkus, PW, and/or
Choice reviews to cover the waterfront, read deeply in your
subject speciality, open your eyes, look at the world. Wink.
And, if you still feel the need of a library journal, then
start one.

That's how Synergy came about. At BARC, we found
that all too often, our card catalog, indexes, and selecting
tools were simply rear-view mirrors. We needed a publication which discussed current issues, movements, and
ideologies currently, and provided bibliographic back-up.
San Francisco is a trend mecca, whether it be communal
living, campus riots, light shows, Indian power, the warehouse movement, food conspiracies, gay liberation, inde-

pendent film making.... You name it, and we've got it--
but not at the library unless somebody has the time and concern to pull together the elusive printed material. For example, on even a highly topical, persistent issue such as
Women's Liberation, the library slumbered along until 1970,
when the requisite commercial interest was generated for
the big publishers to finally get on the bandwagon. A four-
to five-year lag in this case! Meanwhile, there had been
whole magazines, newspapers, small and radical press publications covering the topic. How many mad housewives
lost the old "library faith," etc., when all they could get
on the shelves were happy homebody mags and Helen Gurley
Brown? I'm sure the same type of library lapse was repeated for many other movements which began in the sixties.

In the information game, timing is obviously important. Many librarians realize this, and would like to order
say, a newspaper on Men's Liberation, like Brother (1721
Grove St., Berkeley, Ca. 94709; 25¢/issue, sliding subscription rates. Go see the movie, "Carnal Knowledge," if
you are hesitating). All one needs in this case is a con-
sciousness-raising nudge and the ordering info. That's
what Synergy tries to do.

We also try to put Synergy together as synergistically
as possible, so the resulting publication will differ from,
and hopefully, go beyond solo individual efforts. At any
rate, it's more fun to see what "grows" out of shared responsibility, rather than is hammered out by isolated command. The whole staff decides on a topic by reason of its
social relevance and uniqueness, as well as by the reference
questions and suggestions we get. The topics which proved
truly "relevant" were the ones we researched, wrote up,
and which actually changed us. We've just begun a policy
of revolving editorship, so that every staff member can
have the pleasure of making a magazine. This way, responsibilities and hassles can also be shared, and ego-
tripping kept minimal. However, no editor can really bully
the writers much, because none of us volunteer to work on
an article unless we know or really care about the topic.
Nobody is drafted. Since almost all writing is done on the
librarians' free time, it can't be just a duty thing. Besides, the actual craft of writing is still a hassle for most
of us, so we have to give a damn about setting it down.

What keeps us going is the overwhelming response to
Synergy. We can only print 2000 copies/run and go o.p. in

a month; we get over 50 letters/week.   This is not because
Synergy is that good.   It is amateurish and incredibly uneven.   But it is sought out because there is a huge demand
for social change and counter-culture topics--treated from
the library angle.   Librarians have had their association
journals on "official" super-structure meanderings, their
magazines of technocrats' tips, their big fat magazines to
review big fat publishers' books--in fact, they have hundreds
of library navel-gazing magazines!   Yet, many librarians
care more about the outside world: Who's changing it, how
much, and why.   A growing number do not want to be "disinterested merchants in the marketplace of ideas."   They
are partisan, mainly for the "alternative life styles," which
don't give a damn for domination, but everything for cooperation and tolerance.   These are the ombudsmen of the information game and they are
for sharing its wealth, so that
all can escape the draft, build
a dome, grow dope, learn to
meditate, hear music ... just
think what a Whole Earth
Card Catalog would hold. ...

Obviously these librar-
ians need an independent journal which opts for social
change, describes why and
wherefore, and rounds up
good, little-known resources
to order.   Do you realize no
widely distributed library
mag is independent of associations, institutions, or publishing interests?   Synergy
is dependent on the bounty of
a Federal grant and the approval of S. F. Public Library.
(SFPL is certainly a benevolent master, but there are alter-
cations; two years ago it could not allow the letters LSD,
nor at present allow Synergy reprinted at cost rather than
profit.)

It's true: Freedom of the press is guaranteed only
to those who own one.   Surely someone out there, into cross-
currents-hippie-yippie-skippie library liberation should get
one!   It doesn't have to be off-set sophisticated, and likewise hugely expensive.   Get a good duplicator (mimeo) like

Detail on SFPL card file done by Whole
Earth person (photo - D. L. Maness).

Gestetner ($650 used), preferably one with an electronic
stencil cutter so you can reproduce line drawings and solid
lettering, but that's another $1, 000. If you get an electric
typewriter, it will cut a better stencil, and on an IBM Se-
lectric you can get a change of alphabets like this for
about $20/alphabet. For banner heads and captions, buy
sheets of pressure sensitive letters, like **these** 👉 of "Let-

raset" (95¢ sheet). Use recyclable paper and recyclable
pictures. (Dick Sutphen, Studio, Inc. , Box 628, Scottsdale,
Ariz. 85252, publishes books of funky pictures, (c) free.
Actually most drawings are, in practice, (c) free if you just
give credit.) Create new patterns of seeing. Remember
we ALREADY print too much, so don't just repackage the
same. Above all, take your mission more seriously than
you take yourself.

A fine example of the mighty mimeo medium is the
New Jersey Librarians for Social Responsibility Newsletter,
edited by Martha Williams at Princeton Public Library,
Princeton, N. J. 08540. It is a local call to arms, a cur-
rent awareness bibliographic guide--and its electronic sten-
cil illustrations are mighty leading.... Other communications among (rather than at) librarians are the national SRRT
Newsletter, Librarians Tribe, Sipapu, and The Liberated
Librarians' Newsletter (Mrs. Linda Katz, 2200 Benjamin
Franklin Parkway, Apt. E-1708, Philadelphia, Pa. 19130).
Brian Nielson, a library school student at State University
of NY at Albany, edits a good student newsletter, LSAA
News. Its kind of forum could be used anywhere to give
students a voice and identity, and dead-head curricula would
perhaps fall to the power of the pen. The American
Library Society's quarterly, Concerning Libraries (1411
Northside Blvd. , Apt. 33, South Bend, Ind. 46615, $2. 50/
yr.), edited by 13-year-old John Harlan, is a comer. Another print potential for the young-in-head is the staff newsletter. These can be trippy. The Newsletter of the Falls
Church Public Library (Va.) is a total joy, done for both
staff and patrons. Together. How many public libraries
really feel that way? Synch, from Portland State University
Library (Oregon), seems put together by Merry Pranksters,
Tolkinds, Fire Brands, and assorted god'nose folk. All
these may be the beginnings of an alternative library press
network. Drop in.

If not now, when?

Part I:

LIBRARIES AND LIBRARIANS

PHILOSOPHY, PURPOSE AND FUNCTION
IN LIBRARIANSHIP

by Richard Emery

This, the Library Association Prize Essay, 1971, is reprinted by permission from the (British) Library Association Record, 73(7) July 1971, p. 127-129.

The tendency of librarians to become immersed in the day-to-day realities of their work, to adopt a basically pragmatic as opposed to theoretical outlook, has been pinpointed by a number of writers, none more forcibly than Pierce Butler:

> Unlike his colleagues in other fields of social activity the librarian is strangely uninterested in the theoretical aspects of his profession. He seems to possess a unique immunity to that curiosity which elsewhere drives modern man to attempt, somehow, an orientation of his particular labours with the main stream of human life. The librarian apparently stands alone in the simplicity of his pragmatism: a rationalization of each immediate technical process by itself seems to satisfy his intellectual interest. Indeed any endeavour to generalize these rationalizations into a professional philosophy appears to him, not merely futile, but positively dangerous. [1]

This is not to deny the necessity of facing day-to-day realities, the value of a factual approach to particular problems, or the relevance of facts to philosophy. John Dewey remarked that "... if a philosophy starts to reason out its conclusions without definition and constant regard to the concrete expressions that define the problem for thought, it becomes speculative in a way that justifies contempt."[2] On a lower plane of thought, the formulation of library services for underdeveloped countries must obviously be based on experience in similar areas and developed countries

18

if the formulation is to be successfully interpreted and applied. Such a planning process must involve the collection of data by observation and tapping of human experience, plus its explanation and evaluation.

If, however, the factual approach is not to lead to narrow viewpoints and unjustifiable inconsistencies of practice within one library or the library profession as a whole, then it must be linked to some theoretical framework, which will provide bases for thought as well as interpretation of factual knowledge. Theory aids observation and description as well as providing schemes of analysis by codifying existing knowledge and facilitating its storage and transmission. Theories may contain some elements that do not refer to observables, though this need not necessarily invalidate their usefulness. What remains true is that they still provide a focus for analysis and criticism. Furthermore, elements that do not appear at the present time to be valid or applicable to existing developments may later witness practical orientation.

Philosophy

The concept of philosophy similarly involves links between fact and theory. Although it involves a quest for truth through logical reasoning, rather than factual observation, it can encompass the study of things and their causes, whether theoretical or practical. It may be confusing and somewhat incorrect to equate philosophy too closely with theory, but at an elementary level philosophy may be defined as the theory of a subject matter taken as a whole, containing principles which bind together a variety of particular truths and facts, and requiring a certain harmony of theory and practice. [3]

Philosophers are not agreed as to whether their study of a particular form of activity or class of thing should be concerned with meaning and the related concept of value; hence evaluative appraisals are more easily applied to the notion of function (discussed below). Omitting meaning and its implication of value from a definition of philosophy leaves concepts of critical discussion relating to the true nature of a thing or activity. Philosophical examination involves a critical examination of the general principles and fundamental beliefs underlying a particular subject. It examines causes, in the widest sense, or the ultimate basis upon which the existence of society depends.

Thus a philosophy of librarianship could critically
examine beliefs such as "libraries help promote individuality" or "libraries further the aims of civilization"; the
basis upon which libraries exist, that is conceptions of their
nature in relation to society in general; and the relationship
of librarianship to other branches of knowledge.   Further,
it could usefully examine such formulated statements as
"The cultural motivation of librarianship is the promotion
of wisdom in the individual and the community. "[4]

Yet these discussions would not be completely satisfactory unless consideration was also given to questions of
the nature of civilization, the purpose of the community,
and so on.   In short, fundamental discussions involved in the
questions enumerated in the paragraph above relate to the
bases of society or civilization, of which libraries, like any
other institution, form only a part.   Libraries are an element of society, a function through which society's aims
may be sought and possibly achieved.   As a result philosophical discussions of librarianship will not get very far,
will not be very fundamental, in comparison, for example,
with discussions of political philosophy.

Irwin correctly suggests that the term philosophy be
applied "only to those fields of thought and actions which,
in either their universal or individual aspects, can be regarded as departments of philosophy itself, and to those
major branches of knowledge which have by nature definite
philosophical affinities. "   Insight into what is meant by
"philosophical thought" or "philosophical affinities" is provided
in his discussion of the philosophy of religion, when he defines the area of study as being the origin and purpose of
the universe and the springs of human activities. [5]

Taking a further example, not used by Irwin, political philosophy can be considered in similar terms; political
philosophy is concerned with human activities in so far as
they relate to the grouping of individuals within particular
communities (individual political societies) or relations between communities (international society).

Librarianship, with its more limited areas of activity
and conception, and its study are better viewed in terms of
theory or theoretical principles than philosophy.

So far the discussion of the "philosophy of librarianship" has been related largely to the study of librarianship,
as might be pursued in library school studies.   Its limitations are perhaps even more clearly seen in a consideration
of library activities.   This consideration is not meant to
imply that librarianship is a series of administrative techniques rather than a branch of scholarship or learning,
merely that it demonstrates the banality of the phrase
"philosophy" when applied to librarianship.

Librarianship may include amongst its goals or purposes such themes as the perpetuation of knowledge, the
values of civilization, contributions to the life of particular
communities and promotion of individuality.   Yet the librarian performs secondary tasks, related more to the communication of knowledge than its application or creation. 6
A librarian can obviously create knowledge in the sense,
say, of creating facts and figures relating to a planned
library building, or reporting the social conditions of his
community resultant from a local library-based survey.

The library as an institution is not, however, dedicated to the creation of knowledge as a university might be.
Furthermore, although it seeks to assist in the utilization
of knowledge by effective dissemination, it is scarcely able
to exert a controlling influence over the use made of materials it houses (i. e. the application of knowledge).   The
most one can say is that libraries contribute to the aims of
society or civilization by pursuing a secondary, albeit an
invaluable, function.   They help further the better utilization of existing human resources rather than their creation.
This argument obviously allows that libraries have purposes
and functions.

Purpose

Purposeful, or goal oriented, activity is evident in
many aspects of social life.   Individuals may be motivated
in their actions by personal and immediate, or empirical,
forces, yet the general purpose of society tends to prevail
and mould individual actions by the process of socialization.
If this does not hold true for any particular society in any
particular period of time, if what a majority of people believe about society induces them to act differently from pre-
conceived notions of societal action, then one can speak in
terms of a society breaking up and/or a new one being

established with its own particular goals.   Beliefs referred
to here, or ideas held, tend to come from two sources,
namely individual experience and the experience of others.
As Butler observes, while the first may be primary, the
second is more important.[7] It is more pervading, especially
during a person's formative years; the communicated experience of others helps direct the individual's experience,
and this is another factor favouring acceptance of existing
societal goals.

It is possible, of course, to speak of the purpose of
an individual librarian, his conception of the purposes of
librarianship, and of the purpose of librarianship or the library profession as a whole.   Should the two contradict,
solution to any apparent inconsistencies of thought can be
eradicated by the notion of relative goals; the goals of librarianship may be viewed as a rationalization of the thought
of the majority of librarians, living and dead.

The fact that a basic philosophy cannot exist for a
secondary activity such as librarianship has meant that
many writers, supposedly discussing the philosophy of librarianship, have in fact been directing their attention to
purpose,[8] sets of professional ideals or guides for conduct,[9]
or function.[10]

Purpose is something that man, individually or collectively, sets before himself as an ideal, an object to be
attained.   It forms an end to whose fulfilment material and
human resources are diversely employed.   Ends may be of
a purely practical nature, such as the establishment of a
service for housebound residents in a particular town, or
they may be intangible aims, those which may be said to
place the library in its social context.

Since the latter library goals are of a less deter-
minate nature than, say, those of industry, working on a
profit motive, not only may diversifications be great but
assessment as to the progress a library or the library profession is making toward the attainment of its ideals can be
difficult.   It is possible to examine progress in so far as an
increase in the number of volumes per head of population
is concerned; similarly a more favourable ratio of staff to
readers can be spoken of as progress.   Yet it is certainly
more difficult to say whether a public library is making
an increased contribution to community education and well-
being, or a university library is further contributing to the

volume and quality of scientific research by an increase in
its stock.   Nevertheless, as seen in the opening discussion
of theoretical approaches, this argument, that purposes and
progress towards them are not easily determined, does not
invalidate the value of purpose or aims.

McClellan speaks in terms of the "purpose" of libraries in general and "obligations" of particular libraries, [11]
but really the two terms, plus that of a third, namely aim,
are readily interchangeable.   They all involve elements of
future attainment and ideal practice.

Discussions of library purposes usually indicate that
the library (i. e. largely the public library, although the concept should involve all libraries) is an instrument in society
which should seek to assist in the best utilization of existing
resources and the enlightened development of the individual.
One of the best discussions of public library purpose is that
given by McColvin in his 1952 presidential address to the
Library Association, [12] although he speaks in terms of
function rather than purpose.   Ranganathan's five laws of
library science[13] combine purpose and function.   "Every book
his reader" can, for example, be viewed as embodying the
principle of encouraging individual development and enlightenment, whereas "Save the time of the reader" may be seen
as a functional activity contributing to purposes listed above.
The fact that Ranganathan's laws are often referred to in
terms of philosophical discussion is evidence of lack of
clarity in theoretical discussions of librarianship.

It may further be argued, as it is by Benge, that the
theoretical foundations of librarianship are weak because
there are certain unresolved and possibly inherent contra-
dictions. [14]   "For what purpose" is to Benge a vital consideration in discussing the role of libraries in society.   Yet
he relates this not only to libraries in general, but more
specifically to the use to which material and information
supplied by the librarian is put.   In doing so he successfully spotlights the dilemma of the librarian who is called
upon to supply information for what he regards as a totally
evil purpose. [15]   The dictum of J. D. Cowley, repeated by
Foskett, "no politics, no religion, no morals, " or the notion of "relative goals" referred to earlier, scarcely helps
resolve the problem for the librarian with a conscience.
Butler's statement that "a major phase of the library's
service to any individual reader will be to assist him to an
effective method for achieving his own private purpose, so

long as this is not anti-social"[16] indicates limits of library
service, but provides no theoretical solution to the problem
of library censorship, or definite guidance to individual
action.

Such considerations are important since the library is
part of society and its facilities affect implementation of
society aims.   Since, however, discussion of the latter can
be marked by violent disagreement, to identify weaknesses
in the theoretical foundations of librarianship is not to make
a crushing condemnation of librarianship in general.   From
one point of view, the very fact that there is controversy
surrounding theoretical foundations provides evidence that
there is such a thing as theoretical foundations; from another point of view it indicates that perhaps more discussion of theoretical dilemmas, as opposed to purely administrative arrangements and mechanical techniques, is required.

Function

Earlier it was stated that libraries contribute to the
aims of society or civilization by pursuing a secondary,
albeit an invaluable function.   Libraries pursue a functional
role in society, a means of communication between knowledge and people towards commonly agreed society aims.   If
this is accepted then, of course, library purposes can be
described as societal functions, and in this sense McColvin's
terminology is justified.   Looked at more specifically, librarianship functions need to be viewed at a different level,
one below that of librarianship purpose.

Function explains purposeful action, that is function
is usually thought of in terms of activity by which purposes
are fulfilled.   Not all sequences of behaviour lead to necessary or intended consequences, but the results of action do
provide a means of evaluating functions in the light of their
contribution to library purposes.

The jobs or tasks of individual persons and institutions should be designed with theoretical concepts in mind;
we can then speak in terms of role, duty or work, as well
as function, and more accurately formulate and evaluate
these tasks.   In making such judgments requisites of function should be borne in mind, and consequent evaluations
may be phrased as questions such as: 1   whether the re-

moval or loss of a particular role would result in the disruption or dissolution of a particular department or library, or 2 its change markedly affects library purposes. Judgments may then be made as to whether it is desirable to alter a particular librarian's or department's function, and so on.

The functions of librarianship, means to the ends of library purposes, are normally thought of as being recognition, collection, organization, preservation and dissemination of materials. Thus the Roberts Report stated "the essential function of a public library is to supply to any reader or group of readers, the books and related materials for which they may ask."[17] Such general descriptions provide areas of activity within which standards of service provision may be made. Not all these functions will be relevant to all libraries. Thus a special library may seek to preserve in any permanent form only its own company's report literature and documents; a professional association's library may limit dissemination to its own members. This is an indication of the fact that function is to be related to library purposes.

The functions of a library may be restricted by administrative difficulties (e. g. , staff shortages) or by shortsightedness on the part of the librarian and his ruling committee. Even if they are not subject to such limitations, however, individual library functions can and do vary due simply to different policy formulations in relation to purpose. Thus a public library whose administrative hierarchy views its purpose as being basically of an educational nature may well restrict collection of materials in the fields of light fiction and biography. An academic institution may be geared largely to the pursuit of research, as opposed to undergraduate studies, and this will correspondingly affect library provision; alternatively its librarian may unreasonably emphasize the custodial function of his institution.

Value

The introduction to this essay indicated certain advantages to be gained from a combined theoretical and empirical approach to librarianship and its problems. The essay has attempted to show that some confused thinking exists relative to definition of library philosophy, purpose and function. Such lack of clarity in thought endangers the

precise formulation of library goals and their implementation
by means of realistic functional activities.   Clear formulation of purpose and function aids economical and wise action.
Finally, by indicating areas of purpose and by providing
standards of service, some attention to theoretical concepts
can provide a sense of continuity and unity to the library
profession as a whole and help modify shortsightedness
wherever it occurs.

References

1.   Butler, P.   An Introduction to Library Science.   Univ.
        of Chicago Press, 1933, repr. 1961, p. xi-xii.
2.   Dewey, J.   The Sources of Scientific Education.
        Liveright, 1929, p. 56.
3.   Dewey, J.   "Philosophy."   In: J. M. Baldwin, ed.,
        Dictionary of Philosophy and Psychology.   Vol. 2.
        Macmillan, 1902, p. 291.
4.   Butler, P.   "Librarianship as a Profession."   Libr.
        Q., 21(4) October 1951, p. 246.
5.   Irwin, R.   Librarianship: Essays on Applied Bibli-
        ography.   Grafton, 1949, p. 20-21.
6.   Etzioni makes the distinction between creation and
        application, and communication of knowledge in a
        discussion of semi-professional organizations, i. e.
        those involving less than five years training and
        not involving questions of life and death.   A.
        Etzioni.   Modern Organizations.   Prentice-Hall,
        1964, p. 87.
7.   Butler, P.   "The Cultural Function of the Library."
        Libr. Q., 22(2) April 1952, p. 82.
8.   E. g., Broadfield, A.   A Philosophy of Librarianship.
        Grafton, 1949.
9.   E. g., Foskett, D. J.   The Creed of a Librarian--No
        Politics, No Religion, No Morals.   Library Asso-
        ciation (RSIS, NW Group), 1962.
10.   E. g., Nitecki, J. Z.   "Public interest and the theory
        of philosophy."   Coll. Res. Libr., 25(4) July
        1954, p. 272-3.
11.   Quoted in Sturt, R.   "Module: the Service Unit in
        Future Planning."   Library Association.   Pro-
        ceedings of the Public Libraries Conference, 1970,
        p. 55.
12.   McColvin, L. R.   "The function of public libraries."
        Libr. Ass. Rec., 54(5) May 1952, p. 158-161.
13.   Ranganathan, S. R.   The Five Laws of Library Science.

          2nd ed.   Madras Library Association, 1957.
14.   Benge, R. C.   Libraries and Cultural Change.   Bingley,
          1970, p. 254.
15.   Ibid. , p. 250.
16.   Butler, P.   An Introduction to Library Science, op.
          cit. , p. 106.
17.   Ministry of Education.   The Structure of the Public
          Library Service in England and Wales.   para. 31:
          1958-59 Cmnd. 660.

WHAT PRICE PROFESSIONALISM?

by Renee Feinberg

"In the library you can take a deep breath and walk out and face everything" [Student at Performing Arts High School].

When I wrote up my résumé the summer before last, after my first year as a school librarian, I was so impressed I couldn't reread it to check for grammatical errors. I left that to the friend who typed it for me. She assured me it read correctly. What I wrote had impressed me so much I couldn't read it. I had written this impressive résumé because I was out of a job.

September, 1969. High School of Performing Arts, New York City. In the school system, new staff appointees arrive the Wednesday before the Friday (when old staff return) before the Monday. The library when shown to me was barricaded--large teacher desks, three of them, in a classroom-size library. I smiled at those who found the library for me, and who pointed with pride and said that those adorable travel posters from Greece and Spain had to stay, and split.

The next day I wore my jeans and my special six-pocket Mexican work shirt, carrying my screwdriver, hammer, and pliers, my scissors, penknife, two reels of masking tape, dust rags, paper flowers, posters, crazy contact paper and, ripping off the tallest ladder in the school, ten foot, took down the travel posters, put up ones of movie stars; borrowed a dolly to move out the desks....

FURNITURE CAN'T BE MOVED OFF THE FLOOR!

"Hello, I'm the new librarian.   Do you need a desk?
A file cabinet? A chalk board?"

THE CHALK BOARD WAS BOUGHT OUT OF
LIBRARY FUNDS FOR THE LIBRARY.   DON'T
MOVE IT.

DO YOU REALIZE THERE'S A WAITING LIST
FOR TEACHERS WHO WANT FILE CABINETS?
THE PREVIOUS LIBRARIAN DEMANDED THEM
FOR MAGAZINES.

On Friday, my friend Lillian Shapiro introduced me
to a date stamp, pointed out that books were double stacked
on each shelf, kissed me and left.

Monday.   The opening of school.   I dumped back
issues in boxes for students, put some large art books on
the tables, and turned on the radio.   The first order of the
new term was to OK uncleared library accounts so students
could get their new program cards.   Wow! How-do-you-do
authority! I got to meet a few delinquent library users.
We agreed to talk someday about their debts, library fines,
and overdues.

Some of last year's student aides dropped in to sign
up for service credit and wondered how they were to take
care of circulation and control without each of them having
a desk.   One student explained that a great many overdue
notices had to be sent since books were only checked out
overnight.   The other aide shelved and received books because the students weren't allowed to go to the shelves.   In
her spare time she helped collect the fine money.

I explained why I had removed the desks and put
books on the tables, and asked if they didn't think that, in
a school with only 600 students, we might dispense with
formalities, fines, and overdues, just letting students keep
the books until they had finished them.   They didn't think
so.

I turned up the radio, walked to the fire escape, and
watched a frisbee game in the courtyard below.   It's an old
school, city elementary, baroque type, five floors' worth.
(Sophomores direct new freshmen to the swimming pool on
the fifth floor.)

And so I dusted each morning, seized some bulletin
boards around the school, walked through the halls with my
pass jangling keys ... ["Hey, the librarian wears earrings"]
... sat in the teachers room ... ["Yes, I did go to Scars-
dale High"] ... spent lots of time writing post cards to "Inc.,"
museums, college admission offices ... sent out some innocent questionnaires to students about their preferred paperback titles, to teachers about their favorite magazine titles,
and wondered what the hell I was doing sitting in an empty
library.

"Where's the little lady with glasses with the little
file you'd put your 10¢ into?"
"That Belmondo or Bogart?"
"Look at these movie stars from the olden days."

The Board of Education began its rain of directives,
circulars, memoranda and supplements and new instructions.
Seems I had to spend about $250 on a book order, ON
LIST. Some more money was to be spent OFF LIST. That's
a dollar per pupil or about $600. The New York City list
came in. Wow! Those titles. ... The 1000-page list and
its supplements are an unending series of titles, titles,
titles. I was unfamiliar with the books, books. There
weren't any reference tools in the library, but Bowker was
up the block. During the day I familiarized myself with the
collection, asked the staff and students about needs and
preferences, spent my afternoons in the Bowker library,
and soon gave up. Time is the great leveler of good intentions. Money, too, sets limits. Once I really realized
how few books I could buy with the allotment, I took out
the latest supplement and plowed through those few sections
whose subject content I knew well, and had students from
the drama, dance, and music departments advise me in
other areas.

I think most of my time was spent copying the order
from inside the book to the front and juggling numbers of
copies to make sure I fell within the allotment. It is
always essential to work backwards, from the given money
and time to the preferred books and methods. So much for
hindsight. At the time, however, as a new librarian handling
new procedures, I had to deal with patronizing, noninforma-
tive answers, with deceit and indifference, and with an attitude of don't bother headquarters--even though the decen-
tralized school program had brought specialized high school
libraries directly under "headquarters." But no matter. I

prefer to work things out myself, and the message I was getting was to do that.

LAST YEAR'S BOOK ORDER IS IN THE OFFICE. "I don't think all of last year's money was spent." SHE WASN'T A LICENSED LIBRARIAN. "Well, where's the money? Can I spend it now?" I DON'T KNOW. "Who Knows?" WHO KNOWS?

"Can you prepare a list of books for dance history? Historical fiction?"
"Where's Shakespeare?"
"Hey, man, no Panther paper?"
"Where's WNEW on this radio?"
"You oughta get Psychology Today, New York, Ramparts, Scanlon's, Zapp. We'll make a list. Got any money"?
"You've created a human environment here, but-----WHERE'S YOUR PASS?"

THOSE STUDENTS ARE CUTTING, FOR YOUR INFORMATION. THEY WERE NOT EXCUSED TO GO TO THE LIBRARY.

In time I heard about the school's furniture fund and invited an architect friend down. She planned to pull two stacks out from against the wall and turn them perpendicular to the wall, creating aisles and freeing an area so I could put in two new stacks. I informed the principal in a covering letter, enclosing a scale drawing of the planned change and requesting him to order two new book stacks. He forwarded my request to maintenance.

The students began to come, godblessem, and with them, the excitement of young people capable of articulating their needs and interests, as yet unwilling to demand service. In time ...

"I'm writing a term paper on Women's Lib. You've gotta have something. You wear Women's Lib shoes."
"Renee, is it Canada or jail if I don't register?"
"Hey, where are the sign-out cards for these paperbacks? Take it?"
"I walked out of class."
"No fines?"
"He's got a $10 habit."
"Can I take out five?"

"But I returned it.   I put it on the mess on your desk. "

I love them--their entrances and exits from the fire escape, the messages they left me on the sign-out cards, their patience as I learned the library, learned what they needed and when.   They taught me well.

"Tell Scott he left his shoes under the magazine rack. "
"Why can't we eat here today?"
"Can we stay till four?"
"Listen, I've no time, but I need to borrow that encyclopedia. "
"How do I add a bibliography to my term paper. "
"Renee, you got Portnoy?   The Godfather?   Dr. Hip?"
"I've gotta tear this out. "
"Where's your tracing paper?"
"Can I use your typewriter?"
"That record player stinks. "
"Renee, the WHOOPIE LADIES are out, give me a pass back to class. "
"Can I use the library for my acting class?   They need an environment that's alive to come alive.   Let me try it on your lunch hour. "

By now, in response to student requests, I began to draft counsel in the library.   Hearing conversations about the draft in the library made me realize how little informa- tion was available.

As the students began to organize to pressure for changes in the school, the library became a focal point for planning and comforting.   The place had become the kid's place with radio, flowers, I. F. Stone, posters, a place for a good time, a haven from class.

"Renee, you've got to stay this afternoon.   We need a place to meet. "

They stayed, and they stayed late, though they came from the five boroughs and often worked in the evenings. They spoke of school, of intimidation, of arbitrary rule, of harassment and embarrassment.   They shed tears, and they consoled each other, and they reached out and organized.

They sat down one morning in midwinter, a small group, by the sink in the basement lunchroom. Nobody knew. They held sings about the war, black people, students, me and you. Others dropped by to talk to them, stayed a while, and returned to class.

GET BACK TO CLASS OR YOU'LL BE SUS-PENDED.

The students remained. As the threats escalated, others milled around. By noon, as word had got around, the school sat down with those four students in the basement, protesting the world they had inherited and the school that intimidated them. They spoke to each other, a small community who had recognized each other but hadn't had time to say hello. Parents rushed down to protect those who were threatened with immediate suspension. Even the principal descended from 135th Street to this annex to meet with the students whose school he regulated and whose faces he had never seen.

The students of Performing Arts remained that afternoon and spoke to each other. And everyone listened, and no one interrupted his friend. The teaching staff was extraneous to the educational process conducted that afternoon, and we felt it.

The students agreed on representatives who would present the principal with their grievances about school and the quality of their education. They agreed to try to reach out to those they had turned off among their number, to speak to teachers and administrators. They decided to talk to their parents.

The principal refused at first to meet with them in an open meeting, with the student body in attendance. They waited until he agreed. Though the principal explained tirelessly why things could not happen their way, the students explained why it was necessary to have draft, abortion and drug counseling, to have a governing board involving the entire school community, the right to access to all the school facilities, to print a newspaper freely, to have redress to arbitrary and inconsistent rulings, to correct the racial imbalance of a predominantly white NYC high school, and to update the curriculum. The principal agreed to continue talking. The students submitted their proposals and their blueprints and went back to class.

April 1970. The Cambodia invasion. Vietnam became the Indo-Chinese War, and the students sat down again
in the basement to talk. They organized peace actions and
after-school street theater, planned for a city-wide high
school communications network, and asked that the principal
adopt the crisis curriculum they had presented to help them
"get together" the crises in their world. And they went
back to classes.

Kent State. The students demanded action and refused to return to class. Derogatory comments were
entered on their permanent records, jeopardizing scholar-
ships that many had applied for and carrying untold weight
into the future.

Jackson State. The students walked out of school.
They threw up picket lines. I marched with them for three
days and clung to the building for protection as the construction workers--the same guys who for three years had
shared the luncheonette counters on the block with us--
pelted us with asphalt chips and beer cans. I joined them
at Strike Central in the New School for Social Research.

"Renee, why are you going back into school?"

I had remembered a conversation we had had earlier,
pointing out that the student movement was on its own and
could do its own thing, but that for me there was a conflict
of interest at the outset: that my job was not going to be
put on the line for just any issue, no. My job was not
going to be put on the line regardless of the issue. I'd
wanted to indulge in the fantasy of guerilla professionalism,
working within the system. When I returned to the library,
I had blown that myth. I had felt the need to protect my
job and argue with striking students to protect their scholar-
ships and college acceptances.

They responded.

"You have to know when to make certain all-
out radical decisions, because then you limit yourself, you have a record, you get busted. You're
perfectly justified in saying you're not going to
put your job on the line. For us, in terms of
high school education, it was kind of an all-out
thing to do. The fact that we were striking and
getting mass things in the basement at that mo-

ment meant so much more to us than taking a
stinking Regents. We could have gone overboard
and really messed ourselves up. But here we
are, helping each other for the Regents. We did
what we had to do." **1674896**

In time these young people who had shared the same
school building for four years shared their interests, their
convictions, their money, their sweaters, their homes; they
spoke with other high school students about their actions.
Having petitioned hopelessly, they asked their administration
to allow them to return to school with some token promise
of change, in honor of their own commitment and as an
honorarium to those young people of Nam and Mylai, of
Kent and Jackson State. At an open meeting of the Board
of Education, they again petitioned to be allowed to return
to school with some pledges by the administration that
meaningful changes would be made in the curriculum so
that they could come to understand the world they had inherited. It was not enough now to "go back to classes."

Some Board members even listened to the students
that night. After all, when middle-class, articulate young
people come before them to speak of their concerns and
propose changes and ask for help and guidance, surely we
are all for peace in the world and relevance in education.

June 1970. Business as usual. The students had
trickled back to school. Five of us had been let go--of the
seven teachers who had supported the students, all five who
were non-tenured--and for good bureaucratic reasons. One
of the parents talked about teachers as professionals: why
not bring a malpractice suit against the principal? Those
who had been fired had been respected professionals who had
coincidentally established rapport with the children and stuck
by them. (The principal told parents who confronted him:
had it been up to him, he would have kept the teachers.)

Regents were coming. The library magazines bristled,
new and untouched. We no longer played the radio. The
masking tape had dried and the signs fell down, the "Let's
Be Friends" poster dangling by one corner. The library got
dusty, the center light blew. Quiet cigarettes on the fire
escape ... the unshelved books rested....

"Renee, I'm taking Fanon. Where's Grotowski?"
"I'm not graduating."

"I got 100 on my history Regents and my class grade
was lowered, but I still have my scholarship to Swarthmore."

"Where's Rat?"

"Have you got a job for next year?"

"Hey, I'll see you around."

"Tell Scott to come get his shirt."

"Finished with the Gemini poster?"

TURN IN YOUR LIST OF STUDENTS WHO HAVE NOT
SETTLED THEIR ACCOUNTS.

"There is no list."

STUDENTS WHO CAN'T STAND THIS SCHOOL SURE
SPEND A LOT OF TIME HERE WHEN WE'RE TRYING TO
ENTER GRADES.

"This is their library.   There's room for you to
work."

"Hey, library lady, where you working next year?"

"Renee, we're doing street theater tonight in El
Barrio.   Supper's at my house.   Coming?"

RE-DEFINING THE IMAGE

by Jack Shadbolt

Reprinted by permission from British Columbia Library Quarterly (35:1) July 1971, p. 20-26.

Asked to attent the mini-conference on the future of the library system in Burnaby. At first boredom at the thought then, slowly, curiosity. Why did the general image of library conference arouse a sense of boredom? I use my local library a lot (McGill Branch) and I like it; but what is the image of library today to the public? What could it be to be effective? The problem was thus indicated: for what it's worth I set down my thought process--improvising out loud ...

Since I am an artist I tend to think through images. They help me to generate ideas. Unlike a reasoning man I tend to get the image first. I just walk around with this vague image for a while as it turns up a whole chain of other alternative images until suddenly the old computer comes up with its consensus--that's the image--to which thoughts that have been churned up start attaching themselves and in turn generate further ideas. The image is a probe for testing out possibilities ...

Thinking both sides at once--what is a library today and how will this notion be regarded from the outside view of the public and what aspects of its function have to be dramatised, my first image was that of a Supermarket of Ideas-- shopping for information, for fantasy, adventure, practical help, entertainment, etc., etc.

My notion quickly shifted to that of a Mind Bank-- the term seemed accurate, concise and vivid. The great beauty of images is they encourage invention. Irreverently I thought of a whole instantaneous sequence of connections:

What is your library? Well, to bring its image into currency, it's a kind of Mind Bank, etc.

Visited your Mind Bank lately?
We draw on the international treasury of minds ...
For a very small deposit you, too, can ...
We offer you the best investment for your tax
dollar ...
Where else can you get such a high return of in-
terest ...
A lively interest is always to your credit ...
Deposit a little time with us--we guarantee to in-
crease your rate of interest ...

Just game-playing? Yes, in a way. Yet the image
probe is a useful device. It has already led me to some
useful notions: the word library is no longer a word with
image-appeal. It suggests books--and books alone is not
where it's at. More pertinent perhaps to let the library's
image be carried by other currently more used images--a
bit of a bank, a bit of a market, a bit of a communications
centre, idea exchange, activity centre, information centre,
lively meeting place, community lecture hall, special film
showing, etc. , etc. What would cover all these roles, hold
it together? MIND is a key word, all right--and IDEAS
and IMAGES and INFORMATION.

Yet IDEAS is getting played out by being pushed too
hard--after all, 50 new ideas for cake-making, new ideas
for fixing up your old attic, etc. And INFORMATION is
being overplayed--the information explosion--high-pressuring
you to be an up-to-date--sooner be caught dead than not know
the latest ... too restless. And IMAGES? Too vague.
Suggests only pictures--but could be sloped toward mental
images, imagination, fantasy--a very good possible appeal.
What is the image of fantasy? The free play of the mind.
Now we're nearer: the associations of "free" are good, and
"freedom"--the mind is one of the few areas left where we
can be free today--if, by mind, we mean "imagination. "
Everywhere else we are conditioned. Is the library the
last refuge of our freedom as individuals? A meeting of
varying imaginations ... yes: that aspect is important.
Thinking people are free people. Do it yourself re-defined
in terms of think it out for yourself. Not bad.

To be individual--yes! But what about "relating"?
That's very important. I want to understand other individuals. I want to communicate ... that's a good image--
how to get in touch with fellow thinkers, people like myself--
how to exchange ideas and enthuse about interests. Fine--

that's part of it--a "meeting of the minds."

But not a THINK TANK--that idea generates a lot of highbrow excitement but it's a sort of spectator sport for the public. They don't feel capable of participating. It only enlarges the gulf between them and the highbrows. It raises the eyebrows and lowers the lowbrows ... the word MIND is associated with THINK--a bad image.

Many people aren't aware what the life of the mind is. Their image of it is only connected with THINK--as some kind of tedious homework activity--"hard thinking," "racking one's brains" or having to do mathematics or keeping accounts or "pondering some problem" or "giving some serious thought" .... The truth is that these are usually crisis states which arrive precisely because the mind is not used easily and freely on all the hundred and one little things in the day to day life--un-thought-out things which are allowed to accumulate. People "black-out" against thought. People are driven by the practical urgencies of day to day living. They associate thinking with what they have to do--they have to "think ahead" what's to be for supper? or, is this price label too high? or, what will I give the bridge club to eat? or, I must remember the kid's medicine and to buy toothpaste. Worries and lists and disagreeable "facts to be faced." This is what the mind represents as as image. No wonder they want to escape. I've got enough to think about as it is. Yes, MIND has a disagreeable connotation. They want to go somewhere where they "just don't have to think." "Think, Man! Use your head." "Think before you speak." "Concentrate." "Stop day-dreaming" ... and so on. No wonder people just give up. They hate the mind. They feel the very reminder of the word as a sense of harassment. "Keep up-to-date." They "feel stupid," or they feel it as a sense of inferiority. The information flow overwhelms them. They don't know the facts; or the word Culture (with capital "C") is pushed at them constantly. They feel they just haven't time to catch up and they never will. So they resent Culture--too highbrow--or too impractical ("Hell man I've got too much to do to go to symphony concerts"). ("I just want to go fishing ... sit under a tree .... ")

So a library's of no use to these people. It reminds them only of their harassment that they should be more educated or more cultured or more bright. They only feel more inferior thinking about it. Rather than face it they

"leave it for the kids" or for the "eggheads" or whatever.
At any rate they don't go near it. It is associated with the
word "Mind" and this scares them off.

So the word Mind must be re-defined--after all that
is what the library is about.

The truth is that people can get all the practical
things and advice they need without ever going near a library.
Anyone can live--in fact, today you can hardly die: the
state sees that you stay alive. But do you feel alive? Are
you enjoying it? That is a state of mind.

A new image of thinking is needed. Thinking that
includes feeling, intuiting...

> Think with Ideas
> Think with Interests
> Think with Facts
> Think with Images

Thinking is inventing with ideas. Thinking is dreaming,
speculating, parlaying with images. Thinking is not just
brain work--it means feeling alive.

Images are not just pictures, they are mental pictures. They extend from the realities and facts out toward
the imagination. They return with new insights--inspired
notions. Everyone, whether they know it or not, uses
images to help them think. Imagining helps actuality.

A housewife, cooking, must, in a way, imagine the
dish she is preparing--an image of taste, of smell, of
appearance, or acceptance by those at the table--of satisfaction and pride. The image is a composite--it inspires
her to do her best. The library's approach to her is--we
take it from where you are. If you cook we can lead you
to the lore of cooking. We increase your enjoyment. Sure
you can live--but you can live better.

Even a businessman uses images. His statistical
image--the hard facts--when he gets all his manufacturing
and marketing costs together on a graph it helps him to
think--to spot weaknesses or strengths in his product or its
appeal, to spot new demands and to visualise new products
to meet them. It helps him also to enjoy--to see where all
the pieces of his operation fit together, gives him a sense
of meaning and control.

Even a housewife's budget is a mental image to help her imagine ahead for the future of her children. Her wise planning image even helps the success of her marriage.

A sociologist gets all the evidence together of the way we live and sees it whole as an image of our society-- a living pattern. You can then see it, too, and come to realize where you fit in. Everyone enjoys seeing this pattern. It is our most fascinating image. We all discuss it over coffee "how times have changed," "what's the world coming to?" ... The library is full of ideas on this subject--as it is on any area of interest you can name. That's what it's about! That image of life's fascination is what a good library cum mind centre should awaken as soon as you step in the door ... interesting questions, verbal or nonverbal. Posters, photographs, book jackets, film news, art objects and reproductions, demonstrations, story sessions for children, flowers, Xerox, a flexible space and light that one likes to be in with the evidence of people following interests--listening to music in cubicles, watching video in glass-doored electronic carrels, attractive bookshelves, an informal atmosphere.

Especially the visual presentations should be interesting. It is no longer enough to present a few formal examples of flower arrangement in a glass case or amateur paste-up posters or bad sketch club art--(Group exhibitions, children's art--yes). Movable screen and display facilities should be normal. And the whole world of modern graphic processes is available especially in the photographic realm. Some member of staff should have display and art training. Visual presentation creates immediate impact. Just as dress has come alive so must library buildings, creatively designed and used.

And just as the new liberation of dress emphasises the role that the individual visualises himself in, so the library, to be effective, must cool the stress on goals-- ambition, education, knowledge, literacy, status, success, etc.--and lay its stress on the development of personality. McLuhan has reminded us that "roles not goals" are the present animating impulse. Getting ahead (to what?) is not so important as expanding sideways--getting to know ourselves, to find zest in life, to explore meaning (**EXPLORE** is a good image) and enjoy the rhythm of the senses. To act ourselves.

Are these an abnegation of mind?   On the contrary
they are a flowering of thought processes, coupling them in-
divisibly with the senses and the feelings and even medita-
tion.

Impractical?   By no means, in a society of increasing leisure.   It is only the "practical" people who get bored.
Always just doing.   So what else is new?   Learning how to
be is stimulating, too.

Then there's the whole new area of social involve-
ment--from the university revolution to ecology to politics.
The library cum forum centre has a role here--to provide
open information on all sides--a meeting of the minds for
all factions--an area of reasoned interchange.   Its old hushed
air of sanctity, of implied editorship of taste, must fade into
a new positivism geared to what is currently happening in
the community around.   It must take the capital "C" out of
Culture and generate a new standard of excellence--vitality
of thought, quality of life.   Librarians must not consider
themselves custodians of highmindedness but leaders in
living ... the days of the vestal virgins are long over.   And
they must not get panicky and up-tight about book culture.
Libraries are like justice--"which must not only be done but
must appear to be done."   If they create the feeling of being
alive books will continue to be the most useful tool of the
mind and standards of high quality can be maintained provided
stuffiness is eliminated.   When the emphasis is on ideas
the forward and back interplay between present and past
can keep the classics updated.   Knowledgeable presentation
techniques can assist in this.   Here's how it is today.
Here's how it was then.

On the other hand the image as a chamber of commerce hostess or salesman of all things to all men is even
worse.   The selling of the whole idea of a library on the
level of how-to-do-it practicality is a real danger.   No need
to duplicate what the supermarket is already doing.   The
viable concept is that of the place where the best ideas of
anything you want come together.   If you love to build a
motorboat--O.K.   We can help; but we can also put you in
touch with the whole world of motorboats and their sea ro-
mance--the stories told by aficionados and even the history
if you want it.   We extend out from where you are.   We
can bridge you over to the realm of the mind through the
imagination.   We can help you dream motorboats.   Wherever you are in whatever you do we can help you to move
out into adventure.

To do this the user's interest areas must be tapped. Probably his likes should be noted in a file and he can be kept in touch.   Play it casual.   The over-earnestness of librarians could be played down.   We don't <u>sell</u> you.   People resent being sold.   We intrigue you.   It's here if you want it.   We'll help you get at it.   We'll help with ideas.   We are an agency.

Ideas are the <u>life</u> of the mind.   We all speculate. Even daydreams are an image for speculation--they shape our desires--whether we're dreaming of a new refrigerator, a handsome new kitchen, a fur coat, or successful children, or being adored secretly by a movie idol, or making the great end run in front of a huge crowd ... we all share these dream images.   No one is exempt ... and the library is the prime storehouse for image-dreaming.   Nobody need ever know your secret world--you share it in private with the author, the artist, the musician, the athletic hero, the architect of beautiful houses, the traveller, the business ty-coon, the revolutionary or the mystic.   Here on tape, in books, in pictures, in film, are your kind of people.   You can ease the pressure of life constructively.   For the mind has imagination, feeling, fantasy and exaltation.   It is not just THINK alone.   It is EXPERIENCE.

Libraries must get this notion across not by Madi-son Avenue advertising techniques but by relevance to their situations--by being activation centres of ideas that awaken possibilities--for the mind strives only if personal interest is aroused.   Librarians are life-enhancers.   The aim is not education and uplift but alert and aware weathervanes. We're doing <u>our</u> thing because it interests us to know what's happening.   The library should enjoy itself.   How Tom Sawyer got his fence whitewashed is still a valid technique.

Which means librarians who themselves have in-terests.   The human exchange is vital and the librarian's sociological education and non-academic attitude is essential. A staff should be balanced for their various capacities, and in-service training and continuous exposure to ideas and thought processes should be taken for granted.   The civil service type of hierarchical rigidity should be discouraged.

But who am I to tell librarians what they probably already know?   I was asked to state some ideas.   What happened to me in the process is a prototype situation of an attitude the library should hope to arouse in people within its orbit:

When I was approached I refused flatly.   Not for me!
Too busy.   Besides, what on earth could I say to librarians
(isn't there a better word?).   I had nothing to offer but my
ignorance and I wasn't going to expose that.   I therefore
put it out of my mind.   But once the pressure was removed,
or any sense of obligation, ideas came floating into my head
of their own accord.   At breakfast I jotted some down, free-
wheeling around the idea of a library's function.   No effort.
I just hadn't thought about it before.   It awakened my interest just tossing it around.   By noon I had scribbled these
thoughts.

The point is that my living vitality had increased one
more notch just by this voluntary process.   I had thought
myself inside the problem, identifying myself with librarians.
That's how the mind generates life.   The mind is a marvelous instrument for parlaying out from one suggested idea
to the next, making thought connections.   Can the library
get this concept across to people?   Is it not the prime role
of the library to help bring this state about?   MIND is still
the key word--only a very much expanded and more vivid
image of its aspects and its powers to ignite one to life.

FRONTIER OF FAITH, GEOGRAPHY OF JOY:
A LIBRARIAN'S TESTAMENT

by Patsy Willey

Reprinted by permission from the Wilson Library Bulletin, May 1971, p. 858-863, copyright (c) 1971 by the H. W. Wilson Company.

Why?
Why dropout?
Why librarianship?
Why adopt a child? Why a black child?
Why leave New York? Why Alaska?
Why life?

The last question is mine. All the other reasonable, conventional queries were either asked or thought by others through my life.

What answers are possible to any of them? Perhaps only manufactured rationalizations of what was done, rather than why. Where does one begin to chart the territory of self; how to know the boundaries of one's being or map the frontiers of conviction? Were I to find that ultimate stratum, that molten core at heart's center, I suspect that simply, inexplicably, it is joy. Metaphors and myths and biological empiricism reveal the cyclical certainty of birth, death, rebirth; and my phoenix-life has been so moved by mystery and miracle, that I question choice and submit to-- I am--the pioneer of self, in a personal universe of change.

High school incarcerated rather than educated me. I failed it, it failed me--Patsy, therefore, an early dropout. That first terrible failure, within a system, indeed individualizes you, but as with so many others who find that a failure is a frontier and so begin the first day of the rest of their lives, I found my life beginning.

Freed of school, my education continued in a public library. A childhood nurtured on the rainbow shelf of fairy-tales and fantasy led to an adolescence of autodidactism through the Great Books program.

I read myself into Columbia University ten years later, for a joyful drowning in an unhampered undergraduate education in the School of General Studies.

In graduate school an ambition dating back to third-grade was finally fulfilled.   I took my degree from Columbia's School of Library Service and librarianed a real library--not that third-grader's two orange crates, filled with dog-eared treasures, snowed under chalk dust, sporting handmade cards and pockets.

Third-grader and earnest--I knew a passion for books and still do.   I may be one of the last of the "passionate" nineteenth-century librarians--one who has actually lived in the public library.   Mine was a Hudson River, small-town, Greek Revival mansion--librarianship twenty-four hours a day for 1,900 people.   Joyous!

Alan Ternes, my former husband, and I circulated our own books when the collection failed, did reference work in our kitchen, scrubbed and painted and built and caused a library to be reborn.   In this grand microcosm were revealed all of the frustrations and possibilities of evolving librarianship.   We pioneered a total library service program.

Rules were broken, people had names, not numbers, personal community involvement was a fact, not an ideal.

All my professional activities hereafter will be only sophisticated replications of this early ministry of commitment to life--professionally expressed--through librarianship. This commitment, for me, is the why of librarianship.

In George Wald's urgent speech at Massachusetts Institute of Technology, "A Generation in Search of a Future," he said:

> Our business is with life, not death.   Our challenge is to give what account we can of what becomes of life in the solar system, this corner of the universe that is our home; and most of all, what becomes of men--all men, of all nations, colors and creeds.   This has become one world

for all men. It is only such a world that can now
offer us life, and the chance to go on.

Why Did I Adopt A Child?

Why did I adopt a child? I could not have one of
my own, and my former husband and I wished to have a
family. Why a black child? We took, as do most parents,
that which was delivered. There was no intent on either of
our parts to work out a so-called concerned liberal philosophy. On the other hand, the concept of a contrived matching
of our physical characteristics seemed absurd. The only
requirement was a child who was healthy, whose background
suggested that educational opportunities might be useful in
developing his or her potential. I did not consider a handi-
capped child, because I would continue as a working mother,
in all likelihood, for the rest of my life.

New York adoption agencies, and we interviewed
four, have similar procedural patterns and a similar spec-
trum of standards. An adopting couple or individual is required to make a commitment to one agency. The director
of the agency and our case worker were uniquely caring
people. We elected to swing with them in response to a
climate of openness, warmth, and relaxation of rules. We
felt them to be unusual. As it turned out, we were right.

The adoption route has standard landmarks: group
meetings, individual interviews, home visits, letters of
reference, evaluations. Cara was placed in January. Alan
wished to dissolve our marriage in June. I had, therefore,
to reassess my role. Cara was not legally ours. I was
logical, I was advised, "give the child up"; "it's best for
her"; "she will be a millstone around your neck"; "no one
will ever marry you again"; "you will hurt her, because
you're white and she's black."

After anguished weeks, I realized, how simple:
mothers don't give up their children! I am Cara's mother.
We may have a tough life. Whose isn't? The agency con-
curred. Alan and I divorced. Cara and I made local
history: first single-parent adoption and first trans-racial
adoption in our New York county.

All the bad social problems prophesied have not
arisen. People are not stunned or insulting when they see

my little girl.   She is sunny,   smart,   and glaringly secure.
We've rolled with the punch.   We're making it in the cold
north in that

> ... State so north it curled
> behind the map in hands of snow and wind,
> clutching the end of no place--
> I hold that state before my face and learn
>   my life.

William Stafford wrote those lines in Traveling Through the
Dark.   And now what of our life here?

Alaska Warmth

        Warm.   We are 135 miles south of the Arctic Circle
and our life is warm.   Humanity is accessible.   I backpack
Cara everywhere.   Children are tolerated everywhere.   I
gave a talk at the University of Alaska to some sixty people
for a Head Start tutorial program ("The Public Library's
Role in Support of Community Agencies").   University
faculty, local school administrators, students, tutors, other
babies were there.   Mine had joined a young anthropologist,
his native wife, and their child.   Seeing me, she toddled
down the aisle toward me, arms upraised, called, "Uppie,
Mommie."   I hoisted her to my hip, continued my super-
sell, and no one there, with all that brass and class, generated a negative vibration.   We are involved with a reality
here, women work and are mothers, sometimes simultaneously.   Conflicts are not engendered by what is artifically
correct.

        I recall a rather radical SRRT group which met at
the Chicago (1970) midwinter session of ALA.   I had only
the one chance to see and appraise some of our library
revolutionaries.   Cara's hotel sitter had not arrived, so in
the last half hour of the meeting we audited.   Our library
liberals were somewhat uptight.   Lots of hip talk, all four-
letter words tolerated except B-A-B-Y.   Cold stares,
whispered disapproval, children do not belong.   Professionalism and children don't belong together, it seems.   How
easy it is to get away from life.   Eskimos and Athabascan
Indians know and live an integrated life of professional
survival in the presence of their children.   Do we, as
librarians, because of professional pressures, remove ourselves from the very one-to-one human contact that makes
our work purposeful?

Fairbanks, as a city, has yet to learn to alienate, categorize, separate classes. Cab drivers recognize me from the newspaper and television, roll down their windows and bellow, "Hey, Patsy! How's it coming?" The postman delivered a letter addressed to:

> Patsy
> Library
> Fairbanks, AK

A native lady in the Moocher Bar in Nenana, where all spectators of the annual dog races gather to drink and await the winners, asked me if Cara (who was having a wonderful time with the other kids, natives, and whites) was adopted. I said yes. This lady, a pure Athabascan, said, "That's the way we are all going to make it--race doesn't make any difference." It's a warm bar, the Moocher. We came in out of the cold, -45°, whites, natives, kids, grown-ups, working people, government officials, we were together in the warm.

You can reach and talk to the druggist-millionaire, the U.S. Senator, the governor when he comes through town, the local author who is also an artist (do you know Clair Fejes' books, The People of Noatak and Enuk my Son?), party with the borough chairman, entertain the State librarian, gossip with the Eskimo bank vice president, take a flying lesson from your dentist--people are accessible. Not what you are or who, but simply self is offered, for friendship perhaps, but chiefly, I believe, in recognition that we are here together, linked and needing one another.

I will, I suspect, adopt another child whose race is not mine, so that Cara and her sibling can live that awareness, that we are here together, linked, and needing one another. The child may be boy or girl, Eskimo, Indian, or Aleut, or some combination--but what my children will know themselves to be, primarily, is that he or she is a child of God.

Each night I rock Cara to sleep in an old-fashioned rocker hauled from New York, and I sing her one of our homemade songs:

> What will my babe be when grown
> What will my babe be?

A woman with a love of her own,
That's what my babe'll be.

Where will my babe be when grown?
Where will my babe be?

Living in a land new free,
That's where my babe'll be.

Who will my babe be when grown?
Who will my babe be?

A child of God
Living, loving, free,

That's who'll my babe be.

Pray, Lord, I live to see
My baby when grown.

I write them down.   I'll make my babies their own
mama-made songbooks, I'll give them their poems first
and then the world's.   The spell of words, and book passion,
I hope, is catching.

My baby, my future babies, have a heritage: this
corner of the universe, earth; but possess now, too, the
poetic frontier of space.   Space exerts a force toward
ascension on our children's imaginations.   Their minds--
freed in a surging verticality to the unexplored voids of the
universe, to the possibilities of ever-expanding awareness,
and of soaring perceptions of meaning--will come closer to
the why of life and to joy.

The Passion of Librarianship

Fairytale fed, I find that the antidote to alienation is
in simple values; the belief in right over wrong, in valor
tested, in evil ultimately punished, and in love enduring
and triumphant.   Faith and fantasy are remarkably alike,
both grant a knowing of the intangible and undocumentable.

P. L. Travers, speaking of E. M. Forster's chief
theme, says it is:

The attempt to link a passionate skepticism with

the desire for meaning, to find the human key to
the inhuman world about us; to connect the individual with the community, the known, the unknown;
to relate the past to the present and both to the
future.

This is, for me, an apt description of the caring librarian. We librarians are assemblers, connectors, or
linkers. We are the forgers of the chain of knowledge,
newly strengthened to contain knowledge in all its forms:
the word set in a book, or caught in shapes, sculpture,
sounds, in the creative moment of drama. And if we dare
to rise on a vertical thrust, we might match the magnifi-
cence of the artifacts we assemble.

My mission of service to others is based on Christian
parables. This way of faith was personal. Western Christi-
anity was simply the one most available to me; my carefully
sterilized areligious upbringing has allowed me the freedom
to accept the beauty and truth of all the paths to the divine.

I am committed to a concept of a God of Love, a
God of Joy--a Creator, whose mystery we share when we
love most.

Karl Shapiro has written that "the aftermath of
poetry should be love," and Philip Larkin says, "What will
survive of us is love." Should not the aftermath of our
total life, personal and professional, be the survival of
love?

I've knelt in Communion next to an Athabascan women
of eighty-three, the sole survivor of a whole village struck
by a measles epidemic eighty years ago, whose life is the
emblem of love received and given. I have not known a
humbler moment--before God--to kneel next to monumental
humanity. To see carved on another's face indomitable
courage, faith, and love.

Freedom and faith interlock. I choose my way, I
select for myself that which exists in any institution, social,
educational, theological or professional, and that which I
cannot make congruent with inner vision, I reject. Dosto-
evski's Grand Inquisitor confronts the returned Christ and
admonishes Him for weighing down man with a "free heart
to decide for himself what is good and evil." Must we not,
however, always decide anew? There are no permanent

answers or systems, only new choices.

> Libraries ... where ideas run for safety ... all
> this courtesy and all this trust, tons of trash and
> tons of greatness, burning in time with the slow
> cool burning, burning in the fires of poems that
> gut libraries, only to rebuild them, more grand
> and palladian, freer, more courteous, with corner-
> stones that say: <u>Decide for Yourself</u> [Karl Sha-
> piro].

The poet knows what libraries are, do we? As an
unconventional librarian I accept Emerson's, "There is no
virtue which is final; ... the terror of reform is the discovery that we must cast away our virtues ... into the same
pit that has consumed our grosser vices."

So, away with mid-twentieth century librarianship.
Away with the mausoleum. Away with the carefully balanced selection. Away with frozen dignity, and frozen positions. Let me embrace and grapple with the unexplored
and unexpected, with change and the joyousness of growth.

As in a game of hopscotch, we're going to hop over
the last three decades and hopefully hop into the next century.
The technology is here--we have nothing in Alaska to undo.
We can make the gathering of information and its dissemination a science fiction reality. The ideal of the carefully
balanced collection is a virtue we cast away if it is too
limited. Let's keep it, however, and expand it. Knowledge
and information prepared and delivered to individuals can
be the dynamite which explodes the barriers of ignorant
lives. Let us help bring them to "decide for yourself."
Let us employ social workers--Chicago does; community
organizers; vocational and psychological councilors; reading
specialists. Let's be activists in delivering effective knowledge.

We don't explore the full range of human talent and
needs. We don't offer rigorous, appealing training programs. We insist on limiting employment to high school
graduates. We don't use tax-supported salaries to rehabili-
tate our "misfits." We don't investigate possibilities of
employing the full 24-hour span of the day. We narrow and
bind and chain ourselves to the mediocre successes of the
past.

And, yes, the offbeat, the irregular can be done
with startling success. We have here, in Fairbanks: in-
stituted an eight-member, thirty-eight-week native training
program; established as policy that high school graduation
is not a requirement for employment; we have sought out
seven Neighborhood Youth Corps trainees for fifty-six free
labor hours each overworked week. The kids blossom.
Through a court program our local judges offer the option
of working for the community or paying the fine. Persons
charged with traffic offenses and drunkenness in public
have spent hundreds of profitable hours--for them and for
us--paying off society while contributing to it.

We have fostered a rehabilitation program with the
courts in which we cooperate in a program of reestablishing
self-esteem and societal values to an individual. An Indian
alcoholic and a Caucasian, college-educated shoplifter have
both had an opportunity here for productive experience in
one of the community's most alive and caring institutions.

The organization table and scientific management's
job description are both ways of freezing out channels of
creative chaos. We've got 'em, but we use them for a
launching pad to explore potential.

In remote communities, in suburban shopping centers,
in the ghetto streets, where is the center of activity?
Laundromats. Why don't we merge necessity with our
service. A community center facility could house both a
laundry and library. It will at Fort Yukon.

Fem Lib ladies bring to our attention the desperate
day care needs of our under-school-age population. If you
are three or four and too rich for Head Start and too poor
for private nursery school, who attempts to offer you something? The children's room of the public library. We do
it every day, why not in a big way? Why shouldn't our materials include the toys that stimulate and develop and those
that encourage an understanding of other cultures? We have
some trained staff; why not work out programs for space
and funding?

Our traditional role in adult education can be greatly
expanded by offering facilities to free university programs
with their wonderfully rich, nutty scope (we've offered a
course in gold panning, Edgar Cayce, and knot tying). Let's
grab the ball and get into cassette audio and visual production,

regular and ham radio broadcasting, and television.   Let's
build libraries with broadcasting studios in them.

Let's build libraries with love and passion.   I have
the faith it can be done, and in the trying, I know joy.

AGAINST THE DOGMATISTS:
A SKEPTICAL VIEW OF LIBRARIES

by Daniel Gore

Reprinted by permission, with minor revisions, from
American Libraries 1(10) November 1970, p. 953-957.

> We declare at the outset that we do not make any
> positive assertion that anything we shall say is
> wholly as we affirm it to be. We merely report
> accurately on each thing as our impressions of it
> are at the moment.
> ---Sextus Empiricus, Outlines of Pyrrhonism

If one of us should be asked point black for a metaphor to describe a library, he would probably reply that it
is "a temple of learning, " "a store-house of knowledge," "a
treasury of wisdom, " or something equally grand. Luminous
and inspiring phrases, but using them uncritically brings
needless mischief upon us, for they lead people to expect
something radically different from what actually fills the
shelves of a library. They hide reality behind a bogus
ideal, intimidating ordinary mortals with the suggestion that
we have piled up dry bones for their edification, and out-
raging idealists when they discover we have gilded over the
earthy portion of our libraries with shining metaphors.

Fear and hatred of the written word--and by extension books and libraries--are passions from which philosophers, professors, and librarians are not wholly immune.
An illiterate person is likely to feel awe and reverence for
the art of writing, the making of books, and the building of
libraries. But teach him to read and write and, behold,
we have no longer a guaranteed reverencer of our libraries,
but a potential patron and a possible enemy of that art from
which our profession sprang. Marshall McLuhan is merely
a recent example of the learned man who despises books;

55

the phenomenon itself is ancient. It can be traced biblio-
graphically to the fourth century B. C. , and mythologically
all the way back to the origin of writing.

Advocates of intellectual freedom will better appreciate the difficulty of their position when they consider that
the greatest intellect of the Western World was himself
openly hostile to it. Plato, in the Phaedrus, places in the
mouth of Socrates an argument contrived to discredit whatever virtue the written word may appear to possess. Socrates tells how the god Ammon spoke scornfully to Thoth,
the mythical inventor of writing, when he boasted that his
invention was "an elixir of memory and wisdom. " If the
Egyptians learn to write, says Ammon,

> Their trust in writing will discourage the use of
> their own memory within them. You have invented
> an elixir not of memory, but of reminding; and
> you offer your pupils the appearance of wisdom,
> not true wisdom, for they will read many things
> without instruction and will therefore seem to
> know many things, when they are for the most
> part ignorant and hard to get along with, since
> they are not wise, but only appear wise.

Expounding upon the myth, Socrates concludes that
written words are useless "except to remind him who knows
the matter about which they are written. " The proper mode
of instruction is therefore dialogue between student and
teacher, since books are useful for learning only what one
already knows. And the written word suffers the further
disadvantage--which dialogue escapes--of being "bandied
about, alike among those who understand and those who have
no interest in it, and it knows not to whom to speak or not
to speak; when ill-treated or unjustly reviled it always needs
its father to help it, for it has no power to protect or help
itself. " The argument against writing, placed in the context of Plato's other dialogues, attests to his fear that the
book might offer enlightenment to the masses (for whom he
had no use), and expose to attack his own notions of the true
and the good when he would no longer be around to defend
them. And yet, through a peculiar impulse common to
enemies of the book, Plato commits to writing his fear of
writing, thus equipping us to do what he wished to prevent.

Intellectual freedom, as we understand it, was repugnant to Plato. In the Republic he advocates government

censorship of the stories mothers tell their children, and proposes to banish poets altogether from Utopia. Had there been librarians in his time, he may have expelled them along with the poets, or found tasks for them fundamentally different from those we customarily associate with librarianship. In his last work, the Laws, he proposes strict government control of texts that schoolchildren will be permitted to read, since some authors had already bequeathed to the Greeks "writings of a dangerous character." Plato seems to abandon this troublesome topic with embarrassed haste, as if it awakened in him some painful conflict for which he could find no satisfactory resolution. The topic was to prove even more troublesome to the Renaissance Platonists, who found it necessary to explain away their master's scandalous strictures on poetry and writing in general, because there was clearly no way to defend forthrightly a position that subverted their own passionate interest in the whole of Greek literature.

The foregoing is prologue, to underscore the fact that philosophers are not necessarily our best allies. The dogmatic ones are likely to be our worst enemies, equipped with powerful arguments to overthrow any position we are not philosophically prepared to defend.

We leap now across two millennia to the distinguished Spanish philosopher José Ortega y Gasset, and his celebrated speech "The Mission of the Librarian," delivered to an international congress of librarians in 1935. It is a provocative speech, packed with wisdom and full of philosophical concern for librarianship, and it concludes with a dramatic call to action that has thus far gone unheeded, despite its great emotional appeal. The text has proved to be extraordinarily popular, and is widely available in English, French, Spanish, and other languages. But the Spanish version in Ortega's Obras Completas is indispensable, for there you will find an epilogue, "Qué es un Libro," dropped from the speech and from the English translation of it, that lays bare the philosophical foundation of Ortega's peculiar notions about the mission of the librarian. The epilogue turns out to be a sympathetic rehashing of Plato's condemnation of writing in the Phaedrus, and plainly shows that Ortega, in his speech, is merely extending to librarianship the Platonic feeling about books. With the help of Plato, Ortega has found a proper place for librarians in Utopia.

The concept of "mission" is central to Ortega's

philosophy.   "A mission is just this: the consciousness that
every man has of his most authentic being, of that which he
is called upon to realize. "   And a professional mission is
that which it is <u>necessary</u> for professionals to do, whether
any choose to do it or not.   There is nothing casual about
Ortega's decision to call his speech "The <u>Mission</u> of the
Librarian. "

As the necessities of the library profession have
changed over the centuries, the mission of the librarian
has accordingly changed.   In the fifteenth century, Ortega
avers, the mission consisted chiefly in gathering the harvest
of the printing press.   By the nineteenth century the proliferation of books adds a new necessity: the need to catalog them.   But the book is already beginning to lose what
Ortega styles its original character of "pure facility," and
in the twentieth century the book takes on a negative character, as an instrument in revolt against its creator.   "The
fully negative character," says Ortega, "surges up when an
instrument created as a facility spontaneously provokes an
unforseen difficulty and aggressively turns upon man. "   Pursuing the metaphor of the book turned rebel, Ortega proposes a radical shift in the mission of the librarian:

> Here then is the point at which I see the new
> mission of the librarian rise up incomparably
> higher than all those preceding.   Up until the
> present, the librarian has been principally occu-
> pied with the book as a thing, as a material ob-
> ject.   From now on he must give his attention to
> the book as a living function.   He must become a
> policeman, master of the raging book.

The necessities requiring librarians to become policemen are
then summed up:

> There are already too many books.   Even when we
> drastically reduce the number of subjects to which
> man must direct his attention, the quantity of books
> that he must absorb is so enormous that it exceeds
> the limits of his time and his capacity of assimila-
> tion.   Merely the work of orienting oneself in the
> bibliography of a subject today represents a con-
> siderable effort for an author and proves to be a
> total loss.   For once he has completed that part
> of his work, the author discovers that he cannot
> read all that he ought to read.   This leads him to

> read too fast and to read badly; it moreover
> leaves him with an impression of powerlessness
> and failure, and finally skepticism towards his
> own work.

(A paradox lies in this lament, for if there are indeed too
many books, the problem would be self-adjusting if authors
spent the proper time in bibliographical orientation and
reading. Ortega, whose own works are voluminous, might
at least have stopped writing, just as Plato should never
have started if he really valued his own advice. Appealing
as we may find the philosophical assurance that there are
already too many books, the assertion will not bear logical
scrutiny, since as yet we have no criterion of what constitutes "enough" books.) Ortega continues:

> It is not only that there are too many books; they
> are being produced every day in torrential abun-
> dance. Many of them are useless and stupid;
> their existence and their conservation is a dead
> weight upon humanity.... At the same time, it
> also happens that in all disciplines one often re-
> grets the absence of certain books, the lack of
> which holds up research.... The excess and the
> lack of books are of the same origin: production
> is carried on without regimen, almost completely
> abandoned to spontaneous chance.

Here the peroration begins, and the mystery of the library-
policeman's role in Utopia is cleared up. "Is it too Utopian,"
Ortega asks,

> to imagine in a not too distant future librarians
> held responsible by society for the regulation of
> the production of books, in order to avoid the
> publication of superfluous ones and, on the other
> hand, to guard against the lack of those demanded
> by the complex of vital problems in every age?
> ... It seems to me that the hour has arrived
> for the collective organization of book production;
> for the book itself, as a human modality, this
> organization is a matter of life and death.

> And let no one offer me the foolish objection
> that such an organization would be an attack upon
> liberty. Liberty has not come upon the face of
> the earth to wring the neck of common sense ....

> The collective organization of book production has
> nothing to do with the subject of liberty, no more
> nor less than the need which has demanded the
> regulation of traffic in great cities of today.
> Moreover, this organization would not be of an
> authoritarian character, no more, in fact, than
> the internal organization of works in a good acad-
> emy of sciences.

What are we to make of a philosopher who can see no distinction between regulating traffic in ideas and in automobiles?
Who blandly asserts that regimentation need not be authoritarian? Who tells us there are both too many books and
too few, when he cannot tell us how many is enough? One
senses in Ortega the panic that wells up in a scholar as he
discovers the astronomical dimensions of the bibliographical
universe. And the attendant Utopian urge to return to a
more primitive state of society, where philosophers can
banish poets, and librarians will banish books.

Most of what I have quoted from Ortega appeared
(as excerpts from the speech) in the January, 1936 issue
of the Wilson Bulletin for Librarians. In the same issue
Stanley Kunitz delivered a stinging rebuke to Ortega that
still makes lively reading. Here is the opening paragraph:

> Of what were the librarians at Madrid, the
> sachems and hierarchs of the profession, in in-
> ternational congress assembled, thinking--did they
> stir uneasily in their seats--while José Ortega y
> Gasset, who has been called "one of the twelve
> peers of European thought," delivered his denun-
> ciation of the book? Reading his argument ... I
> wondered whether any in that assemblage had the
> impulse or, what is more, the courage, when the
> speaker had finished, to stand up and defend the
> book against its detractors. I suppose not. Con-
> vention audiences are notoriously phlegmatic; and,
> besides, communication with an international au-
> dience is difficult in any one language. Perhaps
> there was not a handful of librarians present who
> realized that their famous guest was calmly engaged
> in justifying their annihilation.

Later issues of the Bulletin also carried comment favorable
to Ortega's position, whether from librarians who actually
shared his philosophy, or suffered unmanageable cataloging
backlogs, it is difficult to say.

Ortega's entire address (minus the epilogue) appeared
in English translation twice in 1961, [1] but the re-publication
of this astonishing speech drew no audible response from
American librarians.   Perhaps events in Hitler's Germany
and Stalin's Russia are regarded as a sufficient commentary
on Ortega's preposterous program.   But the need still per-
sists for some alternative to the philosophy out of which it
grew, and I will propose one here while discussing the mission of the librarian from my own point of view, that of a
librarian who is neither dismayed by the multiplicity of books,
nor awed by the pronouncements of philosophers.

My general attitude towards books is simply that of
Friar Laurence toward living things:

> For naught so vile upon the earth doth live,
> But to the earth some special good doth give.

There are probably, as Ortega says, many "stupid" books
in the world, and more are surely on the way.   But a useless one (in the absolute sense) is unimaginable.   Even a
penny-dreadful is useful as a bad example, and as a testa-
ment to the kind of civilization that produced it.   Judgment
is needed only to determine how many bad examples any one
library may usefully collect.

A book may contain things foolish, disgusting, appalling; a library of any size must.   You may with constant
vigilance and ceaseless toil keep weeds, insects, and ser-
pents out of your garden plot, but a forest is something else.
So are libraries, and we need the ecological good sense of
Friar Laurence to restrain us from the righteous effort to
purge them of all things vile.

As for the mission of the librarian, I believe it is
still primarily the making of libraries, and I think this is
a task incomparable higher than sitting like some Juno cross-
legged over the nativity of books.   To be sure there have
been librarians willing to let others make libraries for
them--college faculties, for example--but this implies only
that some members of a profession may choose not to do
what it is necessary that they do.   By letting others make
libraries for us, we escape those personal dangers that
beset a librarian who takes his mission seriously.

One fruitful source of danger is a careless choice of
metaphors to describe our libraries.

Consider the perils of publicly declaring that your library is a storehouse of knowledge. Someone will discover on your shelves a book that exhibits blatant, undeniable ignorance, and he will invite you to throw it out because it plainly has no place in a storehouse of knowledge. At that point you may find it is too late to change your metaphor, but you may have to change your job if you refuse to throw the book out.

Those who travel widely in the world of books may agree that a more realistic case can be made for describing a library as a "treasury of learning and ignorance," although that metaphor is unsuitable for use around fiscal officers. We have led them to expect something different for their money.

The disdain of ignorance is widespread but unwarranted. Consider for a moment one example of the small pleasure it can give. Pliny, in the eighth book of his Natural History, speaks of the achlis, "born in the island of Scandinavia and never seen in Rome, although many have told stories of it--an animal that is not unlike the elk but has no joint at the hock and consequently is unable to lie down but sleeps leaning against a tree." And how does one catch an achlis? The thing to do, says Pliny, is to cut some trees nearly through; and when the achlis leans against one to go to sleep, down come tree and achlis together, the achlis no more able than the tree to get up and run from you. While we are smiling at the quaint credulity of Pliny (who himself was always smiling at the quaint credulity of the Greeks), this sobering question invades our mirth: How would one go about proving the absolute non-existence of the achlis? We have been taken in before on matters of well-attested learning-- Piltdown man, for example--and we may be equally vulnerable to matters of well-attested ignorance. Has anyone thought of sawing some trees nearly through, and returning the next morning to see what he may find?

The librarian, above all others in the republic of learning, has need of the great Sceptic formula "I suspend judgment" to guide (but not overpower) him in his professional mission. He may personally deny the achlis if he likes. But woe betide him if he undertakes to drive from his shelves the achlis or anything else simply because he denies its truth.

When the time comes to write a Pseudodoxia Epi-

demica of the twentieth century, the books of ignorance will
be indispensable, while the works of truth will be useless.
And whoever compiles that enormous record of our false
beliefs may discover that, through the alchemy of the decades,
thousands upon thousands of books prematurely celebrated for
their truth have grown strangely ridiculous; while other books,
despised or neglected at their first appearance in the world,
will be cherished for their late-blooming wisdom.

The accumulation of recorded error proceeds at
about the pace at which we discover new knowledge, and the
size of our libraries testifies as much to the magnitude of
our ignorance as of our learning.   I would not wish it otherwise.   Man is a creature too readily disposed to erect imposing monuments commemorative of his own imagined
grandeur.   He needs large libraries to remind him of his
real and imposing ignorance.   Once more, an argument no
one would think of presenting to the holders of the purse
strings.

What argument then should you make, and what
metaphor shall you use to justify your mission as maker
of libraries?   Before attempting any case at all, you might
profitably study Sextus Empiricus, the codifier of Sceptic
philosophy, and see what Scepticism offers in the way of a
philosophical foundation for the libraries you propose to
make. [2]

It is obvious to all of us that a library is a place
in which thoughtful people search for something.   But it is
not obvious what kind of thinkers we can reasonably hope
to accommodate.   Sextus can help us here, with the Sceptic
discovery that every thinker must fall into one of three
categories.   First, there are those who affirm that the truth
exists, and that they are already in full possession of it,
so their search has reached its end.   There is no point in
making libraries for this group--the dogmatists--for they
will eventually find reason to ask you to burn them down.
A case in point is the great library at Alexandria, which,
after a thousand years' glorious existence, was consigned
to the flames at the command of a powerful dogmatist, the
Caliph Umar bin al Khattab.   To him one 'Amr bin al 'Ass
wrote asking what should be done with the books in that
marvelous library.   The Caliph replied, "As for the books
you mention, if their contents agree with the Book of God,
then having the Book of God we are wealthy without them,
and if they contradict the Book of God we have no need for

them, so start destroying them." Which 'Amr bin al 'Ass
did, distributing them throughout Alexandria to be burned in
fireplaces. So great was the collection of books in that
magnificent library that six months were required to burn
them all up. It is said that when the Caliph was told what
had happened, he was pleased.

Seldom is the logic of the Alexandrian dilemma
pushed to so ruthless and absolute a conclusion, but the
light from that disastrous fire should at least help us to
see what is going on, and where we may be heading, when
we are implored or compelled to remove books from our
libraries because they oppose some popular dogma.

The second category of thinkers contains those who
deny the possibility of knowing the truth about anything, and
therefore assert that it is sheer vanity even to begin the
search. We need waste no efforts in building libraries for
them, for at best they will not use them, and at worst
they will denounce us for burdening the public with large and
useless expenditures.

In the third category belong those who persevere in
the search for truth, people who in Sextus's time, and long
before, were known as Sceptics: a term that literally means
"inquirers, searchers." Sceptics have been perversely
misunderstood throughout the centuries as being philosophers
who doubt and deny everything, thus paralyzing every effort
to think and act rightly. The stigma is undeserved. For
the avowed aim of the Sceptics was to free men from the
absurd doctrines of the dogmatists by showing that for every
dogma, one could find another dogma of equal weight in
opposition to it.

If Heraclitus maintains that you cannot step in the
same river twice, since all things are always changing;
and if Parmenides informs you that nothing in fact changes
since motion is logically impossible; then you suspend judgment on the point in dispute, walk or stand still as you
please, and continue to study the enigma of motion if you
are so disposed. [3] If Plato assures you the written word is
useless while speech is perfect for teaching; and if Cratylus
comes along and advises you to give up speech for any purpose whatever, since speaker, listener, and words are all
changing even in the act of utterance; then you suspend judgment on the philosophical issue and talk, write, or hold your
peace, according to the dictates of your common sense.

Through suspension of judgment on non-evident matters, the Sceptic achieved the mental tranquility that permitted him to function sensibly according to the laws, customs, and faith of his people--and to continue his philosophical inquiries.

Neither dogmatist nor nihilist can tolerate philosophically the Babel of books we call libraries. But a Sceptic relishes the conflict of fact, idea, and opinion that goes on in them, for the conflict keeps open for him a way to persevere in his search. Search for what? Search for the truth about himself, and about the universe. If this is so--and in Sceptic fashion I go no farther than proposing that it appears to me at the moment to be so--then what we should try to give this searcher is a library that can metaphorically be called a mirror of the universe, a reflector of things that may appear true or false, pious or blasphemous, beautiful or ugly, depending on who is looking in the mirror.

I have stolen the metaphor from Shakespeare, who tells us that the function of drama is "to hold as 'twere the mirror up to nature; to show virtue her own feature, scorn her own image, and the very age and body of the time his form and pressure." If drama can do these things, a library can surely do as much and more, as is self-evident in that libraries contain dramas, whereas no drama can contain what is in our libraries.

Must a library hold all, or most of the books in the world, to reflect the universe entirely? I think not. Even a tiny mirror held at a distance from a huge object will still reflect the whole object, although not in such minute detail as a larger mirror would if held closer. The aim is what counts. If one is careful and resolute in the making of a modest-sized library, and goes about the task undogmatically, it will faithfully reflect the whole cosmic panorama of order and confusion, of grandeur and triviality.

The flood of books makes the task not impossible, but more engaging. The odds against complete success should be no cause for discouragement. Physicians struggle against disease knowing that all their patients will die anyhow; lawyers try cases in court knowing they will lose half of them; librarians can, if they will, make libraries that accurately reflect most that is known or believed about man and the universe.

Our opportunity to attempt the making of such libraries is unique, or nearly so, in the history of librarianship. It grew out of our national experiment with human
freedom, begun two centuries ago; and in some measure the
success of that uncertain experiment must depend upon what
we make of our unusual opportunity. Frederick Jackson
Turner, in that prophetic book called The Frontier in American History, forewarned that the strains upon our open
society would grow as we moved away in time from the
closing of the frontier, a place where a man could always
strike out for himself and re-establish an open society when
he found his community growing intolerant of his personal
ideals. But hopefully an American who finds his society
closing down on him today can still strike out for the library,
with some expectation of finding there, if nowhere else, an
open intellectual society, a frontier of thought and feeling
with boundaries wide enough to permit perfect freedom of
thought and spirit, to give full scope to the varieties of
dissent necessary to keep alive our imperilled experiment
in human freedom. Russia has lately shown us what the
regimentation of book production can do to contract those
boundaries and make librarians the propagators of whatever
political, academic, or moral dogma is in vogue. Nothing
much stands between us and that same servitude but our own
stubborn will (some will say perverse; let them) to resist
every appeal, every threat, to make the content of our libraries conform to any species of dogma.

A problem universe requires problem libraries.
Making them is the most demanding and also the most awk-
ward necessity of our mission, since in the nature of things
our collections must contain many books that offend our
neighbors and ourselves. The offense will not be lessened
by pretending that our libraries are labyrinths of properly
authorized learning. To develop the nerve we need for
giving the unavoidable offense, and to justify our position
when offense is taken, we must have a philosophy for our
mission that can accommodate all dogmas by assenting to
none. The name of that philosophy is Scepticism.

References

1.   José Ortega y Gasset, "The Mission of the Librarian, "
       tr.   James Lewis and Ray Carpenter, Antioch Re-
       view, XXI, 2 (Summer, 1961), 133-54.   Reprinted
     as a separate in 1961 by G. K. Hall.

2. The best introduction to Scepticism is Sextus himself.
    Philip Hallie's excellent edition of his selected
    writings, entitled <u>Scepticism, Man, & God,</u> presents
    the Sceptic approach with admirable conciseness.
3. I have chosen here for purposes of illustration a philo-
    sophical issue that looks innocent enough on its sur-
    face, if not indeed silly; but it underlies every seri-
    ous defense of totalitarianism, beginning with Plato's
    <u>Republic.</u>   Plato, troubled by the Heraclitean dogma
    of change and decay, concluded that the decline of
    governments and civilizations came about by their
    gradual departure from the Ideal Form in which they
    began.   The natural (and, to Plato, wholesome) cor-
    rective to this process is to establish a totalitarian
    society in which the rulers, by means of force and
    fraud, would completely arrest political and social
    change.   The ruling class will always rule, and the
    slave will always slave.   The stability of such a
    society naturally depends upon the ruthless suppres-
    sion of all statements critical of the rulers or their
    methods.   While a Sceptic would abstain from de-
    bating the philosophical position adopted by totali-
    tarianism, he would not hesitate to point out the
    self-evident suffering of its victims.

"SO (SAID THE DOCTOR). NOW VEE MAY
PERHAPS TO BEGIN. YES?"

by Leonard H. Freiser

Reprinted by permission from Illinois Libraries, 53
(2) February 1971, p. 109-114.

There is nothing in the body of Portnoy which need
remind us of our professional condition. Perhaps some of
you will insist that we too, have a guilt-edged insecurity.
The title of this talk, which is of course the last line of the
Philip Roth novel, is to be taken literally. Up to now we
have been talking about the library--now let us begin to
talk about the library. The king is dead, long live the king.

Make no mistake, we have a very lively corpse and
a most honorable one. It is this very liveliness which
tends to confound both our boosters and our critics. We
innovate, we automate, we sit around tables discussing social responsibility. We have curb service, sidewalk service,
storefront service; we have books in bars, beauty parlors,
housing projects. We have been very busy; we have plunged
into the ocean of social change--and we have done all this
in a toy boat fit for a bathtub. Viewed by librarians our
efforts loom large. Viewed by the people--we are not
viewed by the people.

Our outside critics can point to few weaknesses of
which we are not painfully aware. The critics within our
flock--the library journal athletes; the library directors born
under the sign of the American Management Association and
the Sainted Young--have with varying degrees of accuracy
presented us with head counts of angels on pins. And they
comfort us; their appraisals and proposals are so outrageous
or so commonplace or so inconsequential that we have
achieved a deeper understanding of the meaning of banal.
Our critics and ourselves, however, consider as given, our
present scale of operations (plus 20 or 40 or 70 percent
depending on our recklessness). There are even those who

feel that our toy boat, if outfitted with a rubberband motor, may have a chance outside the bathtub. In a local wading pool for instance.

It is the scale of library operations which concerns me here. I will propose, and attempt to support, that the community library expanded under new legislation and a completely different scale of financing can serve as the focus of community and neighborhood development; that the community library is at the end of one era--a most honorable one--and at the beginning of another. No longer the handmaiden, no longer the boy in the bathtub; now we must begin.

But who are we to say this. What do we have. Ladies and Gentlemen--we have the library. The library as idea and as potential is the greatest good in our society today.

You know--I know, (and do not forget this for one moment) that here is our strength. That we are with the book. The idea. The sensibility. That we have survived with honor the waves of intellectual and social dishonesty which surround us. That we are with the person. Not the number. Not the class. Not the catch pot of bureaucratic diddling--we are with the person. We are also in the community, of the community. Not to regulate, administer, control, or moralize. We are in the community in the same way electricity is there--as a utility.

What the community library stands for--integrity, recognition of the individual, community consciousness, the creative process--is what our society is seeking. And we firmly take our stand for all of this, on the bridge of our toy boat. Some of you will argue that we have been on the big boat of federal library support. Maybe you have, but you've been down in steerage catching crumbs from the second class passengers.

We are the most important agency the country has and it is our job to get this understood. It is our job to get legislation and financial support to enable us to meet our responsibilities. It is our job to go from the thousands of dollars to the millions of dollars; from the millions of dollars to the hundred millions of dollars.

And if this makes us unpopular in certain quarters,

if this puts us into the infighting of school, military, labor, and industrial politics, then we would have made a good beginning. The toy boat library is dead, long live the library.

In the conviction that we are about to enter the golden age of the community library I am not unaware of our weaknesses and the unfinished jobs we have within the present context of our work. Perhaps our greatest weakness is that we do not fully believe in or understand the supreme importance of libraries.

To me, the key to our time is the rediscovery of the human scale. With the rediscovery of the person we seek a style of life which has meaning beyond materialism. We are looking for honesty in ideas, education as well as training, esthetics not packaging, neighborhoods not junk jungles. We are seeking a style of life which leads to healthy communities and which accommodates people. If we set out to create a style of service to help us in our search we would reinvent the library style. The public community library is the only institution available to every person in our society which is not out to sell, convince, deter or train. The library style serves the person, the community--not the institution.

Our country needs us to such a degree that the expansion of library services which is now necessary may well be considered as revolutionary.

Immediately we are faced with our problem: the resistance of some of us to accept active educational and social responsibilities. I do not think that modesty or timidity are solely responsible for this. Rather, it is a credit to the intelligence of some librarians that they are suspicious of anything which can be interpreted as being grandiose. "You are setting up too large an umbrella," one librarian told me.

But their intelligence is keeping them from their intuition and their sense of the moment. The 1970's is the time of the community library. Now is the time to announce to the American people that we accept the challenge of The Right To Read. That by the end of the 70's no person reaching maturity will be without competent individual reading services.

In an editorial "A Nation of Illiterates?" on September 30, 1969 the <u>New York Times</u> states,

> The youth who leaves school without being able to
> read--and read well enough to cope with the de-
> mand of modern life and employment--enters so-
> ciety crippled. Worse, his deficiency is likely to
> impel him to become a drop-out, a frustrated em-
> bittered and easy victim of delinquency, drift and
> crime. At present, an estimated one-third of the
> nation's schoolchildren are embarked on such a
> dismal course, and in the nation's big cities, the
> hopeless army is probably closer to half of the
> total enrollment.

In a <u>New York Times</u> story, "Illiteracy Considered
Nation's No. 1 Education Problem," October 11, 1969, William K. Stevens states,

> In addition to the 24 million illiterates, an esti-
> mated 8 million to 12 million children now in
> school have such serious reading problems that
> they are headed toward functional illiteracy as
> adults. 'Illiteracy is really a much greater
> functional handicap than is the loss of limbs, '
> says Dr. Grant Venn, Assistant United States
> Commissioner for Vocational and Adult Education
> .... How will his program of wiping out illiteracy
> be pursued? 'No one knows yet, ' said an aide to
> Dr. Allen.... Although reading is probably one of
> the most investigated areas in education, relatively
> little is known about the exact process of eye, ear
> and brain by which individuals learn to read....
> It is now widely held that no one method works
> for all children and that a combination of methods
> --primarily phonics and whole-word recognition--
> is usually required, the mix and timing varying
> from child to child. During the last five years,
> concern has concentrated on the intellectual con-
> ditioning that a child brings to the moment when
> formal reading instruction is to begin. It is here,
> many believe, that the root causes of functional
> illiteracy are to be found. Dr. Conrad of the
> Office of Education's bureau of research believes
> this strongly. He would like to see the establish-
> ment of a system of 'early education centers, '
> where pre-school children essentially would play
> at speaking games; where adults speaking fluent,

grammatical English would read to them and talk
with them; where spoken communication would become enjoyable and increasingly sophisticated.

Reading grows on literature, encouraged by individual
attention and a civilized manner.   Learning thrives in an
atmosphere of searching and discovery.   This is the library
we are talking about, nothing less.   We are not committed
to raise anyone to a particular set of pedagogical, occupational, or consumer specifications.   The library's job is to
maintain and transmit learning and information.   I object to
the limited interpretation some librarians have of the job
we can, and must, do.   Reading is the heart of the library,
yet we have stood by while children leave our schools as
illiterates and millions have not found out that they can enjoy a book.   Information is part of the power of the library,
yet we still stand by, waiting for people to come to us,
when we know that out there are millions whose struggle
for better lives and communities requires accurate and understandable information.

We are the powerhouse.   Education and information
are part of the hot core of community regeneration.   It's
our kitchen and now is the time to face up to the heat.

Some of my friends suggest that we can't go out and
say these things; we need proof, feasibility studies.   In our
work there is only one feasible way to run a feasibility study
and that is to get on with the job--go out and do what has
to be done and make it work.   I'd rather have taken part in
important failures than sit around waiting for pallid studies
to dribble in.

There are some librarians who say, "This is not our
job.   We are not teachers, welfare workers, town planners,
or what have you."   In saying that we are not any of these,
my friends are sitting on crucial information and miss the
point completely.   We in this country no longer want to be
unasked, unconsulted recipients of other people's programs.
We do not want to be taught at, we wish to learn.   We do
not want to be taken care of, we want to be part of the
planning.   People want locally accessible facilities and
services which they can use to generate programs which are
satisfying and important to them.   The community public
library is uniquely suited to meet these needs.

But if the library is the answer we are the question

mark. Why do some of our colleagues in New York State wish to abandon childrens' services to the schools? After a three-year study the New York State Commissioner's Committee on Library Development has recommended that school libraries should give total service to children through sixth grade and that public libraries deal exclusively with adult services. Next to the SILENCE sign they will add NO CHILDREN. To me, this represents a profound misunderstanding of the nature of education.

It has not been, and may never be, possible for one kind of institution to be exclusively appropriate for the successful education of children. Education requires the active use of many organizations and professionals other than schools and teachers. The full implication of universal education in terms of institutions and in terms of how people learn, are not yet fully understood

Our time is characterized by threats to our personal identity and sense of community but the public library continues to resist depersonalizing systems. The public library--in terms of personal choice, civil liberties, educational potential, and especially style--may become the chief free comprehensive educational agency in our society. Any abridgment of anyone's right to full use of the public library by commission or omission, by reducing or failing to fully develop services, is an abridgment of civil liberties, the right to learn, and is an act which carries the seeds of an Orwellian and Kafkaish world.

Where so many of our fellow citizens consider the public library to be one of the greatest assets of our society in terms of its penetrating educational influence, as a bulwark and unique defense of the person in an almost closed bureaucratic society, and as a keystone of a true community of people of all ages and conditions--this committee seems to be saying that the public library is less than that.

The New York Committee avoids two basic questions:

1. What does our society require of education, what are the forms of education which apply to our society, and what are the humane and intelligent organizations needed to implement education?

2. What are, and what should be, the responsibilities of the public library in terms of personal freedom of all people

regardless of age, race, religion, sex, income, or residence;
in terms of quick, easy and unrestricted access to literature,
art, music, photography, film, information, etc.: in terms
of building and continuing a sense of community; and very
especially, in terms of its relative lack of authoritarian
bureaucracy and its relative strength of resistance to passing fads and cycles of partisan political pressures in comparison to other public institutions?

Once we clarify our own focus on the primary place
of the library in our society we must develop effective strategies. For instance, the costs of the new scale of community
library services, especially as seen parallel to school costs
may well be the factor which could get us going. The argument that money is hard to get today does not apply to the
changed conditions which now place the community library in
a preeminent position in our society. My argument is not
that public libraries need larger budgets but that the expanded operation puts the library in a different level of
budgeting. I am not suggesting that a library go from five
million to ten million but that it must develop an expanded
program to reach one hundred million. This figure brings
our case into focus. If we can do the things I know we
can do then we have to set the price consistent with the
scope of the job. How would you react to someone who
offered to build a house for you for $327.00? The question
is not that the money is short but that the expanded community library program is an essential and primary social
and education necessity. Our job is to catch up with this
fact. Now we have to change the battleground from incre-
ments on five million to a leap to one-hundred million. We
may have to face a variety of reactions but the important
thing is to reach the right battleground. Let them cut out
budgets--but from one-hundred million.

We are faulted not by what we do but by what we do
not do. I have spoken to many laymen, trustees, who condemn librarians for keeping libraries down. We have among
us those who are unafraid to challenge national and domestic
policies, bigotry, and repression of intellectual and academic
freedom. The one thing which we fear is putting the primary importance of libraries to the test.

Our responsibility to society is to maintain the belief that the enjoyment of intelligence is the proper goal of
education. The rest is training or social control. Our responsibility to society is to join with others to make educa-

tion accessible to all with dignity.   By deeds not words.

Our responsibility to society is to push out the boundaries of library services to the point where they coincide with the education of all individuals.

What this really means is that we take libraries seriously.   That we react with urgency and concern to poor library service and to inadequate support of libraries.

The state of Illinois has one of the highest concentrations of excellent libraries and librarians in the world but it is only a hint of what we must have if our families and neighbors are not to be judged disadvantaged.

Let us place on record our belief in the community library as the primary agency in our society.   Let us study and prepare legislation to accomplish this.   Let us begin to plan the expansion and development of services to meet our responsibilities.   Let us get our present house in order so that we may move without our own fetters.

Yes,   doctor,   we will begin.

HOW REAL IS COOPERATION?

by Ralph Blasingame

Reprinted by permission from Connecticut Libraries 13(3) Summer 1971, p. 8-12.

"Systems," like spring, is in the air. The main difference is that spring will pass; it is an annual event (let us hope), and it comes new and fresh each year. Systems, on the other hand, is always with us. It does not fade into some other something and return new and fresh each year; of course, I may be premature, perhaps the cycle is only longer. Spring is its own definition; it comes to us as a part of nature's cycle. It is unmistakable, if fickle at times. Some group of people--some special "in-group"-- might call winter spring, but all the rest of us would recognize that fiction.

Systems contrariwise, reminds me of Alice's re-action to "Jabberwocky": "It seems very pretty," she said when she had finished it, "but it's rather hard to under-stand!" (You see she didn't want to confess, even to her-self, that she couldn't make it out at all.) "Somehow it seems to fill my head with ideas--only I don't know exactly what they are!"

With due respect to Alice's wisdom--in both being confused and refusing to say so--let me try to suggest what "Systems" may be, what kinds there are (perhaps), and to what extent they may be looking-glass phenomena.

When one takes time to step back from the practice of librarianship and to look at a number of "general" li-braries, one is struck by their similarity. Similarities are:

1. Apparent purposes and services
2. Methods of finance and government
3. Organization

4. Personal utilization
5. Attitudes
6. Even buildings--to some degree.

These similarities, added to a certain feeling of professional solidarity, give the impression that libraries offer fertile ground for cooperation or federation or some kind of getting together. In turn, it seems to me, these impressions lead to the development of the notion of library systems, defined in a number of ways--that is to say, not carefully defined at all as to purposes or services--these are assumed to be compatible, though to my knowledge, few if any library systems are based on knowledge of users' habits.

Ron Miller, in one of the most remarkably honest assessments of a library system I have seen, expressed this situation as follows:

> ... some members would define (the system) as an unincorporated group of people bound together by a constitution, by-laws, prior investment, and an uneasy feeling that money and time devoted to the enterprise could be spent better at home.
> In short, it is faith which holds the organization together, faith that somehow by magic it will all fall into place, and someone will throw a switch and all the lights will go on.

It is possible that the apparent compatibility of libraries as organizations has given us exactly the wrong impression: that it has filled our heads with ideas--only we don't exactly know what they are. Suppose, for a moment at least, that this apparent compatibility as viewed in the abstract becomes absolute chaos when viewed in the framework of any particular institution. Then it may seem that we are calling winter spring. And because it is so unpopular to call it winter, no member of our in-group dares confess with Alice that, "... she couldn't make it out at all."

Nearly all libraries are agencies which are, in turn, part of other agencies--cities, counties, schools, universities. We might, then, view libraries as being creatures of "place" communities, each of which has reasons for establishing service units--of which the library is only one. Our methods of governing communities--now I include all

those just named--require that resources be allocated by
some mechanism related to the place.   Libraries, however,
philosophically and actually, are devices for supporting interest communities: tropical fish fanciers, teachers of
history, physicists and so on.   These interest communities
know no place boundaries and their number is vast.

Now, to try to get back to my original intention.   I
have found a reasonably straightforward definition of system
--by the reasonably straightforward method of looking for
one in a dictionary: it is:

> A set or assemblage of things connected, asso-
> ciated or interdependent, so as to form a complex
> unity; a whole composed of parts in orderly ar-
> rangement according to some scheme or plan.

To me, speaking in terms of libraries, the several
parts of this definition are each important:

First, a system is a set of things--thus, the things
must be compatible, unless the dictionary misleads me as
to the meaning of set.

Second, these things must be connected, associated,
or interdependent.   I stress the last--interdependent--as
meaning that the parts satisfy purposes not complete in
themselves but without which the whole is incomplete.

Third, the parts must comprise a whole, presumably
unlike or superior to any one part--or indeed all the parts
if they are not.

Fourth, in orderly arrangement according to some
scheme or plan.

Now, let me go on to my second theme: the kinds of
library systems.   There are at least three kinds of library
systems--or so it seems to me:

First: Administrative systems--city libraries with
branches; university libraries with branches; businesses
with information centers having some interrelation, for
example.   These have primary allegiance to the place--are
supported by place communities.

Second: Proclaimed systems: the public library
system in New York State, or library consortia, such as
NELINET, for example.   The support here varies and
allegiances are diverse, to say the least.

Third: for lack of a better term, Phantom system--

infinitely more complex many times and often stretching across all kind of place boundaries, these are created by users for their special purposes.

The use of the word system with so many meanings again reminds me of Alice. Humpty Dumpty says that "When I use a word, it means just what I choose it to mean--neither more nor less." She replies, "The question is, whether you can make words mean so many different things." Humpty responds, "The question is, which is to be the master--that's all." In a spirit of generosity, however, he later says, "When I make a word do a lot of work ... I pay it extra."

The first two kinds of systems, incidentally, are bound together by constitutions and by-laws, prior investment, faith, and all those other things Mr. Miller set forth. Thus, productive or not, they tend to be rigid--to operate within bounds of some kind. The last (the Phantom system) if the user has any cunning at all, are by far the most flexible, the ones most apt, I suspect to satisfy all of the parts of my definition of system.

The first two are rigid for a number of reasons. First, since libraries are agencies established and operated by other agencies, the administrative system must satisfy to one degree or another the purposes of the large agency. The proclaimed system, composed of such libraries, must operate within those bounds, plus parameters set forth in its own constitution and by-laws, the sensitivities of the participants and so on. The likelihood of attaining the state of orchestration--the interdependence of parts--suggested in the definition of system is thus doubly limited.

Now, to further complicate our problem, libraries are used by many--certainly not all--people who are members of interest communities, and we librarians sense the pressures of those interests. We cannot resist them, but neither can we really satisfy them because doing so in any full scale fashion would lead us to give away scarce resources allocated to us by place communities.

Yet we keep at it. To quote Mr. Miller again:

> Libraries, over the past six to ten years, have
> been forming groups at a great rate--many of
> them for contradictory purposes. To foster

change, to prevent unwanted change; to depend on
entrenched position to absorb other; to increase
local resources by gaining access to others, to
keep hold of resources which local libraries already own.

Yet with it all, there is an air, in Miller's words, of
Heady expectancy.   Why this apparent thrust?

> 1.   Money--state or federal--to pay for some-
> thing we can't afford.
> 2.   A sense that library problems are some-
> how very much the same and that getting together
> will allow us to solve problems that can't be solved
> if we stand apart.
> 3.   Desire to be inside--to be where it is.
> 4.   Perhaps to relieve our frustrations by
> finding symbols to replace the realities we wish
> were here.

Of course some things have occured.   It is not proper
or fair not to recognize that some benefits have come from
some system.   Legislatures have aided in the support of
local libraries through systems.   In some cases the inaugura-
tion of systems has tempted unusually well-qualified people
to go to places they might otherwise have shunned.   Exchanges of materials and services have been effected.

But (1) how real are these things and (2) are the
accomplishments in scale with the problems we set out to
solve?   Without evaluation we will never know even approxi-
mations of answers to those two questions.   What is the
future in an era of scarcity of unevaluated activities?   If
we say any given system is real and not symbolic, there is
no one to prove us wrong--at least temporarily.

But in an era of scarce resources, this lack of
demonstrable reality could lead to the disappearance of
many of our systems as suddenly and mysteriously as did
Alice's delightful world.   So, if we use system and if we
intend to make it mean something, we should define it, we
should cherish it.   We ought to pay it extra.

THE LIBRARY LOBBY

by Anthony Ralston

Reprinted by permission from College & Research Libraries 32(6) November 1971, p. 427-431.

"The college library should be the most important intellectual resource of the academic community" ("Standards for College Libraries," CRL, July 1959, p. 274). In 1959, when this was written, the library was almost the only general intellectual resource at a college or university. Computers were barely beginning to be important at universities and the battery of instructional communications gear so familiar today was not a major factor on most campuses. Today, the library is still the most important resource of the academic community. I emphasize this point at the outset to try to avoid misunderstanding later. But the question is: Is the college or university library as preeminent as the library lobby--the librarians, accreditors, and their allies--would have us believe? If it is still the most important academic resource, how long will this be true? Is the portion of the university budget devoted to libraries in relation to the other academic resources reasonable? Most basic of all: What is the utility--if one can dare to talk in such terms--of most of the holdings of a university library? My general thesis is that relatively, if not absolutely, the value of much of university libraries is overrated and that, particularly in times of dwindling resources, the university library must no longer be considered sacrosanct, that its claims on the university budget need to be questioned as much or more than competing claims.

The Library Lobby

The power of the library lobby manifests itself both actively and passively. On the active side I had a glimpse of the power recently when I spent two days at a new, small college as a consultant on computer education and computer

usage problems.   It was depressing but not too surprising
to find that the computing budget was negligible, particularly
when contrasted to a library budget twenty to thirty times
greater.   Although there was a lack of perception of the
present and growing importance of computers in all phases
of the academic process, this was not the main reason for
the relative sizes of the computing and library budgets.
Rather, the college is hell bent for accreditation and thus
is forced to give high priority to building the 50,000-volume
collection necessary for accreditation.

Another positive indication of the power of the library
lobby may be found in the budget of the State University of
New York and likely other public institutions also, where
the appropriation for the libraries at the various campuses
is a line item separate from the rest of the budget for the
State University.   Although such special treatment could cut
both ways, in practice, there is no question that this treatment works for the benefit of the libraries by cushioning
them from budget competition with the rest of the university.

Recently (March 1971) in the Communications of the
Association for Computing Machinery there was an article
reporting on a meeting last fall in Houston of the ACM
Special Interest Group on University Computing Centers to
discuss the problem of resource allocation and charging for
use in university computing centers, a topic of no small
interest to academic computing people in times of level or
declining university budgets and declining federal support.
A main point of debate at this meeting was whether a college or university computing center should be run on the
bookstore model (charge users for all services, either
directly or through departmental budgets) or the library
model (let the computing center be a free resource for all
without external funding up to the capacity of the facility).
The arguments on the two sides are not relevant here.
What is relevant is that one never seems to hear arguments
about operating a library on the bookstore model!   Charge
every student or faculty member for every service including
borrowing a book?   Or, let each department have a budget
for library usage against which each transaction would be
charged?   Perish the thought!   The value of the library in
the educational process cannot be measured by such techniques as charging for services.   Or can it?

The Three Faces of University Libraries

One of the barriers to appropriate perception of the university library is its description as a general intellectual resource for the entire university community. Such a description is in fact much more applicable to a university computing center in which all users make use of approximately the same set of resources--the computer and its associated peripheral hardware. But only a minor portion of a university library--that part which serves general undergraduate education--contains resources used by a wide variety of people. Most of the remainder of the library consists of:

(1) Departmental fiefs, sometimes but rarely used by anyone except faculty, graduate students, and undergraduate students in one or, at most, a very small number of departments; and (2) individual research fiefs where the book holdings and perhaps periodical back issues and subscriptions also are provided--often at great expense--for the research needs of one faculty member or a small group of faculty members.

If the above language sounds pejorative, that is not because I am opposed to research holdings in libraries; I'm not, of course. Rather, my point is that the narrow utility of such holdings is seldom admitted.

On many campuses, indeed, the university library holdings are fragmented into smaller libraries, often departmental libraries. On others, such departmental libraries have been fought for but the proponents of central facilities have won. In my context the important point is the existence of the controversy which at least implies the nearly local nature of much of the holdings of a university library. It is, by the way, interesting to note that those who favor departmental libraries usually still wish the local library to be not only administered by the university staff but also supported by it. Departments are usually interested in library budgets only to the extent that funds are available in the university library budget for specific support of their needs.

The contrast with computing is interesting. Departments may have their own computers but they almost always both administer and support them themselves. This contrast between libraries and computers was probably reasonable when generous federal funding was available for the latter but not the former.   But this is no longer the case and a closer congruence between administration and support for departmental libraries and computers seems to be in order.

Library collections--books and periodicals--which support fairly narrow research activities account for a significant portion of library expenditure including some of the most costly on a per book or journal basis.   It needs to be recognized that such collections are quite analogous to the laboratory equipment so important to the research of scientists and engineers.   Again, it is true that, in the halcyon days of massive federal funding for laboratory equipment, no valid argument could be made for considering library collections oriented toward specific research areas analogously with laboratory equipment.   But times have changed and now more thought should be given to treating some library acquisitions and expenditures in a manner similar to laboratory equipment.

My conclusion then is that the support of university libraries should be looked at in three parts: (1) That which truly supports a university-wide academic resource; (2) that which mainly supports departmental needs rather than wider needs; and (3) that which mainly supports individual research.

It is clearly not simple to assign each item in a university to one of these three categories.   Indeed, it is clearly not in the interests of those for whom parts of a library serve as little more than personal research collections to make this distinction.   The result is often individual or departmental demands, particularly at growing universities, for increases in collections in certain areas which just bear no relation to the general academic function of the department.   I heard recently of a humanities department chairman who claimed that a minimum of $750,000 was needed to bring an already substantial collection up to snuff.   It was not clear whether he thought his faculty or students really needed to read any substantial part of this material or whether the tactile pleasure which would be gleaned from handling the books was the real point.   In any case, such requests are only possible because we have lost control of the place of libraries at universities.   Only when we get this under control will the insatiable demands of university libraries for funds be put in a perspective

where they will no longer result in deprivation of other
parts of the university.

Now it is surely impractical to physically divide the
library budget into three parts as implied by the categories
above.   But it is not impractical to estimate the approxi-
mate parts of the library budget attributable to each area
and to make budgetary decisions based on this.   In particular the total university resources available for departmental
support and research support should include the funds now
used to support the latter two categories above.   Departments should be able--perhaps should be forced--to choose
how much of the total support available to them should be
spent on libraries.   From another point of view, some of
the funds expended for other than university-wide library
support might be diverted to support such university-wide
resources--and not just in libraries--or vice versa.

The Utility of a University Library

Let us admit that it is surely very difficult to measure the value to a university of a book or a collection of
books.   Indeed, it is widely felt that attempts to attach such
values to any facet of the academic process is antithetical
to it; education may be a product but who has the temerity to
place a value on it or its components?   Yet one of the reasons for the current financial problems of universities is
their failure to establish priorities.   And such priorities
can only be set by attempting, at least in a relative sense,
to measure the value, the utility of allocating resources
among conflicting competitors.

The single most important point to make about the
utility of the books in a university library is that this
varies greatly among the collection.   Coupled with this is
the fact that very few, if any, libraries consider the utility
of a particular book or periodical when ordering it.   There
are, for example, those libraries which have standing
orders into major publishers for everything they publish
and which subscribe to almost every periodical in print.
Now it is true that often one cannot fairly judge the value
of a particular book or periodical.   The sum of a library's
holdings in an area may be greater than its parts because,
for example, it may provide an environment conducive to
research where a smaller holding will not.   Still this does
not gainsay the fact that large portions of most library

collections are not only unused but, more important, are
such that there is low probability that they will ever be used.

Moreover, the costs of using a university library are
seldom calculated and are, in fact, much greater than most
people realize. For example, a recent survey of major university libraries (CRL, Jan. 1970, p. 28-35) indicated that
the ratio of total library expenditure to the volume of general and reserve circulation indicates a cost of about $4.00
per book circulated. Now, of course, this isn't really a
fair number. Libraries are not just circulators of books.
Many people work in the library itself. Still, however one
looks at it, the cost of providing service to its users is
high. Corresponding figures for computing centers are hard
to come by but, as an example, the University of Colorado
charges a minimum cost of $.60 (which includes $.20 representing the rent charged by the university to the center) for
each job run. This minimum cost is in fact the actual cost
for most jobs, particularly those run by students.

Now who has ever thought of comparing the educational or research value of borrowing a book or periodical
from a library and running a program on a computer?
Maybe the values are incommensurate. But unless there is
an attempt to make such value judgments, it is difficult to
see how any rational decisions can be made on the allocation of resources to libraries and computing.

The Breadth of Usage of a University Library

There should be no university discipline which does
not make some use of a university library. But the amount
of usage and library requirements are widely disparate.
Whereas an historian may need to study broadly and deeply
in a collection of books and documents, many scientists require libraries only quite occasionally and then for very
specific, directed study to a single book or periodical.
Therefore, whereas for teaching purposes the reserve collection may be very important to scientists, their research
needs may be much more limited. In terms of its value
to their work, the library may be quite secondary to many
scientists (and others). Of much more importance may be
their own laboratory equipment and computing facilities.

By contrast, the use of university computing facilities
is not yet nearly so widespread for teaching or research as

the use of the library. Outside the physical sciences, engineering, and the social sciences, many departments make
no use at all of computing facilities. It is easy to predict
that the rapid spread of the use of computing throughout the
academic process will continue until it will be a rare student
and rare researcher who does not have contact with computing. But a more important point is that the number of
departments to which the computer is vital for teaching and
research is not significantly different from those to which
a major library is vital. Thus, if a library is still the
most important academic resource on a college campus, it
no longer stands by itself, far more important than the computing resources.

From the point of view of immediacy, computing
facilities on campus are even more important to those who
need them than is a comprehensive library to those who require it. Lack of adequate computing facilities or fast
service can be a severe, sometimes fatal impediment to
effective research activity. Use of off-campus facilities is
often not a reasonable alternative for both cost and logistic
reasons. The lack of a specific book or periodical at a
particular instant seldom causes similar difficulties. Admittedly, the efficiency of interlibrary loan procedures leaves
much to be desired, but it is relatively unusual for the lack
of specific items in the university library to make a research activity unfeasible. Also, when this is so, the
needed item or items are likely to be of the very rare and/
or expensive kind which puts them in the class analogous to
laboratory equipment rather than in the class of a university-wide resource.

Thus, those parts of university libraries which truly
serve as university-wide resources are on the one hand quite
comparable in breadth of usage to a computing center and,
on the other hand, by no means the whole of the library.

Libraries and the New Technology

I have studiously avoided thus far any arguments
based on the effect of computer and communications technology on libraries. I believe it would be necessary to
reconsider the relative position of libraries and computing
facilities even if there were no indication of a significant
impact by this technology on the structure of a library and
how it transacts it business. And let us admit that the im-

pact of this technology looks much less profound or at least much further in the future than many computing people felt just a few years ago.   But, for example, rapid long-distance facsimile reproduction, such as by long-distance xerography, is not too far away from becoming economic. When it is, the argument for extensive duplication of back periodical holdings or even current specialized periodicals will decrease considerably.   All that need be said here is that none of the foregoing arguments require any of the new technology to be valid, but all will be strengthened as the new computer and communications technology becomes available and economic.

This article is a plea for a reconsideration if not a reevaluation of the relative place of a library in a university. It is a plea to make this reconsideration in an atmosphere free of the shibboleths of the past or the vested interests of the present.   Although it is clear that I believe the result of such a study would be to downgrade this still most important resource, I believe even more strongly that universities must reassess their commitments in all areas if they are to survive the current parlous times in as good shape as possible.

Part II:

TECHNICAL SERVICES/TECHNICAL PROCESSES

THE GREAT GAS BUBBLE PRICK'T;
OR, COMPUTERS REVEALED
--BY A GENTLEMAN OF QUALITY*

Reprinted by permission from College & Research Libraries 32(3) May 1971, p. 183-196.

In which are Exposed the delicious Delusions of those will-o-the-wisps; the Echoes in computerization of Phrenology, Haruspication, and other discredited Ancient sciences; and the moral and Mental decline of our Profession.

> "If it costs you twenty-five percent more, will you stop it?"
> "No."
> "Why not?"
> "Because we believe that sooner or later all libraries will automate."
> --From a real-life, absurd conversation.

On an evaluation visit last spring to a small college (collection 175,000 volumes, peak daily circulation 700), I found the library automating its circulation records, an action tantamount to renting a Boeing 747 to deliver a bon-bon across town. Everyone felt great about it; it was a Good Thing! In a college sorely pressed for funds, wasting this amount of money was actually a serious crime against the common weal.

This situation nicely characterizes the fatuousness of one of the most curious periods in our nation's history--the period that began with a rebound off Sputnik, which seemed for a moment to snatch a tip from our crown of world leadership, to strip us of our masculinity, as it were. In

---

*Ellsworth Mason

90

this period, which has now passed its peak, money meant nothing, the world of formal education was endowed with magical properties, and technology became an unquestioned God (If we can put a man on the moon we can ...). This decade boasted of its technical potency with the false bravado of a male virgin, and if the moon rocket in the Sea of Tranquillity was its sexual symbol, the computer, choked in its navel cord of programs, was its abortion.

This fact has yet to be generally absorbed. It has already become painfully clear that technology is a two-edged sword of Damocles. Grave doubt has been raised that the computer has done even major industries much good.[1] But, oblivious to the signs of change, librarians are proceeding in a kind of stunned momentum like a poleaxed steer, because the computer industry and its public handmaidens have polluted our intellects. In one of the most massive public manipulations in history, the computer has been joined to Motherhood, the True, the Good, and the Beautiful. Operational considerations have been stripped to a stark choice between "the old hand-method" (ugh!) and THE COMPUTER. The effect has been to obscure a whole range of machine and machine-manual alternatives.[2] Technology has been set back many years and intelligence has been uprooted. Any fool who does anything with a computer for any reason (we all know at least one) is automatically a genius; anyone who does not is the last of the dinosaurs.

During a period of study sponsored by a Council on Library Resources (CLR) fellowship which allowed me to study problems in ten major research libraries last spring, my observations convinced me that the high costs of computerization make it unfeasible for library operations and that it will become increasingly expensive in the future.[3] The computer feeds on libraries. We actually devote large amounts of talent and massive amounts of money (perhaps $25 million dollars a year in academic libraries alone) to diminish collections and reduce services, exactly at a time when libraries are starved for both, by channeling money into extravagant computerization projects which have little or no library benefits. While my original expectations were entirely in the opposite direction, after talking at length with some of the finest computer experts in the library world and probing the thinking behind more than forty computerized library operations, it became clear that the application of computers to library processes is a disaster, and that no one is willing to admit it.

The reasons for its adoption are governed by a range of irresponsible, irrational, and totally unmanaged factors, both within the library and in the university, that cannot fail to disgust anyone seriously concerned about the academic world. This article intends to analyze how we learn to stop thinking and love the machine, and to make possible the return of intellect and managerial methods to an area of library practice from which both have been driven.

The Rough Beast with Three Breasts

Unlike most other machines, the computer is not subject to reasonable surveillance at any level of operation. [4] A college president or the manager of industrial research cannot judge with any reasonable degree of accuracy how much computer capacity is required for his needs, nor can his subordinates. This means that basically he must accept his computer configuration on faith and on the urgings of computer industry representatives.

This condition in which the computer wanders free from quality checks extends right down the line of a computer operation to the head of programming, who cannot judge with any degree of precision the quality of the programs written for him. [5] He can tell whether they run (indeed, the principal struggle is to get them to run trouble-free at all), but he cannot tell how they rate in comparison with the range of other alternatives. This free-form condition of control, which is inherent in the occult nature of the computer, accounts for the great range of loose work and random performance observable in computer operations.

Moreover, a computer operation is incapable of becoming stabilized on its own terms. No matter what level of performance is achieved, if a later generation computer is marketed, it is necessary to shift as soon as possible to the new generation, with all the agonies, dislocations, and setbacks involved in the change, and with no assurance that the same level of results can be achieved. There is no choice of remaining as you are if reasonably satisfied with your results because it is extremely difficult to recruit a systems and programming staff (doubly difficult for libraries, which lack the glamor and loose money that have characterized industry until recently). A good staff will abandon a superseded model computer, since to remain would make them professionally obsolescent.

These two floating conditions make computer operations basically uncontrollable. In managerial terms, these
facts alone would argue for discarding out of hand any other
machine in existence, until it was amenable to quality control. But we have been conditioned to suspend completely
the requirements that apply to all other equipment, and
automatically accept the computer as Good, without questioning. We accept the computer as the pot of gold at the end
of the rainbow, the touchstone that turns dross into gold.
Glittering with spangles, draped seductively in the fluff of
unreason, it really has sex appeal, and who applies reason
while gulping the lures of a floozie like Myra Breckenridge?[6]

The New Bloomusalem

When Leopold Bloom, Joyce's common man in
Ulysses, proclaims, while playing God in an hallucination,
"the golden city which is to be, " thirty-two workmen wear-
ing rosettes construct "The New Bloomusalem, " a mega-
structure in the shape of a huge pork kidney. Something
like this debased miracle happened in library computerization in the decade of the sixties, when computers rode tall
in the industrial saddle and librarians flung themselves at
the horse's tail. During that decade, our large problems
were operational (whereas now they are desperately financial) and we looked for a panacea. Noting us sniffing
around the computer, the industry perked up and assured
us they were the answer.

A kind of syllogistic thinking followed--we have
problems; the computer says it can solve them; therefore,
using the computer solves our problems. [7] It's all simple
enough and clear enough if you just have Faith, and of
course, Reason is the enemy of Faith; in fact, it gets in
the way of certainty. In our awe at the wonders of technology, we forgot the deadly threat of Dr. Strangelove's
mechanical hand. Like lemmings moving toward the sea,
we surged to get with it, became scientists, became industrialists, and practiced the best that was known and felt
in the business world. [8] In the whole range of the academic
world, we forgot one of our traditional functions--to suspect the beguilement and evanescence of the moment and
"to keep clean our sense of difference between the temporarily and the permanently significant. "[9] In short, we
embraced with fervor all the sins of the commercial world.
Now, look at the commercial world and at the academic

world and wonder how it is that student rebels connect the
two.

The fascination of the computer, like that of a hooded
cobra, lies in its exotic beauty, which fixes its victim for
the spurt of poison.   On the surface it seems to have many
answers.   It looks effortless, is pleasantly mysterious, it
makes pleasing sounds, it promises great speed, and it has
a reputation for performing miracles.   Despite its beginnings
in 1942 (long before Xerox), it is considered the latest
technological development.   So we got with the new and the
technologically best by adopting the computer.   We did so
to solve simple and clearly defined problems--to save staff
(or substitute for staff that we couldn't hire), to speed processing, and to save money.   Information retrieval was seen
in the distant mist, but these were the clear and central
targets.

But when we used the computer, it didn't save staff,
and it didn't speed processing, and it cost a great deal more
to do the same things we were doing by hand.   Our reaction
was to computerize more.   Although we lost money on every
operation we computerized, the theory grew that if you knit
enough losses together, obviously you would save money.   In
Orwellian doublethink, if you waste money in an attempt to
save it, save better by wasting more.   We still didn't save
staff, and we didn't speed processing, and it cost us even
more money.   Our latest answer is to use newer and bigger
and more expensive computers; it still is not saving us staff
or speeding processing, and we are now spending extravagant
amounts of money.   We bombed library problems with the
computer, and the strategy didn't work.   So we bombed even
more problems with the computer and it still didn't work,
so we are bombing even more.

Just Like General Motors

At this point, the third strange fact about the computer becomes clear.   It is a half-baked machine.   Every
other kind of equipment we use is bought for specific purposes, to perform defined tasks, at a known cost.   Even
highly automated equipment like the MT/ST comes with a
simple program to perform known tasks after a modicum
of training. A wholly baked computer, nicely browned,
would be ordered to specifications, and would come ready
to dust off, to insert the program provided by the manu-

facturer to do what we wanted to be done, and to begin our computerized operation.   Only under such conditions would we consider any other machine.   But we have been brainwashed not to apply the same reasonable standards to the computer.   The cobra has us hypnotized.

When it is dumped on your dock, it can do nothing for you; like, Ford delivers you a Continental and deposits it in your yard.   You leap with joy and shout to the neighbors who come to admire.   You puff with pride, as we do for computers.   "Let's go for a ride," they say.   Somewhat sheepishly, you explain that it is a new proto-electric Continental, with a wonderful fume-free motor, but that there is no battery known strong enough to power it.   When they say, "Why did you buy it?" do you reply, "Oh, I'll do my own Research and Development to produce the battery"?

Such an answer would be insane, but this is exactly what we do for computers. [10]   We assume the responsibility, the elaborate costs, and the human agonies involved in programming to make the machine do what we knew we wanted it to do before we bought it.   In one project now underway, it will take a staff of ten, three years to make anything happen.   Libraries really are getting important when they can play junior GM (without GM's budget) and launch amateur research and development operations, which is what programming really consists of.   No matter how good our systems staff, such research and development must remain amateur.   We don't know enough about technology even to know which field we should work in to solve our problems, let alone which machine we should encourage.   We haven't the meagerest grasp of the perspective required by industrial R & D.   But we have enthusiasm, we have suspended our brains, and we've come to love the computer.

We spend millions making the computer work for library activities, with a guarantee that it will produce a built-in deficit and with only a vague chance that it will improve anything.   We simply can't wait for the finished machine, for the one that really works, the one which when it comes will make computers useless.   We must develop it ourselves, even if we have to sell our libraries (which we are doing) to do so.

How We Are Covered with Locusts
 and How the Invasion Began

How did we get into this mess?   There are prece-

dents in human history.   The mountebank pulls up at the
crossroads and the yokels throng the tailgate to buy snake-
oil guaranteed to cure any disorder of libraries.   Gullibility
accounts for part of it; pressures account for the rest.   The
physical scientists and mathematicians brought the computer
on campus for its computational facility. [11]   Engineering,
which quickly was seized by electronics specialists, bur-
geoned later.   From these three groups came large demands for computer time in the universities.   Administrators, naive and uninformed, began pressures to have all
the computer time on campus used because of its heavy
cost.   They began by offering "free" computer time (an interesting concept at current prices) to any department that
would use it.   This free offer sprang from the prestige
value inherent in using the computer (the industry did supply
the prestige) and from a conviction on the part of administrators (also supplied by the industry) that use of the computer saved money for any operation it touched.

As this free time was used, the demand for computer time overran that available, and bigger, better, and
much more expensive computers were brought on campus.
With even greater increases in expense, administrative pressure (as brainless as all other pressures involved in computerization) intensified, and in some instances became
downright nasty to departments that dragged their feet either
through lethargy or knowledge.   They were joined by the
computer engineering faculty, which in recent INTREXed
years, has become self-deluded to an extreme degree. [12]

Librarians, most of whom are humanistically trained,
are especially sensitive to accusations by technologists and
administrators of refusing the best that is known to business
and technology.   Even when they know better, consistent
pressures unsettle their confidence.   To cool the hot breath
of the president's office, one university made a list of
special materials by computer when they knew in advance
they could do it considerably cheaper by more than one non-
computer method.   To appease the demands of a renowned
and totally impractical engineer, one university went to a
computerized circulation system as the least wasteful operation they could run on the computer.   The fatuous self-confidence of computer experts is considerably jolted when they
have to cope with the demands of library operations, which
are far more complex than anything else they tackle in
terms of their machine.   But so long as they can throw
stones from a comfortable theoretical distance their pressures are compelling indeed.

The Electronic Calf

In a time of waning personal confidence, it takes a very strong man to stand up to a university president and tell him he's wrong when he is convinced by technologists that inertia springs from ignorance. There are only a few men left these days. Therefore, with the prod in our rear, or approaching, we adapted to the new campus ecology, now polluted by technologists. Although some librarians seized the computer for its public relations value (look, mommy: no catalogers!), the more sober members of the fraternity went along with a better conscience by adopting a mystique about the computer that grew partly outside and partly inside librarianship.

This mystique generated, and in turn was generated by, a group of librarians whose livelihood depended on the computer, and whose reason for being depended largely on their ability to believe the computer industry's claims laid out before them. The emergence of this Faith and the band of True Believers have been responsible for the rapidity with which we have gotten into computerization despite all evidence that the fantastic claims for the computer are completely false. This group of the faithful was abetted by enormous sums of government and foundation money that flowed, like Niagara's of champagne (Lucius Beebe's phrase), into computerized projects for a five-year period. With this amplitude of fuel, these neo-Zoroastrians began to burn up the world.

The Revelation

Blazoned across the dark benighted sky of conventional librarianship were the following Truths:

THE FIRST TRUTH--Come to the computer all ye who are heavy laden and It will make everything effortless. 13
THE FACTS--The computer has involved librarians in greater and more prolonged agonies than anything in recent history short of the Florence flood. Agonies of campus politics (flipped from computer to computer), agonies of financing (since the golden angels have gone), agonies of programming, patching programs, reprogramming, redebugging programs, agonies of lengthy machine breakdowns, agonies of deception by computer experts (both in industry and in other campus units) have left deep scars on every

library computer expert I have known. [14] While I was on campus one university was executing the second major cutback of computer capacity within three years, each causing major upheavals and changes in staffs and procedures and the bitterest kind of infighting to control the nature of the computer configuration. The most efficient road to ulcers on a college campus, short of the president's office, is through library computerization.

THE SECOND TRUTH--Thou shalt do everything with the speed of light, if thou butst computerize.

THE FACTS--Response time of computers, which is incredibly fast (as fast as the movement of an electron), is not to be confused with the response time of computerized processes. [15] It is common knowledge that computerized class schedules take weeks longer to produce than the old hand method. In librarianship, these are some of the commonplace delays found strewn all along the trail: Circulation, a delay of one day in the ability of the circulation file to account for the location of a charged book (in one case, the costs of paper led to updating the file only once every three days). On-line circulation, the alternative to batching, is so astronomically expensive that anyone who adopts it should be summarily condemned as a public malefactor. Acquisitions--consistently slower in placing orders. Acquisitions was so slow the spring that I was on campus that, in one case, 20 percent of their periodical subscriptions were cancelled due to slow placement of orders. Book catalogs--longer and longer delays in cumulations because of the costs involved. In the case of one university, an operation highly touted while in action had left a liberal arts college with its book catalog in four (repeat, four) parts. They were at the point of doing what they were sure would be, forever, their last total cumulation because of its cost, while their future lies in a book catalog always in two and three parts. They would like to go to a card catalog, but at 100,000 volumes, cannot afford to. One circulation operation, where the students were cleared faster than previously at the charge-out point, claimed this advantage, without noting that the new system involved the use of book cards in lieu of user-written cards, and that the computer charging console takes longer than most simple charging machines.

THE THIRD TRUTH--The computer will save you money.

THE FACTS--Computer experts laughed when I sug-

gested economy as a motive for adopting the computer. No
one claimed to have saved any money doing anything by computer, and although the analysis of computer costs is, to be
charitable, hair-raisingly casual, estimates of costs of doing
by computer exactly the same thing that had previously been
done manually were extremely high (in one case, five times
the cost).   We now know there is no clear evidence that
the computer has saved industry money "even in routine
clerical operations."[16]

THE FOURTH TRUTH--Well, anyway, once you have
done it, thou shalt have economies in future programming
by having programs convertible to later generation computers.
THE FACTS--Absolutely false! About half of the
third-generation computers in major industries are in an
emulation mode that makes them perform as second-genera-
tion computers because industry, having been hooked on the
enormous programming costs for the second generation, is
unwilling to absorb even higher costs to program for the
third generation, which leads to an interesting view of our
economy (like our libraries), buying the latest to get with it
to avoid losing face.[17]

THE FIFTH TRUTH--Well, anyway, once someone has
done it, programs can be converted from location to location, to you save the expense of programming for yourself.
THE FACTS--This initially was one of the most appealing lures of the computer industry.   A few years ago,
in a correspondence with Robert Hayes of the University of
California, I asked why we all had to make the computer
repeat on machine the motions we were doing by hand.
Since we all need about the same end products at the same
key points in a serials operation, why couldn't one library
program it and present the program in modules, each of
which could accomplish one thing, for us to choose those
we preferred?   At length, in a series of letters, I learned
the elaborate and complex reasons why this could not be done.
All the library computerators I questioned agree that trans-
ferability of programs is completely unfeasible at present
and in the future.[18]

THE SIXTH TRUTH--Thou shalt have cheap computerization by sharing computers with others.
THE FACTS--This, again, was one of the bright
promises laid out by the computer industry, but the deeper
we get into library computerization, the more evident it becomes that sharing computers to reduce costs is a chimera.

Yet within the month, an eminent professor of industrial management who read my CLR report trotted out the old turkey that, with remote access consoles, sharing computers would soon make them economical.

THE SEVENTH TRUTH--Thou shalt save money as you multiply the separate operations that you computerize if you combine them by a systems approach.
THE FACTS--Though a common belief among the aborigines of Computeria and sustained by a well-developed theology, there is no evidence whatsoever to support this belief. 19

THE EIGHTH TRUTH--Thou shalt have greater service for the public by computerizing library operations.
THE FACTS--Most of the libraries computerized seem to have no interest in improving service, as we can see from such things as their average line-staff salaries (mostly at the peonage level), the size of their cataloging backlog (in one case about 300,000 volumes), and the staffing of their campus branch libraries (about half of the staff needed). Money wasted in computerization could greatly improve service if applied to these areas. Also, processes that delay placement of orders, delay accountability of circulation records, and split the card catalog in multiple parts would not seem to be aimed directly at improving service to the public.

The Credo

Throughout the land, the priesthood, with no exception, recited to me "The Credo of Automatic Automators":

I believe in the increasing cost of labor and the decreasing cost of computers.
I believe that in ten years (the time span was standardized) the cost curves will cross in favor of computers.
I believe that even if it isn't cheaper, the by-products of computerization make it worthwhile.

Since my pilgrimage, I have had the same Credo recited by others who were not specifically computerators, so there must be international specifications for its writing. It requires some examination.

First: there really is no "decreasing cost of computers." It is true that, on paper, the unit rental cost of
new generations of computers decreases, but in sounding
out what actually happens in practical applications, it is
evident that the cost of applying the machines has increased
due to various factors, one being the difficulty of keeping
the computer fed without interruption. [20]   But the central
fact is that the overwhelming costs in computerization are
labor costs (machine costs run about 20 percent of the
total), and the salaries of systems analysts and programmers go up even faster than library staff salaries.   Even
after initial development costs are absorbed, the repeated
costs of reprogramming and program adjustment are very
high.   Since the costs of computerized library operations
are far higher than manual alternatives now, and the costs
of computer labor are increasing faster than library labor
costs, computerization will become increasingly expensive
in the future.

Second: we are willing to accept any machine that
will save us money at any time, [21] but if that time is ten
years from now, then 1981 is the time to adopt the machine.   What kind of folly wastes money for ten years on
a machine that it hopes will eventually save money?   Within ten years new machines, now unseen, will emerge in
competition with the computer.

Third: the matter of by-products is the smelliest
red herring of all those dragged across our path by computerators.   The word is invoked with a kind of awe, as
though it descends from heaven to banish all the disabilities
of the computer.   As Melcher put it: "we find ourselves invited to applaud computer applications that are somewhat in
a class with the dog who played the violin--not that it was
done well, but rather than it was done at all."[22]   I keep
having draped before me as accomplishments by-products
that either are of no use whatsoever for a library operation,
or that have a very low incidence of use, or that can easily
be done by hand or by other machines faster and at a
lower cost.   The questions that are ignored must be asked
--what by-products are worthwhile, for what library purposes, at what costs, and for what incidence of use?   In
sum, I find the Credo, like all matters of dogma, an ex-
cuse for suspending the intellect on the part of librarians
and managers.

The Miracles

        At the very peak of library computerization we are
breeding a group of extremely able librarians, whose otherwise fine intelligence is completely blown when they evaluate
their machine. They analyze their daily operations with
command and critical brilliance, but when they talk about
their future, like a sun-crazed prospector dribbling fool's
gold through his fingers, a dull film covers their eyes, and
they babble about miracles to come that are just around the
corner, with not a shred of evidence to support their beliefs. Their faith is the exact equivalent of a witch's faith
in flying ointment. Unfortunately, we have long passed the
stage in which we could run a library from a broomstick.

        Nevertheless, one can respect the priesthood. It's
the acolytes, and at their fringe, the sycophants that make
us feel unclean. Here we are in a range of one-upmanship
and pretentiousness straight from Madison Avenue. [23] Responses to questionnaires about computerized operations
produce amazing answers, if you know what is really going
on in libraries. If someone lays down a transistor on a
typewriter, the department is likely to respond that it has
automated. The computer is used to cover up weaknesses
as cowdung was to plaster frontier log cabins. If catalogers
are low producers, if circulation is in chaos, the tendency
is to computerize instead of reviewing or revising operations, both of which require thinking.

        So, the rules of thumb are clear--if you start a
library from scratch, computerize and you're fifty years old. [24]
If you're upgrading an Ag college, the computer will liber-
alize cows. If you're a frustrated junior college, computerize and it makes you Ph. D. If your faculty is lousy,
computerize and you'll be Harvard. If you're bush league,
computerize and you'll win the Series. If you're stupid,
computerize and you'll feel great. Instant achievement by
machine and cheap attempts to invoke a false sheen of glory
have replaced an intelligent confrontation of the problems in
a large number of weak libraries.

Run, Rabbit, Run

        In view of the irrationality of the forces that led to
library computerization, and the subsequent aggravation of
this situation by self-seekers, it should come as no surprise

that managerial practice has entirely left this field. [25]   Of
the forty-odd computer projects reviewed on my leave in
ten major libraries, not one was begun on the basis of a
managerial decision, after carefully reviewing and costing
the operation to be converted, costing other machine or
machine-manual alternatives (which were obviously available
for many of them), or carefully projecting the costs of the
computer operation after development costs (which one
should be willing to absorb if retrievable over a period of
time).   Since most of the projects were doing only what
had been done manually, price should have been the major
factor in making this decision, yet very little cost analysis
was applied, although all the libraries were hard pressed
for funds.   No computerators were surprised when I reported lack of managerial decisions; it was taken for granted
that there were none in computerization.   Like concupiscence,
the desire to computerize simply must be satisfied no matter what the cost, and this at a time when most universities
and libraries are bankrupt and facing an even bleaker financial future.

Downhill All the Way

My discussions of this problem have produced a number of oppositions over the past few months, the most interesting of which is the concept of comparative incompetence
advanced by a friend of mine.   It makes no difference, the
argument goes, that no careful cost comparisons precede
computerization, because most librarians do not analyze
costs before making other changes in libraries.   The premise, I think, is false; but even if it were true, it is almost
impossible to make even approximately as large a commitment in any other way in a library as that involved in computerization, where a quarter of a million dollars is
meager.

More harrowing than the enormous costs is the fact
that a computerized system is virtually irreversible, the
fourth distinctive disability of this machine. [26]   Once you
begin a systems approach to computerizing operations, you
are hung by the gills on the computer industry's fishstringer
for good.   Once applied, the computer acts as a powerful
agent against change.   The dynamics here are interesting.
One library began to computerize by hiring a systems librarian who hired one programmer when they began to convert their circulation operation.   Two years later, when

the agonies of this conversion had subsided (and the circulation costs were fantastically more expensive than the manual
system, and they were cumulating circulation records only
every three days), the staff of this department was five, and,
having been blooded, was eager to begin computerizing another operation.   Even if you could prove that further computerization was diabolically evil, you still could not stop
this momentum.

    In addition, once computerization begins, the campus
pressures on the library to get with it have been assuaged,
the operation has been tapped for its public relations value,
and personal and institutional egos are heavily invested in
ploughing ahead to disaster.   This is especially true if
the computer project is the librarian's baby.   One highly
touted serials project began on "free" computer time, then
later was charged for the campus computer costs (which
hurt, but were not disabling).   When the campus changed
its computer and this operation had to use commercial firms
for the computer configuration necessary to run its program,
the cost more than doubled previous costs.   After reprogramming for over a year, this serials operation is still
processed partly off and partly on campus.   It is known as
a disaster area among computer experts, but this librarian
stated recently that he thought it had done his library a lot
of good.

    Inertia also results from sheer moral exhaustion.
The prolonged agonies inflicted on any sane person during
the process of converting to computerization push him to the
extremes of human endurance.   After all the bugs are ex-
terminated and the system is running, it is virtually impossible for a survivor of the process to summon up the moral
strength to rethink, reorganize, redevise processes, and re-
staff.   In one case, where superficial cost comparisons convinced an acquisitions operation it was saving money, more
sober thought made clear that it was losing money and
taking longer by computer.   But the department head was
very indignant when I proposed that they could return to
their former system--"After going through all of that?"
Another department head refused even to reconsider and
attempt costs comparisons when, after three years, her
computer system was finally working.

    Then, of course, there are enormous inflexibilities
imposed against change by finances.   Development costs in
one case seem to be running over a million and a half dol-

lars.   You can be sure that it will take quite a jolt to
make a library abandon that large an investment.   In other
instances, the costs of changing to an alternative system
require large amounts of money not in hand, as in the college with the four-part book catalog that would prefer a
card catalog.   Until the totality of waste in operating by
computer becomes so large that the figure really appalls,
the library is not likely to make the sensible move, especially in the fact of the beneficent connotation that (in libraries, at least) is still attached to the computer.

The Brave New World

        Anyone who computerizes at this point in time is
hitching his wagon to a falling star.   The honeymoon is
over, if our seduction by the computer can be so termed.
We have been sucked in by one of the most potent information control powers in recent history.   Computerizing library operations at present and projected costs, and with fore-
seeable results, is intellectually and fiscally irresponsible
and managerially incompetent.   The proper answer to
idiots who beamingly dangle their computerized projects
for our admiration is, "Why don't you do something useful,
instead. "

        The shrinking financial support of the academic
world will drive us to sense even against our will.   On the
campus where I found forty-nine computers (four of them
IBM 360's; one, the largest capacity known), the president
gave the bloodiest state-of-the-university speech to date--
dropping three academic programs, cutting back the current budget forthwith a million dollars, forecasting a
further rollback of 3.5 million over the next three years,
and even this predicated on unusual success in fund raising.

        This is no temporary condition tied to the recession.
More than two years ago, it was apparent that the public
had become disillusioned with technology and education.
They expected miracles of both; yet it is clear that each
is the answer to only a part of our national problems.
Public support for technology, a keystone in education's
expansion, will continue to decline.   Alumni disillusionment
with campus products has seriously diminished alumni support.   Foundations have been turning from the academy to
other social agencies.   The production of bachelor's, master's, and doctorate degrees has overrun the market for

their products.   Elementary and secondary school popula-
tions continue to decline.   Education has costed itself out
of sight, either in tuition costs or in the total costs of
public institutions.   All of these factors guarantee us future
curtailment of programs in higher education and a continual
decline in financial support, except for those programs immediately responsive to immediate problems that enjoy public
favor.   Make no mistake, we are about to shake out the
men from the boys, and the future in libraries (as in other
areas of university services) lies with the managers, who
can make the most out of every cent available.   The computer is the machine that evaporates money the fastest. 27

    In sum, our experience with the computer in library
operations has been one more replay of "The Emperor's
New Clothes, " and what we were led to believe were distant
mountains laden with gold, available merely by boring a
drift in the slope, turn out, upon close inspection, to be
the hairy buttocks of the well-fed computer industry.   And
from such a source we have gotten exactly what we should
expect.

References

1.   Quite obviously, this kind of view is not encouraged
       by industry, but when it emerges, it is extremely
       revealing.   In "Computers Can't Solve Everything, "
       Fortune (Oct. 1969, p. 126-29+), Tom Alexander
       reports the principal findings of a highly disen-
       chanting survey by the Research Institute of
       America of computerization in 2, 500 leading U. S.
       industrial companies.   In "Automation: Rosy
       Prospects and Cold Facts, " Library Journal (15
       March 1968, p. 1105-09), Daniel Melcher, [former]
       president of the R. R. Bowker Company, indicates
       in detail that, although computerization is costing
       the publishing industry more than former processes,
       its effect has been to diminish performance.
           Alexander contends: "But now, after buying
       or leasing some 60, 000 computers during the past
       fifteen years, businessmen are less and less able
       to state with assurance that it's all worth it. "
       (p. 126)   "As the Research Institute of America
       survey revealed, most companies are unsure that
       there is a payoff from computers even in sup-
       posedly routine operations. " (p. 128)   "Relatively

few companies have yet succeeded in devising non-
clerical applications for the computer [because]
programming and equipment costs are so high."
(p. 127)

Melcher contends: "To be candid about it,
however, I think we could have done all this if
anybody had wanted it, even before the invention
of the computer." (p. 1109) "Anything can be
done [by computer], I guess, but that isn't the
issue. What matters is whether anyone in his
right mind would choose that way of doing it."
(p. 1109) "They all hope for tangible economies
in the future--though it is a bit puzzling to note
that the $5 million companies seem to expect
those economies when they reach $10 million,
and the $10 million companies think there might
be economies when they reach $20 million, etc."
(p. 1105) "Computers have unmistakably lengthened
the time it takes to fill an order, and have made
it almost impossible to understand a royalty statement or get an intelligent answer to a complaint
or a query." (p. 1105) "The near-term result
often seems to be that information formerly available by means of a phone call to the order department is reported as unknowable until the computer
makes it next periodic report." (p. 1106) "Batch
processing ... can delay your orders, delay your
deliveries, delay your payments, and cut you off
from ready access to your own data." (p. 1109)

Victor Strauss, a consultant for printing management and contributing editor of Publishers'
Weekly, states: "The computerization offered
neither price advantages nor delivery advantages
to book publishers." "The New Composition Technology: Promises and Realities," Publishers'
Weekly 195:62 (5 May 1969).

2. Circulation is one operation in which librarians
seem to see nothing between a manual and a computerized system, whereas in reality, a large
range of alternatives exists. See also Melcher,
p. 1106: "Other machines also cost less or do
more. The cost of offset printing plates drops
from $1.50 a page to $1 a page to ten cents a
page, even to five cents a page--in an almost un-
believable series of technical breakthroughs."

3. "The old idea that an automated system could be operated at a new lower cost than a manual system is

dead, indeed. " [Allen Veaner, "The Application
of Computers to Library Technical Processing, "
CRL 31:36 (Jan. 1970).]

"Wishful thinking about present and future costs
may give us librarians a black eye with the very
administrators who are urging us to 'get with computers.' " [William Locke, "Computer Costs for
Large Libraries, " Datamation (Feb. 1970), p. 74.]

"I talked to one wholesaler who had really
made his automation work, but who had wound up
with costs a good deal higher than a competitor's.
I asked whether he really thought he could get his
costs down. He said: 'No, but I think the other
fellow's costs will rise--he's automating, too.' "
(Melcher, p. 1107.)

See details of the high costs of computers in
educational processes in Anthony G. Oettinger (of
the Harvard University Program on Technology
and Society), Run, Computer, Run (Cambridge,
Mass. : Harvard University Press, 1969), p. 189-
200. This is the most penetrating analysis to
date of the application of various technologies that
are "force-fed, oversold, and prematurely applied. "
See also the frank statement on the costs of computers, including limitations on the cost reductions
possible in the longterm future, in Frederick G.
Withington (of Arthur D. Little, Inc.), The Real
Computer (Reading, Mass. : Addison-Wesley Publishing Co. , 1969), p. 37-41.

The literature is riddled with irresponsible
accounts of project costs that make no real attempt to include the full range of costs of computerization.

4. This fact was called to my attention by a manager of
    an aerospace satellite systems division.
5. "Programming is still very much an art and one in
    which there seem to be no standards of perform-
    ance. " (Alexander, p. 171.)
6. Just compare. We are lured by the frills of com-
    puterization and forget its enormous basic costs.
    Myra, with her six-foot-seven escort, proposes
    to forget the six feet and concentrate on the
    inches. "The glamor, let's face it, is in the
    computers, but the breakthroughs are elsewhere. "
    (Melcher, p. 1107.)
7. "They [computers] are creatures of their time, and
    they come because they are needed. " (Melcher,

p. 1106.)   Melcher makes the common mistake of assuming that, because we needed something to help us in volume operations, the computer is what we needed.   I contend that it is not.   He states later, "It must be noted, however, that as yet the utilization of the computer to meet those changing needs has been massively disappointing." (p. 1107.)

8.   "The service bureau put out cards through its computer instead of through the far simpler card lister formerly used.   The result was no different, and they charged us three times as much-- but it made us feel kind of big league." (Melcher, p. 1109.)

9.   A phrase by one of our best poets of the 1930s, now reemerging, Laura Riding.

10.   "In effect, each new task for a computer entails the design, development, and fabrication of a unique machine, assembled partly out of the boxful of hardware, partly out of software." (Alexander, p. 171.)

11.   I still accept on faith the remarkable computational facility of the computer, though cautioned by friends in industry that unless the computer is checked at each permutation point in a computation, they cannot be sure that the results are right, because of possible disorders in the machine.   Since checking takes too much time, technologists accept the computer's results, fully aware that often they are working with unreliable data!

12.   This may have eased somewhat, since the extravagantly financed and well-publicized grunts of INTREX at M. I. T. have brought forth a mouse.   The self-delusion of electronics engineers is demonstrated in the fact that, since they have taken over control of the engineering schools, "insignificant" courses, such as Power and Illumination, have been dropped from all of them.   Maybe if we don't look, need for such knowledge will go away.

"When the new specialists were asked to understand before they criticized, some of them were outraged.   'We should learn from you?   You've got to be kidding.   Should we, the Knights of Systems Analysis, soil our anointed hands with that old rubbish?   Learn about it?   We will simply sweep it away in no time with our electronic broom.   We'll put you out of business!' " [Victor

Strauss, "Betwixt Cup and Lip," Publishers'
Weekly (26 Jan. 1970), p. 263.]

13. Similarities to Christian doctrine are due to the fact
that Computer theology is vaguely Christian in
orientation.

14. The most extreme deception encountered involved a
campus computer unit which contracted with the
central library (apparently to get access to its
grant money) to handle a library operation, one
of whose basic requirements was the integrity of
the information stored in the computer (an IBM
360/67). Months after programming began, the
library discovered that the chances of this machine wiping out its storage file are high, a fact
known to the experts from the beginning.

15. See Melcher's statements in footnotes one and three.

16. Alexander, p. 126.

17. "One knowledgeable consultant estimates that about
half the System/360's now installed are still
operating in the 'emulation' mode (i. e. , are
acting as second instead of third generation computers) ... at least a billion dollars worth of new
machine capacity is, in effect, wasted." (Alexander, p. 129.) If we can brainwash people to
be so stupid, why can't we brainwash them to
be virtuous?

18. Allen Veaner discusses this problem in full in "Major
Decision Points in Library Automation," CRL 31:
308-09 (Sept. 1970).

19. "Within limits, the more of our processes we get
computerized, the better chance we have of
matching the costs of the manual system." [Wil-
liam Locke, "Computer Costs for Large Libraries,"
Datamation (Feb. 1970), p. 72.] When pursued
by mail, Locke admitted that he has no evidence
to support this contention.

20. "Despite the fact that, on a capacity basis, the IBM
System/360, RCA Spectra 70, and GE 600 series
are cheaper to lease or buy, they have been the
hardest put to show a demonstrable payoff ... they
are too costly to be sitting idle, but they also
need more highly qualified--and more highly paid
--personnel to operate effectively." (Alexander,
p. 129.)

21. Hofstra is now running final cost estimates on an
MT/ST card production system despite warnings
against it. But we began with careful cost con-

trol of our manual production and will be able to
compare costs to decide whether or not to continue.

22. (Melcher, p. 1107.) His figure, of course, is stolen
from Samuel Johnson.

23. "The rules of the computer game are that you talk
only about what you are going to do, never about
how it turned out. This is a science in which
you publish the results of your experiments before
you make them." (Melcher, p. 1105.)

24. For what happend when computerization begins with
the library, see Dan Mather, "Data Processing in
an Academic Library," PNLA Quarterly 32:4-21
(July 1968).

25. "In companies everywhere the reasons for buying computers were not thought out. From the top, the
attitude was that you can't let the competition get
ahead of you; if they buy computers we've got to
buy computers. The result was great euphoria."
(Alexander, p. 126, quoting a GE internal consultant on computer usage.) "According to the
survey, the majority of computer users believe
they themselves were too precipitous in acquiring
their machines." (Alexander, p. 127.)

26. "Yet once in the grasp of an automated system, there
is no turning back. Entering upon an automated
system in any enterprise is practically an irreversible step." [Veaner, "The Application of
Computers to Library Technical Processing,"
CRL 31:37 (Jan. 1970).]

27. "But do people only want to save money?" plaintively
writes a computerator to me. If at no other time,
certainly when they are bankrupt.

BOOK SELECTION:
A NATIONAL PLAN FOR SMALL ACADEMIC LIBRARIES

by Virgil F. Massman and David R. Olson

Reprinted by permission from College & Research Libraries 32(4) July 1971, p. 271-279.

Although building the collections is one of the most important tasks of librarians, comparatively little attention has been given to this aspect of professional work. The system in current use has been practiced for many years with little systematic scrutiny and with little discussion of possible alternatives. This applies to nearly all academic libraries, but the present article will address itself mainly to problems of the smaller institutions rather than those of the major university libraries.

How are books selected for academic libraries? While patterns vary from one extreme to the other, in most institutions both librarians and faculty members participate in building collections. Many problems arise, for while faculty members play a major role in selection, librarians know very well that faculty selection is often of questionable merit. Among the most conspicuous deficiencies are: (1) many faculty members are already overburdened with other duties; (2) some of them lack acquaintance with the world of books; (3) some do not care (the textbook is enough); (4) a few suffer from a constitutional inclination toward laziness; (5) some select books in their own narrow field of specialization without regard for the needs of students; and (6) some believe that only they are capable of selecting. While this list could be extended, these are some of the major shortcomings of reliance on faculty selection. As Danton has pointed out, the faculty member who fails to find a particular item in the library blames not himself or another faculty member for the deficiency, but the library for failing to procure the wanted title.[1]

How about librarians? Certainly many of the prob-

lems which apply to faculty selection also apply to librarians
--lack of time, inadequate acquaintance with books, and
laziness.   Librarians, however, usually maintain that they
are more likely to consider the needs of students, and that
they are more concerned about building a balanced collection.

Given an ideal balance between selection by faculty
members and librarians, one might expect to develop a
reasonably good collection.   However, because of the com-
plexities of assembling a complementary library staff and
faculty and of maintaining completely harmonious relationships between the two groups, this hope is a virtual impos-
sibility.

Under present conditions the quality of selection in
most academic libraries probably leaves much to be desired,
but this is not entirely the fault of either the faculty members or the librarians, or even the two in combination.
Why?   Part of the defect results from the manner in which
books get into reviewing journals.   This itself has received
comparatively little detailed study.   The Bowker Annual
lists the total number of titles examined in a number of
general reviewing journals, but of course makes no effort
to assess the quality of reviewing nor the duplication of coverage (i.e., whether a particular title received notice in
more than one journal).2   To a considerable extent the editors of the reviewing journal depend upon the publisher to
send new works for examination.   The editor must then
determine whether a particular book is suitable for review
in his journal and give the book to a reader who may or
may not return his evaluation within the specified period of
time.   The latter situation is an especially vexing problem
regarding reviews in scholarly journals.   The specialist to
whom the book is sent for examination is often busy with
more pressing tasks, and may take six months, a year, or
more to read the book, write his commentary, and submit
it for publication--if he gets it done at all.

That the current system is haphazard can be illustrated to some extent on the basis of difficulties encountered
by CHOICE.   This journal farms out reviewing duties to a
large number of librarians and faculty members, and the
editor himself does not know what will be in each successive
issue until virtually the last minute.3   What appears in each
number depends upon copy submitted by reviewers.   If the
reviewer is dilatory, it may take him three months or six
months to send in his report.   This is not to blame the

editor of CHOICE, for he is at the mercy of his geographic-
ally dispersed staff of voluntary contributors. To manage
such a task must take an unusual measure of patience and
dedication. Nevertheless, even when it works well, the
system leaves much to be desired.

Thus, before the librarian has a chance to see the
review and before a book receives a printed notice, the book
must ordinarily be sent out by the publisher, meet the editor's standards, and await evaluation by the critic selected
to review the work. The book review editor himself may
reject many items, not because he necessarily questions
their merit but because the title does not fall into the subject categories or the type of literature (e. g. , scholarly or
popular) deemed appropriate for that journal. Because of
the way the system works a large mass of literature, then,
never comes to the librarian's attention unless he consults
a large number of reviewing journals.

How unpredictable the vagaries of reviewing journals
are can be illustrated by taking five specific examples.
Each of the five titles to be discussed was checked against
the Book Review Digest and the Book Review Index to locate reviews. 4 The first two examples are significant
titles partly because they are of interest to minority groups.
The other three are of value because they deal with certain
aspects of higher education. All five books belong in every
academic library in the United States.

Which journals reviewed these five books? The
first example, published in 1967, was Donald C. Dickinson's
Bio-Bibliography of Langston Hughes. Because it contains
extensive information about one of America's great black
poets it is a basic study which is essential for anyone who
is interested in the broad sweep of American literature, yet
it received a notice only in Nation and Library Journal.
The second work, Vine Deloria's Custer Died for Your Sins:
An Indian Manifesto, was published in 1969 and was reviewed in America, Best Sellers, Library Journal, New
York Times Book Review, Newsweek, Saturday Review,
and Time. 5

The other three books chosen as examples deal with
issues that are of primary concern to librarians and faculty
members. The first, T. Caplow and R. J. McGee's The
Academic Marketplace, discusses hiring practices of institutions of higher learning. It was published in 1958 and

was reviewed in Library Journal and the Chicago Sunday Tribune. The second book, Mark Ingraham's The Outer Fringe: Faculty Benefits Other than Annuities and Insurance, was published in 1965 and was reviewed in Canadian Forum, Journal of Higher Education, Library Quarterly, Science, and Teachers College Record. In this case, as is true for the next item, the subtitle gives a good indication of the content. Mark Ingraham's The Mirror of Brass: The Compensation and Working Conditions of College and University Administrators was reviewed by CHOICE and by CRL.

As already suggested these five items should be available in all college and university libraries, but no single reviewing journal covered all of them. Library Journal noted The Academic Marketplace but not The Outer Fringe or The Mirror of Brass. Of the three books just mentioned, CHOICE reviewed only the latter. (CHOICE was, of course, not yet in existence when The Academic Marketplace was published.) Similarly, the Journal of Higher Education and Teachers College Record reviewed The Outer Fringe but not The Academic Marketplace or The Mirror of Brass. Oddly enough, none of the five journals which reviewed The Outer Fringe reviewed The Mirror of Brass or The Academic Marketplace. Is there any rationale for this, or does it reflect the hazard of chance by which books are reviewed by one or another journal?[6]

Take a half hour to examine the Book Review Digest or the Book Review Index and see how many books which are of value to academic libraries are reviewed only by scholarly journals or only by the general journals. Furthermore, see how many books which are of value to academic libraries are cited with only one review in Book Review Index. (The Book Review Digest normally does not cite titles which received only one review.) If one depends upon reviewing journals as a major source of information for building collections, such an examination may be both enlightening and disturbing to the person concerned about quality selection.

A recent article in CRL discussed the reviews of books in seventy-one scholarly journals.[7] Of the 3,195 titles examined for that article, only about 15 percent received a notice in more than one of the seventy-one periodicals. Thus, 85 percent were reviewed by only one journal. This meager duplication is rather surprising. One

would expect far more overlapping within the journals for
history or for English, for example, or for any other discipline. Because there is not, however, it is necessary to
examine at least several journals for each discipline, and
the total number could easily come to seventy-five or more
for all the various courses offered in the undergraduate
curriculum in most colleges and universities. Even such
extensive examinations of reviewing journals still would not
assure the appropriate range of coverage--to say nothing
about the quality of reviewing.

In discussing the advantages and shortcomings of
blanket order plans, comparatively little attention has been
paid to the deficiencies of the current system of reviewing
new books. A blanket order plan that is handled by a good
dealer is probably capable of giving the library more effective coverage of current books than a system of relying
upon reviews.

The study of the feasibility of centralized processing
in Colorado academic libraries, for example, found that the
approval dealer supplied 40. 4 percent of the titles reviewed
in CHOICE during the first year and 45. 1 percent for the
second year. [8] The writers suggested that the approval plan
needed to improve its coverage because it provided such a
small percentage of the CHOICE titles.

When the list of 3, 195 books examined for the CRL
article mentioned previously and which received favorable
reviews in the journals was compared with CHOICE, duplication approached only 30 percent. Thus the approval dealer
mentioned in the preceding paragraph achieved a higher
overlap with CHOICE than CHOICE did with the scholarly
journals. When the 3, 195 titles were compared with the
Book Review Digest, duplication approached 50 percent. [9]

Then there are also the general reviewing journals
such as Saturday Review, the New York Times Book Review,
etc. In many instances, as an examination of the Book Review Index will demonstrate, a book which is significant to
academic libraries may be reviewed by only a scholarly
journal or by only general journals. Thus to insure effective selection, the library must devise a scheme which will
assure adequate selection based on thorough and regular
examination of the general reviewing organs as well as a
large number of specialized journals which carry reviews.

Under the present system it is extremely difficult to insure the building of first-rate collections. It is, therefore, unfair to place undue blame on librarians for deficiencies in building collections, for the present method is virtually impossible to cope with. The librarian may be doing an excellent job of selecting from those journals which he finds time to read; it is impossible to read them all. To then use the standard procedure of evaluating the collection by checking it against recommended book lists and blaming the librarian if the collection appears to be deficient is affixing blame on a potentially innocent party. Much of the blame might more deservedly rest with the inadequate reviewing system.

A new approach must be found. Although many librarians will object to any suggestion of centralized selection, they should be aware of the fact that publishers and journal editors do a great deal of selecting simply be deciding which works will or will not be reviewed. Over this the librarian has no control.

For a moment, it may be worth examining a few of the major objections to centralized selection. Presumably, the librarian knows his clientele, buys with individual readers in mind, understands their special needs, and is aware of how his people use books. But is there really any documented evidence that librarians (individually or en masse) know their communities as well as they think they do? What constitutes knowing the patrons? Does the opinion of one vociferous faculty member speak for the faculty? To turn to a slightly different area, librarians have strong feelings about whether sets should be classified as sets or whether journals should be classified with books. Is there any substantial evidence that either sets or journals are used more effectively in one way or the other? Is there any "scientific" evidence, in other words, which goes beyond the unsubstantiated assumptions to which we cling so dearly, but which are at opposite points of the issue? Possibly the arguments for local book selection are similar. Possibly the librarian believes he can select more effectively for his patrons than anyone else, but he has no concrete evidence to support his view. Do most librarians select with some shadow of their own image (or the projection of themselves) in mind? Is it possible for the librarian to know what the vast majority of faculty members and students need? The librarian may heed the few whom he knows, but then he should be willing to admit he is doing

that and nothing more.   Much of the same holds true for
selecting for subdivisions of the curriculum.   The general
content of American history is known; the facts are the
same regardless of where American history is taught.   One
professor may stress the Civil War or immigration, but
what if he leaves or if his course is dropped from the
curriculum?   It does happen.   Furthermore, if a professor
or if the entire faculty stresses a particular aspect of
American history, the library still needs the important
works dealing with other aspects of that subject.

Carried to its logical extreme, the concept of selection for present clientele would necessitate the reorientation
of the collection every fall when the new crop of students
and faculty members arrives.   And what happens when this
librarian with his extraordinary insight into the needs of
his clients leaves?   Will he then be capable of immediately
adjusting his extrasensory wave lengths to his new clients
at another institution?   The contention that the librarian is
selecting for particular individuals sounds convincing.   However, if the librarian is indeed buying particular titles with
the needs of one person in mind, is he placing undue emphasis on the unique needs of an individual at the expense of
the common needs of the group?   Library users do have
unique needs, but on the undergraduate level they have more
in common than they have in isolation.   This is what the
"standard works which represent the heritage of civilization"
in the "Standards for College Libraries" is about. [10]   A
well-selected collection of books on American history is
good anywhere, and not because it happens to serve a particular group of students or faculty members in Alabama,
Alaska, South Dakota, or Minnesota.

This paper argues then that the present system of
selection by librarians and faculty members does not produce the quality of collections needed.   This is true for
several reasons which may be summarized briefly.   (1)
Smaller libraries cannot rely on Publishers' Weekly, American Book Publishing Record, or Library of Congress proof-
slips for selection; for if they do, they are buying blind.
(2) Whether librarians like it or not, under the present
system the editors of reviewing journals already engage in
extensive prejudging (selection by inclusion and by omission)
both in determining whether a book will be reviewed and who
will review it.   (3) In order to insure full coverage of current book production, a large number of current general and
scholarly journals must be examined regularly and thoroughly,

and few libraries have the staff time necessary to accomplish such a large task.

A practical alternative might be centralized selection on a national basis. The system might work something like this. The Association of College and Research Libraries or ALA's Library Resources and Technical Services Division would manage the program and would hire subject specialists (twenty individuals with backgrounds in different disciplines should be able to insure good coverage) who would examine all new books currently being published and who would decide which books were appropriate for the undergraduate level. Depending upon the volume of book production, the twenty specialists would select a total of about 5,000 books per year. The total number would fluctuate with the quality and quantity of publication each year, but 5,000 titles would be a reasonable number for purposes of discussion. This is admittedly a round figure, based to some extent on research but also based to some extent on conjecture. A more precise figure could be arrived at as a result of more extensive study. Libraries could buy the package, but they could not make any stipulations about what they would accept or reject. They would take all or nothing. No exceptions of any kind would be permitted.

Such a system would have tremendous side benefits. Why no exceptions? By insisting upon a total acceptance of the package, the program could achieve considerable economies. Attempting to tailor selection to the separate libraries would destroy the program before it had a chance to work, but the package sold to 200 libraries could have tremendous economies of scale. One cataloger using Library of Congress copy could supervise the cataloging of 5,000 volumes (actually 5,000 for 200 libraries equals 1,000,000 books). Complete card sets could be produced with call numbers in place. The circulation card and book pocket could also be included.

The secret of success would be in the processing of 200 copies of the same book at the same time. Producing 200 sets of cards for one title would permit the use of the best equipment and obviously would be far faster and more economical than doing it separately in 200 libraries.

One of the major problems in centralized processing is the matter of exceptions. If the processing center allows exceptions, errors are more likely to occur and every mem-

ber helps to pay for the specialized treatment because exceptions take time and therefore cost money. (For a good
discussion of the problems of centralized processing see the
Fall 1966 issue of Library Resources & Technical Services.)
Furthermore, the simple matters such as spine labeling
and producing circulation cards can sometimes be done more
economically in the local library than in the central system.
However, if this is done en masse, it can be done more
economically.

It is only when the routine can be done en masse and
without a long list of exceptions for each participant that
the routines can be done more economically in the central
system, for only then does automation provide significant
advantages. A computer, for example, has an advantage
over routine manual operations in libraries primarily when
the same task must be performed a number of times. If a
particular task needs to be done only one, two, or three
times, it is likely that the computer will be an expensive
luxury.

It is interesting to note that in her study of centralized processing centers Vann reported that the buyer-
librarian was most likely to be dissatisified with details of
processing rather than with cataloging and classification
itself--as if the location of the book pocket were the essence of cataloging and usability. 11 Uniform processing for
all libraries could ensure a quality product, and it would
not cause significant problems for cooperating libraries.
It would, of course, mean that all participating libraries
would have to accept the same classification scheme, but
this should create no insurmountable difficulties either.

How much would such a plan of centralized selection-
acquisitions-processing cost? Broken down by category, it
might run something like this:

> Selection: twenty complementary subject
>   specialists at an average of $15,000
>   per annum $300,000
> Cataloging: one professional (should be
>   on the same level as the subject spe-
>   cialist and his salary could be aver-
>   aged with that group) $ 15,000
> Catalog card sets, including labor and
>   machine costs: $.10 per set for 200
>   copies of 5,000 titles or a total of
>   1,000,000 sets $100,000

Processing including all labor: $.25
   per book for spine labeling, circulation cards, book pockets, matching
   cards with books, etc. $250,000
Administration $ 35,000
Warehouse and equipment: $3,000,000
   amortized over twenty years $150,000
                                 Total $850,000

Assuming the average price of books to be $10.00 per title and an average discount of 10 percent per title when purchasing 200 copies of each of the 5,000 titles, the centralized acquisitions system would be able to manage all selection, cataloging, and processing for less than the average $1.00 per copy discount (200 copies of 5,000 titles equals 1,000,000 books at $10.00 per book equals $10,000,-000 and a 10 percent discount equals $1,000,000 discount).[12] The total cost of 1,000,000 books, then, would be $9,000,000, and the cost of processing would be $850,000. On a per copy basis this would mean $9.00 per copy and $.85 for processing.

Thus the discount would more than cover selection and all processing costs. The library would be able to build a quality collection with the books coming to the library ready for the shelves and the cards ready for the catalog at less than the list price of the book. This in spite of the fact that the cost estimates above are computed at a rate which is probably higher than they would be in an actual operation.

For example, by using Library of Congress copy and offset printing, one worker can easily run 120 cards per minute. Using a more conservative average production of only sixty cards per minute would mean that one person could produce 3,600 cards per hour (600 sets with an average of six cards per set). At $.10 per set this would mean an income of $60.00 per hour. This would allow a generous $.01 for card stock ($36.00 for 3,600 cards), $8.00 per hour for labor, $8.00 per hour for machine rental, and $8.00 per hour for other expenses. Most businesses would be eager to achieve that kind of return on either investment. Another illustration, the $3,000,000 for the warehouse and equipment, is probably high. At a cost of $50.00 per square foot, $1,000,000 would provide 20,000 square feet. Another $1,000,000 for equipment would be quite generous. Thus $1,000,000 would be left for contingencies.

A larger number of subscribers would further reduce
the per title processing costs, but even with only 200 subscribers, the smaller libraries could nearly disband their
acquisitions, cataloging, and processing centers and invest
that money in books.   Acquisitions and processing costs in
nine Colorado academic libraries averaged $4.09 per book
without considering institutional overhead.   The comparable
Colorado Cooperative Book Processing Center cost was
$3.10, or $2.96 as calculated in the mathematical model.
If two copies of each item could be ordered and processed
simultaneously, the cost of each item would be reduced to
$2.27, disregarding institutional overhead. [13]   A more re-
cent report gives an average cost of $3.10 per book for
1967 and $2.70 during last year's experimental period. [14]
The system described in this article could perform the
same tasks plus the more significant work of selection for
$.85 per book.   At a cost of $49,250 (5,000 titles at
$9.00 each plus $.85 each for processing), participating
libraries would have greatly increased their purchasing
power by practically eliminating the costs of their cataloging
and acquisitions departments.

Using the average cost of $4.09 for the Colorado
academic libraries and without considering institutional
overhead, the processing costs for 5,000 titles would be
$20,450.   Since the system described in this article would
cost only $4,250 (5,000 titles at $.85 each), each library
would save $16,200 in processing costs.   Problems with
financial records would also virtually disappear for the
libraries because bills would come once a month or once a
quarter.   Billing by the centralized system would also be
simple--the same bill would go to everyone.

Saving $16,200 in acquisitions and processing costs
for 5,000 titles would be no small matter for most libraries.
In addition, the library would be assured of a higher quality
of selection.   On any given afternoon, a college's entire
faculty (including the president) and the library staff could
meet in the library, unpack the beautiful new shipment of
books, and read the books rather than the reviews.   And
eventually, this basic, quality collection could become the
minimum acceptable standard for accreditation.   Any academic library which cannot purchase 5,000 books per year
should not be called a library.

Naturally each local library would still need to make
provision for unique or additional educational programs and

for local materials.   However, this would be a comparatively small task.

The twenty subject specialists could examine some 30,000 domestic and foreign titles per year.   This would be an average of 1,500 per specialist.   Using 200 working days per year as a base, this would mean that each specialist would have to look at an average of 7.5 books per day. Assuming a selection of 5,000 titles per year, each specialist would actually approve an average of 250 titles during the course of one year.   Since many decisions for inclusion or exclusion would be fairly routine, the specialists should have adequate time to perform their duties.

The major duty of the administrator for the centralized system would be to insure complete coverage.   It would be his job to make sure that all books which might be relevant to the undergraduate curriculum would get into the system so the subject specialists would have a chance to review them.   This would be the critical factor, getting the books into the system for evaluation.   Aside from this, the administrator would be responsible for supervising all accounts with publishers and libraries as well as routine tasks such as shipping and receiving.   He would also, of course, deal with complaints from librarians.   Once the system was operating effectively (and he would have to have very hard evidence that it was indeed operating effectively), most complaints could be handled in a fairly routine fashion.

If any librarian complained about such matters as the placement of spine labels and call numbers or whether subject entries should be in red rather than in capital letters, the chief administrator for the selection-acquisitions-processing center would write to the complaining librarian's president (with a copy to the librarian) recommending that the institution summarily fire the librarian.

Why not?

References

1.   J. Periam Danton, Book Selection and Collections: A Comparison of German and American University Libraries (New York: Columbia University Press, 1963), p. 71.
2.   Bowker Annual of Library and Book Trade Information (New York: R. R. Bowker, 1970), p. 54.

3. Lawrence E. Leonard, Joan M. Maier, and Richard
    M. Dougherty, Centralized Book Processing: A
    Feasibility Study Based on Colorado Academic Li-
    braries (Metuchen, N. J.: Scarecrow Press, 1969),
    p. 171-72.
4. The Book Review Digest has a number of criteria for
    citing reviews which are explained in its "State-
    ment of Policy" in the annual cumulations, but
    these need not be discussed here.
5. Although the Book Review Digest had not cited it by
    June of 1970, CHOICE did carry a review in
    March 1970.   All the other reviews had appeared
    in October or November of 1969.
6. Possibly reviews of these works appeared in additional
    journals without being cited by Book Review Digest
    or Book Review Index, but no attempt was made to
    do a thorough search of a large number of jour-
    nals to locate additional reviews.
7. Virgil F. Massman and Kelly Patterson, "A Minimum
    Budget for Current Acquisitions, " CRL 31:83-88
    (March 1970).
8. Leonard, Centralized Book Processing, p. 171.
9. The percentages should not be used as absolute fig-
    ures since comparisons were drawn for only a
    small sample.   The point to be made is that a
    substantial percentage of the new books is re-
    viewed by only one journal.
10. "Standards for College Libraries, " CRL 20:276 (July
    1959).
11. Sarah K. Vann, "Southeastern Pennsylvania Processing
    Center Feasibility Study: A Summary, " Library
    Resources & Technical Services 10:472 (Fall 1966).
12. For 1969 an average price of $9. 37 for American
    books was reported by Publishers' Weekly (9 Feb.
    1970), p. 49.
13. Leonard, Centralized Book Processing, p. 244.
14. Mountain-Plains Library Quarterly 15:28 (Summer
    1970).

HOW TO AVOID DUPLICATED INFORMATION

by Carl M. White

Reprinted by permission from RQ, Winter 1970, p. 127-137.

There is an Oriental proverb about pointing toward the oak to curse the ash tree. We are going to look at some works of reference, but we shall be talking all along about an emerging issue in acquisitions--how we are to put up our guard against buying information that is duplicated too heavily to do the collection any good. Nobody is losing sleep over unwanted acquisitions, but creeping redundancy is on its way up. Like creeping inflation or smog, it would please us if it would simply go away by itself. It shows no disposition to do so. The chemistry of the situation tends to make unsought duplication a continuing fact of life, and here are some of the elements that combine to make it so:

1. Indispensability of good library collections. In 1939, a short study published in School and Society asks, "Do colleges buy reference books?" and answers that but half to two-thirds of the sample bought the "must books" on two lists in economics and biology.[1] The care and feeding of information needs these days make this old picture in the album unrecognizable.

2. Better budgets to support collection development. Affluency is changing the style of buying. A large number of libraries settle matters quickly if the book has something good to contribute. The proportion of new information need not be decisive and often is not.

3. Accelerated production of books of all kinds.

4. A changing library market. Production and distribution of many things bought by libraries is still controlled by high professional standards, but commercialization

125

has increased as the library market has become more lucrative.   This is to be expected, especially in a seller's
market like the one we are buying in.   There is a legal
phrase, caveat emptor, that was born of the marketplace;
beware the library buyer must--more perhaps than at any
other time since the library movement got under way.

    5.   Book selection practices.   "Beyond the small
college library," one librarian writes, "the problem of
selecting individual titles from today's mass of publication
is an unrewarding, well-nigh hopeless task for academic
librarians.   In universities, the librarian should get away
from the concept of selection of individual titles in most
cases."[2]   A public librarian puts it this way.   Book selection originated as a by-product of niggardly book budgets.
The eighty-year-old practice began to die as society began
to provide suitable financing, and as of the present book
selection is dead.[3]   It would be less extreme to say we are
hard put to get the job done well and are trying out new
ways to do it, but to stick to the main point, there are
pressures to find a way around evaluating individual titles,
and any slackening of evaluation lowers the guard against
careless publishing standards and possible exploitation.

Methods of Approach

    A cloakroom estimate has it that "when you buy a
new reference book, you get about 10 percent new information."   If you try to pin down how much duplicated information libraries do in fact buy, you quickly discover that the
literature contains but few hard facts on the subject.   Kaser's
review of the literature of acquisitions[4] contains no reference to the subject, and a search of library literature since
1963 turns up nothing either.   In a study of the coverage
of geologic literature for 1961, H. E. Hawkes found that of
60 North American titles, 20 were reported either by Geo-
Science or the Bibliography of North American Geology; 18
were missed by both services, while 22 were reported by
both services.[5]   A University of Chicago study found bibliographical services in the social sciences to be "overlapping,
duplicatory, incomplete, without clearly defined boundaries,
and generally unsatisfactory."[6]   That was in 1950.   Bibliographical coverage has improved since then but duplication,
unchecked, is greater than ever.   Studies made so far are
scattered; they contain sketchy but suggestive information,
and tend to focus on duplication in works of a bibliographical
nature.

The theme of this paper is that duplicated information is getting to be too extensive and too expensive to be dismissed as of no importance and so, the first step is to gain better understanding of the facts. The evidence summarized here is based on case studies. The cases were laid out (1) to obtain data on the degree to which information in widely purchased reference works duplicates information elsewhere in the collection, especially in other reference works; (2) to clarify whether the sorts of information duplicated are few or numerous; and (3) to undertake no more than could be managed on a limited budget of staff time. The study was made possible by the cooperation of Mel Voigt, UCSD Librarian; Gordon Fretwell, Head of Public Services; and three reference librarians--Elizabeth McGraw, Donald McKie, and Philip Smith. These librarians have put us all in their debt by sandwiching many hours of searching in between calls for service at the reference desk.

Bibliographical Information

Table 1 shows the results of taking fifteen periodicals, representing five countries of origin, and checking the information about them that is contained in thirteen sources as follows: Ayer and Son's Directory of Newspapers and Periodicals ("Ayer" for short in the Table); British Union-Catalog of Periodicals, a Record of the Periodicals of the World, from the Seventeenth Century to the Present Day, in British Libraries (British UCP); Deutsche Presse: Zeitungen und Zeitschriften (Deutsche Pr.); F.W. Faxon Co., Librarian's Guide to Periodicals (Faxon); Guide to Current British Periodicals (Guide to CBP); Newspaper Press Directory and Advertisers' Guide (Newspaper Pr.); Annuaire de la Presse Française et Etrangère et du Monde Politique; Annuaire International de la Presse (Presse Fr.); Stamm (Der Leitfaden für Presse und Werbung); Standard Periodical Directory (Standard); Ulrich's Periodical Directory (Ulrich); Union List of Serials (Union list); Willing's Press Guide (Willing); and Willing's European Press Guide (Willing: European).

The table shows that these thirteen sources provide up to seven listings of a single title and also shows up to 100 percent coverage of individual periodicals in the sample. Four of the lists have international coverage. National lists conform to coverage plans of their own, but there is no uniformity as to plan from one list to another, which tends

TABLE 1

A Sampling of Locations Where Information About 15 Periodicals Can Be Found

	Ayer	British UCP	Deutsche Pr.	Faxon	Guide to CBP	Newspaper Pr.	Presse Fr.	Stamm	Standard	Ulrich	Union List	Willing	Willing: European	No. of Places Listed
American J. of Internation Law	x	x	no	x	no	no	no	no	x	x	x	no	no	6
Economic Geography	x	x	no	x	no	no	no	no	x	x	x	no	no	6
English Historical Review	no	x	no	x	x	x	no	no	no	x	x	x	no	7
Facts on File	x	x	no	x	no	no	no	no	x	x	x	no	no	6
Foreign Affairs	x	x	no	x	no	no	no	no	x	x	x	no	no	6
Fortune	x	x	no	x	no	no	no	no	x	x	x	no	no	6
Geographical Review	x	x	no	x	no	no	no	no	x	x	x	no	no	6
Harvard Business Review	x	x	no	x	no	no	no	no	x	x	x	no	no	6
Human Relations	no	x	no	x	x	no	no	no	x	x	x	x	no	7
International Affairs	no	x	no	x	x	x	no	no	no	x	x	x	no	7
International Social Science Journal	no	x	no	x	no	no	no	no	x	x	x	no	no	5
Journal of Educational Psychology	x	x	no	x	no	no	no	no	no	x	x	no	no	5
Oceania	no	x	no	x	no	no	no	no	no	x	x	no	no	4
Schmollers Jahrbuch	no	x	x	x	no	no	no	x	no	x	x	no	x	7
Social Forces	no	x	no	x	no	no	no	no	x	x	x	no	no	5
No. of the 15 Periodicals Listed	8	15	1	15	3	2	0	1	10	15	15	3	1	

to lead either to spotty coverage or to duplicated information to avoid it.

Table 2 takes up the extent of duplicated information. It uses eight items as a basis of comparing the information supplied by these thirteen sources. One item is to be found in but three of the sources while seven items are to be found in ten to thirteen of them, the typical amount of duplication being 80 percent.

The procedure in this case was to take a problem-- the location of certain kinds of information about periodicals --to check the procurability of the information in a selected list of reference works, and to summarize the results. Another procedure is to take a given reference work and check the extent to which the information is duplicated by other reference works or is unique (i. e. , procurable from that source only). Both procedures are used in this study, the second more than the first.

The American Bibliographic Service of Darien, Connecticut, puts out more than a dozen near-print quarterly checklists (with 125 to 500 current books and pamphlets an issue) in the humanities, physical sciences, mathematics, and social sciences. Every fifth page of September 1966 issues of two of these quarterly lists (Ethnology and Sociology, $4 a year, and Economics and Political Science, $8. 50) was Xeroxed, and from these, eight pages (having in all 124 titles) were selected to form a working sample. These titles were then checked against five selective bibliographies and one inclusive English-language bibliography, CBI. Table 3 shows that roughly three titles out of every four were in one or more of the six lists. CBI alone accounts for 62 percent. The ABS Quarterly checklists reach libraries pretty late for book selection purposes but justify their cost mainly on quality selection of international scope. (None of the series reviews or annotates the works listed.) The low correlation between selections published in these two quarterly checklists and their opposite numbers in the two fields raises doubts which collection-builders would find it useful to resolve. We need more published studies on matters of this sort to clarify why duplication is necessary in the first place and why, if we must have it, there is a lack of correlation at points where we would expect to find it. The twenty-eight items not located in any of the six other lists included twelve works in German, three in English, and thirteen in other languages. One of the German titles

TABLE 2

Kinds of Information about Periodicals Supplied by 13 Sources

	Ayer	British UCP	Deutsche Pr.	Faxon	Guide to CBP	Newspaper Pr.	Presse Fr.	Stamm	Standard	Ulrich	Union List	Willing	Willing: European	No. of Places Listed	%
Official Title	x	x	x	x	x	x	x	x	x	x	x	x	x	13	100
When publication commenced	x	x	x	no	x	x	x	no	x	x	x	x	x	11	84
Publisher	x	x	x	no	x	x	x	x	x	x	x*	x	x	12*	92*
Publisher's address	x	no	x	no	x	x	x	x	x	x	no	x	x	10	76
Frequency of publication	x	no	x	x	x	x	x	no	x	x	no	x	x	10	76
Price	x	no	x	x	x	x	x	x	x	x	no	x	x	11	84
Index (annual) indicated	x	no	x	x	x	x	x	x	x	x	no	x	x	11	84
Indexed in other indexes	no	no	no	x	x	no	no	no	no	x	no	no	no	3	23
No. of these 8 items supplied	7	3	7	5	8	7	7	5	7	8	3*	7	7		

*With qualifications.   Union list of serials and New serial titles give publisher irregularly.

TABLE 3

Multiple Listing of 124 Items in Two ABS Quarterly Checklists

a. No. listed by 6 other bibliographies:

Cumulative Book Index	78	62%
International Bibliography of Economics	25	20%
International Bibliography of Sociology	23	18%
International Bibliography of Social and Cultural Anthropology	15	12%
International Bibliography of Political Science	15	12%
Harmon, R. B. Political Science: a Bibliographical Guide to the Literature. Supplement, 1968.	11	8%

b. Of the 124 items

No. found in one or more additional sources	96	77%
No. found in ABS Quarterly checklists only	28	21%
Found in only 1 additional source	43	34%
Found in 2 additional sources	37	29%
Found in 3 additional sources	13	10%
Found in 4 additional sources	3	2%

was a translation of Homan's <u>The Human Group.</u>   Of the
three English titles, two were reprints and one a paperback
popularization.

"The social sciences struggle with less and less success," <u>The ABS Guide to Recent Publications in the Social
Sciences</u> (New York, American Behavioral Scientist, 1965)
states in the preface, "against the overwhelming waves of
documents."   The Guide and its annual supplements stepped
in to help make "the bibliographic response" to this incoming tide more effective.   The 1966 supplement ("ABS" in
Table 4), which lists just under 1,000 articles and books,
forms the basis of one of the case studies of duplicated information.   This supplement selectively lists and annotates
articles from some 308 journals.   The list at the front of
the volume was checked against lists used by ten other indexing and abstracting services (<u>Economic Abstracts</u>, <u>Educa-
tion Index</u>, <u>International Political Science Abstracts</u>, <u>Journal
of Economic Abstracts</u>, <u>Psychological Abstracts</u>, <u>PAIS</u>,
<u>Reader's Guide</u>, <u>Sociological Abstracts</u>, <u>Social Science and
Humanities Index</u>, and <u>International Bibliography of Sociol-
ogy</u>) to determine the amount of duplication if any.   To obtain a more direct measure of uniqueness of content, a
sample of thirty-eight of the articles indexed was checked
to determine whether they have been abstracted in any of
four abstracting services: <u>International Political Science
Abstracts</u> (IPSA), <u>Journal of Economic Abstracts</u> (JEA),
<u>Psychological Abstracts</u> (PA), and <u>Sociological Abstracts</u>
(SA).

Table 4 shows the extent of duplication.   Only fifty-
six of the 308 journals were not indexed or abstracted by
at least one other source.   Only twelve of the thirty-eight
articles were not abstracted in one of the four services
used for checking purposes.   No adequate check could be
made of duplicated information about the books that are included in the list.

<u>The Index of Economic Journals</u>, prepared under the
auspices of the American Economic Association, indexes by
author and subject English language articles in major professional journals published during the years since 1886.
The list of ninety journals indexed in volume 5, 1954-1959,
was compared with lists indexed for the same period in
<u>PAIS</u>, <u>International Bibliography of Economics</u>, <u>International
Index</u>, and <u>Business Periodicals Index.</u>

TABLE 4.   Multiple Indexing and Abstracting of 308 Journals on the American Behavioral Scientist List

a.	Total of the 308 indexed in 8 indexes in the sample (of 10)	4	1.2%
	Total of the 308 indexed in 7 indexes in the sample (of 10)	9	2.9%
	Total of the 308 indexed in 6 indexes in the sample (of 10)	23	7.4%
	Total of the 308 indexed in 5 indexes in the sample (of 10)	27	8.7%
	Total of the 308 indexed in 4 indexes in the sample (of 10)	57	18.5%
	Total of the 308 indexed in 3 indexes in the sample (of 10)	70	22.7%
	Total of the 308 indexed in 2 indexes in the sample (of 10)	62	20.1%
	Of the 308 indexed, the no. indexed by the ABS only was	56	18.1%
b.	Of a sample of 38 articles in these journals, IPSA abstracted	7	18.4%
	Of a sample of 38 articles in these journals, JEA abstracted	1	2.6%
	Of a sample of 38 articles in these journals, PA abstracted	9	23.6%
	Of a sample of 38 articles in these journals, SA abstracted	19	50.0%
	Of this sample of 38 articles, the no. annotated by ABS only was	12	31.5%

TABLE 5.   Multiple Indexing of 90 Economic Journals

a.	Total of the 90 journals indexed in 4 indexing services	11	12.2%
	Total of the 90 journals indexed in 3 indexing services	26	28.8%
	Total of the 90 journals indexed in 2 indexing services	32	35.5%
	Total of the 90 indexed in the IEJ list only	21	23.3%
b.	Of a sample of 10 articles in these journals, Int'l. Ind. indexed	10	100.0%
	Of a sample of 10 articles in these journals, IBE indexed	10	100.0%
	Of this sample of 10 articles, the no. indexed in IEJ only was	0	0.0%

TABLE 6.   Multiple Indexing and Abstracting of 35 Economic Journals

a.

Total of 35 journals indexed in 6 indexing and abstracting services	3	8.5%
Total of 35 journals indexed in 5 indexing and abstracting services	7	20.0%
Total of 35 journals indexed in 4 indexing and abstracting services	12	34.2%
Total of 35 journals indexed in 3 indexing and abstracting services	8	22.8%
Total of 35 journals indexed in 2 indexing and abstracting services	4	13.4%
Total of 35 journals indexed in 1 indexing and abstracting service	1	2.8%
Total of the 35 journals in Journal of Economic Abstracts only	0	0.0%
Total of the 35 journals in JEA covered by Economic Abstracts	29	82.8%

b.   (Duplication of abstracts.   Not available)

TABLE 7.   Availability of Definitions in Other Sources of 50 Terms
in Winick's Dictionary of Anthropology

	Number	Percent of 50
Webster's Third New International Dictionary	39	78%
Encyclopaedia Britannica	31	62%
Zadrozny. Dictionary of Social Science	6	12%
International Encyclopedia of the Social Sciences	2	4%
Winick's Dictionary of Anthropology only	8	16%
Available in the 4 other sources	42	84%

Table 5 shows that roughly a fourth of the journals are indexed in IEJ alone, with extensive duplication of the remaining 75 percent. All of the small sample of articles checked were indexed in all of the four indexes checked (PAIS, International Bibliography of Economics, International Index, and Business Periodicals Index), but this result is explained by a biased choice of articles chosen from journals known to be at least partially indexed by all three. Accurate measurement of multiple indexing of articles would require adequate random sampling for which there was not time.

Table 6 is incomplete. It is based on an abstracting service--Journal of Economic Abstracts, vol. 3, 1965. Adequate testing of duplication would necessitate checking, as was not possible under the circumstances, on the duplication of abstracts. We have an indirect check on this only; twenty-nine of the journals on the JEA list are also covered by Economic Abstracts. Table 6 is limited for the most part to a summary of less revealing information--the extent to which the thirty-five journals are covered by the following indexing and abstracting services: Economic Abstracts, Social Sciences and Humanities Index, 1916-   ; British Humanities Index, 1962-   ; Internationale Bibliographie der Zeitschriftenliteratur aus Allen Gebieten des Wissens, 1963/64-   ; UNESCO's International Bibliography of Economics, and Index of Economic Journals.

Definitions of Words and Phrases

There was but one test made in this area. One column on every tenth page of Charles Winick's Dictionary of Anthropology was Xeroxed, and from the resultant collection of terms, fifty were chosen at random to serve as our sample. Four other reference works were then searched to see whether definitions of these terms could be found and to determine the comparability of the information, when any was located, with that in Winick. Table 7 shows extensive duplication. Only eight terms were found in Winick only. The greatest duplication was with Webster's Third New International Dictionary, 78 percent. For this source, a check was made also of the relative completeness of definitions, with the following results:

Definitions more complete in Winick   6
Definitions more complete in Webster's Third   4

    Definitions of comparable completeness
        in both   25
    Comparison not valid   4

Information about Institutions of Higher Learning

        Social science literature cuts across the interest of
workers in all fields, as those who work with library resources in the area are aware.   This catholicity of appeal
is illustrated by across-the-board use of educational directories, of which we have several of high standard.   What
the public wants to know is of the most varied character,
ranging from the history of an individual institution to the
names of individual professors--or the librarian.   For the
purpose of checking duplication of published information, we
set down several factors that affect an institution's performance; picked out half a dozen institutions of different sizes,
with different programs, located in different sections [Duke,
Fisk, U. of Hawaii, Mills College, Princeton, U. of the
South]; and then searched five well-known directories for
this information.   Directories differ in the degree to which
they bring out the student-teacher ratio, names of professors, size and strength of the faculty, etc.; but insofar as
the sample is indicative, there is a strong tendency, as
shown by the results summarized in Table 8, to duplicate
information that is considered relevant to effective educational performance.   Directory information turns up in
many sources.   For an unexpected example, the Britannica
Year-Book 1965 carries a directory (pages 306-13) of more
than 1,400 colleges and universities, giving eight items of
information about each one.

Reviews of Current and Recent Affairs

        Under the rubric of social science is to be found a
huge collection of material that factually reports developments that have a bearing on the human condition.   Newspapers and other daily reports form the base of the pyra-
mid: these, along with TV and radio, are to the man in
the street the channels of the news.   But above this base
are weeklies, monthlies, quarterlies, and annuals, which
also form part of the system of rounding up the news of
the times, the main difference being one of a longer time
perspective.   Not many years ago, the number of connected
factual reviews for longer intervals was limited, but changing

TABLE 8

Coverage of Selected Information About 6 Colleges and Universities
by 5 Representative Directories

	World of Learning 1968-69	American Colleges and Universities 10th ed.	College Blue Book 12th ed.	Cass. Comparative Guide to American Colleges 1968-69	Lovejoy's College Guide
Standing (Accreditation)	0	6	0	6	6
Admission requirements	0	6	6	6	6
Basis of organization and government	0	6	6	6	6
Degree requirements	0	6	0	0	0
Degree structure	0	6	6	6	6
Enrollment	6	6	6	6	6
Teaching staff	6	6	0	0	6
Library facilities	4	5	4	5	5
Finances	0	6	0	0	5
Physical assets	0	6	0	0	5
Chief executive officer	6	6	0	0	6

times and interests have multiplied them, and with the multiplication of sources has come a wider spread in quality of
reporting.

Our findings are based on two samples. First, a
random selection was made of subjects that periodic summaries might be expected to cover: (1) a résumé of developments in Canada, 1966; (2) NATO activities, 1966;
(3) activities of the Organization of African Unity, 1966;

TABLE 9
Coverage of 7 Subjects
by Selected Annual Reviews

Name of Annual	No. of subjects covered	% of subjects covered
Americana Annual	6	85
Annual Register of World Events	6	85
Britannica Book of the Year	4	57
News Dictionary (Facts on File)	7	100
Die Welt (Deutsches Institute fur Zeitgeschichte)	3	33
World Almanac	4	57
World Book of the Year	6	85

(4) how the Partido Revolucionario Institucional (PRI) fared
in Mexico's 1964 election; (5) civil rights developments,
1966; (6) connected account of the December, 1966, crisis
on publication of Manchester's Death of the President; and
(7) necrology for 1966. Seven annuals were checked for
the information and Table 9 shows that coverage ranged from
33 to 100 percent. Coverage was not all of the same quality.
News Dictionary and World Almanac, for example, contained
reliable factual information, but lacked the thoroughness of
some of the other accounts. The topics that proved most
elusive were, for different reasons, OAU activities, the
PRI, and Death of the President.

A second test was of another kind. Information
services of the sort that first served business and industry
have multiplied since the war. One useful service in the
political field is produced by Congressional Quarterly, Inc.
The heart of it is a Weekly Report of Congressional and

political activity, cumulatively indexed by a Quarterly Index
followed by an Almanac published each spring and covering
the previous calendar year. In June 1965, Congressional
Quarterly published a remarkable volume, Congress and the
Nation, which takes an even longer time span and presents
a factual summary of legislative and political developments
for the twenty years, 1945-64. It was decided to find out
how readily the information packed into Congress and the
Nation can be found elsewhere, and eleven items picked at
random were used for the purpose:

     Number of individual income tax returns in 1946 and
1963 (p. 398)
     Number of civilian employees who were part of the
military establishment as of June 30, 1963, and estimated
annual payroll (p. 1578)
     Glossary of terms (pt. 2, p. 167a-74a)
     Amount of economic aid given to Turkey, 1945-63
(p. 170)
     Summary of the Bay of Pigs disaster (p. 127)
     Measures taken to strengthen the U.S. information
program (p. 208-17)
     Amount of money for aid to students in higher edu-
cation, 1945-65 (p. 1199)
     Salary of the President of the USA in 1964 (p. 1435)
     Size of the Federal payroll for civilian employees,
by year, 1946-64 (p. 1473)
     Name and directory information (including main in-
terests) of principal civil rights groups (p. 1634)
     The amount of the public debt for ten years, 1955-
64 (p. 394)

     The first three items on the above list were not
found in any of the eight other sources checked. The last
item, on the other hand, was found in six of them. The
two central points that emerge from the comparison are
brought out by Table 10. Insofar as our eight sources are
representative, the information summarized in Congress and
the Nation is not widely duplicated. Next, the gamut of information is so wide (news summaries, statistics, directory
information, etc.) that a handful of eight reference works
can hardly be expected to provide an adequate test of duplication. For example, none of the eight works selected contains a glossary of terms, yet one needs go no farther than
an abridged Merriam-Webster to find adequate definitions of
Calendar Wednesday, sine die, cloture, pocket veto, statutes-
at-large, and other technical terms employed by the Congress

--and this is but one source for definition of terms.

TABLE 10
Availability of 11 Items in
Congress and the Nation in Selected Reference Works

	Number of Items Located	The Only Source for How Many Items
Statistical Abstract	3	2
Facts on File	1	0
World Almanac	3	0
Encyclopedia of Associations	1	1
Information Please Almanac	3	1
Economic Almanac	1	0
Statesman's Yearbook	1	0
Historical Statistics of the U. S.	2	1

General Information on Problems
and Activities of Government

Edwin V. Mitchell's Encyclopedia of American Politics (Greenwood Press, 1968) was published by Doubleday in
1946.   Winchell (7th ed. , L233) notes that it "includes brief
articles on the presidents, states, parties, political terms
and slogans, texts of important documents...."   The reprinting of this twenty-year-old work takes account of librarians' recognition of the value of handy compilations of
useful information.

Every tenth page in Mitchell was Xeroxed.   Normally,
one item on each Xeroxed page that contained one or more
separate entries was searched, thus reducing our sample of
fifty-one to a manageable total of nineteen.   Five additional
sources were searched to determine whether they included
information on these nineteen topics: Smith and Zurcher,
Dictionary of American Politics, McCarthy, Dictionary of
American Politics, Safire, New Language of Politics, Adams,
Dictionary of American History, and Encyclopedia Americana.
Two of the Mitchell items were found in none of the five:
"Don't badger them" and "Innocuous desuetude."   The remaining seventeen turned up a total of forty-three times;
three items in four other places and one of them in all

five.   Table 11 gives the breakdown by source.   The investigator (short for the reference librarian who made the search--in this case, Don McKie) estimated that 39 percent

TABLE 11
Frequency of Appearance in 5 Other Works
of 19 Items in Mitchell's Encyclopedia of American Politics

	No. of the 19 Items Located	Quality of the Information		
		Lower	Comparable	Higher
Smith	12 (63%)	8	4	0
Americana	11 (58%)	4	3	4
Adams	11 (58%)	0	7	4
McCarthy	6 (31%)	4	1	1
Safire	3 (15%)	1	2	0
Total	43	17 (39%)	17 (39%)	9 (21%)

(and a fraction) of the time the quality of the information found outside fell below that of Mitchell, but was equal or superior to it 60 percent (and a fraction) of the time.   Safire seems to drag its feet by covering only 15 percent of the items; this is another way of saying that Mitchell is best for pre-1946 material.   In Safire the accent is on material more recent than that.

Librarians find it handy to work with a slender, well-printed, 338-page volume, and this one contains a great deal of well-chosen information when considered in isolation from other sources.   But our necessarily small-scale comparison suggests that, when considered in relation to these, its value is limited, and when it competes with two of the five (Americana and Adams), it seldom walks off with the prize.

Another handy volume in the same general area is Taylor's Encyclopedia of Government Officials, Federal and State, which was announced in 1967 as the first of "a unique series" of biennials.   Drawing on successful experience with slick-paper school annuals, the Taylor Publishing Company portrays the organization of the several branches of government in human terms by listing the names and titles of key personalities and featuring pictures of those of first rank. In this sketchy sense, the volume seeks to be a " 'who's who' of men and women who guide the [political] destiny of

America. " It packs related information on voting, on emblems, former presidents, vice-presidents, etc. , into 200 pages and succeeds in placing before the inquirer a picture as vivid and as pleasing to handle as the latest old-school annual.

But the volume's claim to uniqueness depends on selection and graphic presentation of lively material, not on uniqueness of the information itself, as Table 12 brings out. Not one of the eight sources selected for comparison duplicates all of Taylor's several features, especially in its superb pictures and charts, but the typical source provides about a third of the information. The most nearly unique information is that supplied on state legislators.

TABLE 12
Availability of 21 Items of Information
Provided by Taylor's Encyclopedia of
Government Officials, Federal and State
in 8 Other Reference Works

	Total of 21 Items Found	% of Items Found
Information Please Almanac	14	66
World Almanac	12	57
Congressional Directory	11	52
Statesman's Yearbook	7	33
Washington '68 (Potomac Books, Inc.)	7	33
Congressional Staff Directory	6	28
Kane. Facts About the Presidents	5	24
U. S. Government Organization Manual	4	19

Conclusions and Unresolved Problems

1.   The object has been to focus attention on redundant information in our libraries.   The samples are small but indicate that the accumulating amount is considerable.

2.   The results are suggestive and help define the problem, but more work is needed before solid conclusions can be drawn on the amount of unwanted duplication that is involved.

3.   Up to the present, we have been able to look
upon duplication two ways at once.   Library schools and
reference librarians have been less concerned about duplication than about the availability of adequate sources of information.   It has been necessary to treat redundant information procured while filling gaps in local reference
facilities as secondary to the overriding goal of making a
great public service come into its own.   On the other hand,
our general policy all along has been to use book budgets to
enrich the collection; to this end, we hold down the purchase
of materials such as textbooks and duplicate titles.   We are
driven to inquire whether customary methods of holding
down unwanted duplication are enough.

4.   "Poor man," Benjamin Franklin said, in a
sentence that has become part of everyday language, "you
pay too much for your whistle."   We accept republication
of information on certain grounds: added convenience, a
style of treatment that supplements other sources, etc.
But we are seeing something new--a type and extent of
duplication which obliges us to pay too much for our whistle.
When is duplicated information objectionable?   Publishers
and librarians would benefit if we had better guidelines for
communicating with one another on the subject.

5.   "For many years," another quotation runs, "I
thought what was good for our country was good for General Motors, and vice versa."   For many years, librarians
have thought that what was good for private (read "commercial") development of reference works was good for the
profession.   If we did not like a particular work, the
answer was simple: we were--and are--free not to buy it.
The public service commissions arose to help relate private enterprise in certain fields to the general interest.
There is nothing comparable in the field of books.   The
only available control is over buying or not buying, whereas
the profession needs help in forestalling unwanted production of duplication.   This is another side of the problem that
needs to be studied.

6.   The popularity of blanket orders and approval
plans manifests a desire for something besides the time-
consuming method of evaluating individual titles, library by
library, and a willingness to try out centralized evaluation.
It may be doubted whether the search for centralized, in-
depth evaluation will end there.   Certain subject fields make
liberal use of bibliographic essays to take stock periodically

of contributions that are being made to the literature. Library literature offers some reviews which effectively place new reference works in relation to existing works, but most prepurchase knowledge of them comes from reviews that dwell on their individual merits. It would assist book selection, and would perhaps assist publishers in planning, if there were more reviewing in terms of the contribution which the new work makes to the system of information sources that it is intended to benefit. Can ways and means be found to improve arrangements for book reviewing along this line?

7. Meanwhile our kit of reference tools is being improved. We have a chance to buy works today for which the founders of reference and information service would have given their eye teeth. We will buy them--after sizing them up as best we can in relation to the rest of the collection--but we will buy them and be glad that we can do so. This, however, need not stop efforts to improve the product we buy.

References

1. J. A. Behnke, "Do Colleges Buy Reference Books?" School and Society, 49 (April 1, 1939) 420-21.
2. L. S. Thompson, "Dogma of Book Selection in University Libraries," College and Research Libraries, 21 (November 1960) 441-45.
3. A. P. Sable, The Death of Book Selection, Wilson Library Bulletin, 43 (December 1968) 345-48.
4. David Kaser, "The Literature of Acquisitions," in: Illinois. University. Graduate School of Library Science. "Literature of Library Technical Services." Rev. ed. The School, 1963, p. 7-13.
5. H. E. Hawkes, "Geology," Library Trends, 15 (April 1967) 816-28.
6. Chicago, University of, Graduate Library School and Social Science Division, "Bibliographical Services in the Social Sciences," Library Quarterly, 20 (April 1950) 79-99.

WHEN SOME LIBRARY SYSTEMS FAIL

by I. A. Warheit

Reprinted by permission from the Wilson Library Bulletin, September 1971, p. 52-58, copyright (c) 1971 by the H. W. Wilson Company.

Whenever a new technology develops, especially a popular technology that holds great promise, a number of people including librarians try to make use of it. But with little or no experience, many libraries experience a number of failures--along with some real successes--in the attempt. At the same time, others, viewing this new technology as something undesirable or as a threat to their cherished beliefs, are hostile to it and never miss an opportunity to point out its shortcomings and failures.

Certainly this has been the experience with computer applications in the library. Now, however, it has been over thirty years since Ralph Parker first used data processing in a library, and we have reached a certain maturity. Today all kinds of libraries, from the huge Library of Congress to the smallest special library are involved in the use of data processing. It is well, therefore, to look at the pitfalls that the pioneers experienced in order to avoid them in our own work.

This is not going to be a roman à clef. We are not going to point out specific instances of failures, or name institutions or people. Rather we are going to describe types of failures and try to see what caused them. Although based on actual occurrences, the examples presented are, in reality, pure types based on composite portraits. The purpose is to show the factors that contributed to the failure or lack of success and not to write a history.

Let us get one thing out of the way at once. Many of the so-called early failures were not systems failures at all. When data processing suddenly became respectable for

libraries--and this occurred in 1963 when the Library of
Congress at the Airlie House conference first proclaimed
that it was going to automate some of its operations--the
use of data processing became a sort of status symbol for
progressive librarians. A number of them immediately began thinking of what they would like to do and began discussing their hopes and plans. It was all new and exciting,
and the publicity was extensive. Behind all this publicity
was very little substance. In fact, it seemed that those
who did the most spoke the least, while those who spoke
the most did the least.

All this publicity, however, attracted librarians
throughout the world. As a result, when an Australian librarian, Harrison Bryan, visited the United States late in
1965 to see all the great things about library automation that
American librarians were telling the world, he found very
little to report. Most of these proclaimed systems were
nothing more than hopes, aspirations, or just paper plans.
Admittedly he did not go to the right places. He depended
for guidance on the published literature and the library establishment, who really knew nothing about data processing.
He did not go to the data processing community, who could
have directed him to those places where real work was
being done. Nevertheless, his assessment of the academic
library community, at least, was essentially correct. To
a large extent it represented plans and not operating systems.

Since many of these plans had no support, no chance
of support, and thus could never become a reality, they
cannot be called systems failures. Today, with so many
library applications fully automated, no one pays any attention to proclamations and publicity releases about new systems. Who pays attention when the 135th book catalog is
announced or the 178th mechanized circulation control system, or the 50th information-retrieval tape service? And
these are real systems, not just plans. So many of the
so-called early failures were not failures at all. They
simply never existed.

Lack of Resources

In one sense, however, they can be considered a type of
failure. And that is, the making of unrealistic plans. One
must cut his coat to suit the cloth. There is no sense in
trying to develop a plan or a system for which you know you

do not have the resources.   One must be realistic and
measure the resources that are necessary to implement a
new system.   These resources must include:

1.   A responsible individual, usually referred to as
a systems librarian.   He or she must be part of the
library, know the library's operations, and should
have more than a nodding acquaintance with the tools
he intends to employ, primarily the computer.   This
cannot be a casual responsibility like one more administrative function for a busy administrator or a
part-time visitor from the data processing center.
There have been systems failures where a library
task has been turned over to a data processing person
and no one in the library has had any overall responsibility.   More often than not, this DP person knows
little about automation in other libraries and doesn't
really understand the library.   So the task is more
difficult than it need be, and the applications developed
are often inadequate because no one has really explained to him the total task.   So the first resource
that is needed is a knowledgeable, responsible systems
manager.

2.   The second resource that is needed is the
physical equipment to do the job.   What machines are
available?   What is their configuration?   How much
time can the library have on the machines?   What
operator personnel will be available?   The greatest
danger here is machine time.   Too often, the library
has been a charity ward of the data processing center
and as such has had the lowest priority.   The computer center has not hesitated to dump the library in
favor of higher priority jobs.   It has changed computers with little or no warning, making the library
programs useless.   It has imposed impossible schedules, has left jobs unfinished, and so on.   It is very
dangerous for the library to accept charity.   The library must have a firm agreement as to its rights and
scheduled services on the computer.   If these are not
nailed down, the library runs a great risk of building
a perfectly good system that never becomes operational
or, if operational, is suddenly terminated.
This danger can hardly be exaggerated.   There have
been instances in which the manager of a data processing center has solicited library support, because
the more jobs he had to do, the better equipment he

could justify.   But once the equipment was procured
and installed and more high priority jobs became operational, the library soon found itself pushed right off
the computer.

Closely related to this lack of physical resources
are a number of programs which have appeared but
which suddenly disappeared.   Upon investigation, one
discovers that they were never supported as ongoing
programs, but were allowed to proceed for a short
time as demonstration projects.   In the early days
when library programs were quite simple and relatively
easy to prepare, some of the computer manufacturers
did prepare demonstration packages and used them as
educational and promotional devices.   Unfortunately
they were too often used by individuals to demonstrate
to their administrators that they were actively engaged
in reviewing library procedures and studying what
changes should be incorporated, when actually they had
no intentions at all of changing anything.   In other
words, some of these demonstrations were actually used
as smoke screens and meant to divert attention.

There are, however, some serious demonstration
programs that look very good, but cannot become ongoing operations for a number of legitimate reasons.
For example, a book catalog program was developed
for a consortium of libraries.   All but one of the
libraries found some reason or another not to participate.   One library, however, picked up the plan, developed it further, and has now for several years been
producing an excellent book catalog.

3.   The third resource is the time and money it
costs to develop a new system.   Librarians often do
not appreciate this.   The present manual library systems have been operational now for over half a century.
There is scarcely a technology that has had as few
changes as librarianship.   The great decisions for
library processing were nailed down around 1910, and
only minor refinements have been made since then.
Librarians therefore, are not accustomed to developing
new systems, and often are not equipped or organized
to do so properly.   At the lowest level they often do
not appreciate that they have to make some investment
in manpower and machine time to develop a new system.
Too often, as will be pointed out a little later, the
funds allocated for development have essentially been
used to educate the librarians and systems people and

give them an opportunity to learn the state of the art and not actually to develop a system.

There must be adequate fiscal planning and proper investment. Industry has always recognized that tooling up costs some money and has been willing to invest in it. The librarians must recognize this, but, what is even more important they must use some of the funds, at least as an investment, and not just for the sake of experimentation and education.

Systems have failed not merely because of improper use of resources, but also because of improper design or operation or people failures.

Design Failures

Some systems perform poorly because of inadequate design. The system is too expensive because it does not operate efficiently, or it does not carry out all the functions it should. As an example, some libraries use or have used an excellent text-editing program to convert their records, such as shelflist, serials holdings, etc., into machine-readable form. But this text-editing program was designed to handle large documents and not short records like a catalog card. Therefore, it is not as efficient as it might be for shelflist conversion. Some systems people have not recognized this and continue to use the program unchanged. In one instance, at least, a systems man recognized this deficiency and made a few changes in the program. His library is now converting its catalog records at a much faster rate and at a lower cost.

On the other hand, some poorly designed systems function very adequately and the users are satisfied with them. For the most part they represent an older state of the art and they need updating. It is much like a person who has an automobile that still performs quite adequately and it just does not seem worth the expense and trouble to trade it in for a new car. For example, there is a large library that has automated a number of its operations over the years. As part of its ordering and receiving, it uses a machine that computer manufacturers stopped making over twenty years ago. Although this is a very efficient library with low operating costs and many of its operations are computerized, one can do better than to emulate all of its operations. For some, there are more modern and more efficient methods.

In general, design deficiencies are due to two things.
Either to inadequate skill and knowledge or to the age of
the design and failure to take advantage of new developments.
The question of lack of skill and knowledge opens up the
whole question of operational or people failures. It is here
where one can take corrective action, and it should be looked
at most carefully.

Operational Failures

In Library Journal, November 15, 1970, Brong and
Pasternak published an article "The N-I-H Syndrome." This
was followed by a letter from Abigail Dahl-Hansen in LJ
of March 1, 1971. These two pieces on the (rejecting of
everything) "Not-Invented-Here" syndrome touch on one of
the greatest causes for system failures in libraries. It
does not affect small systems so much, but it has hurt a
number of large institutions and large systems. N-I-H is
due to ignorance, arrogance, and sometimes fear.

An example of ignorance is the library struggling for
six months to install a terminal-oriented circulation control
system. The systems engineers did not know or did not
really stop to consider that there were over 100 such systems operational all over the country, a number of them not
very far away. When they got done they had a good system,
but it turned out to be identical with a number of similar
circulation systems. A case of re-inventing the wheel.

Sometimes, though, the designers of a new system
know that programs and systems exist which do the same
job they want their system to do. But they either refuse
to look at them and study them, or they view these other
systems in a rather critical, hostile way because they consider themselves as being different. Too often the differences are superficial and trivial. This sense of being
unique and different has had a long history in librarianship.
It goes back long before computers. The bibliographic tools
in the old days were all hand-made and tailored to fit the
needs and tastes of the individual librarian. When national
standards were developed and we had ALA rules and LC cards
many libraries would not adapt to these standards. You
still find a number of cataloging departments making trivial,
stylistic changes in LC cards. Happily, under economic pressures this wasteful work is being eliminated.

Refusal to accept standard formats and procedures, however, is still a very real problem. For example, several libraries in a city want to form a consortium. Everything has been agreed upon, except that the catalogers cannot agree on the form of the main entry. In another example, a very progressive library adopted a serials program from a sister institution. The program did the job very satisfactorily; however, the library also borrowed the serials records in order to select those entries which were identical to its own. But one institution listed year first and then volume, and the other volume first and then year. The parochial decision to clean up and change the records cost them more even than if they had keypunched their own records.

Another example: a library refused even to consider using or analyzing certain systems because they were designed for State university libraries, and this library served a private university.

A combination of ignorance and arrogance is seen when a system is demonstrated at a small institution or in a laboratory environment. The visiting librarians and systems people do not fully appreciate the system design, but are very conscious of the fact that the program is operating in a library much smaller than their own and at an institution of little or no prestige. They too often conclude that the system is good for the little library, but is really quite inadequate for their big and important library. The irony of it all is that some excellent systems have been developed at small places. Knowledge and brains are not exclusive to any single group.

Another example of combined ignorance and arrogance is when we minimize the tasks that have to be done by the other person. Librarians have suffered from this for a long time. Too often their job is viewed as a high-class clerical function. Too often data-processing people have approached a library problem with a very simple-minded concept of what constitutes a library record and how a library operates. The tendency then is to underestimate the task, which can lead to very embarrassing delays and failures in implementing a system.

Conversely, the library systems personnel and programmers can underestimate the amount of effort and programming skill needed to prepare the support programs so

that the computer can handle the various application programs.   A case in point: an institution orders hardware that
is cheaper but which does not come with a full operating
system.   The systems people blithely decide that they can
write the necessary operating systems programs quickly and
easily.   Unfortunately, they find the job much more difficult than they anticipated.   The computer stands around idle
or is used at a low level for a long time.   The application
program gets delayed because everyone is busy trying to get
the operating system completed.   The institution may also be
stuck with some exotic hardware that cannot use standard
peripherals and all standard inputs must be converted.
Sometimes, therefore, the cheapest initial cost turns out to
be the most expensive final cost.

Some of the N-I-H syndrome is due to fear; that is,
the fear of being "sold" something.   This is somewhat less
true of special libraries in business and industry, but is
very characteristic of academic librarians.   Very often they
hold the representatives from commercial organizations,
such as hardware manufacturers and software houses, at
arm's length or even refuse to see them for fear they will
be brainwashed and sold something rather than properly advised.   This can happen, of course.   The best protection
is to have the commercial representative tell you what other
libraries are using the system he is proposing and to check
with them.   If he cannot give you this information, then be
wary.   But do not neglect the commercial sources of information.   Often they have the most experience and have developed the highest skills.

A case in point.   A private consultant convinced a
librarian and a governing board that he would design and
build the most advanced library system that present technology could offer.   But they had to be very careful and not
talk to any of the standard manufacturers or software organizations because they would not approve his very advanced ideas.

He and the library signed a contract for a very
substantial sum and he proceeded to design a system.   It
was, as they say in the trade, an absolute kludge.   Just
bits and pieces of various machines hooked together.   He
could not get the system to work.   The contract was cancelled.   Court suits were threatened.   The librarian re-
tired.   The library subsequently installed a good standard
computer program.

Sometimes the systems design is good but the planning, scheduling, and administration is poor.   There is a case in which one problem was so interesting and challenging that a major part of the effort was devoted to it--to the neglect of the total system.   The irony of it all was that the problem, which was hardware-related, was one that the library would not have to consider until the system became fully operational.   In the meantime, industry as a whole was working on the same problem and would provide adequate solutions when the library was ready for it.

So often the brilliant, knowledgeable person gets hung up on research and development or promoting a pet scheme when he is supposed to be doing system design.   Large sums have been allocated for system design to prepare working library applications, and no working system has appeared. The funds have been used up for research, development, and, sad to say, for the education of the people concerned.   There are much cheaper ways of getting educated.   It is this confusion between research and education on one hand and actual system design and implementation on the other which has consumed more grant dollars than one cares to think about.   If only these two aspects could be kept properly separated, as they are for the most part in industry, then we would have a great many more successful, economical, working library systems.

Even--in fact, especially--among some of the most knowledgeable persons, there is a tendency to be very critical of standard, available programs and systems.   These people, therefore, decide to build their own supporting programs like file management systems, I/O supervisors, and even operating systems.   They do this because for their specific applications these specially built customized jobs are, or might be, more efficient than the generalized programs.   What happens is that they spend a disproportionate amount of their resources--time and money--in building the tools to do their job.   Also, they learn later that as their needs grow and change, those efficient supporting programs must also be changed.   Good standard file management and supervisor systems are generalized and can perform a variety of functions.   Maybe you don't need them all, but you might in the future.   Also the responsible vendor of these systems "supports" them and will modify them as required.

One could go on in this vein for some time and discuss other problem areas.   There is the overly clever de-

signer who is essentially a problem solver and enjoys
showing how he can make the computer do things it really
shouldn't do.   Or the one who insists on refining standard
codes and formats because his designs are more efficient
than any standard product.   The designers who insist on
employing the latest fad and do not provide any fallback
position in case it doesn't work.   The people who are always waiting for tomorrow's hardware.   The problems encountered when one depends on temporary staff who leave
you in the middle of a job.   The system that has no documentation so that only one person knows how to operate it.
The errors compounded by overlooking and neglecting reviews and check points while the system is being built, and
for debugging and testing when the system is completed.
Conversely, there are those who can never release a program because they want to keep on refining it.   There are
the systems people who neglect the working library staff,
the very ones who have to operate the system.   Without their
cooperation, they can wreck the best system in the world.
With their cooperation, they can make anything work.   And
so on and on.

          The topic is a large one, and perhaps this rather
negative approach is not the best way to present it.   A
more positive approach would be to clearly set forth those
things which should be done to build a good system.   This
is an even bigger topic, and, hopefully, it will first be
taught in our library schools.

PROGRESS IN DOCUMENTATION: "INFORMATICS"

by D. J. Foskett

Reprinted by permission from the Journal of Documentation 26(4) December 1970, p. 340-369.

Introduction

The term "informatics" was first advanced formally
by the Director of VINITI, A. I. Mikhailov, and his colleagues A. I. Chernyi and R. S. Gilyarevskii, in their paper
"Informatics--New Name for the Theory of Scientific Information, " published at the end of 1966. [67]   An English
translation was circularized in the beginning of 1967.   As
the authors state in this paper, they are not the first to
use this term, and they quote a review by Professor J. G.
Dorfmann of their own book Fundamentals of Scientific Information[68] in which Dorfmann criticizes the use of other
terminology, such as "documentation, " "documentalistics, "
"information science, " and so on.   Although the authors do
not object to the use of the word "Documentation" in the name
of the International Federation for Documentation [Gilyarevskii
has proposed to FID/RI that "Informatics" be added], nevertheless they claim that this term has not found application
in the USSR and indeed they apologize for spending some
time in discussing its suitability as a name for "the new
scientific discipline which studies the structure and properties of scientific information as well as the regularities of
scientific information activity, its theory, history, methods,
and organization. "   It is clear that the authors have made
a thorough survey of the literature, as might be expected,
and they argue fairly about the meaning of most of the
terms that have at one time or another been advanced to
name this "new discipline. "   Their definition is as stated
above but they are careful to add the rider that Informatics
does not investigate the specific content of scientific information, only the structure and properties.   In their paper they
also advance definitions for "information, " "scientific information, " "scientific information activity, " "information officer, "

and "information scientist. " They have backed up their proposal by changing the title of their own book for its second edition,
and the title of the information science fascicule of the Referativnyi Zhurnal, which is now called Informatiki.

In 1967 Professor Mikhailov circulated a memorandum
on the theoretical basis of Informatics with a view to producing
a volume dealing with research on the topic for the FID Conference due to take place in Moscow in 1968. As is known, this
conference did not in fact take place, but a series of papers
was collected together and published by VINITI as FID 435;[71]
this was issued as a document by the Study Committee FID/RI
on "Research on the Theoretical Basis of Information. "

This was naturally a very important volume, but in a
sense it was something of a disappointment when compared with
its Prospectus: in this, the action headings were as follows:

Informatics and laws of science development
Interrelation of Informatics with other fields of knowledge
General concept of information
Theory of information retrieval systems
Linguistic problems of Informatics
Information languages and classification problems
Psychological problems of Informatics
Study of information needs and inquiries
Efficiency of the scientific information activity, its cri-
    teria and indices
Theoretical basis for reasonable presentation of scien-
    tific information
The role of hardware in science information activity

The immense importance of this tabulation will be obvious:
perhaps for the first time an outline of this field of study
was put forward which did not limit itself to the mechanical
handling of scientific and technical information, using "scientific and technical" in the narrow Western sense. As
was perhaps inevitable in a volume composed of solicited
papers, the coverage is sketchy and uneven, but the first
paper of the volume by the same three authors sets out in
more detail the subject "Informatics: its scope and methods. "
In this, although full recognition is given to the importance
of mechanized techniques in the modern era of vast quantities of publication, nevertheless the basic approach is to
set Informatics in its social context, and not to regard it
as a technology. They emphasize that "the subject matter
of Informatics are the phenomena and general laws of scientific information activities, rather than these activities themselves which may and should be performed by experts and

scientists in the respective domains of science and technology"; Informatics is not concerned with the truth or falsehood of information nor of its novelty or usefulness. "What is important is the fact that there is a certain piece of scientific information which is to be timely brought to its potential user in the most effective way and in a suitable and sufficiently complete form." After elaborating these arguments they conclude: "It follows from the above definition of the subject area or scope of Informatics that the latter belongs to the category of social sciences, since the object of its study--i. e. , Scientific-Information Activities-- is a phenomenon peculiar to and occurring only in the human society." Such a statement may well come as a surprise to those who claim that their activity is so scientific that it is unintelligible to and beyond the scope of all but science graduates with years of research in laboratories behind them; also to those who have advanced the notion that this activity is a technology, concerned only with production and therefore aimed at using the best type of machinery for the production of as large a quantity of output as possible. On the other hand it will certainly be welcomed by all those who regard librarianship, enquiry work, scientific information service, and similar activities (by whatever name they may be designated) as something which has to do with human beings and their peculiar needs, and not with the mere production of objects as in an assembly line.

This paper was clearly a milestone, for not only was the FID 435 quickly published, but a further two volumes appeared in 1969, also as a production of FID/RI.[70] These two volumes, International Forum on Informatics, reprint some of the papers from FID 435 but have a very much wider scope and cover nearly all of the sections named in the original Prospectus. It is still, however, a collection of separate contributions, and therefore some sections receive considerably more attention than others, in particular the sections on the general concept, the theory of I. R. systems, Information needs and inquiries, scientific information activity, and hardware. A further volume,[69] printing a series of lectures, has just been issued by Unesco. The present review has been inspired by the conviction that this discussion needs to be continued, and that there lie at this moment considerable dangers in the direction that most research in this field is taking, that is to say, the reduction of information to a commodity and the emphasis on the technology of processing information without regard to its

meaning or destination.   As Fairthorne[30, 33] has often
pointed out, many have rushed into this field without defining
their terms or even, in some cases, of knowing precisely
what they were talking about.   It is quite possible that the
term "Informatics" itself will not eventually prove to be the
accepted one; in France and West Germany for example
"L'informatique" and "Informatik" are not used in the sense
of Mikhailov et al., but in some publications are used in
the sense in which we use the term "information theory,"[77]
in others as a collection of disciplines which relate to the
automatic processing of information, (Poly and Poulain,[76]
Arsac, Demarne[66]).   Arsac, for example, claims that Informatics is concerned only with the transfer of marks de-
noting information and not at all with the message carried
by the information; this clearly would exclude Informatics
from the area of the social sciences.   Demarne widens the
scope of the field, but in the same direction, by stating
that it is concerned with everything to do with the design,
production, and use of computers.

        East Germany, on the other hand, has followed the
Russian lead, and has re-named the journal ZIID-Zeitschrift
as Informatik.   The East German translation of Mikhailov
et al. 68 is called Grundlagen der Informatik, while that
issued simultaneously in West Germany is called Grundlagen
der wissenschaftlichen Dokumentation und Information.   In
his Foreword to the latter, however, Professor Dr. Adolf
Adam comments on this terminology and gives the opinion
that the Soviet usage is preferable: to use "Informatik" as
merely meaning computer science is too restricting.

        In the West, (apart from theoretical works on the
nature of communication, such as those of Cherry[17] and
Meredith[64]) almost the only attempt to sketch out a new
discipline of this scope has been Jesse Shera's concept of
"Social epistemology" advanced as long ago as 1952 jointly
with Margaret Egan--"a new discipline, perhaps a science of
communication," based on the biological necessity of the human brain to engage in information-processing activity in order
to develop properly, and the fact that this also extends to
the human collective, society. [86, 87]   The externalization of
the individual human process in oral speech, and its extension by means of graphic symbols, have made possible the
growth of a distinctively human culture, "a duality of action
and thought, bound together by the communication processes."
It is difficult to understand why Shera's thesis should have
gained so little overt acceptance, for in his writings he has

actually covered most of the ground defined by the VINITI
team; his two last books were collections of articles, and it
may be that, to mark a turning-point in the social sciences,
a whole book is still required (a comment in this direction
is offered by R. D. Whitley[100]).

Gropings after a similar synthesis have been made
from time to time, usually very tentatively, as by Kochen:[53]

> 'Information science' does not now exist as a sci-
> entific discipline in its own right. We believe
> that it may emerge as such, perhaps as a syn-
> thesis of concepts and methods originating in
> automata theory, logic, mathematical linguistics,
> graph-theory, list-processing techniques, and the
> theory of cognitive processes. It deals with the
> principles and facts underlying the analysis and
> design of information systems.

Kochen's two anthologies do, however, provide useful collections of wider scope than the usual "information science"
volume. [52, 53]

The long controversy that has raged between librarians and information officers has been sterile because although there was a definite consciousness of improvement
over traditional operations, there has never been brought
forward any evidence to show that the practices concerned
were genuinely new, and not merely improvements. The
controversy has in fact related to what Mikhailov et al. call
"scientific information activity," bearing in mind that "scientific" in the Russian sense relates to the whole of knowledge and is not used in the narrow Anglo-Saxon sense of the
natural sciences. This activity is "operations performed to
collect, process through analysis and synthesis, store, retrieve, and disseminate scientific information." In relation
to these I stand by what I wrote in 1958 that

> these services may take many forms and often
> reach the highest levels of scholarship; and it is
> my opinion that the information officer who or-
> ganizes and performs them has taken librarianship
> to its most advanced state, but has not founded a
> new and qualitatively distinct profession. [38]

A new discipline does not arise simply because practitioners
of the old get better at their jobs, but because dynamically

new relations arise with other fields.   In this sense, the
activity "information storage and retrieval" is better librarianship, but "Informatics" is developing as a new discipline, in that, for the first time, people are now studying
the behaviour of information itself and the properties, or
"morphology, " as Fairthorne puts it, of information flow. [32]
To a great extent this has been brought about by the advent
of the computer, though not entirely so, as many computer
people seem to think.   Since we are occupied with the
meaning of texts, that is to say what texts are about, and
what use they are to people who are looking for information
about their subjects, our approach must necessarily, in so
far as measurement is concerned, be statistical and not
merely arithmetical; it has long been recognized that the
mere counting of books issued over the counter does not
give an adequate assessment of the quality of a library
service.   The advent of computers has made it possible for
us to deal in much larger numbers than before, and to
manipulate the numbers much more easily and effectively,
and has therefore brought within our reach the possibility
of much more detailed and systematic analysis of techniques, [31] but it must not be forgotten that this does not
mean that the techniques are the same thing as the analysis.
Considering the vast quantity of resources in money and
man-years that have been devoted to computer research in
this field, the results have been paltry, to say the least.
In some cases, moving into the operational field has bought
disaster.   Nevertheless no one would deny that computers
have brought about the final necessary break with the previous generally-accepted pattern of thought, and have not
only enabled us to improve existing types of service but
have also made possible new services.   On the social level,
they have introduced us to new types of colleague; computer
specialists and other experts in several different disciplines
are taking a new interest in the handling of information, not
only as mere arithmetical or statistical data to be processed
but as presenting a genuinely new and exciting challenge to
their own expertise.

        More than this: in recent years, it has become in-
creasingly obvious that many "information specialists" do
not take very often the advice that they so readily offer to
others, and consult the literature of the subject.   Of all
professions, we should avoid the snare of over-specialization,
since a vital part of our activity is to detect relevance, for
specialist effort, in the literature of other fields.   Whether
or not the actual term "Informatics" becomes accepted or

not, the recognition of a new emergent discipline should
rescue us from a narrow and inward-looking concentration
on techniques as ends, and clarify the distinction between
a mere technology of moving marks from here to there, on
the one hand, and on the other a multi-faceted activity place
in a meaningful social context.

Scope

In his contribution to FID 435, A. Merta criticises
writers who limit the scope of this field to the collection,
processing, and dissemination of information, or information, or information sources.[65] He would include, as integral parts of the process of information flow, "the act of
origination of information, both factual and descriptive, as
well as patterns, means, and effectively of information movement on its way between the creator and the user." This
"social and dynamic aspect" prevents the reduction of the
discipline into a mere collection of technologies; it also implies that we, as exponents, should have and demonstrate a
proper understanding of what is involved--the process of
intellectual creation, the formulation and presentation of
material for the act of communication, and the relation between recorded information and the needs of users, as well
as the well-known technical processes involved in collection,
processing, and dissemination.

It is a measure of our failure to appreciate this
point that, in works on creativity in science (and still less
in the arts), one rarely finds any reference to the role of
libraries and information services.   J. D. Bernal in his
classic work, The Social Function of Science,[9] discusses
methods of communication, but principally from the organizational aspect; in dealing with the Librarian, however, he
did look forward to the prospect of a colleague who
would not only organize publications, but also draw up reports on current work from the viewpoint of the laboratory
and, as a corollary, make its work known to the outside
world.   This discussion has been brought up-to-date by
Herbert Coblans' contribution to a book in which fifteen
scientists assess the effects of Bernal's work twenty-five
years later.[43]   "User studies," such as those presented to
the International Conference on Scientific Information, Washington, 1959,[51] have generally been arithmetical in approach,
and producer- rather than consumer-oriented.   An exception
is the sociologist Herbert Menzel, whose Washington paper

is reprinted in The Sociology of Science, [3] one of the most
thorough-going reviews yet published. In particular, the
papers by Talcott Parsons, "The Institutionalization of
Scientific Investigation," and by R. K. Merton, "Science and
the Social Order," are well worth studying in the context of
Informatics as well as of science as a whole.

    On the other hand, the concern felt by scientists over
their information needs breaks out from time to time, usually
at a specially convened conference or symposium.   The most
famous, perhaps, is the 1948 Scientific Information Conference
of the Royal Society, but important contributions were also
made by the 1955 IUPAC Conference in London on the documentation of pure and applied chemistry--now almost forgotten because never published as a single volume--and the
1966 Ciba Foundation Symposium on communication in science, which had particular reference to documentation and
automation. [29]   Most of the contributions were on organizational aspects, but much of the discussion (also reported)
and the papers of D. J. de Solla Price and W. T. Knox deal
with the problems facing the individual scientist in both
transmitting and receiving information.

    Many research workers in all fields have discussed in
print their views on what they do, however, and there are
several comparisons between scientific and artistic creativity: e. g. Aldous Huxley, [49] John Beloff, [5] P. B. Medawar, [62]
C. D. Yeoman, [98] C. P. Snow, [88] and the "two cultures controversy."   Some have suggested that the differences are
less important than the similarities: Abdus Salam, on the
"Art of the Physicist," says that each major breakthrough is
"achieved by some great physicist who goes through the
spiritual agony of creation."[83]   The editor of the Scientific
American has expressed the opinion that scientific creativity
manifests itself in the discovery of a new principle and not
in the manufacture of an atomic bomb.   All writers agree
that creativity resides in the act of synthesis, that is, the
perception of relationships hitherto unnoticed, and the uni-
fication, into a coherent system, of elements that were not
previously unified. [81] Creativity does not reside in the
mere assembly of a heap of particular instances; as Paul
Weiss[99] says, "scientific knowledge grows like an organic
tree, not as a compilation of collector's items."

    Man's desire to investigate Nature arises from his
unique ability to work out a purpose in his mind before
setting about a project; he does not proceed merely by trial

and error, but makes a plan which incorporates expected results.   His works help him to control his environment and to predict, so that he is not taken by surprise by the events of each new day.   Because Man is a social being, control of his destiny involves others, and is therefore a social process.   It is primarily because of this that science has to win public acceptance, to become what John Ziman[102] calls "public knowledge"; that is, it has to be published in such a way that others can repeat work and confirm or refute the results.   Karl Popper[78] goes so far as to make "falsifiability" the test of true science, though it is hard to understand how this could be generally applied; the continued existence of the human race depends on simple truths such as that water boils at 100°C under normal atmospheric conditions.

Science nowadays, "big science" that is, has also to rely on public acceptance because it has become a social institution in its operation, and not solely in the area of communication.

But science as "public knowledge" must be the description of a reality existing outside ourselves, for if the idealist philosophers were right and there were no such reality, there could be no point in trying to communicate our notion of it to others.   We are only able to communicate our own knowledge, of course, but we hope that by the exchange of knowledge with others we may continually arrive at more nearly accurate pictures of the truth about the world.   By publication we make possible the process of cross-checking results and correction of errors.   Our conception of reality, therefore, does not simply remain of our own making.   To this extent, natural science, unlike Art, is not dependent on the peculiar structure of a single individual mind, though this certainlu influences its presentation.   It depends mainly on those intellectual features that are common to all, which enable us to perceive the world outside us, to form abstractions from these percepts, and to symbolize them in a manner intelligible to others. [8]   Only in this way can there come into existence a "common stock of knowledge, " which resides in the literature and is stored in libraries.

One of the best-known attempts to analyse the development of knowledge is T. S. Kuhn's The Structure of Scientific Revolutions. [56]   Kuhn suggests that research in any field results in the formation of a pattern of knowledge,

or "paradigm, " that wins general acceptance and so becomes "public knowledge. " This provides a satisfactory
explanation for the phenomena studied by specialists in the
field, but inevitably discrepancies are found which the
paradigm cannot explain satisfactorily.   It is recognized "that
Nature has somehow violated the paradigm-induced expectations that govern normal science. "   More research uncovers
more violations, and tension begins to build up between the
paradigm and the tested observations that denote its failures.
Finally there comes a moment when these failures can no
longer be regarded as aberrant, and the paradigm is over-
turned by some genius who produces a new theory which can
account for more observations than the old.

        This account has two important features in the con-
text of Informatics (apart from the fact that this discipline
might itself be regarded as an example): first, originality
consists in explaining the departures from a paradigm; and
second, that the overthrow of a paradigm cannot be achieved
without the necessary discovery of instances that contradict
it.   In order to recognize the contrary instances, it is
necessary first of all to know the paradigm--the normal
expectations that are in the mind of the research worker
when he plans his programme.   This is the consensus; that
is, knowledge that has been put to the test by other experts,
and accepted as explaining the phenomena they purport to
explain--at least as far as these are known at the moment.
A paradigm does not rest on implied guesswork, but on
tested and proved hypotheses; it attains "consensibility" by
the hard work of researchers who accumulate masses of
detail and record them in the literature so that they may be
confirmed or challenged by others.   A paradigm is based,
in fact, on information, and unless that information is
organized in the most helpful way, the creative worker will
lack the basis from which he may take off on his own individual path.   This is why matters have come to something
of a crisis situation in the world of information control.
Since the store of information increases so rapidly, while
the capacity of the human brain increases little, if at all,
how can the creative worker be sure that he is genuinely
advancing the frontiers of knowledge?   How does he know
that what he has discovered, or hypothesised, is actually
new, and not merely new to him?   If libraries and information services are to play any part in this process--and this
is undoubtedly what they aspire, and claim, to do--then it
is essential that they should regard themselves as an integral part of the process, and not some other compart-

mented expertise, with its own laws, dedicated merely to
increasing the quantity of material processed.   Research
workers are unlikely to turn to us for help if they feel, as
many certainly do, that we, for our part, cannot be expected to have or cultivate an understanding of their problems when we are so manifestly preoccupied with those of
our own invention.

A wider perspective is therefore essential, not only
for developing a sympathetic understanding of what each individual research worker is up to, but also for making our
own work effective.   Any librarian or information officer
knows from his own practice that this is the case.   A true
understanding of the world comes not merely through observation and hypothesis, but from actively engaging in that
world and testing hypotheses in action.   As M. Cornforth[24]
has succinctly put it, "the laws of thought are the rules for
drawing correct conclusions from practice."   Information
is more than the mere itemizing of sense perceptions, or
responses to given stimuli; it requires processing by a
human mind, before it can be made into part of a consen-
sible pattern or paradigm.   It may not be the province of
Informatics to decide the truth or falsehood of recorded information; it must, though, be ready to assess relevance
and pertinence.   It seems a pity that this useful distinction,
introduced by C. W. Cleverdon[21, 22] in his comparative study
of indexing systems, has fallen out of favour, because it
certainly draws attention to a significant difference.   By
"relevance" applied to any piece of information, I would
understand that it is acceptable as part of the consensus of
an area of public knowledge; by "pertinence," that it meets
the specification of a particular individual who is trying to
complete a pattern in his own mind.   Relevance is the criterion for selecting material to be published in an indexing
or abstracting service, or a review of progress in a subject, since the compilers are not relating their selection to
the needs of any individual, but to the consensus.   Pertinence is the criterion used by a librarian or information
officer when making a selection to suit the needs of his
own clientele, and in order to use this criterion correctly,
he must be aware of how they look at their subjects.   When
they use recorded information, they are trying to advance
their own understanding through the medium of what other
people have said about their subject.

Now this is far more than a mere question and
answer, or stimulus-response situation.   When a writer

sets down for public scrutiny and criticism what he thinks,
he is usually doing one of two things. Either he is writing
a descriptive account of matters not described before, that
is, he is adding to our collection of particular instances;
or he is developing a hypothesis to account for certain
phenomena that he has observed taking place, that is, he
is trying to construct a pattern of interrelationships. This
is more than the description of objects, though even the paper
which enumerates the characteristics of a particular instance
has to take note of the fact that the universe is dynamic,
and not static, and that before one can start to explain interrelationships, one has, so to speak, to detach the elements from their natural context, and dissect them in an
unnatural state of isolation.

Concept Formation

          Man is also himself part of Nature, and the con-
cepts that he forms in his mind to account for his environment do not lie around in his head "like peas in a bag" as
L. S. Vygotsky[97] puts it, but are all closely linked with
each other to form a picture that approximates to the reality
he is trying to describe.   Modern psychological theory has
come to reject the behaviourism of Watson, Hull, and
Skinner and what L. von Bertalanffy[10, 11] and Arthur Koestler[54] have called the "rattomorphic" view of Man as an
animal that merely reacts to external stimuli, like a machine.   Such reactions would give us only what Vygotsky
calls "spontaneous concepts," but in order to transform
these into "scientific concepts," they have to be generalized
and made to form part of a system.   In this way, it becomes possible to make a general picture of the world, to
formulate purposive behaviour, and to conceive structures in
the imagination without having to go through the motions of
actual construction.   The roles of identification, seriation,
and classification have been studied in great depth by, for
example, J. P. Guilford[45] in California, and Jean Piaget and
his colleagues in Geneva. [50]   Piaget has shown that the
learning process depends primarily on the accumulation of
data given by the senses, by observation, and by experiments.   We record through our senses the notions of shape,
colour, size, and so on, and we perform certain actions
which relate these notions to particular objects: we see an
object which is round in shape and reddish in colour, and
by linking these qualities with those discovered by the
actions of peeling and chewing, we identify the object as an

orange. That is, we classify it, and we learn to form
classes of objects either by analysis, by separating out from
a group those items which exhibit the same properties, or
by synthesis, by collecting together into groups from here
and there those items with the same properties. Both
collection and separation can be made on the basis of different characteristics, and thus we form multiple and not
single hierarchies, lattices and not trees. As Fairthorne[33]
remarked in one of his earliest papers, this also applies
to bibliographic classifications, which "have no unique com-
plement, and are therefore lattice systems, and not Boolean
algebra." This fundamental point has often been forgotten
by those under the spell of computers, whose activities, of
course, do reduce to the manipulation of binary digits, in
the manner of true mono-hierarchical dichotomous classifications like the Tree of Porphyry.

If Piaget's work has particular significance for the
study of concept analysis, that of Guilford is equally note-
worthy, since it has formed the psychological basis for the
theory of relational analysis advanced by J. E. Farradane.[34]
In his "structure of intellect" model, Guilford also rejects
the reductionist views of the behaviourists, and tends to
discount most psychological theorizing based on animal research: "people are not rats (with a few exceptions), nor
pigeons (again with a few exceptions)." He has applied
factor analysis to the classification of human abilities, producing a three-dimensional lattice system capable of holding
120 different "cells," or combinations of types of i) materials of thought, ii) operations of thought, iii) products of operations. Units of information are the basic material which is
processed in the mind to form relations, systems, trans-
formations, and implications. The creative mind is capable
of analysis and synthesis, of handling ideas with flexibility
and fluency, and above all of forming and evaluating complex structures of concepts. Guilford has also compared
the human memory to the operations of a computer store,
but emphasizes

> the importance of classes and sub-classes and
> their organization into larger systems as aids in
> giving information the identification that is helpful
> in searching operations ... since classification is
> so important in providing addresses of information
> in memory storage, considerable emphasis should
> be given to habits of forming classes and relation-
> ships between classes.

Linguistic Aspects
<u>   </u>

Thus in so far as a writer understands what he is
writing about, it is because he has been able to form accurate concepts from his observation and experiment, and
to fit these concepts into a structured system which he himself understands as a unified whole, that is, as we say, it
makes sense to him.   The medium by which he can do this,
and also the medium by which he can make his ideas seem
sensible to other people, is language. [40]   The communication of knowledge is more than merely handing on a message (hence the irrelevance of much of "information theory"
for our purpose[12]); a message can be handed on in Morse
Code or in a foreign language by someone who understands
neither.   True communication relates to the apprehension of
meaning, when a structured scheme of concepts becomes
assimilated into the mind of the recipient, who can then
adjust the scheme already in his mind to incorporate the
new data.   It is significant that most modern linguistic
theory has been derived from psychological and social
factors, and has virtually superseded the historical-compara-
tive study of "philology" developed with great success in the
nineteenth century.   The description of individual languages
has given way to the analysis of structure and the consideration of language as a system with precise and identifiable
rules for its operation.   This process is generally considered to have begun with the great Swiss linguist F. de
Saussure, who rejected the notion that the study of language
was the study of the derivation and history of words, and
drew attention to the inseparableness of meaning.   The fact
that Man is able to handle signs (symbols that refer to
natural phenomena) in the absence of the phenomena themselves constitutes a vital difference in mental features from
the animals, and Saussure claimed that "the social side of
speech" is a science <u>sui generis,</u> a distinctively human
activity (unlike mere <u>vocal sounds</u>).   He gave the name
"Semiology" to the science that "studies the life of signs
within society."   While acknowledging Saussure's pioneering
contribution, J. R. Firth[35] described his sytem as "static
mechanical structuralism," and his successors, in the
linguistic school of Prague,[95] the Copenhagen Linguistic
Circle[47] and the English school of General Linguistics[82]
have all gone on to develop further what may be described
in a general way by Firth's phrase, "the contextual theory
of meaning."   This emphasizes that language is not so much
a science of constructing schemes of grammar and syntax,
in which individual words are described in relation to their

own forms and to other words, but rather a study of the constantly developing means of communicating ideas between human beings, each of which is endowed with a unique personality and therefore with a unique interpretation of the world. "I venture to think" says Firth, "that linguistics is a group of related techniques for the handling of language events. "

In the United States, the study of language was particularly influenced by the "descriptivists" who made several studies of the unwritten languages of the American Indians, and continued the development of structural analysis through the several levels of letters, sounds, words, phrases, sentences. Two of the principal representatives of this tradition, Bloomfield and Harris, were explicitly behaviouristic in their approach to linguistic description, viewing all utterances as expressions of responses to particular stimuli. In recent years, their position has been strongly attacked by the most famous of present day linguists, Noam Chomsky, [18] who goes on from structural grammars to "transformational grammar, " in which he tries to provide a set of rules which can explain the differences between sentences which have apparently the same grammatical form (compare "the poet is popular in Japan" with "the poet is tall in Japan"). He has introduced the concepts of "deep" and "surface" structures, the former being a system of propositions which enumerate the notions to be communicated, the latter a system of categories of signals which enable the former to be conveyed intelligibly to other people. Inevitably, Chomsky has been drawn to emphasize once more the social nature of linguistic phenomena, and its "creative" aspect: a child can master its mother tongue without having any notion of what language is (probably, as Halliday[46] says, the most difficult intellectual achievement of its life) and can readily form sentences correctly, even though it has never heard them before. Chomsky has been criticized (Meredith, [64] Hockett[48]) for trying to reduce linguistics to a mathematical degree of precision, and of failing thereby to come to grips with the realities of social communication.

These problems were faced in the earlier work by Vygotsky, [97] first published in Moscow in 1934, but not made available in English until 1962, which so far has received more attention from psychologists and educators than from professional linguists, although Firth did draw attention in a 1950 paper on "Personality and Language in Society" to the work of Russian linguists, particularly commending their criticisms of Saussure. Vygotsky set out to find a theory of language that would account for the human ability to convert the world of personal experience into a set of communicable symbols that would represent the real world to someone else. This involves a transition from a collection of perceptions, sense-impressions derived from experience of the environment, to a structure of concepts connected by relations established in the mind, but corresponding to relations actually existing in objects outside of the mind. Such a transition is made possible through the medium of language; the basic units are not those derived from the analysis of the symbols themselves (i. e., semantic and phonetic elements), but analysis whose products retain all the basic properties of the whole phenomena described. This "unit of verbal thought" Vygotsky defines as "word-meaning," in which thought and speech unite into verbal (and therefore communicable) statement. Word-meanings do not merely denote objects, but classes of objects, generalizations which enable the mind to construct systems of inter-related concepts, and convert "spontaneous" into "scientific" concepts. It is the presence of a system that converts mere apprehension into understanding, both in the development of the mind from child to adult, and in the reception of a communication by the reader or listener.

A different approach has been made by the Cambridge Language Research Unit, [90] who have been applying the techniques of computational linguistics, the analysis of word frequency and word association in texts, by means of computers. This team has demonstrated the tendency of families of notions to occur as clumps of terms, and have gone on to derive automatically what they call "keyword classifications." Encouraging results have been obtained in using these schemes for information retrieval, and if this technique proved to be capable of adequate refinement, it might well offer an alternative method of using computers for analysing computer input as well as producing computer output.

The importance of linguistic studies in information control has already been underlined by Bar-Hillel[2] and by Gardin[27, 41] whose Syntagmatic Organization Language (SYNTOL) stems directly from Saussure. For two of his main types of relations, Gardin uses Saussure's terms, "paradigmatic" and "syntagmatic," and these bear a marked resemblance to Ranganathan's use of facet analysis;[79, 80] the first, in the formation of the schedules of the Colon

Classification, the second, in the use of facet analysis for the classifying of individual documents. Ranganathan long ago called bibliographic classification an artificial language of ordinal numbers, and the use of computers for mechanical translation as well as for information processing has led to the widespread concept of a "machine-readable language." Many writers now speak of indexing or retrieval languages rather than of classification and subject headings, although the basic function remains the same, namely, to provide what Salton[84] calls "language normalization": "If the natural language is used as a primary input to an information system, any content analysis system must include methods for consistent language normalization." The success of such methods can only be based on the extent to which they succeed in matching, rather than distorting, the subject content of the input text. This means using both analysis and synthesis; Ranganathan, it will be remembered, has advanced from his original technique of "faceted classification" to what he calls "analytico-synthetic" classification, an enumeration of terms in categories, based on a system of postulates and rules for combination. As is well known, his categories are based on the fundamental notions of Matter, Energy, Space, and Time, with "Personality" as his own term for each level of whole entities whose nature as an integrated whole determines the Basic Class, and thus the content of the Matter and Energy facets of that class. These are, of course, not the only possible categories, as de Grolier[44] has shown.

Classification

The development of theories of indexing languages has reflected the growth of knowledge itself.[20, 37] The great contribution of Melvil Dewey lay in his recognition that it would be possible, by using decimal notation, to enumerate terms--names of objects--in a structured scheme that closely paralleled the arrangement used by the classificatory sciences: a genus-species relation. An elementary form of transferring the idea of classification from objects or entities to documents appears in those documents, that are simply straightforward descriptions, and most of the foundation papers in the classificatory sciences are of this kind; they are descriptive, that is to say they enumerate the characteristic features of different species at various levels of complexity. In chemistry, for example, we have descriptions of the elements; in botany, descriptions of individual plants which are rather more complex than chemical elements; in biology, descriptions of individual living species which are more complex than plants. Thus classification of the true genus-species type of hierarchy is still suitable for documents of this kind, documents which are descriptive because they are enumerating the sort of characteristic which we use in making a hierarchical classification. And, indeed, this type of classification is necessary. In recognizing that we need more than true generic classification, we must not throw out the baby with the bathwater. Some people have suggested that we no longer need generic classifications at all, simply because generic classification by itself will not cater for the needs of modern literature; but generic classification still remains an important part of subject analysis, even though only one part.

In information retrieval the inclusion of generic hierarchies is absolutely essential, if we are to make the maximum use of mechanized retrieval systems. The reason why this kind of classification is still suitable is because information about the basic forms, the basic entities in any field of knowledge makes the foundation of the inductive method of reasoning, which is the mode of reasoning characteristic of the classificatory sciences. In other words, we have descriptions of a number of objects or entities, and from these descriptions we can draw up a system which will cover all of the entities, in respect not only of their structure but also of their behaviour and their interaction. We can make generalizations about them and thus we come to make a science. This includes library science. There has been a lot of criticism, directed by people who do research in librarianship, and hope to make librarianship into a science, of what is called the "how I run my library good" type of article. This type is commonly found in the literature of librarianship, and has indeed often been open to the criticism that the authors are writing about their own library service as if it were the ideal, which everybody else should copy. But we do need descriptions of individual libraries, because only by examining the individual objects or entities in the class of libraries, can we draw general correct conclusions about the nature of libraries, and how to organize them.

Information Retrieval

A great deal has been written about modern systems

of index language construction;[26] Jack Mills[72] has recently
provided a full review, and all that need be said here is
that no such language will be successful unless it takes into
account modern work in psychology and linguistics. The
dangers of the behaviourist approach have been heightened
by the advent of the computer, particularly in what has been
called the man-machine interface, a misuse of language almost as monstrous as the grossly reductionist philosophy
behind it. This implies that the typical information retrieval
situation is one in which the system itself is the active element; that it is the computer that asks the questions, and
that the human user merely sits pushing buttons in a typical
stimulus-response mode. He does not know what he has to
say next until the computer has asked its next question--
which will of course be based on what term-associations are
in the computer memory. In real life, as any information
officer or librarian knows, it is the user who asks the
questions and they are based on what is in this own mind;
the store supplies answers as best it can, but does not
normally try to make the user change the questions he wants
to ask. The advantage of a printed source over a console
display lies mainly in its ability to provide, at a glance, a
wide-range of readily accessible data; the console can only
do this by becoming large enough to produce a poor imita-
tion of the printed page. After much research, J. Toman,[93]
of the Czechoslovakia Academy of Sciences, in Vol. I of the
International Forum, comes to the conclusion that individual
request answering by computer is always inefficient, apart
from exceptional circumstances. This conclusion, though
borne out in practice in many organizations, rarely reaches
the literature; the reason may be that most of the published
works describe what Toman includes as exceptional circumstances, namely, a) computer time is not charged, b) expense
is no object, c) vast quantities of requests are batch processed (as by an international organization such as EURA-
TOM).

        This does not, naturally, mean that we should reject
the help of computers; indeed, most of the major works on
the theory of information storage and retrieval are based on
the assumption that we shall need to use computers if we
are to achieve our objectives of control and dissemination of
knowledge under contemporary circumstances. The theoretical foundations have been explored by many writers,
notably Becker and Hayes,[4] Vickery,[96] Foskett (A. C.),[36]
Loosjes,[59] Scheele,[85] and the new volume from VINITI.[92]
Significant articles appear in the proceedings of many bodies,

in librarianship, information science, and computer science, not least among them the Committee for International Co-operation in Information Retrieval among Examining Patent Offices, ICIREPAT. Not so much attention has been paid to the process of information transfer itself, and when we come to practical applications of the theory, we find once more an almost exclusive concentration on the technology of how to do it, rather than an examination of what is to be done, and why. This is part of the "information-commodity" phenomenon in which it is taken for granted that information is a good thing, and the problem is to produce as much of it as we can; it is, or becomes, its own justification.

Communication activities, however, are not an iso-lated behaviour pattern, as Janice Ladendorf[57] insists in a brief but very pertinent review. "They are deeply tied to social, professional, and institutional relationships," and it is out of these relationships that information needs arise. Reality exists outside of ourselves, but our knowledge of it is in itself a social construct, and the transfer of knowledge must involve social relations; even the face-to-face oral en-counter will not bring about understanding unless there is a considerable stock of previous knowledge held in common, and assumed to be so. Language is part of this common stock in that we all understand what language is (otherwise the early explorers of unknown lands could not have had con-verse with the natives), as well as being itself the medium by which the exchange may be carried on.

As Ladendorf rightly says,

> the literature is full of various user studies, most of which are so primitive in experimental design and techniques that they do not produce results which can be compared and used to establish gen-eral principles of behaviour. The flow of informa-tion in science and technology is not as simple as it might be. . . .

Such studies as have been made, such as those presented to ICSI and those of Martyn and Slater[61] (as well as the unpub-lished investigations of C. W. Hanson for Aslib) tend to con-firm what one could deduce from scholars' own writings, that their reliance on libraries and information services is a good deal less than we care to think. If "information" has acquired status value rather than intrinsic value, we should expect a cut in resources in time of financial stress;

and indeed this is what happens.   On the other hand, the
Dainton Report, [28] in a now notorious paragraph, defends the
idea of full national coverage of published literature only
for science and technology, and not for the humanities, because they are less directly related to the nation's economic
well-being.   This is a very limited basis for the planning of
information services, but it does at least have the merit of
relating to social needs.   The Report claims, rightly enough,
that the country's prosperity depends on science, industry, and
commerce; it does not, however, go on to consider at what
point a country becomes prosperous enough to indulge itself
in comprehensive information services for the social sciences
and humanities.   If Informatics is itself a social science, it
would seem certain that we must both justify its claim for
support as a necessary part of the economic basis of prosperity, and also examine its relationship with other subjects
on either side--that is, both sciences and humanities.   It
is not without significance, after all, that even the poorest
nations are ready to devote relatively large resources to the
preservation of their works of art and their cultural in-
heritance.   (This trait is not so noticeable in advanced,
"prosperous" countries.)

Sociology of Information Transfer

        The necessity for social justification is emphasized
by the public attention now being given to library and information services.   Other countries, as well as the UK,
have had government or quasi-official commissions examining their position, and Unesco has also helped in organizing conferences to consider the planning of national systems.   The first section of C. V. Penna's Unesco Manual[75]
makes the case for library provision on the grounds of the
services given to the various groups of users.

        But there is still an inadequate appreciation of the
actual social role of the librarian/information officer.   In
many advanced systems, he seems to be regarded solely as
a producer of secondary documents, such as bibliographies,
abstracts, and literature surveys, and this role is certainly
made more accessible by computers.   On the other hand,
some of the products of such activity are less than successful,
and lie mouldering on the shelves because, though convenient
for the producer, they are not so for the user.   Ranganathan
has spoken of libraries as "externalized memories, " but this
does not quite do justice to their function in its two-fold

aspect: retrospective searching and current awareness. In so far as the analogy is correct, however, it certainly implies that the information service must behave in a human, and not mechanical, manner; that librarians and information officers should be outward-looking, not involved in their "own work," but in the work of the team of which they claim to be members. Several papers contributed to the thirty-sixth IFLA Conference in Moscow dealt with this, in particular those of N. I. Tyshkevich, [94] O. S. Chubaryan, [19] and S. A. McCarthy. [60] In the year celebrating the centenary of the birth of V. I. Lenin, the Russians relate their social role to Lenin's insistence that libraries are an integral part of the extension of mass education and are therefore essential to the building of the Soviet state. Certainly, the statistics of Soviet libraries, and the resources devoted to them and to organizations like VINITI in the information field, are impressive. The concept of an active rather than a passive service was extended to the public libraries by N. N. Solovyova, [89] who uses the term "recommendatory bibliography" for public library activity which complements the educational system and plays a positive part in helping the worker to continue his education throughout his life. McCarthy, the Director of the US Association of Research Libraries, confines his remarks to research libraries, but his insistence on the need for planning on the basis of user studies, at national and international levels, have importance for all information services. "Libraries generally have been concentrating too much of their resources on the recording and organization of collections; too often they have left readers to their own devices in making use of the materials assembled for their benefit." This applies a fortiori to information services based on computers: witness G. W. King's extraordinary vision of some hapless reader in the automated Library of Congress, attempting to extract the relatively simple answer of a text of Hamlet. [52]

In embarking on the sociological study of information services, then, we have to look first at the larger problem. [6, 91] As Dan Bergen[7] has shown, we can apply General Systems Theory at this level as well as at the level of the design of indexing languages. An information service can be analysed (and usually is) as a collection of activities linked together in order to process "information," variously defined (or undefined), but eventually transformable into marks on tallies. One identifies, collects, and examines the tallies (books, periodicals, etc.), codes their contents in an indexing language, stores the coded contents in a retrievable

form, and issues them either as current awareness service
or as the results of a retrospective search. This is the
limit of analysis of those who wish to reduce Informatics to
a technology (Informatology), but even those who stress the
scientific aspect--i. e. the detection and enunciation of prin-
ciples--usually do so within the same limits. In raising
Informatics to the level of a social science, however, we
have to look at the information science /library system in a
new light: not only as an integrated and self-contained whole,
in isolation (a legitimate study, of course), but as an integrated whole which forms a unit in a wider network of units,
which together then form another, more complex, whole--
the communication system by which knowledge circulates.

We have already glanced at the processes that bring
a research worker to the point of wanting to tell others
about his work, and it is then that he needs to rely on a
social network. Although several studies have emphasized
the importance of the personal contact and face-to-face discussion, nevertheless, if results are to become accepted,
they have to be submitted to the scrutiny of the general
public and not merely of a few friends. Here, two different motivations may enter. On the one hand, some
branches of research are subjected to censorship, usually
on grounds of national security; on the other, the research
worker wishes to "make his name"; to win the acclaim of
his peers and, nowadays, to earn an international passport
into other groups working in the same field.

The censored paper prevented from publication still,
however, needs to be subjected to examination by competent
experts; hence the practice of building up "informal" communication networks, for the circulation of reports. These
originally became popular in the British Research Associations, who carried out research on behalf of their members,
and issued the reports to members only, in the first instance. Of course, the practice had existed before in industry and defence, but on the whole these reports had
tended to be tested in practice, by trial and error in the
factory, rather than by the scrutiny of other, "objective,"
experts in the same field. Atomic energy research introduced two new factors: first, the size of the operation,
with its consequent enormous increase in the numbers of
documents; and second, the need to disseminate information
on as wide a scale as possible in the public interest, since
much of the research is civilian-oriented and not subject to
military censorship. Problems of reports have often been

discussed, and their rise in importance can be seen from the growth of a few index entries in the first edition of the Aslib Handbook[1] to a whole chapter in the third.

For non-censored reports, the main justification was speed; authors claimed that they could bring their work to the attention of all those who needed to know it much more quickly if they did not have to attend to all those matters that are insisted on by editors: good manners in presentation, correct English, consistency in citations, and so on. This justification was implicitly a criticism of journals; for while book publishing usually takes longer, authors who have waited to collect all their materials into book form are prepared to wait for the normal printing, binding, and distribution processes. Journals, on the other hand, have always been regarded as speedy means of publication; some, like the "letter to Nature," still are, but many have delays comparable to those of book publishing. Thus the importance of informal means of communication, especially for young and unknown authors, cannot be denied, in spite of criticism. Mullins[74] investigated the role of such networks in terms of disciplines, university departments, and the professional status of the members, and found that both direct and indirect relations were non-random, that members tended to communicate more with those who agreed with them than with hostile critics, but that while the choices of addresses were usually of those of equal or similar status, higher and lower level choices also existed and were not merely local. Thus they represented real colleagues, and were not confined either to close friends or to seniors who could advance careers.

An interesting attempt to formalize informal communication broke out two or three years ago in several specialized fields. "Information Exchange Groups" (IEG) were formed for the pre-publication exchange of reports. When the sponsors appealed for members in the professional press, however, they met with such a hostile response that their movement failed to win the support they hoped. Opposition came mainly from those who, like Ziman, maintained that the normal system of submission to editors, refereeing, and revision works well enough, and forms a protective barrier between the practitioner and an unevaluated proliferation of half-baked opinion and superficial enumeration of the commonplace. (This danger is exemplified by Research in Education, published by the US Educational Resources Information Center.) Editors and referees have indeed been

called "gate-keepers"; and Garvey and Griffith[42] suggest that
the development of an informal IEG into the gate-keeping
group of a regularly published new journal is a normal feature of progress, especially in a new, usually more specialized field.   These two authors have probably carried out
the most detailed investigations on the sociology of communication, for the American Psychological Association and the
Johns Hopkins University Center for Research in Scientific
Communication.   The latter exemplifies the "self-fulfilling
prophecy" so common in social science by publishing its
own series of "Preliminary Reports" and "Technical Notes."
It is supported by many professional societies, from various fields. Garvey and Griffith gave a progress report to the
CIBA 1966 Conference[29] and subsequently published an updated version of the same materials in a professional
journal;[42] once more proving the truth of their own discovery that work reported at a conference is later published
as an article.

These authors also believe that a communication system is an ideal subject for sociological investigation: the
activity is social, the main elements of the system are
social units, the system is regulated by authoritative social
norms, and it is a closed system--that is, scientists both
produce and use the information in the system, and the
two main products of science, information and manpower,
continuously interact and generate the momentum of the
system.   In terms of system theory, however, this could
only be regarded as a closed system conceptually, for the
sake of a particular study.   In real life, as in real library /
information services, the effects of the system on its elements are inevitably carried over to some extent to other
systems.   Each scientist, for example, is a member of a
biological system (his family), a locality system (his neigh-
bourhood) and so on, while each communication system,
whether research laboratory or professional society or whatever, is also an element of a still larger system: the firm,
the Armed Forces, the general "body-politic" of science,
even the whole nation.

Two recent papers by R. D. Whitley[100, 101] of the
Manchester Business School have followed up the work of
Garvey and Griffith by a study of British social science
journals.   Whitley's conclusions do not fully accord with
the others; in particular, he points out that books are still
as important as journals in the social sciences, that the
use of referees is not universal, and the manner of their

use also varies, and that papers that lie within the bounds
of the "paradigm" tend to be more popular with editors than
those which purport to offer theoretical or epistemological
advances. But he agrees in appreciating this field as rewarding for sociological endeavour, and we may probably
look forward to further publications. It is not without either
sociological or informatical significance that Whitley quotes
no references from "information science" sources, and Garvey and Griffith very few.

Information Services

Thus, leaving aside well-recognized means of oral
communication such as meetings, conferences, and chats at
the bar, the author has a relatively few, clearly-defined
means of documentary communication with others, which
can be sub-divided another way into two groups: those
directed at a readership known to him personally or by
reputation (usually the informal channels), and a "general
public" whom he does not know but expects to be interested
in what he has to say about his work. A library/informa-
tion service operates in a similar manner. On the one hand,
it goes all out to collect those documents which are known
to be of direct interest to the users, which they cannot do
without; on the other, it also collects in a general way documents that the librarian/information officer judges, on the
basis of his own professional skill, to be relevant to the
fields he covers, whether or not they happen at this particular moment to be pertinent to the work of any of his users.

These two facets of acquisition policy are clearly
related to the two main activities of current awareness and
retrospective searching, and the role of the library/informa-
tion service is to institutionalize the process of making access points through which an author can normally expect to
be brought into contact with potential readers, and vice versa.
The fact that many scientists, at least, do not regard libraries as among the most important sources of information
indicates that they do not yet regard "the literature" as an
integral part of science (although Ziman's book[102] will certainly help), nor do they probably realize the full extent of
the literature available that would help them. Their sources
are limited to those colleagues whom they know, and those
tools which they have come across, often by chance in the
first place, and which they have taken the trouble to learn
to use. This may seem a pessimistic view when one looks

at the very many excellent information services that exist, and are obviously highly valued by their users; but this is the situation revealed by user surveys, and one does not have to search very far in our own literature to find plaintive cries about the shortsightedness of scientists (and other scholars) who do not appreciate what their libraries can do for them.

As McCarthy and others have urged, the advent of computers gives us a chance to alter this situation, provided we understand what we are doing. There will surely be no point in providing vast quantities of secondary source material, such as abstracts and indexes, if we intend merely to load them on to the desks of people whom we already pity for their inability to cope with primary sources. This is particularly true when the secondary stuff is manifestly inefficient, like KWIC indexes or unevaluated "research" reports. As I remarked above, we are lost if we choose to regard "information" as a commodity to be produced in the largest possible quantities, and, like super-salesmen, regard our users as simpletons to be gulled into buying all we produce, whether useful or not. We need a deep and sympathetic awareness of the aims of authors and readers, personal skills to detect and remedy the gaps in the social process of communication, and a highly sophisticated, international, organization--a network of organizations would be more correct--to which we provide access points for each and every user, according to his particular needs. (Unlike motor cars, "information" will never be acceptable if it is provided in "any colour you like, provided it's black.") Some subject specialists recognize this; at the important conference on Foundations of Access to Knowledge[73] held at Syracuse University in 1965, two eminent American sociologists, Norman W. Storer and Talcott Parsons, speaking on "the disciplines as a differentiating force," urged the need for much closer collaboration between academics and information specialists, in order to help academics out of the narrowmindedness into which the pressures to specialize (among them the quantity of literature) are pushing them. This required, they said, that the information specialists should learn more about the nature of academic subjects, so that they would be acceptable as colleagues with a characteristic contribution to make. Courses at library schools on themes like "the universe of knowledge," pioneered by Ranganathan in India, and by D. W. Langridge[58] in Maryland and London, are an obvious necessity for the preparation of future professionals--more so, I would think, than courses in

mathematics and engineering, which purport to fit them for
tasks they would be foolish to attempt, and should leave to
mathematicians[14, 15, 31] and engineers.[63]   We need all the
assistance we can get from such specialists, but do not
need to become them ourselves.   There is a recognizable
difference between understanding the nature of a subject,
and being an expert in the practice of it; otherwise, every
research worker would be an information specialist himself.
A good example of fruitful collaboration is provided in the
field of Comparative Education; Thelma Bristow and Brian
Holmes[13] have participated over several years in seminars
on the use of the specialist literature, and have collaborated
in a bibliographical guide to their field.   This guide is
particularly interesting in that it includes a chapter on the
use and value of imaginative literature.

        An examination of actual needs would lead to a funda-
mental reappraisal of some techniques, and throw new light
on others.   It would resolve, for example, the maddening
tendency of some information scientists to confuse statements
of fact with discourse about subjects.   A computer printout
which states the answer to a sum, or a list of specific
heats, is not the same class of information as one which
states the authors and titles of articles containing discourse,
and it ought to be just as obvious that criteria that apply to
one do not necessarily apply to the other--the precision with
which one can ask the appropriate questions, for instance.
It is the case, without doubt, that computers can relieve all
of us of much of the drudgery of data compilation and consultation, but this by no means implies that the role of the
information specialist is changed into that of a computer
programmer, or keyboard operator, or oilcan wielder.   As
we know from experience, information service has a more
positive role to play, in which there is a genuine dialogue
based on intellectual awareness, and not merely a question-
and-answer rigmarole.   I suggest that we can look forward
to applying the excellent methods developed in the area of
what is translated from Russian as "factographic" information, to the development of what, for want of a better word,
I choose to call "insight."   This is the quality that characterizes the creative mind, which is able to perceive relations hitherto unnoticed and to effect syntheses of details
from different fields to produce abstractions and theories
of a higher level of generalization.

Forms of Organization

        If this is the type of activity that will characterize

future information services, more than the manipulation of ever-increasing quantities of data, it will be necessary to rely on organizational forms appropriate to the purpose. These must surely develop along the lines of international cooperation, and not competition. In countries where centralized planning and administration is the rule, as in the USSR and Eastern Europe, national documentation centres, such as VINITI, have been established to ensure that the state receives the maximum possible benefit from all information sources. With its full-time staff of nearly 3,000, and able to draw on some 20,000 part-time specialists, it is not surprising that VINITI has been able to achieve eminently satisfactory results in all aspects of secondary documentation, abstracts, fast notification service of new publications, literature reviews, as well as carrying out a great deal of research on the use of computers for information storage and retrieval, and computer-cathode ray tube link-up for rapid printout without the need for chains of type.

The countries of Eastern Europe have tended to imitate the organizational pattern of VINITI, but have not attempted to duplicate the comprehensive abstracting service, Referativnyi Zhurnal. They have, however, produced abstracts in major foreign languages of work published in their own countries, which seems a sensible way for a group using a minority language to communicate at the international level. Some specialized tools have also been produced, like the Index Radiohygienicus of the Institute of Radiation Hygiene in Prague.

In the USA, suspicion of central government activity dies hard. The Federal Government has had more than a small share in subsidies, however, and many contributions to our literature carry footnotes thanking the US Air Force, or the National Defence Education Act, or similar hospitable umbrella, for the necessary finances. After the Weinberg Report on "Science, Government, and Information," the President established his Committee on Scientific and Technical Information (COSATI), which has issued several reports and also commissioned a further study of a national document handling system. The Systems Development Corporation examined several schemes, and recommended, as its own choice, a federal co-ordinating agency. This was rejected: COSATI preferred to encourage what was already going on (competition for research and development grants by private institutions or universities), and carried on thinking about a national plan without any central direction.

The US Office of Education, however, did go ahead. Its Educational Resources Information Center (ERIC), set up after a good deal of investigation, public discussion, and private argument, has copied most of the VINITI operations, even to unnecessary excess, as in Research in Education. The operation is based on universities known to be centres of excellence, who collect, abstract, and distribute in their special fields. The ERIC linking and co-ordinating activity does not inhibit local initiative, but, as its Director[16] says, "the day of 'we'll do it alone' in Education is past."

Inescapably, in modern civilization, the lives of individuals are bound up with the activities of central authorities, and whatever our own personal philosophies may be, we have to recognize that such a development is bound to be best for certain functions. [39] In some areas--roads, post-- the State has played the major part since antiquity. The fact is that nowadays the State has changed, in some degree, from being merely an organ for coercion (to pay taxes, for example) on behalf of a governing élite, and has become, in democratic societies, an instrument for effecting the common good on a scale beyond the reach of individuals. This does not, in our field, apply only to the largest and wealthiest States: several of the smaller European countries have also set up national documentation centres for Education, [25] as well as Science and Technology.

As we know, the British Government has taken a characteristic position, in the middle of the road. It has established OSTI, and the Library Advisory Councils, but prefers to encourage and support rather than take direct action. Its very effective support lies in operations like the National Lending Library for Science and Technology, and the Documentation Processing Centre in Manchester. OSTI has encouraged numerous research projects and the setting up of UK bases for international services such as MEDLARS, UKCIS, and INSPEC. [23]

These illustrate the latest stage in the institutionalization of specialist communication, its elevation to the international level. It is not exactly new; the Commonwealth Agricultural Bureaux, though nearly all located in the UK, have catered for an international market for many years. These have not, however, been supra-national in the same sense. At last, it has been realized that, as far as the

organization of secondary documentation goes, it is as absurd for each country to attempt self-sufficiency as for each
library. The advent of computer technology makes it easier
for international cooperation, in which each country may look
after its own productions, as in the MARC project, or may
establish a national centre for processing the output of a world
collecting and distributing centre, as with MEDLARS, UKCIS,
and INSPEC.

It is natural that these and similar efforts should
lead, in the end, to the international organizations themselves. [23] The International Federation of Library Associations and the International Federation for Documentation both
have a long and impressive history, but have not so far made
much impact on the actual organization of services; the International Council of Scientific Unions had likewise given
only limited attention until recently, though its Abstracting
Board has brought about certain improvements by its good
advice. In 1965, ICSU decided to take more positive action,
and set up a Committee on Data for Science and Technology
(CODATA) on an international basis; in the UK, the Royal
Society has accepted the responsibility for organizing the
British contribution. In recent years, moreover, a number
of inter-governmental organizations such as Unesco, OECD,
the Council of Europe, and COMECON, have all started
paying attention to the establishment of supra-national organizational networks. The International Labour Organization, for example, has for several years been producing abstracts in Occupational Safety and Health, based on contributions from centres from many countries all over the
world. The Council of Europe has proposed a European
Documentation and Information System for Education,
EUDISED. [25] This has not yet crystallized, but it seems
likely that it will first form a network of institutions already
existing--national documentation centres (probably including
ERIC), and abstracting services now operated independently,
such as Sociology of Education Abstracts. Then an attempt
will be made to co-ordinate all existing and proposed systems (abstracts, indexes, etc.) so that the literature of
each country is covered, all contribute to the same store,
and each contribution is compatible with the others.

These and similar "subject" systems are probably the
best way of reaching the individual specialist; he knows that
his specialist colleagues are involved--he may be involved
personally--on the production side, and respects the authority
of the organization under whose aegis the system works.

Subject systems, and "local" systems like EUDISED and
ERIC are, however, themselves potentially part of a still
larger system, which might not have any particular production role itself, but would co-ordinate the efforts of producing systems.   Such a vision is that of UNISIST--The World
Science Information System being studied by a joint committee of Unesco and ICSU.   This committee was set up in
1967, with the aim of carrying out, first of all, a feasibility
study to see whether such a centre might be possible.   It
was emphasized from the start that it would have an advisory and coordinating role, assisting existing services and
sponsoring new ones where necessary: it would not set out
to provide an actual information service for the whole world.
Several working parties were established, and reported by
the end of 1968, when the joint committee commissioned
J. -C. Gardin to review the reports and proposals, and to
prepare a final report on the feasibility study, to be published by the Joint Committee.   It is expected that this will
be early in 1971.   Advance reports indicate that Gardin
views the centre as feasible, provided that it retains a
flexible organization responding readily to local needs.
Among the areas surveyed are: bibliographic description
for computer processing, information services in developing
countries, problems of language (both translation and indexing), classification, and research.

Thus the organizational pattern for the future appears
to be taking shape at the subject, national, and international
levels.   It remains to be seen whether the various vested
interests can be made to develop in compatibility with each
other, so that we may avoid wasteful duplication and the
building up of enormous edifices of blocks of information
that either no one wants, or no one will use because of
their faulty construction.   The responsibility for this lies
on the shoulders of librarians, information officers, information scientists--all, that is, who would lay claim to be
specialists in the new discipline of "Informatics. "

Apologia

I am well aware that this review has left out a great
deal of what many readers will have expected to find.   It
did not seem necessary to discuss the vast number of books
and papers that deal with information storage and retrieval,
library management (with cost-benefit analysis), bibliographical description, reprography, computer programming,

and the design of forms. All of these have their part; but
a new discipline emerges, tentatively and shakily, from a
synthesis of parts from diverse fields into a new, coherent
whole, and not as a mere enlargement or improvement of
parts, or even of an existing whole. I have tried to draw
attention, albeit briefly and superficially, to those areas of
other disciplines which seem to have a genuine significance
for our developing profession. Whatever name may ultimately win approval does not particularly matter; it is the
content and the purpose that count: the social organization
of the products of individual minds so that the whole of society may benefit, that there may be added a quality to life,
as Whitehead once put it, beyond the mere fact of life.

References

1. Ashworth, W. A. , ed.   Handbook of special librarian-
       ship and information work.   Aslib, 3rd edition,
       1967
2. Bar-Hillel, Y.   Language and information.   Reading,
       Mass. , Addison-Wesley, 1964.
3. Barber, B. and Hirsch, W. , eds.   The sociology of
       science.   NY, The Free Press of Glencoe, 1962.
4. Becker, J. and Hayes, R. M.   Information storage and
       retrieval: tools, elements, theories.   Wiley, 1963.
5. Beloff, J.   "Creative thinking in art and in science. "
       British Journal of Aesthetics, vol. 10, 1970, p.
       58-70.
6. Bergen, D.   "The communication system of the social
       sciences. " College and Research Libraries, vol.
       28, 1967, p. 239-52.
7. Bergen, D.   "Implications of General Systems Theory
       for librarianship and higher education. " College
       and Research Libraries, vol. 27, no. 5, 1966, p.
       358-388.
8. Berger, P. L. and Luckmann, T.   The social con-
       struction of reality.   Penguin Press, 1967.
9. Bernal, J. D.   The social function of science.   Rout-
       ledge, 1939.
10. Bertalanffy, L. von.   General Systems Theory.   NY,
       Braziller, 1968.
11. Bertalanffy, L. von.   Robots, minds and men.   NY,
       Braziller, 1967.
12. Brillouin, L.   Science and information theory.   NY,
       Academic Press, 2nd edition, 1962.
13. Bristow, T. and Holmes, B.   Comparative education

through the literature: a bibliographic guide.   Butterworth, 1968.

14. Brookes, B. C. "Bradford's Law and the bibliography
of science." Nature, vol. 224, 1969, p. 953-6.

15. Brookes, B. C. "The viability of branch libraries."
Journal of Librarianship, vol. 2, 1970, p. 14-21.

16. Burchinall, L. G. "The role of the federal government
in information systems in education." ASIS, vol.
21, 1970, p. 274-8.

17. Cherry, C. On human communication. MIT and John
Wiley, 1957.

18. Chomsky, N. Language and mind. NY, Harcourt,
Brace, and World, 1968.

19. Chubaryan, O. S. "Library science in the system of
sciences." 36th IFLA Conference, Moscow,
September 1970.

20. Classification Research Group. Classification and information control. Library Association Research
Pamphlet No. 1, 1970.

21. Cleverdon, C. W. "Evaluation tests of information retrieval systems." Journal of Documentation, vol.
26, no. 1, March 1970, p. 55-67.

22. Cleverdon, C. W. , Mills, J. , and Keen, E. M. Factors
determining the performance of indexing systems.
Cranfield, College of Aeronautics, 1966.

23. Conference on International Developments in Scientific
Information Services. London, June, 1970. Aslib
Proceedings, vol. 22, 1970, p. 355-422.

24. Cornforth, M. The open philosophy and the open
society. Lawrence and Wishart, 1968.

25. Council of Europe. EUDISED: European Documentation and Information System for Education. Stras-
bourg, 1969. Vol. 1. Report of the working party
on the application of computer techniques to educational documentation and information; Vol. 2. National reports; Vol. 3. Technical studies.

26. Coyaud, M. Introduction à l'étude des langages documentaires. Paris, Klincksieck, 1966.

27. Cros, R. C. , Gardin, J. -C. , and Levy, F. L'automa-
tisation des recherches documentaires: un modèle
général, "Le SYNTOL." Paris, Gauthier-Villars,
1964.

28. Dainton, F. S. , chairman. Report of the National Libraries Committee. HMSO, 1969.

29. De Reuck, A. and Knight, J. , eds. Communication
in science: documentation and automation. J. and
A. Churchill, 1967.

30. Fairthorne, R. A. "Content analysis, specification, and control." Annual Review of Information Science and Technology, vol. 4, 1969, p. 73-109.

31. Fairthorne, R. A. "Empirical hyperbolic distributions (Bradford-Zipf-Mandelbrot) for bibliometric description and prescription." Journal of Documentation, vol. 25, no. 4, December, 1969, p. 319-43.

32. Fairthorne, R. A. 'Morphology of information flow." Journal of the Association for Computing Machinery, vol. 14, 1967, p. 710-19.

33. Fairthorne, R. A. Towards information retrieval. Butterworth, 1961.

34. Farradane, J. E. Report on research on information retrieval by relational indexing. City University, 1968.

35. Firth, J. R. Papers in linguistics, 1934-1951. OUP, 1957.

36. Foskett, A. C. The subject approach to information. Bingley, 1969.

37. Foskett, D. J. Classification for a general index language. Library Association Research Pamphlet No. 2, 1970.

38. Foskett, D. J. Information service in libraries. Crosby, Lockwood, 2nd edition, 1967.

39. Foskett, D. J. "The role of the state in the provision of specialist library and information services." Nigerian Libraries, vol. 3, 1967, p. 116-23.

40. Freeman, L. Information and the language sciences. Elsevier, 1968.

41. Gardin, J. -C. SYNTOL. Rutgers, The State University, 1965.

42. Garvey, W. D. and Griffith, B. C. "Scientific communication as a social system." Science, vol. 157, 1967, p. 1011-16.

43. Goldsmith, M. and Mackay, A., eds. The science of science. Souvenir Press, 1964.

44. Grolier, E. de. A study of general categories applicable to classification and coding in documentation. Paris, Unesco, 1962.

45. Guilford, J. P. Intelligence, creativity, and their educational implications. San Diego, Knapp, 1968.

46. Halliday, M. A. K. "Language and experience." Educational Review, vol. 20, 1968, p. 95-106.

47. Hjelmslev, L. Prolegomena to a theory of language. Madison, University of Wisconsin Press, 1961.

48. Hockett, C. F. The state of the art. The Hague, Mouton, 1968.

49. Huxley, A. Literature and science. Chatto and
     Windus, 1963.
50. Inhelder, B. and Piaget, J. The early growth of logic
     in the child: classification and seriation. Rout-
     ledge and Kegan Paul, 1964.
51. International Conference on Scientific Information. Re-
     ports and papers submitted. Washington, National
     Science Foundation, 1959.
52. Kochen, M. The growth of knowledge. Wiley, 1967.
53. Kochen, M. Some problems in information science.
     NY, Scarecrow Press, 1965.
54. Koestler, A. The ghost in the machine. Hutchinson,
     1967.
55. Koestler, A. and Smythies, J. R. , eds. Beyond re-
     ductionism--new perspectives in the life sciences.
     Hutchinson, 1969.
56. Kuhn, T. S. The structure of scientific revolutions.
     Chicago UP, 1962.
57. Ladendorf, J. M. "Information flow in science, tech-
     nology, and commerce." Special Libraries, vol.
     61, 1970, p. 215-22.
58. Langridge, D. W. , ed. The universe of knowledge.
     School of Library and Information Services, Uni-
     versity of Maryland, 1969.
59. Loosjes, T. P. On documentation of scientific litera-
     ture. Butterworth, 1967.
60. McCarthy, S. A. The role of national and academic
     libraries in scientific progress and in education.
     36th IFLA Conference, Moscow, September, 1970.
61. Martyn, J. and Slater, M. "Characteristics of users
     and non-users of scientific information." In:
     Looking forward in documentation, 38th Aslib Con-
     ference. Aslib, 1964.
62. Medawar, P. B. "Science and literature." Encounter,
     vol. 32, 1969, p. 15-23.
63. Meetham, R. Information retrieval: the essential
     technology. Aldus Books, 1969.
64. Meredith, G. P. Instruments of communication: an
     essay on scientific writing. Pergamon Press,
     1966.
65. Merta, A. "Informatics as a branch of science." In:
     Ref. 71, FID 435.
66. "Les métiers de l'informatique." Avenirs, no. 213-
     14, Avril/Mai, 1970.
67. Mikhailov, A. I. , Chernyi, A. I. , and Gilyarevskii, R. S.
     "Informatics--new name for the theory of scien-
     tific information." Naukno-tekhnicheskaya In-

formatsiya, no. 12, 1966.
68. Mikhailov, A. I., Chernyi, A. I., and Gilyarevskii, R. S. Osnovy informatiki. Moscow, VINITI, 2nd edition, 1968. (Formerly Osnovy nauknoi informatsii).
69. Mikhailov, A. I. and Gilyarevskii, R. S. Guide for an introductory course on informatics/documentation. Paris, Unesco, 1970.
70. Mikhailov, A. I., et al., eds. International forum on informatics. 2 vols. Moscow, VINITI, 1969.
71. Mikhailov, A. I., et al., eds. On theoretical problems of informatics. FID 435. Moscow, VINITI, 1969.
72. Mills, J. "Library classification." Journal of Documentation, vol. 26, no. 2, June, 1970, p. 120-60.
73. Montgomery, E. B., ed. The foundations of access to knowledge. Syracuse UP, 1968.
74. Mullins, N. C. "The distribution of social and cultural properties in informal communication networks among scientists." American Sociological Review, vol. 33, 1968, p. 786-97.
75. Penna, C. V. The planning of library and documentation services. 2nd edition revised and enlarged by P. H. Sewell and H. Liebaers. Paris, Unesco, 1970.
76. Poly, J. and Poulain, P. Initiation à l'informatique. Paris, Dunod, 1969.
77. Ponte, M. and Braillard, P. L'informatique. Paris, Editions du Seuil, 1969.
78. Popper, K. R. The logic of scientific discovery. Hutchinson, 1969.
79. Ranganathan, S. R. The Colon classification. Rutgers, The State University, 1965.
80. Ranganathan, S. R. Prolegomena to library classification. Asia Publishing House, 3rd edition, 1970.
81. Reid, L. A. Ways of knowledge and experience. Allen and Unwin, 1961.
82. Robins, R. H. General linguistics: an introductory survey. Longmans, 1964.
83. Salam, A. "The art of the physicist." New Scientist, vol. 35, no. 554, 1967, p. 162-3.
84. Salton, G. Automatic information organization and retrieval. McGraw-Hill, 1968.
85. Scheele, M. Wissenschaftliche Dokumentation. Schlitz/ Hessen, Scheele, 1967.
86. Shera, J. H. Documentation and the organization of knowledge. Crosby, Lockwood, 1965.
87. Shera, J. H. Libraries and the organization of knowledge. Crosby, Lockwood, 1965.

88. Snow, C. P. The two cultures: and a second look.
     CUP, 1964.
89. Solovyova, N. N. The role of bibliography in the edu-
     cation of the population. 36th IFLA Conference,
     Moscow, September, 1970.
90. Sparck Jones, K. and Jackson, D. M. "The use of
     automatically-obtained keyword classifications for
     information retrieval. " Information Storage and
     Retrieval, vol. 5, 1970, p. 175-202.
91. Storer, N. W. The social system of science. Holt,
     Rinehart, and Winston, 1966.
92. Teoiya i praktika naukno-tekhnicheskoi informatsii.
     Moscow, VINITI, 1969.
93. Toman, J. "Information systems: stages, methods,
     levels. " In: Ref. 70, vol. 1.
94. Tyshkevich, N. I. "The role of scientific and tech-
     nical libraries in education and technical creative
     work of the Soviet people. " 36th IFLA Conference,
     Moscow, September, 1970.
95. Vachek, J. The linguistic school of Prague. Indiana
     UP, 1966.
96. Vickery, B. C. On retrieval system theory. 2nd
     edition, Butterworth, 1965.
97. Vygotsky, L. S. Thought and language. MIT and
     John Wiley, 1962 (Moscow 1934).
98. Yeoman, C. D. "Creative thinking and the teaching
     of science. " Educational Review, vol. 21, 1968,
     p. 13-24.
99. Weiss, P. A. "The living system: determinism
     stratified." In: Ref. 55, p. 3-42.
100. Whitley, R. S. "The formal communication system of
     science: a study of the organization of British
     social science journals. " The Sociological Review
     Monograph, no. 16, September 1970, p. 163-79.
101. Whitley, R. D. "The operation of science journals:
     two case studies in British social science. " Soci-
     ological Review, vol. 18, 1970, p. 24-58.
102. Ziman, J. Public knowledge: an essay on the social
     dimension of science. CUP, 1968.

SCHOLARLY REPRINT PUBLISHING IN
THE UNITED STATES

by Carol A. Nemeyer

Reprinted by permission from Library Resources and
Technical Services 15(1) Winter 1971, p. 35-48.

My purpose here is to highlight selected findings of
a survey whose objective was to identify and describe the
nature and extent of the scholarly reprint publishing industry in the United States.   Two years adrift among reprint
publishers with the advantage of communicating from a position of "no advocacy" has provided an opportunity to gather
factual data and opinions as well as form impressions about
the industry and its active participants.

Background and Need for the Survey

The reprint industry is a twentieth-century phenomenon, the camera-born offspring of the publishing-bookselling-
printing triumvir.   By the decade of the sixties, the period
of this survey's focus, few, if indeed any other part of the
publishing industry seemed in such a dynamic state of
growth, change, and turmoil as the reprint sector.

The major factors that spurred the industry to unpre-
cedented levels of action in the 1960s were:

1.   Technological innovations, improvements in offset
printing and micropublishing processes and resulting economies made short pressruns of specialized, small-edition
titles feasible to produce and sell.
2.   The injection of large amounts of government
funds into the nation's education sector nourished the library
and book worlds.   Upgraded curricula at all educational
levels, the formation of many new libraries, and the expansion of existing library collections created demands for
more copies of older scholarly works than generally could
be satisfied through normal book trade channels.

Prospective customers found reprints of scarce and rare titles acceptable as: (a) replacement copies of deteriorating original works, (b) additional copies of works permitting preservation of originals, (c) new copies for new or expanding library collections, and (d) space savers in microform.

Reprint editions offer the possibility of wider distribution of specialized scholarly works with a predictably small market potential; too small to attract most regular publishers who need to allocate resources to works of new authorshop.

The Gaps

The reprint industry has operated largely with an unexamined sense of its positive contributions to the scholarly world. To date, negative aspects of the industry and more newsworthy ones perhaps, have received the most attention. This fact, I believe, has created the industry's most dominant personality traits--defensiveness, suspicion, and a kind of adolescent self-consciousness. Reprint publishing is a part of the publishing world; yet is apart from it.

In July 1968 when this survey was proposed, reprint publishing was found to be plagued by, and partially responsible for, serious information gaps that cloaked the industry with a veil of mystery. Plaintively people asked, "How do you find out if a particular title has been reprinted? By what publisher? In what format? At what price?" It seemed that the lack of reliable, consistently reported reprint information was a deterrent to cooperative relations among reprinters and between reprinters and their prospective customers.

Four of the major reprint information gaps that yawned widely two years ago are still not satisfactorily resolved:

1. There is no association of reprint publishers to provide overall industry information, to field questions about individual firms, or to recommend or enforce standards of performance.
2. There is no complete, accurate directory of reprint publishers.

3. There is no comprehensive, enumerative list of reprinted titles, current or retrospective.

4. There is no published list of titles that are out-of-print, out-of-stock, or in the public domain in the United States.

These voids create tensions within the reprint industry that exceed what is normal in competitive businesses, and waste publishing house and library staff time and money.

Discovering the Universe of Reprint Publishers

For the foregoing reasons, this survey was begun in a partial vacuum. The identification and description of the industry had to depend primarily upon obtaining factual data and reliable opinions directly from as many reprint publishers as could be found and who were willing to cooperate in the survey. As of this writing (August 1970) 274 U.S. reprint publishers have been identified. (In June 1970, 269 publishers comprised the universe.)

Early in the survey, personal interviews were conducted with 92 publishers, booksellers, printers, and librarians; 48 were found to be reprint publishers. The interviews were loosely structured, but intended to elicit standardized responses to the fact-seeking questions. Opinion questions were deliberately open-ended to encourage publishers to provide additional information, to suggest or expand upon problems, and to describe their firms with a measure of individuality. The interviews proved extremely valuable for these purposes, and in the subsequent design of a 29-item questionnaire.

Obviously the industry did not stand still while interviews were arranged and conducted. New firms entered the field or popped into view at a fast pace, making it clear that not every firm could be personally interviewed. A questionnaire was structured, pretested, and mailed, in October 1969, to an additional 250 firms and organizations believed to be reprint publishers. Returns were received from 157 firms, a gratifying 62.8 percent response from an industry that is disorganized and highly competitive. Thirty-one respondents eliminated their firms from further study, stating that they are not reprint publishers. These are useful negative responses since most of the names were culled from existing lists of reprinters.

The 274 identified firms will be listed, and in many cases described, in the Directory of Reprint Publishers which will appear as an Appendix to the full report.[1]

Summary of Selected Findings

1. <u>Types of reprint firms</u>. Eight types of organizations that publish reprints have been distinguished. Table 1 lists the eight categories and the frequency of their occurrence within the publisher universe studied. Type of firm information is known for 233 firms (unknown for 41 firms). The first group, called "commercial" for lack of a better designation, includes firms that are primarily publishers. Since all the firms have been included in this survey <u>because</u> they publish reprints, this label tends to confuse. Some examples might clarify the type of firm included in the first group: Humanities Press, Citadel Press,

TABLE 1
Number of Reprint Publishers by Type of Business

Type of Business	Number (N=233)
Commercial Publisher (COMM)[a]	122
COMM:BKSL[b]	7
Bookseller (BKLS)	42
BKSL:PRTR	2
University Press (UNIV)	17
Micropublisher (MICR)	16
MICR:COMM	1
Association or Society (ASSN)	9
ASSN:BKSL	1
Printer (PRTR)	7
PRTR:COMM	3
Library (LIBY)	2
LIBY:MICR	1
Foundation (FNDT)	2
FNDT:MICR	1

[a]Specialist reprint houses and trade publishers with separate reprint programs are included in this category.
[b]Dual listings are assigned to establishments that indicated their "primary" business is divided into two functions.

and World Publishing Company are essentially trade publishers, with special reprint programs. A few firms engage
also in "other" business, such as Macoy Publishing and
Masonic Supply House and Argonaut, Inc. , a coin dealer.
About sixty firms, or one-half of the commercial group are
specialist reprint publishers.   For them, publishing reprints
is a primary or sole business.   Examples are Garrett Press,
Kennikat Press, and Maxwell Reprint Company.

The commercial publisher group (122 firms) accounts
for slightly more than one-half (50. 4 percent) of the 233
firms.

As is true of the overall publishing industry, clear
demarkation between types of firms cannot always be drawn.
Companies venture into related fields: printers issue titles
under their own imprint; booksellers take a publishing
gamble; and libraries and associations publish.   Mindful
of these provisos, Table 1 at least suggests the diversified
structure of the reprint industry.   People with a wide variety of backgrounds and primary interests are currently
engaged in reprint publishing.

Forty-two booksellers (plus ten firms that are also
printers, publishers, and one association) publish reprints.
Most are antiquarian bookmen who, recognizing the demand
for titles they have cataloged as original copies, utilize re-
prographic techniques to provide customers with titles.

The micropublisher group (sixteen firms, plus one
equally involved in publishing hard copies) does not include
all micropublishers currently in business.   It was realized
early that the micropublishing industry, while closely related
to hard copy reprinting, also bears distinctive characteristics.   The firms included in this survey have been found
to be heavily engaged in programs of microrepublishing.
Examples include the Micro Photo Division of Bell & Howell
Company, University Microfilms, 3M/IM Press, and
Readex Microprint Corporation.

Some firms issue the same titles in hard copy and
microformats.   For example, Greenwood Publishing Corporation's Radical Periodicals of the United States series
is available in hard copy, microfiche, and microfilm.
Other firms may be considered microrepublishing specialists,
such as University Music Editions, Inc. , publishers of a
microfiche reprint series, and, a recent entry into the field,
Mikro-Buk.

Libraries, associations, foundations, and societies
are increasingly engaged in publishing reprints. The
emerging role of libraries as publishers, an interesting
and significant development, is more fully discussed in the
final report.

The printer-turned-publisher is a direct result of
offset printing technologies. The lures have obviously been
great for there are now seven printers (plus three equally
engaged in commercial publishing) who issue reprints.
Several firms, Crane Duplicating and Edwards Brothers,
for example, are primarily service printers, manufacturing
to other publishers' specifications but heavily involved
in republishing.

The significant point, aside from the diversification
of the industry noted above, is that reprint publishing can be
a business for anyone with an original to copy and photographic capabilities to reproduce an edition. This fact tells
us nothing of quality or expertise needed to select, market,
and distribute reprint editions successfully, but does explain
the highly competitive and fragmented nature of the industry.

In discussing some reprinters-who-would-be-publish-
ers, Hayward Cirker, Dover's innovative president, likened
these characters to vanity press operators, with librarians
supplying the funds rather than authors. It is central to
understanding the reprint industry that there are some reprinters who engage in piratical practices, who undercut
prices and involve theirs and other firms in cutthroat tactics;
however, the vast majority of reprint publishers appear to
conduct themselves as responsible businessmen.

2. Geographical location of reprint firms. The 274
firms have headquarters in 39 states. Reprint houses, like
other types of publishers, are heavily concentrated in New
York, which has almost three times the number of firms (92)
as California, home of 34 firms. Exactly 50 percent (137
firms) are located in 8 Northeastern states; some 20 percent (53 firms) are based in 7 Western states. The remaining firms are scattered nationwide, with the next
heaviest concentrations in Illinois, Michigan, and the District of Columbia. [2] In states with only one reprint publisher, firms are generally (not always or exclusively) engaged in reprinting regional material, or are a part of book-
selling or printing firms.

Because reprint houses do not generally have the same need as regular publishers to be close to megalopolitan clusters of authors, authors' agents, and advertising agencies, the high degree of urban concentration is somewhat unexpected. Because reprint firms frequently contract printing and binding away from home, and arrange for warehousing outside expensive urban areas, location of headquarters is perhaps a less significant industry feature than might be presumed.

There is, however, an important aspect of the geography of the industry that needs further study: What is the relationship between reprint publishers' locations and their use of libraries for borrowing material and for conducting research? Presumably, libraries in the areas of heaviest reprint publisher concentration are subject to the greatest number of dealings with reprinters.

Therefore they might be most desirous of establishing formal arrangements to deal with reprinters. On the other side of the coin, these librarians might also be exceptionally effective in improving communications between libraries and reprinters. A mutuality of interests exists. What is needed is more knowledge of how to maximize the gains currently being made in smoothing relations between reprint publishers and librarians.

3. <u>Format of reprint editions.</u> Reprints are issued in the following formats by 216 firms for which these data are available: Hard covered books (183 firms); paperbound books (103 firms); microfilm (reels: 31 firms); microfiche (15 firms); micro-opaques (3 firms); microcards (8 firms); ultramicrofiche (3 firms); and xerographic (electrostatic) prints (12 firms).

Microfilm is either an intermediary step to hard copy productions (Bell & Howell's Duopage Books and University Microfilm's OP Books) or an end product (Research Publications, Inc.'s League of Nations materials on film). Many firms issue material in different formats. Some firms issue parts of series or titles in microform and supporting finding aids in hard copy (United States Historical Documents Institute's Dual-Media project reproducing the Proceedings of the U. S. Congress).

Casebound books are the most frequently produced reprint format. The publisher's choice of format is dependent

upon many factors: the nature and quality of the original;
production facilities and capabilities; the prospective market;
projected costs and prices; and competition.

There is a wide variance in the quality of reprint
products.   Aside from quality of content, physical quality
is a matter of utmost importance to library customers and
is, fortunately, a subject of increasing concern to responsible reprint publishers.

4. Form of material reprinted. Reprint publishers'
catalogs are rich with titles which were originally published
as monographs, books in series, periodicals, government
documents, newspapers, manuscripts, annual reports, travel
accounts and diaries, music scores, library and advertising
catalogs and genealogical records.   They have been reproduced as exact facsimiles, anthologies, extracts, and
abridged or enlarged editions.   The imaginative resurrection
of many forms of original material is both a benefit and a
vexatious problem for librarians who, pleased with increased
access to scarce original source materials, are troubled by
the lack of indexes to older works and the lack of consistent
bibliographical descriptions.

5. Number of titles reprinted.   It is difficult to
arrive at a precise figure of how many titles have been reprinted by United States publishers.   First, one has to sur-
mount the recurring dilemma of title-counting (titles versus
volumes, titles in series, etc.).   Then, one must realize
that publishers, responding to questions about their total
title output, might have tended to check off a higher rather
than a lower range, for reasons of "prestige, " business
pride, comparative status, or whatever.   Therefore, it
must be stressed that the estimates of title output that follow are subject to cautious interpretation.

Using the UNESCO and Publishers' Weekly system of
title counting, publishers were asked to check an A through
J range of titles, where A equals fewer than 10 titles, and
J equals more than 5,000 titles.   Title output information
was supplied by 201 firms.   From their responses, I estimate that these 201 firms have reprinted at least 85,000
titles since their programs began.   If microrepublished
titles are added, the figure is closer to some 120,000 titles.
Table 2 shows the number of companies that say they publish in each title range.   My estimate of 85,000-120,000+
titles is considerably higher than previous estimates, which

generally have put the output at between 35,000-40,000 reprinted titles. [3]

The 85,000+ estimate was made by multiplying the
number of titles in each range (A-J) by the number of companies that say they publish in that range.   For this reason,
and because only 201 companies supplied these date, I believe the estimate is, if anything, on the low side.

From Table 2 it is clear that the largest cluster of
firms (58) publish between 10 and 49 titles; the smallest
number of firms (3) publish between 1500 and 2999 titles.
About 78 percent (157) of the 201 firms that answered this
question have published fewer than 300 titles each.   Most of
the J-range respondents are micropublishers, who tend to
issue many titles, but in very few (often single) copies.
These figures therefore tell us nothing about the number of
copies published.

The most significant result of this "numbers game" is
that, without a doubt, reprint publishers have issued a great
many titles, probably more than are generally recorded in
the bibliographical reference tools of the book trade.   Reprint publishers compete for book dollars from library budgets.   Reprint publishers are an important segment of the
total publishing industry, at least in terms of title output.

6.   Edition size.   "Short run" and "small-edition"
publishing are examples of terms in common usage in the
publishing industry that are without precise definition.   Edition size generally defines the number of copies of a title
manufactured at one time, and is a major variable factor in
manufacturing costs.   Size of editions is also an important
determinant of sales price per copy.   If the total number of
copies of reprints were known, and if the total number of
titles and sales price per title were known, then it might be
possible to answer a frequently asked question: "How 'big'
is the reprint industry?"   To date the findings do not provide sufficiently reliable data to answer this question
authoritatively.

To get a better idea of what short runs or small-
edition publishing means to the participants in the reprint
industry (who generally describe their industry in these
terms) publishers were asked to indicate the size of their
typical initial pressrun for reprint editions; 149 firms supplied this information.   Publishers checked edition size

ranges from A (fewer than 100 copies) to G (more than
2,000 copies). The largest cluster of firms (41) checked
range F, a pressrun of 1,000-2,000 copies; 36 firms regularly print in range D (500-749) copies; 16 firms issue
fewer than 100 copies. The majority of publishers in the A
range are micropublishers issuing titles on demand.

TABLE 2
Estimated Number of Titles Reprinted by U. S. Publishers

No. of Titles (and Range)		No. of Companies	Possible No. of Titles in Each Title Range
Min.	Max.		
Less than	10 (A)	45	45 - 450
10 -	49 (B)	58	580 - 2,842
50 -	99 (C)	19	950 - 1,881
100 -	299 (D)	35	3,500 - 10,415
300 -	499 (E)	6	1,000 - 2,994
500 -	999 (F)	12	6,000 - 11,988
1,000 -	1,499 (G)	10	10,000 - 14,990
1,500 -	2,999 (H)	3	4,500 - 8,997
3,000 -	5,000 (I)	4	12,000 - 20,000
More than	5,000 (J)	9	45,000 - 45,000*

Total No. of Companies   201
Total No. Titles, Minimum Range   83,575
Total No. Titles, Maximum Range   119,557*

*Because J range is open-ended there is no way to
ascertain the top limits. Therefore, only the lower limit
(45,000 titles) was added to the sum of ranges A-I
(74,557) to arrive at an estimated maximum range of
119,557 titles.

These data were further interpreted in the light of
conversations with printers and others in the publishing industry; with the result that I believe the D range, or 500-
749 copies, is a realistic estimate of the typical short-run
print edition for scholarly titles. Some publishers arrange
to print but not to bind all copies until sufficient orders are
received. Some titles are held in sheets for later decisions
regarding type of binding. There is at least one publisher-
printer-bookseller who prints an edition with three or four
different title page imprints, all his, who actually cuts

away all but the title page bearing the imprint for which an order is received.

Sixty-five firms that regularly issue pressruns of over 750 copies are relatively small (fewer than 100 titles). From the data collected it appears that there is no significant correlation between the size of a firm (measured in number of titles published) and the size of the pressrun. The size of pressrun correlates more significantly with the form and the format of material reprinted. In general, hard-cover editions are produced in smaller pressruns than paperbound editions. The choice of binding is, in turn, based upon the projected "popularity" or "scholarliness" of a title. Among other findings, the data indicate that (1) many publishers do not bind all the titles they print; (2) many publishers set the sales price for their titles on an anticipated initial sale, spread over the first and second year after publication, these copies bearing the price burden for additional copies in the inventory; (3) publishers base estimates of pressrun size on information gleaned by "advance market testing," which creates the "announced but not yet published" syndrome that distresses librarians. This practice is not a matter of past practice, but is an ongoing industry marketing device. However, there are indications that more publishers are telling this story more truthfully. Publishers more often announce that a title is forthcoming, asking for "expected intentions to buy" rather than forcing customers to encumber funds. Surely this marketing approach is preferred by librarians.

7. <u>Markets for reprints</u>. College and university libraries (including junior colleges) are the primary markets for most reprint publishers. Public libraries rank second in importance. Then, in descending order, individual customers (faculty, scholars, authors, etc.), bookstores, schools, and wholesalers. One of the minor surprises in these data is that thirty-eight companies report that individuals are their primary market. Ten firms report they do not sell <u>at all</u> to colleges and universities, and two firms sell <u>only</u> to these markets.

Publishers would like to expand their school and public library markets but are unsure about how to reach them. Wholesalers, some questionnaire respondents noted, "should not be considered markets, since they sell to the other categories listed." While it is true that wholesalers get trade discounts, I believe most publishers think of

wholesalers as a market outlet.   Perhaps the point is de-
batable.

        To reach their prospective customers, most publishers
issue catalogs or fliers, which range in style and quality
from crowded mimeographed sheets to professionally created
reference tools.

        The cost of catalog production and distribution is
high.   Many publishers have queried me (sometimes I have
become the interviewee instead of the interviewer) regarding
the effectiveness and utilization of their catalogs by librarians.   Gabriel Hornstein, president of AMS Press, informs
me that the monthly newsletter alerting service costs his
firm about $12, 000 a year to produce and distribute.
Albert Boni, president of Readex, reports that his 1969-
1970 catalog cost about $16, 000; Fred Rappaport, Johnson's
vice-president, notes that their fall 1969 "Red Dot" catalog
costs a little more than $1. 00 each and that a major cata-
log costs about $18, 000 to $30, 000 to prepare, print, and
mail.

        It is easy to understand therefore why many com-
panies would appreciate feedback from catalog users, feedback that terminates in sales, of course, but also information about user satisfaction or reasons for dissatisfaction.
One may be reasonably assured that suggestions or comments
about the organization of catalog information will be attended to at the executive level in many firms.

        8.   Public domain.   Publishers have reacted strongly
to the question of payment of royalties or fees to authors,
heirs, or original publishers for reprinting titles that are in
the public domain in the United States.   The complex matter
of copyright and the differences between U. S. and international copyright fall beyond the study's scope, but it is important to note that there is no such thing as international
copyright that will automatically protect an author's writing
throughout the entire world.   British works published before
1956, when the U. S. joined the Universal Copyright Convention, are unprotected in this country, even though a
British publisher might hold a copyright abroad.   Publishers
of English-language books and periodicals manufactured outside the U. S. and not eligible for UCC exemptions may secure ad interim copyright here, affording them short-term
protection only.

Problems occur in the reprint industry because some publishers do not follow what other publishers believe is the "spirit" of the copyright laws. Firms that choose not to pay royalties for public domain material are perfectly within their legal rights. Other firms do pay royalties or fees for works in public domain, feeling a moral responsibility to reimburse authors and publishers for original work or monetary investment. Some of these firms apparently also find future dealings with original publishers enhanced.

Several publishers say they check the records at the Copyright Office; if they find that a British publisher has taken pains to secure short-term protection, they pay him royalties or request his permission to reprint his titles.

Many trade and university presses have not renewed copyright on works which, in past years, seemed unlikely to be candidates for new markets. These works, now in the public domain, became grist for reprint publishers' mills. Long lists of university press titles currently appear in reprint catalogs, to the chagrin of some original publishers who have since joined the reprint ranks. But, once in the public domain, a work remains in the public domain.

The issue of "ethical" versus "legal" payments for public domain material elicited the following representative comments from reprint publishers:

We always pay if we can find a rightful owner--an author or his heirs, or the original publisher--if the firm still functions.
We pay when necessary.
The practice is desirable but impractical. Costs of production and short pressruns (in this case, 300-500 copies) make a royalty difficult outside of copyright.
The law is clear and has a moral and ethical basis as well as a legal one. It would be absurd to pay.

Some firms offer a courtesy fee or token payment. The majority of the respondents say they favor payments, but there are firms (particularly among the "new" entrants) that feel payments are absolutely wrong and will pay nothing unless a work is under United States copyright protection.

9. Is the title well running dry? Reprint firms are increasingly interested and involved in publishing original

works.   To find out if this trend relates to availability of
older titles, publishers were asked if in their opinion "the
well is running dry" as this statement applies to "titles of
merit" in their future publishing programs.

Responses from 118 publishers range along a continuum: 65 firms think there is plenty of reprint work left
for their programs to prosper for years; 15 firms feel the
well may be running dry; and 10 feel the well is dry already.   Other firms expressed indifference to the question
or said they "don't know. "   Some representative responses
follow:

Hell no, good books go OP every day.
Well is not dry, but bibliographical imagination is
needed.
Programs are limited only by lack of funds, not a
lack of titles.
The real possibilities of photographic republishing
are only now being realized.   Areas of study are expanding, and thousands of valuable books go OP every
year that scholars and libraries will continue to need.
Statement applies to the fast-buck reprinter who
lacks an appreciation or real insight in the contents of
the books he reprints.   For him, after the Voigt-Treyz
thing, there is nothing.
It is dry already!

Four firms that find the well running dry were
founded before 1960, and publish hard-cover and paperbound
books.   Two firms are in the music field; two issue Western
Americana.   Five firms founded in 1960 or later also see
the well running dry.   Four of these, publishing hard-cover
books only, issue history and/or political science, literature, sociology, and black studies.   One firm publishes in
the field of sports and recreation.

10.   Association of Reprint Publishers.   Recently
there has been much talk about the possibility of reprinters
forming an association or council of publishers.   Firms
were questioned as to their willingness to participate in discussions which might lead to an association.   Of 155 firms
who responded to the question, 78 said they would probably
agree to discuss, 51 firms would probably not, and 26
firms are either indifferent or unsure.

In April 1970, at the invitation of the ALA Reprinting

Committee and the American Book Publishers Council (now
the Association of American Publishers) more than 70 firms
attended an informal meeting in New York City, at which the
idea of an association surfaced as a primary topic of interest. On the matter of forming an association, AAP's president, Sanford Cobb, offered the advice of AAP's legal counsel to interested reprint publishers. He also suggested the
possibility of divisional status for reprint publishers within
AAP. The ball is in the hands of the reprinters; it is up
to them to decide whether or not a group involvement is best
for their long-range interests.

Conclusions and Recommendations

I have not talked here of the personalities involved in
reprint publishing. In my two years of discussions with reprinters, I have discovered the obvious but often overlooked
fact that reprinters are people, not the amorphous group of
faceless "theys" generally pictured. Some are calm, some
nervous; some are arrogant, some modest; some are
scholars; most are businessmen. Some are dedicated to
serving scholarship, while others are probably the piratical
"buck-aneers" who have tarnished the industry's reputation.
It is a hopeful sign for the future of reprint publishing that
the latter group of "quick buck" bookmen are a minority.

Competition within the industry remains keen. The
same economic facts of life affect librarians, who need to
control book-buying budgets carefully. These signs point to
greater selectivity on the part of the publisher, who must
build lists, as well as on the part of prospective customers,
who must seek quality but spend judiciously. To the extent
that less responsible reprint publishers are squeezed out of
the industry because of inferior products or poor business
practices, these belt-tightening economic pressures will be
helpful to the reprint industry's future.

Increasingly, publishers of hard copy reprints are
also issuing micro-reprints. [4] More reprinters are publishing original works. [5] These trends in the industry suggest
that the lines that divide reprint publishing from regular
publishing are becoming increasingly indistinct. Some reprinters who now issue original material are showing fewer
signs of "guilt" about reprinting. As they gain more confidence in their procedures and as their products and marketing
capabilities improve, reprinters may become less hysterical

about what their competitors are doing, making communication among reprinters more feasible than earlier.   With
more open communication channels, the industry might be
willing to share some "secrets" with customers.   To the
extent that customers are made aware of why some phases
of reprint publishing are inherently different from regular
publishing, the problems become solvable.

Now, a few simple suggestions.

1.   People in the reprint industry are still generally
bemused by the mystiques of library science.   Many reprinters have questioned how librarians select titles; what information is wanted in the reprinted books; what reprinters
should be doing about Library of Congress cards; and how
microforms should be listed and described.

These queries suggest the need for a series of tutorial workshops or seminars, perhaps conducted by the
ALA Reprinting Committee, in cooperation with interested
librarians, members of the Library of Congress, publishers
of book trade reference works, and anxious reprint publishers.
Together, such a group can iron out some of the "nuts and
bolts" problems which loom large for publishers and irri-
tate librarians.

2.   Many library and other professional associations
have committees currently concerned with reprints.   (The
Music Library Association, The American Association of
Law Libraries, the ALA Social Responsibilities Round Table
Task Force on Minority Materials, and others).   Some of
the committees appear to be duplicating efforts.   Many are
subject-oriented, but their findings would be of interest to
a wider audience.   Therefore, I suggest a central reprint
committee projects clearinghouse and reporting service.
Perhaps the ALA Reprinting Committee could serve as the
"umbrella" for such a group effort.   A newsletter describing committee projects and findings would be useful, particularly if it is also distributed to reprint publishers.

The current state of bibliographic controls imposed
upon reprints is both chaotic and penurious.   Reprint publishers must find ways to make certain that their titles are
either consistently recorded as "regular" books in standard
book trade reference sources, or they must spearhead a
search for alternative bibliographic control methods.   This
is an area of interest where librarians and publishers can
and should work together.   The benefits can be mutual.

Acknowledgments

The author gratefully acknowledges the advice and general cooperation given by members of the reprint industry. Special appreciation is expressed for the advice and assistance of the faculty at Columbia University's School of Library Service as well as to the ALA Reprinting Committee. Research has been aided by an officer's grant from the Council on Library Resources for which the author is extremely grateful.

References

1. The final report will be submitted as a doctoral dissertation to Columbia's School of Library Service, and subsequently will be published in book form by the R. R. Bowker Company. (Spring 1972 is a tentative publication date.) The Directory of Reprint Publishers will include the name and address for each firm, and where known, the name of the person in charge of reprint programs or head of firm, the founding and/or reprint date, type of publisher, format, form of material reprinted, number of titles (in letter ranges), kind of new matter added, subject specialties, and comments about mergers, subsidiaries, etc.

2. Book publishing geographical distribution is described in U.S. Industrial Outlook 1970, issued by the Business and Defense Services Administration, U.S. Department of Commerce. For sale by the Superintendent of Documents, U.S. Government Printing Office, Washington, D.C.

3. Publishers' Weekly estimates some 35,000 reprints on sale in the U.S. at the end of 1968, contrasted with only a few hundred titles available early in the 1960s. See "Facsimile Reprinting: The Newest Revolution," Publishers' Weekly, 194:31-6 (December 30, 1968).

   A guesstimate of only 15,000 reprints was made by reprint publisher Burt Franklin, in "Ten Years of the Hard Cover Scholarly Reprint, A Retrospective View and a Proposal for Improvements in Processing Orders," The Reprint Bulletin, XIII:1 (July-August 1968).

4. Reprint editions of public domain titles are not copyrightable, except for substantial new matter added.

There is nothing therefore to prevent a reprint
from being microfilmed by another publisher, except lack of motivation or demand in the marketplace. Some microrepublishing by hard copy reprinters may be undertaken in self-defense, to discourage piracy. What does one call a pirate who
pirates another pirate--a repirater? Someone
recently suggested "meta-pirate!"

5. Some newcomers to "original" publishing fail to acknowledge the fact that there is bad original publishing just as there is bad republishing. Bad
republishing is perhaps the less pardonable, since
it is an intentional or ignorant duplication of
previous mistakes.

WORDS AND DOCUMENTS

by Herbert Coblans

The Fifth Aslib Annual Lecture, June 9, 1971, reprinted by permission from Aslib Proceedings 23(7) July 1971, p. 337-350.

Those of us who look back on a lifetime of work in librarianship, documentation and education--what is nowadays called communication--are often tempted to try to define our terms. Subconsciously we are probably trying to separate the sheep from the goats. Precision in terminology is necessary, especially in the sciences. But what I am going to talk about is more akin to the arts. I would like to take a more general, broader view of our function, our stake in the continuity and the quality of civilization as a whole.

Our stock-in-trade can be simply described--words packaged in documents. These documents, and they include all forms of recording, are stored in libraries, and it is by the quality of the description of their contents that they are made usable. More and more we are beginning to understand how difficult this is, how little we know about the laws of this "description." In and around this complex process we have built up a sort of theology--we believe in many gods, major, minor and, of course, false ones. With the concession that bias and prejudice are hard to avoid, I shall state my credo, but I would like to think that it is shared by a fair number of my colleagues. The major ones are: the word and the literacy it implies, the primacy of information, knowledge as a common heritage and free for all, and order. The minor ones include tradition, the "user," the author and standardization. Some of the false ones are: the unique system universally applicable, the perfect metalanguage which will solve all indexing problems, and probably the machine.

There is bound to be some conflict between major and

minor, as for example between standardization of routines
and the standardization of natural language.   Standardization
is an absolute priority but only in matters mechanical (intellectually trivial levels) and administrative.   Clearly we
sin against the spirit of an industrialized society, with its
efficiency through mass production and interchangeability,
by condoning the folly of the confusion in microforms, by
accepting the anarchy of commercial enterprise which en-
sures that no compatability exists between the various codes
and practices in data processing.   Or to come nearer home,
how can we justify the insistence on individualistic local
cataloguing rules which ensure that the same book is ex-
pensively catalogued de novo in academic libraries all over
the world?

Switzerland is an example of a country which maintains a good measure of low-level standardization, but not
in language.   The problem is how to achieve the right compromise between laissez-faire and planning.   Above all, as
a profession we must steadfastly oppose the shallow materialism that makes a philosophy out of taxes on knowledge,
public enlightenment and education.   The fact that a small
country like Switzerland has four official languages (and a
number of additional variants)* is very significant.

Natural language should not and cannot be standardized.   Any such attempts would be treason against the human spirit, and, of course, it would not work.   Just as
nature has evolved in a panoply of forms (which man has
all too often succeeded in making extinct) so speech is the
evolving characteristic of man in all his glorious diversity--
what Shaw in Pygmalion called "the divine gift of articulate
speech. " That implies a multiplicity of growing and changing
languages.   Esperanto, or any other artificially standardized
language, can only function as a common language of communication at a very inadequate level.

---

*Julian Huxley in his Memories[1] records a fascinating ex-
ample of such variants in bird song: "As we tramped round
the estate I heard an unfamiliar song: I went off with my
binoculars and discovered that it was a common chaffinch,
singing in what might be called a local dialect.   (These local
song-forms are handed down by tradition, the young birds
remembering their parents' song-type when they start singing
next spring.)   The Africans were delighted to find that
British birds, like African tribes, have their own dialects. "

Perhaps the most valuable insights into the problems of information retrieval came with the growing understanding of the key role of natural language in the fifties and the early sixties, undoubtedly stimulated by the pioneering work of Cleverdon and his team in the Aslib Cranfield Project. Already in an address given in 1938 Niels Bohr,[2] the great Danish theoretical physicist, had pointed out that:

> As regards reason compared with instinct, it is above all essential to realise that no proper human thinking is imaginable without the use of concepts framed in some language which every generation has to learn anew.

In the post-War period the euphoric impact of computer achievements was both salutary and seriously misleading. It has introduced, if only by negative influence, a flowering in the discipline of linguistics and once again "language" and "mind" have become closely linked, especially in the work of Chomsky,[3] in contrast to the more behaviouristic school of B. F. Skinner,[4] also at Harvard. In a recent book Chomsky[3] has stated that:

> ... an appreciable investment of time, energy and money in the use of computer for linguistic research ... has not provided any significant advance in our understanding of the use or nature of language.

On the other hand, it would probably be fair to say that the rigour demanded in the handling of textual material in a computer has shown up large gaps in linguistic studies, especially in syntactics and semantics.

> Honesty forces us to admit that we are as far today as Descartes was three centuries ago from understanding just what enables a human to speak in a way that is innovative, free from stimulus control and also appropriate and coherent.

If Chomsky's contentions are correct, they have far-reaching consequences for machine translation, automatic indexing and "free text searching."

A very instructive insight into the problem, particularly in its implications for computerized information retrieval, was provided a few years ago by A. G. Oettinger,[5]

Professor of Linguistics at Harvard University. He examines the simple and apparently unequivocal sentence:

Time flies like an arrow

and shows that there are three possible syntactical structures,
and therefore three entirely different meanings for this statement.

	ADJECTIVE	NOUN	VERB	NOUN	ADVERB	
1.		Time	flies		like	an arrow
2.	'Time'	flies	like			an arrow
3.			Time	flies	like	an arrow

(To clarify the meaning of each of these sentences a rough
French translation follows: 1. Le temps s'envole comme
une flèche; 2. Les mouches (genus) 'Temps' aiment une
flèche; 3. Chronométrer, avec la rapidité d'une flèche,
les mouches.)

He goes on to say:

> No techniques now known can deal effectively with
> semantic problems of this kind. Research in the
> field is continuing in the hope that some form of
> man-machine interaction can yield both practical
> results and further insights into the deepening
> mystery of natural language. We do not yet know
> how people understand language, and our machine
> procedures barely do child's work in an extra-
> ordinarily cumbersome way.

While the vigour and variability of natural language
defies standardization, and hence automation, it is our
privilege as documentalists to live with it, our responsibility to elucidate it, and to campaign against its abuses.
It is particularly instructive to collect examples of living
language, and in recent years there has grown up a rich
crop of such cross-fertilization between English and French,
English and German, etc. Thus, recently, the publication
of a new French dictionary led to an inspired invention.
For some time the famous Littré, the French OED, has in
effect been displaced by the seven-volume Robert. Now (in
1969) they have issued a one-volume version--le petit
Robert, and obviously it is known as "le mini Bob"!

Another example would be the idiomatic translation of

new and evolving concepts.   The French are supposed to
have a saying: "A translation is like a woman: if faithful,
it is not beautiful, and if beautiful, not faithful. "   Well, I
have come across a "translation" which is both delightful
and faithful to the national temper of France.   Their version
of "work to rule" is "grève du zèle, " which one might render
roughly as a "strike with excessive fervour."   Such is the
genius of language, and inevitably the computer remains
illiterate in the face of it.   Or more correctly, it is not
the computer but rather our inability to devise algorithms
which can analyse language and simulate its generation.

Above all, within the English language, even in our
own field, new terms, both good and bad, are continually
being coined.   A topical one is "anti-preprint. "   It appeared
in 1970 in a new periodical[6] with the title "Preprints in
Particles and Fields and Anti-Preprints. "   The anti-preprint
section contains the bibliographical references to the published versions of former preprints.   Thus we have come
full circle and I offer a new definition of a periodical: "A
periodical is a collection of anti-preprints. "   But seriously,
the anti-preprint is a real contribution to the relief of the
bibliographical confusion which the widespread and haphazard
distribution of preprints has caused.

If a common language of communication is not a
meaningful aim, are there any viable solutions in the real
world, where technology is fast eliminating the traditional
frontiers, both linguistic and political?   Clearly there are
no unique and simple solutions.   At best, we can foster a
few of the great languages of human discourse.   The choice
tends to be inevitable rather than equitable--English, French
or Spanish, Russian, and very soon Chinese.   These will
probably be increasingly accepted as the languages of international exchange.   Each national group with a "local"
language could then choose at least one international language as its "switching language. "   (Such unusual peoples
as the Dutch and the Scandinavians would probably continue
to handle a number of European languages.)

This would mean that the main tools of documentation,
the forms of information transfer, need only be standardized
in a few key languages.   Then it would be up to each local
language group to make the necessary arrangements for
linking with its chosen international language.   Of course
it must be realized that this would stir up powerful political
and psychological forces, as language has always been both

an instrument of rapprochement and of "cultural imperialism."
The newer media of mass communications have only aggra-
vated this further. The best safeguard is that the number
of international languages should not be restricted too much.
However, each new one added enormously increases the
burden of translation concordance and interpretation.

The implications for the documentalist who has to
ensure access to the subject content of documents are basic
and far-reaching. From the language of the original document there must always be an analysis and conversion to the
meta-language (standardized description) of indexing and
classification systems. Our present techniques are still
rather crude approximations--alphabetical subject headings,
hierarchical classification schedules, co-ordinate indexing,
citation indexing, etc. The great hope since the fifties,
especially in technical and industrial libraries, has been
that the computer would provide the answer, be it by automatic indexing or by what is now called "free text searching." I shall be discussing this question in more detail
later.

II

It is just about ten years ago that a Canadian professor of
English issued a book, The Gutenberg Galaxy, which we as
librarians must take seriously, particularly as its author
has achieved the fame (or the notoriety) of a modern
Spengler. Marshall McLuhan[7] has become a much quoted
prophet and he is certainly a master of the striking half-
truth and the dogmatic overstatement, not least in the areas
that are relevant to the "word" (especially in its spoken
form) and the "document." None the less, two such per-
ceptive and critical writers as J. Miller[8] and G. Steiner[9a]
concede that his insights, though often based on doubtful
history or bad theory, are stimulating; and that he is helping to provoke the literary Establishment into a re-examina-
tion of such fundamental questions as:

What is a book?
How do we read?
What is the function of literature?

Therefore it might be useful to consider some of Mc-
Luhan's aphorisms, particularly those that relate to our field
and express in more extreme language what many of the

"machine" men and the "futurologists" are saying in their own way:

(a) The medium is the message.

(b) One can consider language as a technical medium which exists independently of the mind which uses it. *

(c) The phonetic alphabet began the fatal dissociation between the senses. Most civilized people are crude and numb in their perceptions, compared with the hyperaesthesia of oral and auditory cultures. For the eye has none of the delicacy of the ear.

(d) By translating all aspects of the world into the code-language of one sense only--the reading eye--the printing press has hypnotized and fragmented Western consciousness. [9]

(e) The Roman Empire crumbled because supplies of papyrus from Egypt were cut off.

(f) "Authorship"--in the sense we know it today, individual intellectual effort related to the book as an economic commodity--was practically unknown before the advent of print technology. Medieval scholars were indifferent to the precise identity of the "books" they studied. In turn they rarely signed even what was clearly their own .... The invention of printing did away with anonymity, fostering ideas of literary fame and the habit of considering intellectual effort as private property. [7c] (McLuhan's explanation of copyright is very relevant. It is no accident that the computer storage and publication of information, on-line "dialogue" with computers through terminals, has led to the most serious crisis in the law of copyright in this century.)

But it is in his insistence on the medium that the essence of his approach lies. For him the technology of communication determines the way people think, behave and see the world. He implies that the microphone, the radio, and more recently, television and computers are making the book, the periodical, the learned paper, obsolete--and he would add "good riddance." Similar warnings have come from the computer experts. Thus a former director of research at IBM, J. C. R. Licklider, [10] in his book Libraries of the Future, stated the case for "non-libraries" of "non-

---

*This formulation of McLuhan doctrine by Miller[8] is typical of his assumptions.

books. " An earlier, though related misconception was very
fashionable in the sixties--conventional libraries are heading
towards a breakdown, engulfed in a literature explosion.

The early demise of such vestigial relics as the book
has often been prophesied:

> Books will soon be obsolete in the schools. Schol-
> ars will be instructed through the eye. It is pos-
> sible to teach every branch of human knowledge
> with the motion picture. Our school system will
> be completely changed in ten years. [11]

That was Thomas Alva Edison writing in 1913. (Essentially
what McLuhan has done is to add the ear to the eye as
manifested in the medium of television.) There is little
doubt that the central position of the book as educator in a
humanistic sense is being eroded. In a series of articles
which appeared in The Times Literary Supplement on the
"the future of the book, " Steiner[9b] pointed out that recent
estimates put the literacy of over 50 per cent of adults in
the USA at the level of 12-year olds. In other words, we
are facing a growing sub-literacy in Western culture [a
tendency which McLuhan would probably welcome]. (In the
other world of the developing countries, illiteracy is actually
growing both relatively and absolutely.) Steiner quotes the
rather special example of France with its old tradition of
the personal book collection. A 1969 survey established that
the per capita consumption of books is of the order of one
per year, indicating a sharply declining readership. But
all this does not make the book redundant--it shifts the
emphasis from hard back to paper back, from ownership to
borrowing. Public libraries in the UK still lend approximately 500 million books per year. [12]

Of course, for the forward-looking enthusiasts the
book was never fully "with it" anyway--they are more concerned with the periodical. For more than thirty years the
question has been repeatedly asked: Is journal publication
obsolescent?[13, 14] During the past ten years we have had
some very revealing user studies. The research projects
of the American Psychological Association[15] on the structure
of formal and informal communication of the literature of
psychology have provided very relevant results. They
showed that just over 80 per cent of communication between research workers lies outside the scientific paper.
In other words, the average psychologist gets less than 20

per cent of his ideas and information from reading his literature.   This more than confirms what has long been sus-
pected--scientists in general do not read, they talk.   It
also explains the rather depressing statistical fact that, on
average, each scientific paper is referred to, i. e. cited,
only <u>once</u> per annum in its useful lifetime.

None the less, this does not mean that the periodical
as a form of publication is becoming obsolete.   As long as
human perception (our animal physiology) and the way in
which scientists work remain much the same, the scientist,
the scholar will depend on the <u>orderly</u> presentation of new
information.   The history of the periodical bears this out.
Ziman[16] has put this point rather delightfully:

> It is extraordinary to consider that the general
> form of a scientific paper has changed less, in
> nearly 300 years, than any other class of litera-
> ture except the bedroom farce.

Those who see this problem purely as one of collection, storage and communication, for which the computer
can certainly provide efficient solutions, are neglecting the
essential nature of learning and research.   What is the difference between a learned periodical and a collection of
papers, stored in a computer on tap to anyone who is prepared to learn the rules of on-line dialogue?   The contents
of a scientific periodical are controlled and modified by those
who produce the knowledge, the scientists themselves.   Above
all, they co-operate within the framework of the traditions
of the learned society with its editors and its referees.   The
final result of all this intellectual effort (correction, clarification, condensation) is a published paper, easier to read,
to understand and to use.   It has become the first step in
the transmutation of information into that recorded knowledge
which is continually re-appraised and slowly matures into
the consensus which is scientific thought at any given moment.

It is not so much how the subject content of a periodical can be efficiently retrieved[17]--the vast arena of conflict which I should like to call "Cleverdonia. "   Rather the
formal paper, as presented in the published periodical and
later evaluated in the annual review, is an essential part of
the discipline of confrontation with one's own peers as
critics.   In this way, data and information become knowledge
and understanding--alchemy becomes chemistry!

III

While insisting that it is not the medium but rather the content that matters, I want to stress that organization or order is what makes the content meaningful. The often quoted example of Copernicus illustrates this point. [18] Essentially he made sense out of the complex helices of Ptolemy by moving the origin of the co-ordinate system--a revolutionary insight. As has been rightly said, the organization is the information. It is thus not an accident that the creation of order has always been and will remain one of our major aims. Classification is a basic part of that order.

It is true that we happen to be in a temporary phase where classification is rather a "dirty" word, especially among information scientists.   They are, of course, obsessed with the fascinating problems of information retrieval from sets of documents, as collected in large technical libraries.   Admittedly the use of the words of a natural language in automatic text processing--indexing with computers--is very attractive, as it promises reduction of costs by eliminating a number of expensive information specialists and benefiting from international sharing by exchanging magnetic tapes.   But in the long run, I am convinced that hierarchical classification must be part of the training and the conceptual framework of librarians and documentalists. Each generation must organize knowledge broadly in a meaningful way, preferably in some internationally acceptable form, if they are to be able to serve their clients properly.   Excessive specialization on the one hand, and the growth of border disciplines on the other hand, make this even more imperative.

In the history of documentation there is a periodic change of emphasis as to how much intellectual effort must be applied to recognize patterns of order and thus obtain efficient retrieval.   Present research, above all the work of Cleverdon[19] and Salton[20], point to:

> ... the surprising conclusion ... that, on the average, the simplest indexing procedures which identify a given document or query by a set of terms ..., obtained from the document or query texts are also the most effective. [20]

This means that the single term (the word) is more effective than the concept as an indexing device.   Also it greatly favours the computer approach, where single words can be handled more effectively than composite headings.   There is growing evidence to suggest that automatic indexing methods are no longer inferior to manual means; actually both are equally inefficient in extracting the documents relevant to a particular question.   But since searching for words in titles of articles involves less intellectual effort, it can be done fairly easily by programming a computer.   In terms of cost/ benefit, this explains why "free text searching" has become so popular.   Thus very recent studies in Oxford by Lynch and Smith[21] have compared the computer service of the Chemical Society (University of Nottingham) based on the magnetic store of Chemical Titles, with a manual search of the literature.   They found that more than 90 per cent of desired information can be retrieved mechanically at a level satisfactory for most commercial and scientific purposes.

Particularly in certain subjects, like chemistry and law, where texts contain a high proportion of fairly standardized words, usually rich in information content, this approach seems to be worthwhile for large technical units with narrowly defined subject interests.   As a solution of the indexing problem for the whole range of the bibliographical record, the computer technique remains crude, makeshift and inadequate in my view.

More hopeful are the ideas worked out in an indexing technique which uses controlled terms and faceted classification in full association.   Jean Aitchison[22] calls this retrieval language tool the "Thesaurofacet."   It is interesting but not surprising to see how all the efforts during the past twenty-five years to eliminate classification are ending up in hierarchy coming back in a hidden form or, as in this case, quite openly.   Admittedly it requires human indexes to assign index terms and so will cost more in comparison, when computer costs fall further, as they are bound to do. However, it must be accepted once and for all that, if scientific research and technological applications are worthwhile, then the cost of recording the results in documents and making their contents adequately accessible by subject is basically just as important as the original research, and is part of the cost of that research.

Another interesting development is the project of the Groupe d'Etude sur l'Information Scientifique of the CNRS working under J. -C. Gardin in Marseilles.   (Since 1965 a number of international meetings have been arranged.)   The

Groupe has compiled an outline Intermediate Lexicon for
information science, which would permit the conversion of
indexing terms in one system to a different one; e. g. from
the keywords of a thesaurus A to a list of subject headings
B, or thesaurus F in French to thesaurus E in English.
This would depend on the viability of an intermediate indexing language, [23] which would have to resolve a range of
semantic ambiguities and hierarchical incompatibilities.   Its
value, in reducing wasteful duplication and profiting from
international sharing of the indexing load, would be considerable.   Thus subject analysis and indexing carried out
by one centre could be taken up ("translated") into the retrieval language of another centre, anywhere else in the
world.   OSTI has provided a grant for the testing of such
a principle at the School of Librarianship of the Polytechnic
of North London.

                              IV

So far computers have not been as effective as was originally hoped for in the more "intellectual" aspects of information retrieval; the achievements understandably are mainly
in the mechanization of administrative routines, housekeeping
in libraries and in printing.   But on the other hand, their
potentialities can hardly be over-estimated and their impact
on social organization could produce a structure very different from our own.

         Technically, that is in terms of hardware, it is quite
feasible for all types of recorded information, the contents of
documents, images, sound, stored in one computer centre,
to be transmitted at high speeds to libraries, schools, even
individual homes anywhere in the world.   Within an average-
sized country the telephone lines can be the channel.   For
very long distances it would be done through communication
satellites. [24]   Since that memorable day, the 6th of April
1965, when the first satellite of this kind, "Early Bird, "
was launched at Cape Kennedy, the number of words that
can be transmitted through a microwave channel has increased to something like 4 million per minute.

         It is not too fanciful (see Martin and Norman, [25]
The Computerized Society) to think of the Post Office towers
that carry these microwave antennae as the symbol of our
electronic age, dwarfing the Gothic spires and the Eiffel
towers of the nineteenth century.   However, the question we

should be asking is, how can we use such power to communicate, to what purpose, and for whom? As always in
human affairs, technology must be related in a meaningful
way to the facts of life: usefulness, costs, maintenance
and reliability, standardization and intelligibility. To maintain such a world network there would have to be a large-
scale re-organization of existing, and a creation of new,
national information services at the broadcasting and the
receiving ends. This would presuppose an investment in
man power and equipment, and a freedom of international
exchange almost unthinkable in our present climate of
national rivalry, all in a world which is more than half
illiterate and where the gap between the "haves" and the
"haves-nots" is widening.

But let us take a narrower view and see what has
been done and what can reasonably be expected from computers in the advanced countries. Already in the early
fifties when the first experiments in mechanized information
retrieval were under way, teaching machines had obvious
attractions. They fit naturally into the theories of behaviouristic psychology[4] and the already mentioned concept of
language as a technical medium rather than a creative form
of mental organization. One American critic[26] has put it
another way:

> The impetus to mechanized education was first
> supplied by Sputnik and the Ford Foundation; the
> first created the hysteria, and the second provided
> the money.

Here was a market of great promise for the electronic industries. By 1962 there were over one hundred commercial
companies making such machines. The advantages of CAI
(computer-assisted instruction) were widely discussed in the
literature; it was all very reminiscent of the inflated claims
made for computerized IR. They are, of course, closely
related areas of man-machine interaction.

As usual the most searching evaluation of these developments has been made in the USA. A very useful report by A. G. Oettinger[27] of Harvard appeared last year in
the Harvard series of "Studies in Technology and Society."
When he gives it the sub-title "The Mythology of Education
Innovation," he is not being a reactionary Luddite. He is
speaking in sorrow rather than in anger, from the full consciousness of the insider who has worked with all the re-

sources of the famous Multi-Access Computing system, the
Project MAC at MIT.   Cambridge, Mass., with its Chom-
skys and Skinners has become the great centre for these
controversies, as Cambridge, England, was <u>the</u> focus for
atomic physics in Rutherford's day.

The great promise offered by CAI is the "individu-
alization of instruction"--each child should be able to move
forward at its own pace of learning.   Computer terminals
in each classroom linked to central information pools would
change the whole process of education.   But would they
change the sorry picture of the public (in the American sense)
or primary schools as we know them in most parts of the
world?   That can be done only by smaller classes, better
trained teachers, by adequate school libraries, etc., and
all that costs money.   So far these technical devices have
not lowered the costs per pupil, in fact rather the reverse.
A few years ago RCA was leasing this sort of educational
machinery at $50 per year per student. [27]   CAI can no doubt
be made effective, but it would need a very large investment
in programming effort.   According to Martin and Norman[25]
present costs are of the order of $10 per pupil hour and
would have to drop down to $1 to become feasible.   The
result is that computers at present are mainly used in education for clerical and administrative routines, thus closely
paralleling the position in documentation.

Yet in some ways the situation is more encouraging
in the handling and publication of information.   In particular,
printing using computer-aided typesetting is going from
strength to strength.   In the early days a whole generation
of librarians felt a real sense of bibliographic revulsion at
the sight of line-printer output with its 48 characters (all
caps), its closely packed lines and poor impression.   But
nowadays "the computer can ... speak in the cultivated language of bibliography, and not merely, as hitherto, in a
bibliographic pidgin English."[28]   Not only can the highest
quality of printing and the widest range of characters be
met, but an entirely new dimension of flexibility and selectivity is possible.   From a single typing, with all the
necessary printing and indexing instructions added, a periodical with, in due course, all its cumulated indexes can be
printed with speed and accuracy.   The contents can be re-
arranged in the computer store in any desired manner and
printed out in any specified format.   Parts of this store can
be duplicated automatically for use by other indexing, abstracting or current awareness services.   And all this at

prices that are becoming competitive with conventional printing. By the end of the sixties already more than a thousand
computers were being used in printing shops in different
parts of the world, about two thirds of them for newspapers.[29]
It is these capabilities which have resulted in an increasing
number of international subject services based on duplicate
magnetic tapes. In a sense they are by-products from the
compilation and printing of periodicals like Index Medicus,
Chemical Titles, the INSPEC trio of abstracts and the INIS
Atomindex, or in a different way the internationally shared
cataloguing included in the MARC tapes.

In a general and very significant sense there are two
important consequences. Firstly, the conversion from manual to computer operation must be preceded by a critical
examination of the purpose and the structure of each procedure broken down minutely step by step. This is grandi-
loquently called Systems Analysis, but we have long known
it as a standard routine in applying the scientific method.
Such studies are very rewarding, especially in situations
where the accretions of decades have built up conventions
and traditions, where means too often become divorced from
objectives, as for example in librarianship.

Secondly, almost as a throw-away, computer control
provides a wealth of statistical information of direct use for
management and policy-making.[30] In any large public or
university library the mechanization of the circulation records would provide benefits out of all proportion to the extra
cost incurred. Such parameters as the growth of the literature in various subjects, user distribution and population
growth, book demand in relation to supply (reserved books),
obsolescence, inter-library loan strategy, can be continuously
checked. Trends can thus be measured and long-term
planning need no longer be based on global and inadequate
annual statistics.

However, it is in this virtue that a great danger
lurks--the electronic invasion of privacy. The computer is
a ruthlessly efficient tool for the ultimate control of all
aspects of our lives. This clear conflict between a mechanical efficiency and personal freedom is becoming more
and more obvious. The advantages of a single information
file which would integrate the data of scores of government
departments (vital statistics, police record, education, library usage, tax and bank status, medical, employment and
social security history, and so on) are obvious; but so is

the nightmare of such a world of total information. A Cambridge sociologist and a computer specialist have analysed the position very well in their book, The Data Book Society. [31] Their recommendations are entirely reasonable. Personal information should not be assembled in one master file but remain in separate and unrelated computer stores. Each store should have elaborate protection, admittedly costly, against infiltration, misuse and corruption of the facts. It must be accepted that there are certain records that are so sensitive that they should not be put into computers at all.

V

Documentation almost from its beginnings has been very much concerned with science, both in its methodology and its content. Our criteria, our ideals are circumscribed by the scientific method; our clients, especially in the large centres, the information Establishment, are mainly scientists and technologists; our literature is full of the problems of "science information." For those of us who grew up between the Wars the scientific gospel was one of those "gods" that I spoke of at the beginning. The shattering events of forties have made some of us more sceptical.

It is perhaps necessary and salutary to look critically at these tenets so as to avoid the twin dangers of Scylla and Charybdis. On the one hand, there is that "scientism" which has been defined[32] as "the belief that science knows or will soon know all the answers." On the other hand, there is the negative view, often associated with youthful protest, that blames science for all the sins of society. [33] Not long before his death last year, one of the founding fathers of modern physics, Max Born, recorded his honest doubts and fears in the book Physics in My Generation. [34] He compares the introduction written in 1921 for his book Einstein's Theory of Relativity with a postscript to his The Restless Universe of 1951, a time gap of only thirty years.

> In 1921 I believed ... that science produced an objective knowledge of the world, which is governed by deterministic laws. The scientific method seemed to me superior to other more subjective ways of forming a picture of the world-- philosophy, poetry, and religion .... In 1951 I believed in none of these things ... deterministic laws had been replaced by statistical ones ...

> physicists ... had contributed nothing to a better
> understanding of nations, but had helped in inventing
> and applying the most horrible weapons of destruc-
> tion.   I now regard my former belief in the superi-
> ority of science over other forms of human thought
> and behaviour as a self-deception.... Still, I be-
> lieve that the rapid change of fundamental concepts
> and the failure to improve the moral standards of
> human society are no demonstration of the useless-
> ness of science in the search for truth and for a
> better life.

There is no doubt that the middle of the twentieth century
was a watershed both scientifically and morally; and I think
we should start accepting the consequences!

Scientific discoveries are unpredictable and cannot be
planned in the ordinary way, but their applications in industry
are controllable, if we so wish.   Science and technology
move on without pause, the latter feeding on the former
through complex and not very efficient information channels.
We must foster the former and limit the latter to serving
human ends.   It is here that there comes the implacable
clash between the sociologist, the ecologist and the classical
economist who demands more economic growth, more technology.   But this sort of laissez-faire is a dangerous luxury.   It can wreck urban and rural life, foul up our ecology
and impose the unending burden of repairing "the damages
wrought by the technology of yesterday. "[35]

Pure and applied scientists with a social conscience
have long been warning us.   In 1968 the editor of Science[36]
drew attention to these implications in an editorial entitled
"The Inexorable Exponential. "   He pointed out that the elec-
trical power industry in the USA had been increasing its installed capacity at around 7 per cent per annum (a doubling
every ten years) creating enormous problems in siting, air
and water pollution.   He goes on to say that, if we are concerned about our long-term future, we should regard rapid
growth in any industry with suspicion and slow down before
it is too late.   It is encouraging to find that so distinguished
an economist as Galbraith has been expressing the view, in
his Fabian Lecture in 1970, that unrestricted economic
growth can be an evil in advanced countries.   Elsewhere he
has argued that it does little for those at the bottom of the
economic ladder, and the remedy is "taxation that is seriously and energetically redistributive. "

In conclusion may I try to draw the threads together. For the forseeable future, books and periodicals will not disappear, they will be extended and supplemented. New technology will modify rather than revolutionize our methods of treating information. In this context civilization can be seen as an accretion and an integration of evolutionary changes. We are not just the keepers of the documents; we must also be the interpreters who match the reader with the document through the handling of words and symbols. By our classifications, by our indexing we must contribute to that synthesis which presents each generation through its books, each culture through its artefacts.

And now let me put a more personal question. What are the geriatric joys for those who work with books and are at home with the printed word? For myself a few of them would be: the new and significant correlations that spring from order and hierarchy, the insight and understanding that are the gifts of time and experience, the recognition of the same basic concepts which continually recur in new forms, the growth of a sturdy internationalism in spite of all the setbacks.

My final plea is that human relationships should always take precedence over mechanical efficiency. I can illustrate what I would like to call the "machine fallacy" in the following way--a sort of analogy. The latest marvel of reprography is PCMI (Photo-Chromic Micro Image). I have here the complete Holy Bible on a sheet of laminated microfilm (2" x 2"). This is a highly efficient medium for storing 1, 245 pages. But efficient for what purpose? This medium is not relevant for those to whom the Bible means so much. They can carry it around with them but they cannot read it. I am not questioning the technical excellence of PCMI when used in its right and limited place. Therefore let us not bow down too easily before these golden calves.

Above all let us keep librarianship and documentation with a human face!

References

1.   Huxley, Julian. Memories. London: Allen & Unwin, 1970, p. 266.
2.   Bohr, Niels. Atomic physics and human knowledge. New York: Wiley, 1958, p. 28.

3.   Chomsky, N. Language and mind. New York:
        Harcourt, Brace, 1968.
4.   Skinner, B. F. Verbal behavior. New York: Ap-
        pleton-Century Crofts, 1957.
5.   Oettinger, Anthony G. "The uses of computers in
        science." Scientific American, 215, 3, Sep-
        tember 1966, p. 160-72.
6.   Rosenfeld, A. et al. "Preprints in particles and
        fields." In: Handling of nuclear information.
        Proc. of a Symposium, Vienna, February 1970.
        Vienna: IAEA, 1970, p. 405-16.
7. (a) McLuhan, H. Marshall. The Gutenberg galaxy: the
        making of typographic man. London: Routledge,
        1962.
   (b) McLuhan, H. Marshall. Understanding the media:
        the extensions of man. London: Routledge,
        1964.
   (c) McLuhan, H. Marshall and Fiore, Q. The medium
        is the massage: an inventory of effects. Har-
        mondsworth: Allen Lane, Penguin Press, 1967.
8.   Miller, Jonathan. McLuhan. London: Fontana /
        Collins, 1971.
9. (a) Steiner, George. Language and silence. Essays
        1958-1966. Harmondsworth: Penguin Books,
        1969, p. 261-7.
   (b) Steiner, George. "The future of the book." The
        Times Literary Supplement, 2nd October, 1970,
        p. 1121-3.
10.   Licklider, J. C. R. Libraries of the future. Cam-
        bridge, Mass.: MIT Press, 1965.
11.   Beswick, Norman. "The certain standards in con-
        text." Journal of Librarianship, 2, 1970,
        p. 167.
12.   Benge, R. C. Libraries and cultural change. Lon-
        don: Bingley, 1970.
13.   Pasternak, S. "Is journal publication obsolescent?"
        Physics Today, 19, 5, May 1966, p. 38-43.
14.   "Demise of scientific journals." Nature, 228, 12th
        December, 1970, p. 1025.
15. (a) Garvey, William D. and Griffith, B. C. "Communi-
        cation in science: the system and its modifica-
        tion." In: Communication in science. Proc.
        of a Ciba Symposium, London, November 1966.
        London: Churchill, 1967, p. 16-36.
   (b) Garvey, William D. and Griffith, B. C. "Scientific
        communication as a social system." Science,
        157, 1st September, 1967, p. 1011-16.

16.   Ziman, John. Public knowledge: the social dimen-
            sion of science. Cambridge: CUP, 1968.
17.   Cranefield, Paul F. "Retrieving the irretrievable,
            or the editor, the author and the machine."
            Bulletin of the Medical Library Association, 55,
            April 1967, p. 129-34.
18.   Thompson, Frederick B. "The organization is the
            information." American Documentation, 19,
            1968, p. 305-8.
19. (a) Cleverdon, Cyril W. , Mills, J. and Keen, E. M.
            Factors determining the performance of indexing
            systems. (Research Project report.) Cranfield,
            1966, 2 vols.
     (b) Cleverdon, Cyril. W. "Evaluation tests of informa-
            tion retrieval systems." Journal of Documenta-
            tion, 26, 1970, p. 55-67.
20.   Salton, G. "Automatic text analysis." Science,
            168, 17th April, 1970, p. 335-43.
21.   Lynch, J. T. and Smith, G. D. W. "Scientific in-
            formation by computer." Nature, 230, 19th
            March, 1971, p. 153-6.
22.   Aitchison, Jean. "The thesaurofacet: a multipur-
            pose retrieval language tool. Journal of Docu-
            mentation, 26, 1970, p. 187-203.
23.   Coates, E. J. "Switching languages for indexing. "
            Journal of Documentation, 26, 1970, p. 102-10.
24.   Campbell, Harry C. "Possibilities of international
            diffusion and documentation of scientific inno-
            vations by communication satellites. " Inter-
            national Literary Review, I, 1969, p. 21-34.
25.   Martin, J. and Norman, A. R. D. The computerized
            society. Englewood Cliffs, NJ: Prentice Hall
            International, 1970.
26.   Seligman, Ben B. Most notorious victory--man in
            an age of automation. New York: The Free
            Press, 1966.
27.   Oettinger, Anthony G. Run, computer, run: the
            mythology of educational innovation. Cambridge,
            Mass.: Harvard University Press, 1969.
28.   Clapp, V. L. In: Annual report of the Council of
            Library Resources 1963. Washington: CLR,
            1964.
29.   Coblans, Herbert. "National planning of mechanised
            documentation." In: Schneider, K. Die ZMD
            in Frankfurt am Main. Berlin: Beuth, 1969,
            p. 50.
30.   Maidment, Wm. R. "Management information from

housekeeping routines. " Journal of Documentation, 27, 1971, p. 37-42.

31.   Warner, M. and Stone, M. The data bank society.
London: Allen & Unwin, 1970.

32.   Medawar, P. B. "Science and literature. " Encounter,
January 1969, p. 15-23.

33.   Burhop, E. H. S. "Don't blame science for the sins
of society. " Scientific World, 15, 2, 1971, p.
9-11.

34.   Born, Max. Physics in my generation. London:
Longman Group, 1969.

35.   Gabor, Dennis. Innovations: scientific, technological and social. London: OUP, 1970.

36.   "The inexorable exponential" (Editorial). Science,
162, 11th October, 1968, p. 221.

THE EVALUATION OF PUBLISHED INDEXES
AND ABSTRACT JOURNALS

by F. W. Lancaster

Reprinted by permission from the Bulletin of the Medical Library Association 59(3) July 1971, p. 479-494.

This paper discusses criteria relevant to evaluation of the effectiveness of published indexes and abstract journals, and suggests procedures that might be used in such an evaluation. It is based largely upon a report prepared for the National Library of Medicine [under contract with Westat Research, Inc., Bethesda, Md.] and deals specifically with the recurring bibliographies (RBs) produced by MEDLARS in various specialized areas of biomedicine. These recurring bibliographies, which may be regarded as a form of group SDI, are produced by computer matching of incoming indexed citations against a pre-established search strategy. A citation is automatically selected for publication in a recurring bibliography when the index terms assigned match the search strategy established for that bibliography (1). The heading, or headings, under which the citation will print are also established by the search strategy. While the procedures were developed for the evaluation of these particular bibliographies, they should be equally applicable to the evaluation of other printed indexes and are, therefore, presented for general consideration.

Background

Only in the last decade has much attention been paid to the problems of evaluating information products and services on a reasonably objective basis. Most of this somewhat sparse work has concentrated on the evaluation of retrospective search systems. Little has been done on the evaluation of the performance capabilities of published indexes, bibliographies, and abstracting services. However, in a sense, this is much more important work; the number of scientists

using a published bibliography generally far exceeds the
number using a retrospective machine search system.
Much of the work that has been done has been devoted to
studies of coverage or overlap (duplication) between various
publications. The coverage of a published index is certainly
an important attribute that must be considered in any complete evaluation and a number of useful studies of this type
have been conducted; see, for example, Bourne's recent
reports on the Bibliography of Agriculture (2, 3). However,
coverage is only one attribute to be considered. Coverage
studies will show whether or not a particular item is contained in a printed index but will not tell us whether this
item can be found in the index by a user consulting the most
likely headings. Only Martyn (4) has extended conventional
overlap and coverage studies by a consideration of the important indexing factors.

A possible explanation of why little work may have
been done in this area is that in many ways it is more
difficult to evaluate a published bibliography than it is to
evaluate retrospective searching in a system such as
MEDLARS. One very important reason is that we have control over the MEDLARS demand searches and can observe
this use relatively easily. The published bibliographies, on
the other hand, are used in offices, homes, and libraries.
We have no control of this use and we cannot observe it
directly.

In discussing evaluation of published bibliographies
we have concentrated more on the primary use made of these
bibliographies by the scientists who receive them directly.
Secondary use, through libraries, while important, has been
relegated to minor consideration

Performance Criteria for Published Indexes

Recurring bibliographies can be used either for current awareness purposes (i. e. , they are dissemination devices) or for retrospective searching (i. e. , retrieval tools).
In general, the principal direct use by individual recipients
should be for current awareness while the principal secondary
use, in libraries, will be for the purpose of retrospective
search. However, these are not watertight compartments.
Some direct recipients may well use the publication for
retrospective search on occasions, while some nonrecipients
may regularly consult the latest issue in a library for current awareness purposes.

One element in a complete evaluation program would be a survey (by questionnaire) of a sample of the users of the publication and a sample of the nonusers. From the users, the questionnaire would gather data on type and frequency of use, general satisfaction or dissatisfaction with the publication and suggestions for possible improvement. The questionnaire administered to nonusers (within the relevant subject population) would attempt to determine reasons for nonuse, what other sources these individuals use for information gathering, and how (if at all) the publication might be made more responsive to their needs. This type of survey would be an important element in the overall evaluation program. It will be discussed in more detail later.

Let us first consider the current awareness requirements of a user of a printed index. First, the publication must have an adequate coverage of the literature of interest to the individual scientist. A bibliography that covers, say, only 10 percent of the literature of interest to an individual may be of comparatively little value--the return in relevant literature may not compensate for the time expended in finding it. A second factor of importance is the recall capabilities of the index. This is governed by the indexing policies and procedures themselves and really reduces to whether or not the user can find the articles of interest to him under the headings he thinks most appropriate and chooses to consult. In the course of a year, a particular index may cover 60 percent of the literature of interest to scientist **X**. However, the amount of this literature which he can find (because it appears under headings that he consults) may be very much less than this.

A third factor of concern to the user is the amount of effort he must expend in order to find x relevant citations. This effort may be measured in terms of the total number of citations he must scan in order to find x relevant citations (i. e., the precision of the search) or in terms of the amount of time he must spend to locate x relevant citations. Either of these measurements of effort will allow us to derive an efficiency index for the bibliography in terms of unit cost per relevant citation. This unit cost for one scientist might be ten minutes per relevant citation, or a total of 350 citations scanned to produce one relevant citation (where the mean screening or scanning time is approximately thirty-five citations per minute). For another scientist the yield may be much greater, say two minutes per relevant citation or a total of seventy citations scanned to produce one relevant citation (with the screening time still averaging thirty-five citations per minute). The bibliography obviously has a greater efficiency for the second scientist than for the first. The first scientist may have very precise interests that are covered under quite broad headings in the bibliography, or he may have interests that cut across the subject breakdown. The second scientist, on the other hand, presumably has interests that coincide much more closely with the subject breakdown allowed by the subject headings used.

From the viewpoint of current awareness, the fourth factor of concern to the user is that of novelty. The published bibliography is of value as a current awareness tool if it brings to the attention of a user references to articles that are new to him, but of little value if the references relevant to his interests are mainly to items with which he is already familiar (e. g., published in journals that he regularly reads or disseminated as preprints).

To recapitulate, the user of a recurring bibliography as a current awareness device is primarily concerned with the following properties of the index:

1. its coverage
2. its ability to yield relevant literature (recall)
3. the amount of effort he must expend to discover this relevant literature measured in precision or time
4. its novelty factor

The scientist who uses the bibliography for retrospective search purposes will be concerned with this same set of performance criteria. He is certainly interested in the ability of the index to reveal relevant literature (recall) and he is interested in the unit cost (per relevant citation) required to retrieve this literature in terms of time and precision. He may or may not be concerned with coverage. If, as is quite possibly the case, he wants to conduct a comprehensive search on a subject, he will be very much interested in the coverage of the index. On the other hand, if he is looking for "a few good articles" on a subject, he is not really too concerned with the coverage factor. Of course, the same scientist, for some searches, may want fairly comprehensive coverage; for others, he may be satisfied with much less. In retrospective search, the novelty factor is less important than it is in current awareness.

Nevertheless, the requirement is still present to a certain
extent. Presumably, in conducting a retrospective search,
a user will normally want to retrieve documents that are
new to him and that add to his knowledge. This is not always the case: in some searches he may want to confirm
that nothing exists on a particular subject or that nothing
exists that he is not already aware of.

     In the above discussion we have attempted to show
that the user of a published bibliography has the same set of
performance requirements whether he uses it for current
awareness or retrospective search purposes--the ranking of
these requirements may change from use to use, but the
basic requirements remain the same. Next, we will consider some methods that might be used in evaluate a printed
index in terms of these requirements.

Evaluation Procedures

     In this type of evaluation, we are faced with the prob-
lem of distinguishing between an optimum performance (i. e.,
a theoretically "best" performance achieved under ideal conditions) and real-life performance which will probably be
less than optimum. As an example, let us assume that for
a certain subject area there are forty relevant citations in
a particular issue of a recurring bibliography. These are
all potentially retrievable--if the searcher hits upon all the
correct headings! However, the scientist conducting a
search on this topic may only be able to find thirty of these
citations and therefore achieves a 75 percent recall. A
trained medical librarian or a MEDLARS search analyst,
who could be presumed to have greater familiarity with the
subject headings, might be able to find, say, thirty-five of
these citations and raise the recall level to 87 percent.
The other five citations are shown to appear below headings
under which one could not reasonably expect any searcher
to look. We could say that, for this particular search, it
is possible to achieve an optimum performance level of 87
percent recall but that the actual performance achieved by
the user was only 75 percent recall.

     It is much easier to study optimum performance
levels for published indexes than it is to study performance
levels actually achieved by users. For the former, we can
make use of librarians and information specialists and maintain a reasonable amount of control over the whole operation.

To study actual real-life use is more difficult, requires the voluntary cooperation of working scientists, and is outside the full control of the evaluator.

Another aspect must be borne in mind in the conduct of this type of study. The ability to identify "relevant" citations in a published index (without abstracts) is largely dependent upon the quality of the title of the article as an indicator of content. Suppose, for example, we are conducting a search on the effect of thyroid hormones on the large and small intestine. One relevant paper is entitled "Anti-thyrotoxic activity of hemoglobin in the rat." This title gives no indication of involvement of the intestine. The searcher would realize its possible relevance if it appeared under an intestinal term (e.g., INTESTINE, SMALL or INTESTINE, LARGE or INTESTINAL ABSORPTION) but may be less likely to do so if it were found under THYROID HORMONES. On the other hand, in certain of the recurring bibliographies, the tracings (i.e., record of all the index terms assigned) are given along with the citation to which they belong. In this example, the citation might be recognized as relevant when an intestinal term is present in the tracings even though the citation does not print under an intestinal term.

In an objective evaluation of the performance capabilities and real use of published bibliographies we would ideally like to derive performance figures for a number of actual uses of the publication (for current awareness or retrospective search) representing coverage, recall, precision, user time and novelty. How can we best derive these figures? Below we will consider and discuss a number of alternatives.

Synthetic Searches

By far the easiest way to derive most of the performance figures would be to use synthetic searches rather than real-life searches. These would be much easier to control but would be less satisfactory than the real-life searches in many respects. In using synthetic searches we would be evaluating optimum use rather than actual use. Nevertheless, synthetic searches can tell us a great deal about the index and may be worth using in conjunction with some real-life searches. The use of synthetic searches is, in any case, probably the most satisfactory method of studying the coverage of a published index.

A synthetic search is probably best if it is based
upon a comprehensive bibliography on some specific subject
within the scope of the index to be evaluated.   Such a bibliography could be one attached to a review article on a
specific subject area.   For example, suppose we are interested in evaluating the coverage of the Index to Dental Literature.   We use the Bibliography of Medical Reviews to
arrive at a list of review articles dealing with subjects
within the general scope of the dental sciences.   We examine these articles and select those references cited that
fall within the time span that we wish to study, say 1965-
1969.   We might, without further ado, accept these references as relevant to the subject of the review article or we
might employ a jury of subject specialists to determine
relevance (on a three-point scale of: major relevance,
minor relevance, not relevant) of each cited article to the
subject covered by the review (some articles may be cited
for secondary reasons such as particular laboratory technique used and may not be directly relevant to the central
subject of the review).   Let us suppose that one of the review articles chosen to evaluate the coverage of the Index
to Dental Literature is a review on oral manifestations of
diseases of the blood.   In the bibliography to this review we
find twenty references (which we judge to be relevant to the
subject matter) published in the time period to be covered
(i. e., 1965-1969).   The coverage of IDL in relation to this
subject can then be assessed by using the author index to
determine which of the twenty citations have and have not
been included.   Suppose we find that sixteen appear in IDL
but four do not.   Our apparent coverage factor is, then
16/20 or 80 percent in relation to this subject matter.   We
must then do an analysis to determine why the four other
citations were not included.   Some may have been omitted
because they are from journals not indexed by NLM or because they are items of the type not regularly indexed (e. g.,
conference papers), while others may have been excluded by
inadequate indexing (an "oral manifestation" term was not
used when it should have been used) or because the search
parameters used to prepare the recurring bibliography are
defective.   Whatever the reason, we must undertake an
analysis to determine reasons for less than 100 percent
coverage.   Obviously, we cannot evaluate coverage on the
basis of a single review article.   But we can obtain a very
good idea of coverage by the use of review articles covering
various aspects of the broad subject field.

This is an adequate method of studying coverage and arriving at a meaningful coverage factor for a recurring bibliography. It can be used independently of the methods employed to derive figures for recall, precision, search time and novelty. However, there is one possible pitfall that we must avoid. We must not use a review article if the reviewer, in compiling his review, has made use of the recurring bibliography to be evaluated. If we did this we would be strongly biasing the results in favor of the index we are testing. Therefore, we must contact the author of a candidate review and determine whether or not he made use of the recurring bibliography in his compilation process. If he did, this review is of no value for our purposes.

The synthetic search topics (i.e., statements of the central subject matter of each review article), and the bibliographies derived from them, can also be used to establish recall, precision and search time for the index under investigation. Suppose that, for a particular search topic, we know sixteen relevant citations included within a recurring bibliography (we have established this by checking the author index) in a three-year period. We present this search topic to a medical librarian or a MEDLARS search analyst and ask him to search the recurring bibliography in order to locate articles relevant to the subject. The searcher is given a special form upon which he records the headings he consults, brief identification of each citation he chooses as probably relevant, and the time of beginning and end of search.

From the completed form we can derive a number of useful performance figures. First, we can compare the list of known relevant citations with the list of citations selected by the searcher and thus we can derive a recall ratio for the search. Of the sixteen known relevant, the searcher has found fourteen, so that the recall ratio of this search is 14/16 or 87 percent. However, the searcher may also have identified and listed some additional, possibly relevant documents. These articles must be obtained and judged for relevance on the same basis as the original recall set (i.e., by a single judge or a jury). Let us suppose that, in addition to the fourteen articles previously known to be relevant, the searcher has uncovered another six. We now know that the search has retrieved a total of twenty relevant items. Having this knowledge, we can now compute a precision ratio for the search and also a time cost per relevant citation. Suppose the searcher has spent a total of one hour on the

search and has scanned a total of 2, 000 citations (i. e. , all
the citations under the headings consulted) to find twenty
relevant ones.   The cost per relevant citation is then three
search minutes and the precision ratio of the search is 20 /
2000 or 1 percent.   Novelty will not enter into the situation
because this is a synthetic search and does not represent a
real information need of the searchers.

We must realize, if we use this technique, that what
we evaluate is the ability of one single searcher to conduct
a search on this subject.   This is not necessarily an optimum performance of the index because of human failures in
searching.   To compensate for this, we can have the same
search conducted independently by, say, three different
analysts, compute recall, precision, and search time for
each and average these results over the three participants.
This would give us a reasonable average search performance
under optimum conditions (i. e. , conducted by people familiar
with the bibliography and its vocabulary).   We would obviously want to conduct an analysis to determine why certain
relevant citations, included in the RB, had not been retrieved and would attribute these failures to inadequacies in
the indexing, vocabulary structure, inability to recognize a
relevant document from its title, search parameters of the
bibliography, or search strategy used by the analysts, as
the case may be.   Such an analysis would tell us a great
deal about the utility of the bibliography as a finding tool
(or as a current awareness tool), the costs associated with
finding relevant citations, and factors causing relevant citations to be missed.

Through the above procedures, we can evaluate the
ability of medical librarians or MEDLARS searchers to retrieve relevant citations by the use of a recurring bibliography and we can establish cost factors for the searches in
terms of search time per relevant citation retrieved or total
number of citations consulted per relevant citation retrieved.
However, this tells us nothing about the performance of a
medical specialist in conducting the same search.   Perhaps
he will perform less well because he is less familiar with
MEDLARS and its vocabulary.   On the other hand, he may
perform better because he is more likely to be able to
recognize relevant citations when he sees them.   To test
the abilities of the medical specialist to use the tool, we
could have each test search carried out (using the same
procedure as those used by the information specialists) by
three medical specialists, average their results, and compare

their average performance with the average performance of the former group. Again, we will do an analysis to determine why certain relevant items may not have been retrieved. This study would provide an interesting comparison of the RB as a search tool when used by librarians and when used by scientists. From this we may be able to determine what needs to be done to improve the RB as a finding device (e. g. , the possible need for more extensive cross-referencing).

Note that we need not necessarily use review articles as the basis of our synthetic searches. Instead, we could contact a number of specialists, within the area covered by the recurring bibliography, and request a list of recent citations that the specialist considers relevant to his precise research interest. This list could then be used as the basis of the aforementioned studies of coverage, recall, precision and search time, a statement of the specialist's research interest being used as the basis of a synthetic search. Again, however, we must make sure that the list of references was not compiled through the use of the bibliography being evaluated.

Real-Life Usage

By using synthetic searches we can learn a great deal about the coverage, recall, precision and search costs associated with a recurring bibliography. We can also locate factors that may be contributing to failures in use of the tool. However, we still have not learned very much about how the bibliography is actually used, in real life, by working scientists and what success they have in using it. How far we can go along these lines depends largely on how much cooperation we can get within the scientific community.

Consider a scientist who regularly scans a particular recurring bibliography for purposes of current awareness. His scanning will be done in one of two ways. Either, (a) he will have a list of headings that he regularly consults and will only scan citations under these, or (b) he will virtually scan the whole publication looking for pertinent headings and pertinent citations under them.

Whichever method he uses, to evaluate the efficiency of the tool as a current awareness device, we would like to determine:

a. which headings he consulted,
b. which citations are selected as being relevant to his
    interests,
c. which of these citations were to articles with which he
    was already familiar,
d. how many additional citations of relevance to his in-
    terests are listed in the bibliography but were not
    found by him (either because they appear under head-
    ings not consulted by the user or because the titles
    of the articles did not reflect the subject content ade-
    quately),
e. how much time he spent scanning the publication, and
f. the total number of citations under each of the head-
    ings consulted.

If by some method we can obtain the above information from a representative group of users, we will be able
to calculate all the performance figures we need to express
the efficiency of the recurring bibliography as a current
awareness device:

1. Recall: $\dfrac{b}{b + d}$ 3. Novelty: $\dfrac{b - c}{b}$

2. Precision: $\dfrac{b}{f}$ 4. Unit search time: $\dfrac{e}{b}$

How can we obtain this information from the user of
a recurring bibliography? Whatever method we decide to
use, we will need a considerable amount of cooperation on
the part of the recipient of the bibliography. Whether or
not we can find enough people (say twenty-five to thirty per
bibliography) willing to expend the effort remains to be
seen. If the individual will scan the bibliography anyway,
for his own current awareness purposes, the amount of
additional effort on his part may be within his tolerance
level.

Perhaps we can try the following procedures. The
scientist will be given a special copy of one issue of the
publication. This copy he will make up in various ways and
return to the evaluator. Preferably, we should try to give
the individuals cooperating advance copies of the publication.
We certainly do not want them to see another copy of this
issue before the one they will handle under test conditions.
Attached to the front of the issue will be a special form for
the user to complete. This form will record a full statement

of his current interests (i. e. , the interests he is seeking to satisfy, for current awareness purposes, in examining the publication). In addition, the form will record the exact time he spends in examining the publication. If he scans it on several separate occasions, rather than at one sitting, he will record all times involved. Nothing else need be recorded on this form (with one exception noted below); all other data will be recorded in the bibliography itself.

First, the scientist will be asked to circle all the headings he consults in scanning the bibliography. If he scans only certain subheadings under a main heading, the main heading and subheading will both be circled. If the scientist would normally search all headings in the publication, rather than have him circle everything we will ask him merely to check a box on the cover form. (The scientist will be told to follow his normal information-gathering pattern; if he normally consults all headings he should do so for our purposes also).

Within each heading consulted, we will ask the user to code certain citations with appropriate marks, as follows:

A--This is a paper I was unaware of prior to scanning this bibliography. I have since examined the paper and found it of major relevance to my interests.

B--This is a paper I was unaware of prior to scanning this bibliography. I have since examined the paper and found it of minor relevance to my interest.

AX--This is a citation to a paper of major relevance to my interests. I was aware of the paper prior to scanning the bibliography.

BX--This is a citation to a paper of minor relevance to my interests. I was aware of the paper prior to scanning the bibliography.

C--This paper looks as though it may be of some relevance to my interests but I have not been able to see a copy of the full paper yet.

D--This paper is not directly related to my current research interests. However, I am glad to know of its existence for other reasons.

All other papers (the items not marked by the user) will be presumed (at least for the moment) to be category F, of no interest. The marked issue of the bibliography will be returned to the evaluator, who would undertake to provide to the user a photocopy of every paper marked C.

On seeing the paper the user will be asked to rate it as an
A paper, a B paper, or an F paper (of no interest).   These
data will allow us to derive a <u>precision ratio</u> for the
searcher's use of the index (i. e. , the number of relevant
citations discovered over the total number of citations
scanned), a novelty ratio (the number of new papers over
the total number of relevant papers found), unit search time
per relevant citation, and a serendipity factor (relating to the
number of D items found).

        We still will not know the <u>recall ratio</u> for the scien-
tist's use of the index.   Did he find all the relevant references included in this issue or only a portion of them?   To
determine recall, we can conduct a MEDLARS machine
search on the subject of the requester's statement of interest.   (In the evaluation of other indexes, where no machine data base exists, this phase would have to be done by
parallel search in other indexes and subsequent elimination
of items not contained in the index we are evaluating.)   In
addition to this interest statement, the search analyst will
have the benefit of a list of citations already known to be
relevant to the search topic.   The job of the search analyst
will be to conduct a comprehensive search designed to retrieve anything of possible relevance to the interest of the
user (no holds barred).   The search will be run, however,
only on that portion of the data base that was used to generate the issue of the RB under examination.   It is perfectly conceivable that some additional relevant citations
will appear in this demand search.   They were not found by
the user because he did not consult the necessary headings
or because, from title alone, the item did not appear to be
relevant.

        When the search printout is received, we will take
the following steps:

    1.   Eliminate all citations that seem to be obviously
         irrelevant.
    2.   Eliminate all citations to papers that the requester
         has already passed direct judgment on (i. e. , papers
         already rated A, B, AX, BX, C or D).
    3.   Obtain photocopies of the remaining items and have
         these assessed by the user on the same scale as
         before.

        We will make the assumption that relevant papers
found by the user in his manual search plus any additional

relevant papers found by the machine search will together
constitute the entire set of papers, contained in the issue
under study, that are relevant to the current interests of
this user.   We can now derive a recall ratio as follows:

$$\frac{\text{Number of relevant papers found manually}}{\text{by scientist}}$$
Number of relevant papers found manually +
number of additional relevant papers found
by MEDLARS search

By these methods we can obtain a complete picture
of the requester's success in using this issue of the RB as
a current awareness device:
- recall ratio
- precision ratio
- unit time involved in finding each relevant citation
- novelty
- serendipity

Coverage has not been determined but this aspect of
the system will be dealt with by other methods, as described
above.

Of course, we will not be able to evaluate the success
of a recurring bibliography meaningfully on the basis of the
use of one issue by a single user.   Ideally, we would like
to have a group of users willing to go through this exercise
with a number of successive issues of an index.   But can
we reasonably ask any one person to go through this exercise more than once?   Instead, we might get meaningful
overall results by recruiting thirty scientists in three groups
of ten each.   The study would be staggered so that each
group examined a different issue (i. e., the first group would
work on the first issue in a particular year, the second on
the second issue, and so on).   When results are averaged
over the entire set of thirty users, this procedure will tend
to compensate for the fact that the utility of a recurring bibliography to any one user may vary substantially from issue
to issue.

The most important part of the study will lie in the
analysis of results.   This analysis will tell us the overall
coverage of the bibliography, what is being excluded and why,
the recall of the bibliography and why certain relevant articles may not be found by users even though present in the
tool, the novelty factor, the serendipity factor, and how

much effort the user must expend to find relevant literature.

By the above procedures, we have evaluated the recurring bibliography as a current awareness tool rather
than a retrospective search tool.   Can similar methods be
used in the evaluation of retrospective search?   We have
already discussed the possibility of using synthetic requests,
for which we have a set of known relevant documents, as the
basis for an evaluation of retrospective search capability.
However, it would be preferable if we could evaluate on the
basis of real usage based on real information requirements.
This will be difficult.   It requires that we be able to identify
certain scientists who regularly use the recurring bibliography
for retrospective search purposes and who expect to be using
the tool for retrospective search in the near future.   These
scientists must be willing to do this search under controlled
conditions and provide us with certain data.   Inevitably, a
search done under controlled conditions may be slightly different from one done at other times because of the "spot-
light effect. "   Nevertheless, this is something we will have
to put up with.

Our initial user survey (described in more detail
below) will presumably identify certain scientists who do use
the index retrospectively and expect to use it for this purpose in the near future.   (An alternative procedure is to en-
list the cooperation of a number of librarians who will approach people actually using the index and request their
participation in the evaluation.)   A number of the scientists
would be asked to cooperate by recording the results of the
next search undertaken.   A cooperating scientist will use a
form on which he will record the exact subject upon which
the search is being conducted, the volumes of the bibliography
consulted, the headings consulted, brief identification of citations selected as being relevant, and the time expended in
the search.   For purposes of the test, the user will list all
citations identified as relevant or probably relevant from the
printed index.   He will include citations to articles with
which he is already familiar but will distinguish these on
the form.   Once he has seen the actual articles, he will
mark the form to indicate which items he considers of
major value, which of minor value and which of no value.
(Some may turn out not to be relevant even though the title
suggested possible relevance.)   For any articles he has been
unable to locate, no final relevance assessment will be provided at this point.   Copies of the articles would be supplied
later to allow this assessment.

The completed form will be returned to the evaluator who will initiate a comprehensive MEDLARS search on the subject of the request, restricting this to the time period covered by the searcher.   The search results will be examined and obviously irrelevant items will be eliminated. Also eliminated will be citations to articles for which relevance assessments have already been made by the user. Photocopies will be made of the retrieved and possibly relevant articles and submitted to the requester for his assessment (if too many are involved, a random sample will be taken) along with the items that the user found himself in the bibliography, judged "possibly relevant" but was unable to locate in full copy.   The user will be asked to rate all of these articles on the scale: major value, minor value, no value.

On the basis of these results, a complete picture can be obtained of the user's success in conducting this particular search.   The following performance characteristics will be derived:

1.   The recall ratio, i. e. ,

$$\frac{\text{Number of relevant articles found by user}}{\text{Number of relevant articles found by user and additional number found by MEDLARS search}}$$

2.   The precision ratio, i. e. ,

$$\frac{\text{Number of relevant articles found by user}}{\text{Total number of citations under the headings scanned}}$$

3.   The novelty ratio, i. e. ,

$$\frac{\text{Number of relevant articles found by user that were previously unknown to him}}{\text{Number of relevant articles found by user}}$$

4.   The cost (in time) per relevant citation found, i. e. ,

$$\frac{\text{Total search time in minutes}}{\text{Number of relevant articles found by user}}$$

These parameters express the degree of success of the user's search in terms of his ability to locate relevant citations and the time and effort involved in this process. The most important part of this study will again be the

analysis undertaken to determine why certain relevant articles
were not found by the user.   Such failures may be due to
inadequate indexing, defects in the search strategy used to
construct the bibliography, inadequacies in the vocabulary of
the index, lack of cross-references in the bibliography, poor
searching technique used by the scientist himself, or inability to recognize relevant citations from the information
given in the bibliography.   Once this analysis has been
undertaken, we will have a much better idea of the factors
that determine whether or not a real-life search, undertaken
by a working scientist, is successful or not.   Hopefully,
this study will point to ways in which the index can be made
more responsive to the needs of the user.   Obviously, the
more searches we can have conducted under these test conditions, the more useful data we will have for analysis purposes.

Survey of Users and Nonusers of a Recurring Bibliography

We have postponed the discussion of this aspect because, although sequentially it would precede the other aspects of the study, the exact content of the user survey is
somewhat dependent upon the particular data we need to collect
to support these other aspects.   However, the survey of selected users and nonusers will be a very important part of
the complete evaluation of the use of a recurring bibliography.
In general, we would like to know who the users are, and
how they differ from nonusers, how they use the bibliography,
how frequently they use it, which parts they use, and their
overall impressions on the adequacy of content and organization.

Using the mailing list of the bibliography under review, a random sample of the users would be selected to
receive a mailed questionnaire.   The exact size of this
sample will vary with the size of the mailing list and the
required number of completed questionnaires.   In this questionnaire, which requires very careful design, we want to
learn at least the following:

1.   Who the recipient is (i. e., name, qualifications,
     position).
2.   What his current areas of interest are.
3.   Whether he uses the bibliography himself or passes
     it on to a colleague or subordinate.
4.   For what purpose he uses the bibliography (current

awareness, retrospective search, or "other purpose").

5. How frequently he uses it and where he uses it.
6. If used for current awareness purposes,
   (a) a detailed statment of the current research interests which the user is attempting to satisfy in consulting the bibliography;
   (b) how frequently the bibliography is consulted for current awareness purposes, how much time the user spends on an average issue, and whether the scanning is conducted in one sitting or spread over several sessions;
   (c) the user's methodology of scanning--whether he scans the entire issue or only selected headings (if the latter, we will ask him to list the headings regularly checked);
   (d) the parts of the bibliography used--subject section only or subject section plus author section (where both are included);
   (e) the parts of the record used (e. g., where tracings are given, does the scientist make any use of these in determining relevance);
   (f) the user's subjective opinions on the bibliography, its organization and format, and how it might be improved, including his subjective assessment of the efficiency of the tool as a current awareness device (his estimate of what proportion of all the current literature of interest to him is brought to his attention for the first time by the bibliography);
   (g) other current awareness tools and methods that he regularly uses, including journals and indexes that he reads or scans;
   (h) whether he would be willing to participate in a controlled study of the efficiency of the bibliography as a current awareness device.
7. Similar questions relating to retrospective search usage will also be included.

This questionnaire should be pretested on a small group of users before it is distributed to the larger sample. On the basis of such a pretest, it is usually possible to improve the questionnaire by clarification of questions which appear to give difficulty or which lead to ambiguous answers. Another useful technique which may be worth applying is the group interview process. A group interview with a small number of users can be used to further refine the questionnaire. Such a group interview should follow the pattern of questions set in the questionnaire but should be less highly

structured to permit free discussion among the group.   The
entire group discussion, relating to utility and limitations of
the bibliography, should be recorded, using a tape recorder,
for later in-depth analysis.

We will also want to survey a sample of nonusers
of the publication.   To do this, we will need to compare the
mailing list of the index with membership lists of appropriate
professional bodies so that, for example, we can identify a
sample of endocrinologists who are not using the Endocrin-
ology Index.   We will then want to develop a questionnaire
(which can also be pretested on a small mailed sample and/
or by group interview) to be addressed to this group of
nonusers.   From this questionnaire, which would be sent
out with a specimen copy of the publication, we will want to
learn the following:

1. Who the nonuser is (name, qualifications, position).
2. Whether or not he was aware of the existence of the
   publication.
3. If he was aware of its existence, why he has found
   no reason to use it, what other sources he uses for
   current awareness and retrospective search, and how
   (if at all) the publication could be improved in order
   that it would be of use to him.
4. If he was not previously aware of its existence,
   whether he now intends to make use of it, and if
   so, in what way (e. g. , how does he intend to obtain
   a copy, will he use it for current awareness or
   retrospective search).
5. Any other comments that the nonuser would care to
   make on the publication, its content, organization
   and format.

Summary of Sequence of Procedures to be Used
  in Comprehensive Evaluation of a Recurring Bibliography

1. Select samples of users and nonusers of the publication.
2. Design and pretest survey questionnaires by preliminary
   mailing or group interviews.
3. Administer mailed questionnaires to sample of users
   and nonusers.
4. Analyze results of these surveys and identify users
   willing to participate further in the evaluation program.
5. Study coverage of the bibliography through the use of
   specific review articles, or other bibliographies, by

methods described earlier.
6. Use synthetic requests to study "optimum use" of the
    bibliography and conduct an analysis to determine the
    factors that appear to have most influence on perform-
    ance.
7. Through a select group of users willing to cooperate,
    study the effectiveness of the index as a current aware-
    ness device (by methods described above).
8. Through a select group of users willing to cooperate,
    study its effectiveness as a retrospective search tool
    (by methods described above).

    Procedure 8 will be the most difficult to implement
and we may have to rely entirely on synthetic requests in
order to study retrospective search capability. Several of
the above tasks may proceed concurrently. For example,
the user and nonuser surveys can be conducted at the same
time as the study of coverage. Since the user survey will
identify types of users and hopefully establish their willingness to cooperate, this task should precede tasks 7 and 8
above.

Some Recent Work on Evaluation of Published Indexes

    As mentioned previously, while coverage studies are
relatively common, other aspects of evaluation of published
indexes have been generally neglected (although Torr et al.
presented some possible procedures in 1964 (5)). In the
last two years, however, the subject appears to have received increased attention and a number of interesting
studies have appeared. These are not comprehensive evaluation programs of the type outlined above, but they are worth
considering because they touch upon some of the elements
identified as necessary in a complete evaluation of a published index.

    Davison and Matthews (6) report a very interesting
investigation in which the topic "computers related to mass
spectrometry," for which 183 unique references were known,
was searched in twelve of the major indexes to chemistry
and spectroscopy. The most interesting results were as
follows:

1. No one source located more than 40 percent of the
    known references.
2. The world's largest chemical indexes, Referativyni

Zhurnal Khimii, Chemical Abstracts, and Chemisches
Zentralblatt produced only 5. 5 percent, 24 percent,
and 4. 5 percent of the references, respectively.

3. The 14 percent retrieval from CA was only obtained
    by checking every item under terms indicating mass
    spectrometry and also terms indicating computers in
    three years of the indexes. This required checking
    about 5, 000 items--about ten hours' work. Direct
    lookup (of the association between computers and
    spectrometry) gave only about half the numbers of
    references. In other words, the precision of the
    search in CA was about 44/5, 000, or less than 1
    percent, while the unit cost (in time) per relevant
    citation retrieved was about thirteen and one-half
    minutes (forty-four citations found in ten hours.)

4. All the references from Chemisches Zentralblatt
    were unique to that source, because they were so out-
    of-date that none of the other sources covered them
    in the period searched.

5. Searching of Chemical Titles, simulating a computer
    search of CT tapes, gave 11. 5 percent of the total
    number of references found--just over one-quarter of
    the retrieval from the best source.

This was a most interesting study that went into the problems of "findability" (recall) as well as the problems of
coverage.

Elliott (7) compares Psychological Abstracts with
Bulletin Signalétique on the basis of coverage, number and
subject distribution of abstracts, and publication delay.
Psychological Abstracts was found to be superior on all
counts. Elliott concludes that, for English-speaking organizations, BS is only useful in complementing PA in
coverage of European journals in medicine, the humanities,
and ornithology. However, this investigator takes no account of the important aspect of findability. Perhaps it is
easier to search in BS and therefore one is able to find
relevant citations at reduced cost (in search time). Moreover, Elliott makes no reference to how the publications
are used. Since both tools are probably used more for
retrospective search than for current awareness, the factor
of publication delay may be somewhat less important than it
seems on the surface.

The coverage of virology literature in Biological Abstracts and in the BioResearch Index was analyzed by

Carroll (8). Approximately 2,300 virology papers were located in a five-month span of the two indexes. The papers were drawn from 495 different sources representing forty-four different countries. Abstracts of virology-related papers were found in no less than twenty sections of Biological Abstracts other than those dealing directly with virology. This analysis of the scatter of the virology literature in BA is extremely pertinent to the evaluation of published indexes in general. It is all very well to show that BA covers x percent of the published literature in virology, but how much of this is actually findable by a user consulting the most likely sections or headings of the publication? Carroll's study suggests that it might be extremely difficult to obtain high recall in many virology-related searches and that the unit cost (per relevant) citation of such searches is likely to be quite high.

Barlup (9) reports a small test on the relevancy of cited articles in Science Citation Index. Here "relevancy" is taken to mean "related to" the subject content of the cited articles. The authors (physicians) of twenty-five medical articles were sent copies of up to ten articles that cited an earlier article of their own and were asked to judge the relatedness of these articles to the subject content of their own paper. Eighteen (72 percent) of the physicians responded. In all, 161 (70 percent) of the 230 articles were evaluated and returned. Of these, 72 percent were judged very closely related to the subject matter of the cited article, and 22.4 percent were judged slightly or indirectly related. From the actual articles, only about 5 percent were judged "not related" at all, although approximately 18 percent were judged not related from their titles only. Once more, this points to the difficulty of determining relevance from titles alone. The study is very pertinent to the factors of precision and unit cost per relevant citation in searching of published indexes although the findings are, of course, peculiar to the Science Citation Index.

The Bibliography of Agriculture (B of A) has been studied comprehensively by Bourne (2,3) from the viewpoints of characteristics and extent of coverage and of overlap with other services. Checking against pertinent agricultural references in an abstract journal and in three annual reviews, Bourne discovered that B of A covers only 48 to 58 percent of the available literature relevant to the interests of agricultural researchers. The material not covered was not fugitive literature but predominantly English language, mostly from journals and conference proceedings, and much of U. S. origin. A check of publication lists from USDA, a research laboratory, and several state agricultural experiment stations and extension services indicated a B of A coverage factor of from 45 percent to 74 percent for this type of material. On the other hand, a study of the degree of overlap between B of A and fifteen other major services, based on 5,000 citations, indicated that approximately 54 percent of the items covered by B of A are not covered by any other service; in fact, no single service overlaps the B of A data base by more than 20 percent. In investigating B of A time lag, and comparing this with time lag for inclusion of agriculture-related literature in eleven other services, it was found that B of A, on the average, published later than eight of these services. Based on a sample of 617 citations covered by both services, it was found that Chemical Abstracts, which includes abstracts in addition to the citation data provided by B of A, publishes 3.7 months earlier on the average.

Bystrom (10) has studied the ability to find citations on soil science and plant nutrition in four agricultural indexes: Biological and Agricultural Index, Bibliography of Agriculture, Chemical Abstracts, and Soils and Fertilizers. This is an interesting study in that it does attempt to evaluate recall as opposed to coverage only. The approach is sound, but the sample searches reported are too few to allow us to draw any valid conclusions on the relative merits of the various approaches to indexing.

Purely subjective "evaluations" of published indexes have been conducted by Drage (11) and by Cluley (12).

Drage compared two methods of displaying a subject index to Sugar Industry Abstracts. Fifteen "senior" users evaluated the two alternatives and checked the one they preferred. Cluley summarized an Aslib study on user reaction to Analytical Abstracts. A questionnaire to subscribers determined how the publication was used and recorded user reaction to arrangement and format, subject and journal coverage, time lag, indexes and form and content of the abstracts. Respondents were also asked to compare the utility of Analytical Abstracts with that of Chemical Abstracts and 60 percent indicated that they preferred the former for current awareness purposes, while 42 percent preferred it for retrospective search purposes. Compared with CA, the chief virtues of AA were found to be its

specialized emphasis on analytical methods, the quality of
the abstracts, and the ready availability of the journal resulting from its modest price.

Subjective evaluations of this type, based on some
form of user survey, are of value in establishing user attitudes or preferences toward publications. However, they
have limited diagnostic value. That is, they usually tell us
comparatively little that will allow us to increase publication effectiveness.

As mentioned earlier, one factor affecting the findability of relevant citations in a published index is whether
or not the citation can be recognized as relevant from the
surrogate provided. It is possible that a particular citation
appears under the heading consulted, but that the searcher
is unable to recognize it as relevant from title or, possibly,
abstract. In this connection it is important to recognize,
as Harley (13) points out, that the index entry (subject heading, keyword, class number or whatever) should really be
considered an extension of the title. This point was discussed earlier. Obviously, in any evaluation of a published
index, we must take account of the quality of the document
surrogate as an indicator of content. Some recent studies
have shed further light on this.

Saracevic (14) investigated relevance predictability
using ninety-nine requests from twenty-two users and searching these against an experimental IR system. In all, 1,036
documents were retrieved over the ninety-nine searches.
The requesters were asked to predict relevance first on the
basis of titles alone and then on the basis of abstracts.
Finally, they made actual relevance decisions on the complete
document texts. Relevance judgments based on all three
services were made for 843, or 78 percent of the documents.
Of 207 documents judged relevant from the full text, 131
were judged so from titles and 160 from abstracts. The
implications are as follows: given titles, users will recognize about 66 percent to 75 percent of the relevant items;
given abstracts, they will recognize about 80 percent to
85 percent. These figures are in line with findings in the
actual evaluation of operating information systems. An
index may operate at a potential recall of 90 percent (in
terms of the citations contained under the headings consulted by the user) but the actual recall (in terms of the
citations actually recognized by the searcher) may well be
less than this--say 75 percent of 90 percent, or an actual
recall of about 67 percent.

In evaluating his on-line retrieval system, BROWSER,
Williams (15) was able to measure the value of patent abstracts as content indicators. In less than 1 percent of the
abstracts read by patent attorneys in his test were the attorneys led to irrelevant patents. Of course, this tells us
nothing of how many relevant patents were missed because
of inadequacies in the abstracts. Williams also tackles the
thorny problem of abstract quality. He suggests a way of
measuring the "information value" of an abstract by sum-
ming the information values of all the word roots occurring
in the abstract. The "information value" is a numerical
value which is inversely proportional to the number of occurrences of a rootword in the complete corpus of abstracts
--the rare words get higher information values. If the information value of an abstract is below some pre-established
threshold it will not be sufficiently discriminating, being too
similar to many others in the file. Williams, who was
dealing specifically with patents, suggests that a low information value abstract should be returned to the writer and that
he should be asked to add further valid terms that will
distinguish, if possible, this abstract from others in the
file.

In the evaluation of any type of published index,
there is grave danger of confusing the evaluation of the
index per se with the evaluation of the use of the index by
one particular user or group of users. This danger is particularly present in the measurement of recall and precision
for published indexes. A recent study by Jahoda and Stursa
(16) failed to make the necessary distinction. Two indexes
to a collection of 3, 204 documents in chemistry were
evaluated. One was a keyword-from-title (KWOC) index,
providing multiple access points (an average of 4. 55 per
document) based on words occurring in titles. The other
was a conventional alphabetical subject index with one
access point (subject heading) per document. Thirteen
graduate chemistry students searched fifty-five questions
in these two indexes. For each question, a number of
"known relevant" documents existed. The students searched
and attempted to select relevant documents based on the
bibliographic descriptions contained in the indexes. Recall
ratios, precision ratios, and search times were collected.
As far as recall and precision goes, the two indexes were
not statistically significant. However, the alphabetical subject index had statistically significant better search times
except for those questions in which only one relevant document was noted.

It is indeed no surprise that only search times differed. The most reasonable way to compare two indexes of this type is by measuring the cost involved in obtaining a particular recall ratio in each. Cost can be in terms of search time (yielding a unit cost per relevant citation retrieved) or in terms of precision. However, precision must be measured on the basis of the number of citations consulted in the publication and not the number of citations selected by a human searcher. It is not particularly meaningful to compare the performance results of two searches, one based on a set of documents chosen by a group of searchers in the course of searching a keyword index and the other based on a set of documents chosen by the same group of searchers in the course of searching an alphabetical subject index. By so doing you are measuring, more than anything else, the ability of searchers to use the indexes and to recognize relevant documents from the citation data given. In this test the search times are valid but it is not surprising that recall and precision (of screened output) should not be too much different for the two indexes. Had recall and precision been measured by other methods (as specified above) the results might well have been much different.

A similar defect occurs in a study by Virgo (17) which attempts to compare the success of machine searching in MEDLARS with hand searching in Index Medicus. The Index Medicus "precision figures" were based on the number of relevant documents found by requesters in a set of documents selected from Index Medicus by a team of searchers. Instead, the precision figures should have been based on the number of relevant documents contained under the headings consulted by the team of searchers--otherwise the precision figure is meaningless since it gives no indication of the amount of effort expended to obtain a particular recall ratio. Did they scan twenty-five irrelevant citations for each relevant one found or did they scan 250 irrelevant for each relevant found? There is a difference, reflecting efficiency of the index, which is not shown in the figures presented.

Summary

The various factors affecting the effectiveness of a printed index are illustrated in Figure 1. Whether or not a scientist uses the index in the first place is dependent upon the coverage it provides. Presumably, he will not attempt to make use of an index if he feels that its coverage is

unlikely to be adequate in the area of his current interests.
Having decided to use a particular index, the user is faced
with the task of translating his information need into a search
strategy in the language of the index to be searched (i. e. ,
he decides which terms he should search under).   Usually,
he will not prepare a formal search strategy before approaching the index.   Nevertheless, the terms that he does
look under, in the conduct of his search, comprise a search
strategy derived heuristically.   The user's ability to translate his need into the language of the index depends upon a
number of factors, including: (1) his ability to express his
need verbally, (2) the degree to which the vocabulary of the
index matches his requirements (particularly the factor of
whether or not the vocabulary is sufficiently specific to
match his precise requirements (3) his ability to search
systematically, and (4) the assistance and guidance given by
the index itself, particularly in its organization, structure
and cross-referencing.

When the user actually matches his search strategy
against the index (i. e. , consults a series of headings) the
success or failure of the search is obviously dependent on
the characteristics of the indexing employed.   Indexing policy
will affect performance, particularly the policy regarding
exhaustivity of indexing (i. e. , the number of access points
provided).   Indexing quality and accuracy obviously also
affect performance.   The searcher may not retrieve everything on skin transplantation, for example, even though he
consults all the correct headings because indexers have not
always assigned these headings when they should have been
assigned.   Again, the vocabulary of the index is an important factor in the indexing process as it is in the searching process: perhaps the vocabulary is inadequate to express
many of the concepts occurring in the literature indexed and
losses occur because items are hidden away under headings
the user could not reasonably be expected to consult.

Finally, given that the searcher consults all the correct headings we have no assurance that he will recognize
all the relevant items contained under these headings.
Whether or not he recognizes them as relevant depends
largely upon the quality of the document surrogate provided.

It should be noted that these various factors affecting
performance are cumulative.   That is, in a search of a
printed index (or a consultation of the index for current
awareness purposes) some of the relevant literature may

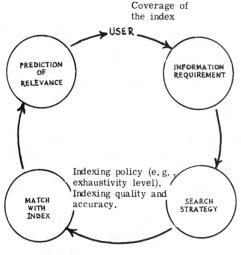

Coverage of
the index

USER

PREDICTION
OF
RELEVANCE

INFORMATION
REQUIREMENT

MATCH
WITH
INDEX

Indexing policy (e. g. ,
exhaustivity level).
Indexing quality and
accuracy.

SEARCH
STRATEGY

User's ability
to verbalize his
requirement; ability
of the vocabulary
to describe con-
cepts of interest
to the user; assis-
tance and guidance
given by the index
(organization and
structure); user's
ability to search
systematically.

Ability of the vocabulary to describe
concepts occurring in documents.

Figure 1

be missed because of poor searching strategies, some because of vocabulary inadequacies, some through indexing
policy and indexing quality, and some through deficiencies in
the document surrogate. The combination of these various
factors makes it extremely difficult to conduct a search that
will yield 100 percent recall (i. e. , a search that will un-
cover all the potentially relevant items contained in the
index). Moreover, all of these factors also affect the time
it takes to conduct a search and thus govern the unit cost
per relevant citation retrieved.

In this paper we have tried to describe performance
criteria for published indexes, to present factors affecting
the performance of published indexes, and to suggest possible procedures that might be used in a complete evaluation
of the effectiveness of an index. We have also mentioned
some recent work that is relevant to the evaluation of printed
indexes in general. These investigations deal usually with
a single aspect of the evaluation (e. g. , the quality of the
surrogate, user attitudes, coverage). No comprehensive
evaluation of all factors affecting performance of any published index has been conducted, to our knowledge, so far.
This is virgin territory for the researcher.

References

1. Lancaster, F. W.   "MEDLARS: a multipurpose informa-
    tion system."   INSPEL 4:22-27, Jan. 1969.
2. Bourne, C. P.   "Characteristics of Coverage by the
    Bibliography of Agriculture of the Literature Re-
    lating to Agricultural Research and Development."
    Palo Alto, Calif., Information General Corpora-
    tion, June 1969.   PB 185 425.
3. Bourne, C. P.   "Overlapping Coverage of Bibliography
    of Agriculture by 15 other Secondary Services."
    Palo Alto, Calif., Information General Corpora-
    tion, June 1969, PB 185 069.
4. Martyn, J. "Tests on abstracts journals: coverage,
    overlap and indexing."   J. Doc. 23:45-75, March
    1970.
5. Torr, D. V. ; Fried, C. ; and Prevel, J. J.   "Program
    of Studies on the Use of Published Indexes."
    Bethesda, Md., General Electric Company, In-
    formation Systems Operation, 1964.
6. Davison, P. S., and Matthews, D. A. R.   "Assessment
    of information services."   Aslib Proc. 21:280-3.
    July 1969.
7. Elliott, C. K.   "Abstracting services in psychology: a
    comparison of Psychological Abstracts and Bul-
    letin Signalétique."   Libr. Ass. Record 71:280-3,
    Sept. 1969.
8. Carroll, K. H.   "An analytical survey of virology lit-
    erature reported in two announcement journals."
    Amer. Doc. 20:234-7, July 1969.
9. Barlup, Janet. "Mechanization of library procedures
    in the medium-sized medical library.   VII. Rele-
    vancy of cited articles in citation indexing."   Bull.
    Med. Libr. Ass. 57:260-263, July 1969.
10. Bystrom, M. "Agricultural information. Can you find
    it with the index?" Spec. Libr. 59:712-7, Nov.
    1968.
11. Drage, J. F.   "User preferences in published indexes,
    a preliminary test."   Inf. Scientist 2:111-4, Nov.
    1968.
12. Cluley, H. J.   "Analytical Abstracts: user reaction
    study."   Proc. Soc. Anal. Chem. 217-2, Nov.
    1968.
13. Harley, A. J.   "MEDLARS: a comparison with hand
    searching in Index Medicus."   Inf. Scientist 2:59-
    70, July 1968.
14. Saracevic, T.   "Comparative effects of titles, abstracts

and full texts on relevance judgments. " <u>Proc.</u> <u>ASIS</u> 6:293-9, 1969.

15. Williams, J. H. , Jr. , and Perriens, M. P.   "Automatic Full Text Indexing and Searching System. " Gaithersburg, Md. , IBM Federal Systems Division, 1968.

16. Jahoda, G. , and Stursa, M. L.   "A comparison of keyword from title index with a single access point per document alphabetic subject index. " <u>Amer.</u> <u>Doc.</u> 20:377-80, Oct. 1969.

17. Virgo, J.   "An evaluation of <u>Index Medicus</u> and MEDLARS in the field of ophthalmology. "   Master's dissertation.   Chicago, Graduate Library School, August 1968.

SOME OBSERVATIONS OF THE
DEVELOPMENT AND NUTRITION OF BOOKLICE

by Z. P. Baryshnikova

Reprinted by permission from Restaurator 1(3) 1970,
p. 199-212.

With the exception of a few species Psocoptera live
in woods, in parks and in gardens on trees and bushes,
where there is a relatively high degree of air humidity.
They live off fragments of animal or vegetable matter, particularly on microscopic mould fungi and on pollen.

Some Psocoptera are synanthropous. They usually
live in houses, in museums, in libraries and in other buildings, where they are almost unnoticed because of their
hidden way of life. The most widely distributed vermin of
this group in buildings is Troctes divinatorius Müll. It is
also called the mould louse or the cabinet louse, though its
similarity with a louse is only superficial.

Literature on the biology and the ecology of the booklouse is rather sparse. The most thorough and interesting
examinations on the ecology of this species have been carried out by Ghani (1951) and Brown (1952) and on its
anatomy by Kolbe (1880) and Noland (1924).

The booklouse is cosmopolitan. In buildings it is
found on walls, in cupboards, behind baseboards, behind
fixtures and behind water supply equipment. This insect is
almost omnivorous, living on practically all kinds of animal
and plant matter. The booklouse may be found in collections
of insects, and other dried animals, in herbaria and in
stack-rooms, between books and papers, especially in moist
places. It destroys books, wallpaper and photographs,
eating out the glue and the starch. It may also be found in
dried fruits, in flour, in grain and in other products. However, some authors assume that the booklouse lives exclusively on mould fungi and does not destroy material that is

to be preserved.   We do not agree with this opinion, as it
is contradictory to our observations.

In stack-rooms the booklouse appears sometimes in
large quantities.   Insufficient knowledge of the way of life of
this species made us study the influence of different tem-
peratures and different degrees of humidity on the booklouse.
Knowledge of these factors may be of considerable value in
creating such conditions in library buildings as are unfavour-
able to the development and the reproduction of this vermin.
We have also studied the nutrition of the booklouse.

Experimental Method

A culture of booklice in weighing bottles, on wheat-
flour, on dried meat, on cloth and on woolen material was
placed in an insectarium with room temperature and moist
air.   For our experiments we took insects from this culture and placed them in chambers of plasticine which we
put on slides.   The chambers were 8 mm in diameter and
4 mm in height and covered with a dense cloth of silk or
satin.   Crumbs of wheat-flour or dried meat were used as
food.

We made daily observations of the booklice and
studied their nutrition on wall-paper, newsprint and paper
made of rags, and on the same sorts of paper processed
with farinaceous glue, with and without antiseptics and with
the sodium salt of carboxymethyl cellulose.   We made
further studies of their nutrition on new and old russet-
tanned leather and new chrome leather, on old and new
parchment, on calico, on imitated leather, on natural and
on artificial silk, on cloth, on wheat-flour and on dried
meat.

One series of experiments was made under room
conditions, i. e. , at the temperature and percentage of
humidity of the insectarium.   Another series of experiments
was made at the temperature of the insectarium and 80% air
humidity.   The experiments lasted approximately 2 years.
For our work we used imaginal booklice from the stock
culture fed on wheat-flour and dried meat.   The insects
were put in chambers of plasticine, which were covered
with a dense cloth of silk.   The chambers were circular
with a diameter of about 8 mm and placed on slides.   Each
chamber contained 1 imaginal specimen.   Also chambers

intended for 10 specimens were used.   These were oval,
up to 3 cm long and 1. 5 cm broad.

Observations of the Development of the Booklouse

Our first subject was to examine the influence of air
humidity on the viability of the booklouse.   To this purpose
20 imagines were placed in chambers of plasticine and later
in desiccators with a constant air humidity from 10% to
100% (with an interval of 10%).

Above 30% of humidity the insects developed normally.
Nymphs developed from the eggs laid by the imagines.   The
largest number of eggs was laid at air humidities of 80%
and 90%.   In chambers with 100% air humidity we observed
an intense growth of mould fungi whose hyphae conpletely
covered the nutritional substrate and filled the chamber.
It is probable that the development and the reproduction of
the insects was suppressed by drop formation (Table 1).

TABLE 1:   Survival rate of Troctes divinatorius Müll. at
           different percentage of relative humidity [20
           samples were used at the experiment]

Air humidity in %	Mortality in %	Day of death	Progeny (no. of nymphs)	Remarks
10	100	14	-	90% died on 6th day
20	100	10	-	90% died on 6th day
30	100	14	-	90% died on 6th day
40	-	-	19	
50	-	-	19	
60	-	-	10	
70	-	-	17	
80	-	-	48	
90	-	-	55	Nutrition on mould fungi
100	-	-	15	Drop formation and excessive development of mould fungi

Smaller quantities of mould fungi have been observed in the
chambers at 90% humidity.   In this case the fungi had no

strong effect on the insects, on the contrary, they were used
for nutrition.

In 1952 Brown studied the influence of 25 different
combinations of temperature and humidity on various phases
in the development of <u>Liposcelis</u> (<u>Troctes</u>) <u>divinatorius</u> Müll.
He showed that the most favourable condition for oviposition,
incubation of eggs, development of nymphs and lifetime of
the imagines is a conbination of 85% of air humidity and a
temperature of 20-25° C.

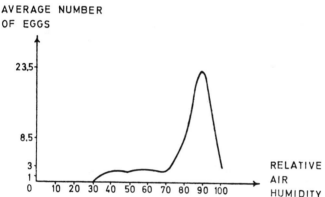

Fig. 1.   Fertility of <u>Troctes divinatorius</u> Müll. at
different percentages of air humidity and room temperature.

After the results of the first experiments we studied
the influence of air humidity (from 10% to 100% with intervals
of 10%) at variable room temperature.   To test the humidity
in this series of experiments we took 3 of the oldest nymphs
at a time and kept each in a separate chamber.   These
nymphs developed into imagines and laid eggs (the reproduction of the booklouse is parthenogenetic).   Each egg was
them placed in a separate chamber.   We noted the lifetime
and the fertility of the imagines at each stage of humidity.

At 10%, 20% and 30% humidity all the nymphs died,
their average lifetime being 6, 6, 8, 3, and 13 days respectively (Fig. 2).   The nymphs lost water, and they became short and flat.

At 40% humidity all the nymphs developed into imagines which laid eggs.   No female laid more than 3 eggs.

The second generation was less viable; only in one case a nymph developed into imago. It lived 355 days, but did not lay a single egg (Fig. 1 and 2).

The maximum lifetime of an imago of the first generation at 50% humidity was 300 days. The largest number of eggs laid was four. The nymphs of the second generation had rather a long lifetime (181 to 193 days), but they died before they had reached maturity. Of this generation only 1 nymph developed into imago. However, it died after 370 days, and it never laid eggs.

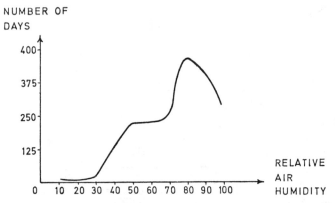

Fig. 2.   Lifetime of imagines at different percentages of humidity and room temperature.

The imagines originating from the nymphs used for the experiment lived 160-341 days at 60% humidity. The largest quantity of eggs laid by a female was 5. All the nymphs of the second generation died before they had been transformed into imagines, though some of them lived quite long (up to 252 days).

At 70% air humidity the lifetime of the first generation was longer than at lower degrees of humidity. Some insects lived more than 470 days. Part of the nymphs of the second generation died. The nymphs which reached maturity were alive for more than 245 days. At this percentage of humidity a third generation was developed, but much more slowly. For instance, one nymph reached only the second stage of a nymph after 141 days.

At 80% humidity the development of the booklouse was considerably faster. Simultaneously the lifetime of the imagines was increased. In most cases they lived for more than 470 days. In our observations we noted a partheno-genetic development of 5-6 generations. The quantity of eggs produced by a female reached 20-23.

At 90% humidity the development was also fast. Within 18 months 6 generations had developed. The life-time of the imagines was quite long (180 to 257 days). The number of eggs laid by a female was larger than the num-ber of eggs produced at 80% humidity (Fig. 1).

The average number was 25-30, and in one case it was as high as 114. At this percentage of humidity mould fungi developed in the chambers on the nutrition substrate, and the nymphs as well as the imagines lived on spores and hyphae of fungi. We found the following species of mould fungi: Aspergillus flavus Link, Penicillium meleagrinum Biourge and P. tardum Thom.

The development of the booklouse at 100% humidity was suppressed by intense growth of mould fungi, which almost filled the chambers, and by drop formation. Book-lice of the second generation died after 300 days, at the imaginal stage. In the second generation only 1-3 eggs were produced. In the third generation there was only one nymph. It lived for 164 days and did not reach maturity.

The most favourable condition for the development, the lifetime and the fertility is a humidity percentage of 80-90%, at varying room temperature.

We also made a series of experiments at a constant temperature of 25° C. at 40%, 60% and 80% humidity. Our observations, which we had to stop for technical reasons, lasted 8 months. We took 6 imagines at a time and kept them in separate chambers, at each percentage of humidity. As soon as the booklice had produced their first eggs, they were transferred to the general culture, whereas the eggs remained in the chambers. We noted the speed of the de-velopment of each stage, and observed their lifetime and fertility.

It is probable that air humidity has not an immediate effect on the time of the development of the booklice. The time of development of the eggs does not differ considerably at different percentages of humidity (Table 2).

TABLE 2:   Duration of the development (in days) of the
           booklouse at a temperature of 25° C.

% air humid.	Generation (no. of replica- tions) and Eggs		Number of nymphs by stage				Imago
			1st	2d	3d	4th	
40	I (6)	11. 5	10	-	-	-	-
60	I (6)	11. 0	17	34	37	-	-
80	I (6)	11. 4	4. 6	3	4. 2	4. 5	1. 2*
80	II (83)	11. 3	13	6. 8	5	5	-

*Editor's note: This must be the preoviposition period,
cfr. the lifetime in Table 3.

As the nymphs grow their development becomes
slower and slower.   At 60% air humidity the development
takes 17, 34 and 37 days; these figures apply to the first,
the second and the third stage, respectively.   In the first
generation the development of each stage of nymphs takes 3-
5 days at 80% humidity.   In the second generation the development of nymphs of the first stage laster longer than it
did for the preceding generation.   In the second generation
the average time of development (from the oviposition to the
imago stage) had increased two times as compared with
the first generation.

At 80% humidity the booklice reached maturity after
29 days in the first generation, after 58 in the second generation and after 41. 6 days in the third generation (Fig. 3).
In the first generation the difference between the extreme
values is very small.   In the second generation it increases
abruptly.   In the third generation these sizes are noticeably
approximated.   The development of the booklouse is os-
cillating.

The booklice reached maturity at 80% air humidity.
At 60% air humidity one imago was developed.   It is therefore difficult to judge of the lifetime of the imagines and of
their fertility.

A comparison of the lifetime of the imagines according to generations at 80% humidity shows a reduction in
their lifetime (Table 3).

At the same time the fertility is reduced, which
clearly appears from Table 3.

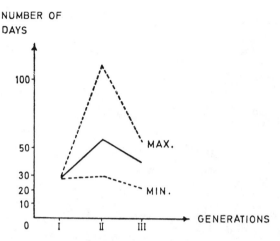

Fig. 3.   Change of the periods of development according to generations at 25° C. and 80% air humidity.

TABLE 3:   The lifetime of imagines and their fertility at 80% humidity and a temperature of 25° C.

Generation (and no. of replications)	Lifetime			Fertility		
	max.	min.	avg.	max.	min.	avg.
I (6)	165	37	95. 7	75	7	38. 7
II (22)	113	4	65. 1	71	3	23. 6
III (12)	67. 6	35. 7	50. 2	27	2	18. 5

A graphic representation of these sizes shows gradual approximation of the extreme sizes and the average size of the third generation (Fig. 4 and 5).   In the last series of experiments the optimal humidity at a temperature of 25° C. was 80%, but, apparently, constant conditions have a depressing effect on ensuing generations, which is seen from the reduction of the fertility and the lifetime of the imagos. It should, however, be noted that the difference between the first and the second generation is larger than the difference between the second and the third generation.   In our opinion it might be supposed that the difference between ensuing generations will be reduced more and more and that the curve will oscillate around a medium level, which is lower than the original level.

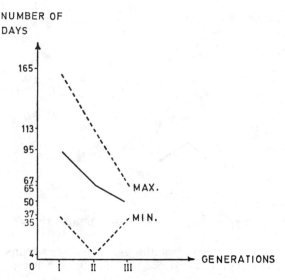

Fig. 4.   Change of the fertility according to generations at 25°C. and at 80% air humidity.

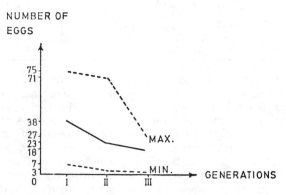

Fig. 5.   Change of the lifetime of imagines according
to generations at 25°C. and 80% air humidity.

The Nutrition of the Booklouse

Studying the nutrition of the booklouse we have observed that of the diets tested wheat-flour and dried meat (Tables 4 and 5) were most favourable for their development.

In our experiments some generations were developed on each of these substrates.   The number of generations in the second series (at constant humidity) could be determined only with difficulty, as the generations were mixed, and the number of specimens increased to 100-200.   Under room conditions (variable temperature and air humidity) we observed 2-3 generations.   Further observations were stopped, though the insects were still alive.

We noticed considerable damage on the cloth, which they tore asunder and changed into single small fibres.

We also noted that essential damage had been done to artificial and natural silk.   The booklice devoured the eggs they had laid; besides, they fed on the mould fungi Aspergillus restrictus G. Smith, which developed in the natural silk.

Inconsiderable damage was observed on the fleshside of old and new russet-tanned leather and in new chrome leather.   We found a large quantity of excrements, the colouring of which was the same as the colouring of the leather.   As they apparently did not digest the leather we concluded that they had used their eggs as nutrition.

In old and new parchment the damage was insignificant.   However, we found plenty of excrements of a white colouring, and we observed that letters had been stripped off old parchment, so that only traces of them were left.

The damage done to the calico and the leatherette was hardly noticeable.   But there is no doubt that these materials had been damaged, since we found many blue excrements in the chamber with the leatherette and a large portion of excrements of a light colouring in the chamber with the calico.   The colouring of the excrements corresponded to the colours of the materials eaten.   In the chamber with the leatherette the mould fungi Aspergillus restrictus G. Smith were developed.

TABLE 4: The nutrition of the booklouse at room temperature and air humidity

Material	10 nymphs in each chamber			1 nymph in each chamber		
	Degree of damage done to material	Lifetime in days	Number of generations	Degree of damage done to material	Lifetime in days	Number of generations
Art paper	-	376	2.3	-	49.6	1.3
Art paper with flour glue without antiseptics	-	365	2.3	-	120	1.6
Art paper with flour glue with antiseptics	-	353	2.6	-	201	2.0
Art paper with sodium carboxymethyl cellulose	-	361	2.3	-	73	1.3
Newsprint	-	381	2.0	-	71	1.3
Newsprint with flour glue without antiseptics	-	353	2.3	-	124	1.3
Newsprint with flour glue with antiseptics	-	353	2.0	-	162	2.0
Newsprint with sodium carboxymethyl cellulose	-	364	2.3	-	152	1.6
Paper made of rags	-	394	2.0	-	151	1.6
Paper made of rags with flour glue without antiseptics	-	324	2.3	-	153	1.6
Paper made of rags with flour glue with antiseptics	-	236	1.6	-	247	2.0
Paper made of rags with sodium carboxymethyl cellulose	-	372	2.6	-	219	2.0
New russet-tanned leather	x	420	2.6	x	207	1.6

Old russet-tanned leather	x	262	2.3	–	152	1.6
New chrome leather	x	349	2.3	x	119	1.3
New parchment	–	346	2.3	–	166	1.6
Old parchment	–	346	2.3	–	156	1.6
Calico	–	250	2.0	–	19	1.0
Leatherette	x	363	2.3	–	166	1.6
Natural silk	x	358	2.3	–	179	2.0
Artificial silk	x	339	3.0	x	160	2.0
Cloth	+	339	2.0	+	135	2.0
Wheat flour	+	483	4.0	+	339	3.0
Dried meat	+	445	3.3	+	144	1.3

Signs: No damage: –, Partial damage: x, Considerable damage: +.

TABLE 5: The nutrition of the booklouse at room temperature and at 80% air humidity

Material	Degree of damage done to the material	Lifetime of all generations in days	Number of generations
Art paper	-	549	2. 0
Art paper with flour without antiseptics	-	451	2. 0
Art paper with flour with antiseptics	-	189	2. 0
Art paper with sodium carboxymethyl cellulose	-	619	2. 5
Newsprint	-	376	1. 5
Newsprint with flour glue without antiseptics	-	223	1. 5
Newsprint with flour glue with antiseptics	-	258	2. 0
Newsprint with sodium carboxymethyl cellulose	-	383	2. 0
Paper made of rags	-	460	2. 0
Paper made of rags with flour glue without antiseptics	-	280	2. 0
Paper made of rags with flour glue with antiseptics	-	262	2. 0
Paper made of rags with sodium carboxymethyl cellulose	-	623	3. 0
New russet-tanned leather	x	589	3. 0
Old russet-tanned leather	x	473	2. 5
New chrome leather	x	451	2. 0
New parchment	-	451	2. 0

Old parchment	x	533	2.0
Calico	-	311	2.0
Leatherette	-	371	1.5
Natural silk	+	606	2.5
Artificial silk	+	396	2.0
Cloth	+	606	3.0
Wheat flour	+	more than 679	not established
Dried meat	+	589	not established

Signs: No damage: -, Partial damage: x, Considerable damage: +.

We have not observed damage in all kinds of paper.
We quite often found that eggs had been eaten by the booklice.   On paper processed with the hemicellulose pasti
sodium salt of carboxymethyl-cellulose common salt was
crystallized out.   This is apparently explained by the fact
that a technical product was used.   At 80% air humidity a
large number of mould fungi were developed on all the
samples of paper.   On art paper we found the fungi Penicillium notatum Westling, on newsprint the fungi P. meleagrinum Biourge, Hormodendron Bonorden, and of the
group Aspergillus glaucus we found: A. repens (Cda) de
Bary and A. restrictus G. Smith.   On paper made of rags
we found Penicillium notatum Westling, P. meleagrinum
Biourge, Aspergillus flavus Link, and Hormodendron hordei
Bruhne.

We made one series of experiments with different
quantities of nymphs in one chamber (1 or 10 nymphs in
the same chamber).   When we compared the results we
saw that at a higher density the lifetime was considerably
longer, the damage was more noticeable, and a large quantity
of material was destroyed.   The single specimens lived
averagely two times longer than the specimens that were
kept together.   At a higher density we used the dead bodies
of insects for nutrition, and at the end of the experiments
we were not able to detect a single dead body.   However,
we sometimes found capsules of heads.   Besides, the booklice would quite often eat the eggs they had produced themselves.

In two series of experiments the density of insects
was the same, but the cultures were kept either at 80%
humidity or at variable room humidity.   At a constant degree of humidity the lifetime was longer.   Booklice are
sensitive to humidity and prefer air humidity which is not
below 40-60%.   In the course of 24 hours room humidity
oscillated between 40% and 85%.   The degree of damage was
the same in both series.

The lifetime of Troctes divinatorius Müll fed on
paper processed with sodium salt of carboxymethyl cellulose at 80% humidity considerably surpasses the lifetime
at variable humidity.   This is due to the fact that they
lived on spores and hyphae of mould fungi, a very large
quantity of which was developed on these samples of paper.

Conclusions

1. At room temperature the optimal air humidity for the development of the booklouse Troctes divinatorius Müll is 80-90%.

2. At constant conditions the duration of the development changes from generation to generation.

3. Of the materials of which books are made booklice prefer cloth, artificial and natural silk and leather, new and old russet-tanned leather and new chrome leather; old parchment is partially damaged.

4. The higher the density of insects and of humidity the greater the damage done to the materials and the longer the lifetime of the booklice.

Literature

Brown, Carl D.: "Temperature and relative humidity as factors in the ecology of Liposcelis divinatorius (Müller) (Corrodentia, Atropidae)." Iowa State College journal of science 26 (1951-52):175-76.

Ghani, M. A. and Harvey L. Sweetman: "Ecological studies of the book louse, Liposcelis divinatorius (Müll.)." Ecology 32 (1951):230-44.

Hawkins, John: "Corrodentia as pest of ground feed." Journal of economic entomology 32 (1939):467.

Kolbe, Hermann Julius: "Monographie der deutschen Psociden mit besonderer Berücksichtung der Fauna Westfalens." Jahres-Bericht des Westfälischen Provinzial-Vereins für Wissenschaft und Kunst 8: 1879 (1880):73-142.

Mallis, Arnold: Handbook of pest control: The behavior, life history, and control of household pests. 2. ed. New York: Mac. Nair-Dorland Co. 1954. (Pp. 369-76: Psocids or book lice. Order Corrodentia).

Merrill, E. D.: "On the control of destructive insects in the herbarium." Journal of the Arnold Arboretum 29 (1948):103-10.

Noland, Ruth Chase: "The anatomy of Troctes divinatorius Müll." Transactions of the Wisconsin Academy of Sciences, Arts and Letters 21 (1924):195-211.

Rosewall, O. W.: "The biology of the book-louse, Troctes divinatoria. Müll." Annals of the Entomological Society of America 23 (1930):192-94.

Rumyantsev, P. D.: Biologiya vrediteley khlebnykh zapasov. Moskva 1959.

Part III:

COMMUNICATION AND EDUCATION

A FEMINIST LOOK AT CHILDREN'S BOOKS

by the Feminists on Children's Literature

Reprinted by permission from School Library Journal
January 1971, p. 19-24, published by R. R. Bowker
(a Xerox company), and copyright (c) 1971 by the
Xerox Corporation

> Our history has been stolen from us. Our heroes
> died in childbirth, from peritonitis, overwork, op-
> pression, from bottled-up rage. Our geniuses were
> never taught to read or write. We must invest a
> past adequate to our ambitions. We must create
> a future adequate to our needs.
> --The Old Mole,
>   Cambridge, Massachusetts

Is the portrayal of females in children's books
sexist? That is, are girls and women assigned only traditional female roles and personalities? And when the female foot fails to fit that often too-tight shoe, is the girl
or woman then seen as an unfortunate, troubled human
being?

These questions were the basis of a group effort to
scrutinize some of the more highly praised children's books.
In our view, a non-sexist portrayal would offer the girl
reader a positive image of woman's physical, emotional,
and intellectual potential--one that would encourage her to
reach her own full personhood, free of traditionally imposed
limitations.

In selecting books to examine, we consulted a number of influential lists. These were the Notable Books of
1969 (American Library Association), the Child Study Association's annual recommendations for that same year, and
the Newbery Award winners.

It was a shock to discover almost immediately that

relatively few of the books on these lists even feature female characters--let alone what we would consider <u>positive</u>
female characters. Of all 49 Newbery Award winners,
books about boys outnumbered books about girls by about
three to one. On that score, the years have brought little
improvement. The ALA list for 1969 gave us a ratio of
over two to one.

The Child Study Association list for the same year
proved more difficult to analyze. It is very long, divided
into innumerable categories, and many of the books can't
yet be found in the libraries. However, we made a separate
check of several categories. Under the heading of "Boys
and Girls" we found a male to female ratio of two to one.
Under "Growing Up" the ratio was over three to one. And
"Sports," of course, like certain bars we could formerly
name, was 100 percent male. The rest of the book list
may not follow the pattern of this sampling, but suspicion
runs high!

The thoughtful introduction to the Child Study Association list makes the following statement: The books a child
reads "should not shield him from knowledge of destructive
forces in the world, but rather help him to cope with them."
We agree, for the most part. But why does the sentence
read "shield <u>him</u>" and "help <u>him</u>"? Sexism is such a destructive force in the world, that we feel the implicit sexism
is this sentence should not be overlooked.

The introduction states also that a book's "possible
emotional and intellectual impact on a young reader" must
be considered. Right on! Not even a problem of gender
there. The CSA continues: "from its inception, it has been
aware of the mental health aspects of reading and asks that
books for children present basically honest concepts of life,
positive ethical values, and honest interpersonal relationships."

We ask no more than that. The CSA has clearly
been struggling to encourage greater sensitivity toward
racism in books for children. If only their future book
selections could be made with an equally growing sensitivity
to the impact of sexism! Many of the present selections
fail to realize the promise of their own introduction. The
list is guilty of sexism--if only through indifference.

Of course, a greater sensitivity to sexism would

greatly curtail the current lists of recommended children's
books--at least for the next few years.   Yet, a scrupulous
attitude on the part of prestigious organizations would surely
serve powerfully in raising the general feminist consciousness of the children's book world, making forever obsolete
Eve Merriam's recent and accurate comment that "sex prejudice is the only prejudice now considered socially acceptable. "   Habit dies hard.

We'd like to apologize for seeming to pick on CSA.
It's just that such a praiseworthy introduction deserved
attention in terms of its implications for the female image.
Nor were we being picky in our examination of specific
books: checking the prevalence of so virulent a disease as
sexism requires the isolation of even potential carriers.

What would we like to see in children's books?   What
were our criteria?   We wanted to see girl readers encouraged to develop physical confidence and strength without
the need to fear any corresponding loss of "feminity. "   We
would have liked to see the elimination of all those tire-
some references to "tomboys. "   Why can't a girl who prefers baseball to ballet simply be a girl who prefers baseball to ballet?

Many women have to--or simply prefer to--earn a
living.   Can't we encourage girls to find satisfaction and
fulfillment in work, and lay forever the suspicion that work
outside the home for a woman is primarily proof of her inability to love a man, or to land a sufficiently lucrative
one?   Women do study seriously, work with enjoyment--or
at least pride in their competence--get promoted, and (of
course) fight sexism at work and in their families in order
to progress.   Let's show them as no less "feminine, "
despite the assertiveness and firm sense of self required
in this untraditional role.

Margaret Mead has written that "man is unsexed by
failure, woman by success. "   That's another brutal truth
we'd like to see changed.   And while we're about it, let's
not overlook the fact that boys, too, are denigrated and
cramped by sexism.   Our current rigid role definitions require that a boy be all that a girl should not be: unafraid,
competent at "male" jobs, strong.   A weeping boy is a
"sissy. "   Words like "sissy"--and "hero, " too--should be
dissected and exposed for the inhuman demands they make
on growing boys.   Children's books could help.

We object to a woman's being defined by the man she marries, or the children she bears, or the father she once obeyed. Let's see women who are people in their own right --independent of such compensatory affiliations. And if a woman doesn't want children, or even a husband, must this be seen as peculiar? Why not encourage girls in a search for alternate life styles? Give a girl all the possible options you give a boy for her future life choices, all his freedom to inquire and explore and achieve. Her options don't have to be slanted toward certain currently socially imposed preferences.

There are books on superwomen. Okay. Superwomen do exist. But many more books are needed on women who simply function very well and freely wherever they choose--or are forced--to apply their abilities.

We are bitterly tired of seeing depictions of the woman as castrator. Even a well-known writer, whose portrayal of girls we frequently admire, slipped badly in some recent picture books. In one of these, the mother reproves her son for spilling the mud he is playing with--even though the scene is outdoors! In another, little sister (and we know where she learned her lesson) reproves brother for accidentally spilling paint off his easel. Little girls are as capable of making a casual mess and as freely lost in creative play as little boys. A picture book that does that beautifully is Rain Rain Rivers by Uri Shulevitz (Farrar, 1969) which we were delighted to find on both the ALA and CSA lists. (We were as pleased to find the two previously mentioned books ignored by both lists.)

And when, as must sometimes happen if books portray real life, there is an overcontrolling or too-bossy woman, she should not be made a fool or villain. A little understanding--of her problem, her frustration at not being allowed to play an equal role in her family or her world, and her consequent misuse of energy to project her ideas and ego through the lives of others--is long overdue.

How about books showing more divorced and single-parent families? And, for heaven's sake, every divorced or widowed mother does not solve her problems through remarriage--or even wish to do so. (Few do, you know!) Maybe she can start on that career she never had--and discover a new concept of herself. The difficulties and the loneliness are real, as are the child-care problems. But let the woman find a new self-reliance in fighting her own battles--and joy in winning at least some of them.

There is also the question of language. No more automatic use of "he" to mean "child," or "mankind" to mean "humankind." If at first the alternatives seem forced--and they will--they won't sound that way for long.

Despite our criticism of socially assigned roles, we don't mean to diminish or ignore the mother or housewife. She is often a strong, wonderfully rich human being. Her role can be vital, and sometimes she finds satisfaction in it. But let's not insist on that as her role. Men can also cope skillfully with household tasks--and not necessarily look for a woman or daughter to take them off the hook.

Sexist Books

The books we read--most from the lists mentioned earlier--fell, or were pushed by our merciless analysis, into several categories. One, plain and simple, was the Sexist Book, in which girls and women are exclusively assigned traditional female roles--although the material may, unhappily, be fairly true to life.

We were forcibly struck by the purposeful sexist propaganda between the covers of some of the recommended children's books.

Young women who have found it an uphill struggle to identify with the popular female image will recognize it as propaganda--and not simply as a natural reflection of life. Unfortunately the girl reader is not yet so experienced. Books that outline a traditional background role for women, praising their domestic accomplishments, their timidity of soul, their gentle appearance and manners, and--at the same time--fail to portray initiative, enterprise, physical prowess, and genuine intellect deliver a powerful message to children of both sexes. Such books are a social poison.

Take, for a horrible example, the attitude exemplified in the following line: "Accept the fact that this is a man's world and learn how to play the game gracefully." Those words fell from the lips of a sympathetic male character in Irene Hunt's 1967 Newbery winner Up a Road Slowly (Follett, 1966). Or take this juicy bit from the 1957 winner

Miracles on Maple Hill by Virginia Sorenson (Harcourt, 1956).

> For the millionth time she was glad she wasn't
> a boy. It was all right for girls to be scared or
> silly or even ask dumb questions. Everybody just
> laughed and thought it was funny. But if anybody
> caught Joe asking a dumb question or even thought
> he was the littlest bit scared, he went red and
> purple and white. Daddy was even something like
> that, old as he was.

Does that passage describe real life? Indeed it does!
But a good book for children should comment and leave the
child feeling something is wrong here. This one does not.
In fact, we voted it our supreme example of the most
thoroughly relentless type of sexism found in children's literature. The girl, Marly, never overcomes her hero wor-
ship of brother Joe or her comparative inferiority. And it
certainly would have been relevant to explore the toll that
maintaining hero status takes on Joe's character.

Such perfect examples, of course, are not the rule.
But there was a surplus of books whose thesis might seem
less obvious, but whose refrain was predictably the same.
A little girl in the 1955 Newbery winner, The Wheel on the
School (Harper, 1954) asks her boy playmate: "Can I go,
too?" And the response is "No! Girls are no good at
jumping. It's a boy's game." Meindert DeJong leaves it
at that--and another eager little girl reader is squelched.

Those fictional girls who join the prestigious ranks
of male adventurers often do so at the expense of other
members of their sex. And small wonder, the tomboy-
turned-token-female is simply the other side of the coin.
The message is clear: if a girl wishes to join the boys in
their pranks and hell-raising, or to use her imagination and
personality in leading them, she renounces all claim to supposedly feminine characteristics--tears and fears and pink
hair ribbons. The line between traditionally assigned sex
roles is drawn sharp and clear. The girl who crosses that
line is forced to desert her sex rather than allowed to act
as a spokeswoman for a broader definition.

Take Lulu's Back in Town (Funk & Wagnall, 1968).
The proof provided by author Laura Dean to show Lulu's
final acceptance by the boys is the clubhouse sign: "FOR

BOYS ONLY.   No Girls Allowed.   (Except Lulu.)"   This is
seen by the author, who unfortunately happens to be a woman, as a satisfactory ending.   But our committee was not
so pleased.   (Except to find that neither ALA nor CSA had
listed it.)

Cop-Outs

The Cop-Out Book is often the most insidious.   At
its worst, it promises much and delivers nothing.   But the
better ones are the most infuriating, for often they are only
a step away from being the exact kind of literature we'd
like to see for girls and boys about girls.   The actual cop-
out may be only a crucial line, a paragraph, the last chapter.   But somewhere a sexist compromise is made, somewhere the book adjusts to the stereotyped role of woman,
often for the sake of social pressure and conformity.   The
compromise brings with it a change, and this change is not
only disturbing, but often distorts the logical development
of the character herself.   Suddenly her development is re-
directed--or, rather, stunted.

The many Cop-Out Books we found are probably a
fair reflection of the social uncertainities and inner conflicts
of writers, publishers, and reviewers in our sexist society.

Caddie Woodlawn by Carol R. Brink (Macmillan,
1935) is a Newbery winner.   Not a recent one, but still
extremely popular.   Caddie is a young pioneer girl, allowed
to run free with her brothers.   She is happy and strong in
her so-called tomboy role.   Though her mother pressures
her to become more of a "lady," the reader feels serenely
certain that Caddie will remain her own person.   Alas, as
the book draws to a close, Caddie's father pleads: "It's a
strange thing, but somehow we expect more of girls than of
boys.   It is the sisters and wives and mothers, you know,
Caddie, who keep the world sweet and beautiful.... "   Thus
subdued, she joins the insipidly depicted girls at the weaving
loom.   True, the boys do ask her to teach them how to
weave.   Apparently they may choose to join women at their
work, but no longer may Caddie choose to run free in the
woods.   And we are left feeling cheated.   Why should it
be the right choice for her obediently to join the "sweet and
beautiful" women of the world on their pedestals?   Why
shouldn't she continue to struggle for a life in which she
might fulfill some inner potential?

The linking of a girl's growing up to the abandoning of her "tomboy" ways is a depressingly frequent theme in these books. As a stage in growing up, tomboy behavior appears to be acceptable. But the girl must in the end conform to more socially approved behavior. In a widely used bibliography compiled by Clara Kirchner in 1966 entitled Behavior Patterns in Children's Books there is an entire section called "From Tomboy to Young Woman." Here are two random descriptions:

> A Girl Can Dream by Betty Cavanna (Westminster, 1948): Loretta Larkin, tops in athletics but poor in social graces and jealous of a classmate who shines socially, finds out that being "just a girl" can be fun.

> Billie by Esphyr Slobodkina (Lothrop, 1959): Billie, who wore faded jeans and played boys' games because she didn't like being a girl, came to think differently after she took ballet lessons to limber up a sprained ankle.

These books fit into the following categories: Womanliness, Growing Up, and Popularity.

Young readers of such grievous cop-outs are forced to believe that the spunk, individuality, and physical capability so refreshingly portrayed in tomboy heroines must be surrendered when girls grow up--in order to fit the passive, supposedly more mature image of a young woman. But where is that earlier energy to be spent? Is depression in the adult woman perhaps linked to the painful suppression of so many sparks of life?

In a way we could call the Cop-Out Book the "co-op" book, for it permits the tomboy reader to believe she can pass comfortably over into that other world at a safely future date. Real life is rarely like that.

A new book recommended on both the ALA and the CSA lists is Constance Green's A Girl Called Al (Viking, 1969). The main character comes across as a nonconformist who truly enjoys her individuality, and throughout most of the book she eschews traditional female worries-- how she looks, hooking boyfriends, etc. Wonderful. But the ending is a neat little all-American package. Al gets thin, gets pretty, and now she will be popular. All these

sudden switches hit the reader in the last few pages.   Her
pigtails make room for a feminine hairdo.   Her closest
friend explains: "Her mother took her to the place she gets
her hair done and had the man wash and set Al's hair, and
now she wears it long with a ribbon around it.   It is very
becoming, my mother says.   She is right.   But I miss Al's
pigtails.   I wanted her to wear it this way but now that she
does I'm kind of sorry.   She looks older and different, is
all I know. "

Again, we are led to believe that another character in
our long line of individual heroines will conform to the role
society has rigidly defined for her.   We find it hard to buy
the sudden change in Al.   And we also miss the pigtails.

Sometimes it is the focus of a book that makes it a
cop-out.   When we read the 1959 Newbery winner, Elizabeth Speare's The Witch of Blackbird Pond (Houghton Mifflin,
1958), we praised Kit's independent spirit, her rejection of
bigoted values, and her truly striking courage at a time
when women were burned for witchcraft.   From a feminist
standpoint, the book is marred only by the plot's revolving
around the standard question: "Whom shall Kit marry?"   In
too many books we find the male character worrying about
what shall he be--while the female character worries about
who shall he be.

Only a few hairs are out of place in Next Door to
Xanadu by Doris Orgel (Harper, 1969), also listed by ALA
and CSA.   The main character faces the too-often very real
hatred of preteen boys toward girls.   She meets it with
strength, earning respect.   The only boy-crazy girl in the
book is deemphasized.   But one scene allows our society's
pervasive sexism to come shining through.

At a going-away party for one of the girls, a woman
parades as a fortune-teller.   "She took out a bowl, put it on
the table, filled it with all sorts of strange little things.
Then she said 'Who among you dares to delve into the
secrets the future holds in store?' "   Here were the fortunes
of the girls: The girl who pulled out two safety pins would
be "the mother of a fine pair of twins. "   Chalk meant another would be a teacher.   The one who picked a little sack
of soil would be "a farmer's wife. "   One pulled a penny:
she would be very rich.   One picked a little plastic boy doll
and she would meet a "fine young man. "   "Great happiness"
was in store for the one who got a bluebird's feather.

When one of the girls pulled out a jack, the fortune teller chanted: "Butcher, baker, candlestick-maker; tailor, sailor, teacher, preacher; doctor, lawyer, carpenter, smith--she would have kept it up, but Helen guessed it. Betsy would marry a jack-of-all-trades. "

Not be a jack-of-all-trades, but marry one. Not be a farmer, but be a farmer's wife. The only vocation predicted was that of teacher. Unfortunately, fortune-tellers will be like that, until we have feminist fortune-tellers. That would certainly bring brighter futures.

At the risk of carping, we felt that such a fine book as A Wrinkle in Time by Madeline L'Engle (Farrar, 1962), the 1963 Newbery winner, had a hint of acceptance of woman's second-class status. This is almost the only science fiction book in which a girl is the main character. We even find a mother who is a scientist, perhaps one of the only scientist moms in juvenile fiction. But why did father have to be a super scientist, topping mom by a degree or two?

Positive Images

Happily, if not of course, there are some books for children which show female characters in flexible, diverse roles. They allow for character development beyond the stereotype, and do not disappoint us in the end.

At first we tried calling these "Non-Sexist." But we found many books were not precisely either Sexist or Cop-Out, though somehow they did not quite fit our exacting feminist standards, usually because they did not deal with the questions they posed in a sufficiently clear, real and affirmative way. The rare book that did succeed, even in this, is our Positive-Image Book.

Certainly, these categories overlap a bit. A Wrinkle in Time really belongs among the Positive-Image Books. We just couldn't resist putting down papa's degrees. Unfair, we admit, because of the especially fine, honest relationship between Calvin (the boy who is a friend, as opposed to Boy Friend) and the girl protagonist. They respect each other's heads, and his ego does not stand in the way of her saving the day with an act of courage that rescues her little brother from it. We also applauded the image of the mother as a brilliant scientist who instills pride in her children.

Another Newbery we salute is the 1961 winner, Island of the Blue Dolphins by Scott O'Dell (Houghton Mifflin, 1960), one of the rare books showing a girl with strong physical skills. She kills wild dogs, constructs weapons, kills a giant tentacled sea fish, and hauls a six-man canoe by herself. The Indian girl protagonist, Karana, spends 18 years alone on a bleak and lonely island. And there we are indeed tempted to ask why such a marvelous heroine can only be encountered alone on an island--and never in the midst of society?

While on the subject of positive images, there is a new book we hope will appear on the 1970 recommended lists. Rufus Gideon Grant by Leigh Dean (Scribners, 1970) is about a boy, but we were taken by the following reference to a woman: "There inside this magazine was this lady, climbing giant trees and playing with wild chimpanzees...." And Rufus asks: "Can a boy be a zoologist?"

If we had time we would also like to discuss such essentially positive-image books as Strawberry Girl by Lois Lenski (Lippincott, 1945), From the Mixed-Up Files of Mrs. Basil E. Frankweiler by E. L. Konigsburg (Atheneum, 1967), Vera and Bill Cleaver's Where the Lilies Bloom (Lippincott, 1969), and Pippi Longstocking by Astrid Lindgren (reissued in paper by Viking, 1969). Padding our Positive-Image list a bit we might add commendable classics like Lewis Carroll's Alice in Wonderland (first published in 1865), Anne of Green Gables by Lucy M. Montgomery (Grosset & Dunlap, 1908), and Rebecca of Sunnybrook Farm by Kate Douglas Wiggin (Macmillan, 1903). Of course there are some positive books that escaped our notice, just as some of the negative ones may have slipped by, but we wanted to cover a fourth and extra category that seems to overlap all the others.

Especially for Girls

This category appears on a number of publishers' lists and on lists of recommended books. It's called "especially for girls." The reason advanced by librarians and publishers for having such a category at all is that while girls are perfectly happy to read "boys' " books, no self-respecting boy will read books about girls.

In our male-dominated society, unfortunately, this is probably true. But listing a separate group of books for girls provides boys with a list of books not to read, further polarizing the sexes.

There seems only one possible justification for a separate category of books for girls: to spot and recommend those books which, according to our highest, most stringent feminist standards are not sexist. Pursuing this logic, when children's literature no longer supports sexism, there will no longer be any reason to list books "especially for girls."

The current lists of girls' books promoted by publishers, show a preponderance of stories about love, dating, and romance. And there are the companion books about young girls with problems like shyness, overweight, glasses, acne, and so on, that are supposed to interfere with romance. Certainly, problems facing young girls should be dealt with in the books they read, but we resent the implication forced on young girls that romance is the only fulfilling future for them. Boys, too, are involved in romance, but their books are about other things.

The lists for girls also include career books about nurses, secretaries, ballet dancers, stewardesses. Why not more female doctors? Bosses? Pilots? Aquanauts? Present books simply reinforce the sex roles imposed by society--and even then virtually all the careers end in a cop-out. When the girl marries she gives up the career. But must marriage and career be mutually exclusive? These books are justified by their publishers in terms of the market--they are meant to sell rather than to edify. We happen to believe that career books that edify will also sell, and far more lastingly, as women gain in the struggle for their freedom.

But what about those lists of currently recommended books that are intended to edify? In 1969, for example, the Child Study Association listed eight books "Especially for Girls." Of all of these, we were disheartened to find that only one was free--or almost free--of sexism. Two more were Cop-Out books. The rest were middling to very bad.

Let's start with the best. The Motoring Millers by

Alberta Wilson Constant (Crowell, 1969) not only shows delightful girls and women behaving responsibly and delight-
fully--and doing many things the men do, but the question of
sex roles is specifically aired. In the story, the winner of
an auto race turns out to be a young girl. When the wife
of a college president says to her: "I want you to know
that I am highly in favor of your driving in this race. Wom-
en should advance their cause in every field," the winner
replies, "I didn't think about that. I just love to drive.
Taught myself on our one-cylinder Trumbull when I was
ten." We welcome both reactions.

     Two more books on this list, A Girl Called Al and
Next Door to Xanadu, have already been described above as
Cop-Outs, though we did consider them both almost commendable. To those three acceptable books, we would also
add Julie's Decision by Rose A. Levant (Washburn, 1969)
except that we were disturbed by what seemed a paternalistic
white attitude especially inappropriate in a book about a
black girl.

     But, after these titles, the CSA girls' list deterio-
rates into sexism. It is shocking to find "recommended for
girls" a book like The Two Sisters by Honor Arundel
(Meredith, 1969), which not only reinforces the stereotype of
girls as romantic, clothes-crazy, and spendthrift, but whose
moral says that, when all is said and done, love is a
woman's proper vocation and her future ought to be subor-
dinated to her husband's. The young heroine in The Two
Sisters has just told her father that she may abandon her
university scholarship to follow her husband who has gone
off to find a better job in another city. Her father says
gently: "Geoff's quite right to be ambitious and you're
right not to stand in his way. A man who doesn't get a
chance to fulfill his ambition makes a terrible husband."
It doesn't occur to either that a woman who sacrifices her
potential can also end up making a terrible wife.

     John Rowe Townsend's Hell's Edge (Lothrop, 1969)
is just as bad. The motherless teenage heroine cooks all
the meals and does the housework for her teacher-father,
whose domestic ineptitude is paraded as one of his endearing
qualities. A pair of sisters in the book are set up with
mutually exclusive stereotyped female traits--and then shot
down for them. One is described as a "half-wit" for being
concerned with looks and clothes; the other sister, a book-
worm, is denigrated for not caring about her looks or

clothes.   Damned if you do and damned if you don't.

In another CSA recommendation, the boys in the family are considered more important than the girls, even though the book is supposedly for girls.   (Well, it happens in real life too!)   The name of that prize is <u>One to Grow On</u> by Jean Little (Little, Brown, 1969).

In <u>A Crown for a Queen</u> by Ursula Moray Williams (Meredith, 1969), the plot revolves around--get ready--a beauty contest with the boys as judges!   The most memorable (and most offensive) line occurs when the heroine, Jenny, finally get the beauty crown.   As we might predict, she "never felt happier in her life."   This is scarcely the positive female image we'd be looking for, even if we could all be beauty queens.

As our consciousness of "woman's place" changes, our recommendations of books for girls must change.   As must books themselves.   Eventually, we will have no more need for any list recommended "Especially for Girls."

ON THE VAGARIES OF CHILD-CARE BOOKS

by Shirley Olofson

Reprinted by permission from American Libraries, December 1970, p. 1036-1044.

Soranus, writing anxiously in the second century on the topic of the baby's first bath, sounds very modern in his insistence that his way, an immediate and thorough salting, is the only way to bathe a child, and woe to the children of the Germans and Sythians who persist in their ridiculous habit of plunging their neonates into cold water, to say nothing of other poor babes who are bathed in brine and wine. [1]

Despite the fact that few studies show any scientific justification for the continuous fluctuations of child-rearing practices in child-care literature, [2] these vacillations, coupled with repeated dire warnings for the child whose parents fail to follow the most modern practices comprise the most conspicuous characteristic of child care publications. The middle-class mother, to whom the greatest amount of this advice is aimed, must put up with dozens of nagging, urging, threatening voices, all squabbling with each other, and all more than willing to place the total responsibility for society's ills squarely on her shoulders. Population explosion to one side, is it any wonder we hear so much about abortion on demand?

If one looks for comfort to the theory that while parents may well read these books, when the chips are down they will forget all admonitions and revert to their own natural ways, one is soon disabused of such comfort. The image of infants in the 1920s tied to beds, spread-eagle, to prevent them from sucking their little thumbs, or touching their little bodies, even from rubbing their little thighs together, [3] is enough to set one sucking one's own thumb. Were that not enough, sociological studies show that class patterns of child-rearing practices changed in the early

294

1940s, when middle-class mothers became more permissive.[4]
According to Bronfenbrenner:[5]

> ... mothers not only read these books but take
> them seriously, and ... their treatment of the
> child is affected accordingly. Moreover, middle-
> class mothers not only read more but are also
> more responsive; they alter their behavior earlier
> and faster than their working-class counterparts.

It might seem that mankind would, by this time, have
come up with some immutable laws governing child care,
but this has not been the case. It is not the case because
society, and the views of its members, are subject to change,
and child-rearing practices are governed by society's conception of (1) the basic nature of the child; (2) the ideal
adult member of the society; and (3) the procedures needed
to turn the child into the ideal adult.[6] Each of these concepts is subject to variation, and all are related to other
conditions, such as economic trends, scientific knowledge,
attitudes toward sex, or the society's place at any given
time on the war-peace continuum.

During colonial Puritan times, the child was thought
to be depraved from birth, and if left to develop naturally,
it was thought he would become a pleasure-seeking adult,
covered with snake tracks. The ideal adult of that time,
however, was pious, industrious, and disciplined. To
change the baby beast to the ideal adult could only be accomplished by imposing hard work, denial of the pleasures
of the flesh, rigid discipline, and plenty of hell-fire and
brimstone. The child must, at any cost, be "broken, "
and many of them were.[7]

Since Puritan times there has been remarkably little
change in the concept of the ideal adult; he remains responsible, moral, and hard working. According to Winch,
"It is true that there have been some changes, such as
the evaluation of spontaneity--disapproved, officially at least,
in Puritan culture and approved, officially at least, in contemporary middle-class culture--but there appears to be a
large core of middle-class ethic on which all generations
have agreed. "[8] Winch goes on to point out that there has
been a considerable amount of variation in the concept of
the basic nature of the child, ranging from little devil to
little angel and points between. The third concept, the procedures by which the child becomes an adult, is especially

susceptible to change, based as it now is on medical knowledge and psychological insight, which is often cited but
rarely tested by the writers of child-care books.

Robert Sunley has examined the child-care literature
during the forty years preceding the Civil War.   The rubber nipple was patented in 1845, and the first acceptable
formula was developed around 1860.[9]   But the big problem
was not whether to breast or bottle feed, but whether the
mother herself should nurse the baby or turn that job over
to a wet nurse.   As it is in the twentieth century, advice
in the nineteenth was contradictory, ranging from indulgent
treatment to stern discipline.   "Solitary prayer and Bible
reading were proposed to counteract the child's desire to
masturbate."[10]   It is not clear whether it was the mother
or the child who was supposed to do the praying and reading.

The 1890s were the salad days of motherhood, when
mother knew best and she could tend her children without
fear of contradiction from authorities, secure in the thought
that her instincts were right.   According to Celia Stendler,[11]
who analyzed the literature from women's periodicals from
1890 to about 1950, the mother of the 1890s was primarily
concerned with the development of good moral character,
and the term "well-adjusted personality" had not yet been
developed.   "Good moral character" included courtesy,
honesty, orderliness, industriousness, and generosity.   The
Christian home was imperative; the mother supreme.   A
loose schedule was advocated for the child, and "discipline"
involved the use of rewards, rather than punishments.[12]
Feeding procedures were not seen as related to personality
and character development.

In general, this same pattern continued in the early
1900s; character development was often discussed, and a
good home was usually the means to that end.   "Love,
petting, and indulgence will not hurt a child if at the same
time he is taught to be unselfish and obedient.   Love is the
mighty solvent," one editor wrote.[13]   But, beginning in the
1900s, another, older theme also became evident; children
were getting away with too much, and discipline was again
interpreted to mean punishment.   Ridicule, restraints, and
pepper on the liar's tongue were deemed proper disciplinary
measures.

From 1890 to 1910 God was seen both as the pro-
vider of little children and the parents' help in raising them;

following 1910 such references rarely appear.[14] With the
disappearance of God, however, all hell began to break
loose. While in 1900 only 22 percent of the child-care
books advocated strict scheduling, by 1910, fully 77 percent
did. Though there was still an emphasis on good character
development, love was no longer the proper disciplinary
procedure.[15] Martha Wolfenstein, who studied the 1914,
1921, 1929, 1938, 1942, 1945, and 1951 editions of the
United States Children's Bureau's Infant Care, found that "In
this first period, 1914-21, the danger of the child's auto-
erotic impulses was acutely felt."[16] More was needed to
combat this than mere solitary prayer, and mechanical restraints, including binding the child hand and foot, were
suggested. As for nail biting, Stendler cites the following
quotation: "Get some white cotton gloves and make her
wear these all the time--even in school. They will not only
serve as a reminder but also will make her ashamed when
people ask her about them."[17] Obedience was to be exacted
at all times. Love, especially physical manifestations of it,
were discouraged, for too much would "lead to precocity in
the older child and dullness in the man."[18]

There are several possible reasons for this sudden
change in child-rearing advice. Stendler cites the turn-of-
the-century zeal for reform, combined with the fight against
the high infant mortality rate then prevalent. Whatever the
reasons, this new dogma was advanced "just as vigorously
and positively as the previous one, and with just as little
scientific backing for it."[19]

By 1920 the child-care media were unanimously in
favor of early toilet training, rigid schedules, and ignoring
the child's screams of protest. Women had the vote, and
many of the periodical articles were devoted to child welfare, child labor, and child health. Articles on physical
development focused primarily on nutritional problems.[20]
The love of scheduling had become intense, and handling
the infant was forbidden, not because it would lead to "precocity," but because Watsonian behaviorism led to the interpretation that to pick up a crying child would condition
him to crying.[21] A baby would be properly trained if
everything was done strictly by the clock. Freud's influence
was also felt, and mothers were warned against "any act
tending to produce in after years, what the psychoanalysts
call infantile fixation."[22]

These influences were heightened by the great in-

crease in the prestige of science during the twenties and
thirties; moreover, the twenties had brought the era of the
flapper, and young women looked with scorn on their grand-
mothers' ideas of child care as old-fashioned and unscien-
tific. 23   The apex of antiseptic rigidity, however, was
reached in the 1930s. Interest in physical development
reached a high, and, for the first time, the emphasis was
on personality rather than character development.   Severity
was still the guide word, but the focus had shifted from
autoeroticism to bowel training; regularity in all things
had become the thing.   The baby was now seen as capable,
if not carefully controlled, of dominating his parents.   A
child was properly trained only if he lost the struggle for
dominance. 24

But even in the thirties, new voices were joining
the chorus, piping a new tune for mothers to dance to.
Among them was Karl Menninger who stressed, for the
first time, the child's emotional adjustment and new,
psychological principles of child rearing.   By 1940, personality development came charging to the forefront, and,
although about a third of the child-care articles still advocated modified behaviorism, two-thirds championed self-
regulatory, permissive procedures. 25   Wolfenstein notes
that the baby of the forties was "remarkably harmless, in
effect devoid of sexual or dominating impulses.   His main
active aim was to explore his world; autoeroticism was an
incidental by-product ... the baby needs attention and care
... mildness is advocated in all areas; weaning and toilet
training are to be accomplished later and more gently. "

These trends continued into the 1950s, but parents
began to have some misgivings.   Perhaps, after all, it
was not so much what you did, but the spirit in which you
did it, that was all-important.   The main emphasis in the
fifties was on the mother's reactions, rather than the child's
actions.   It was all right for the child to touch himself, but
if it bothered the mother she could give him a toy to hold.
And the squabbling voices rang full force in the mother's
ears: "Something must be wrong with you if it bothers you;
look to yourself, for if your child has problems, it is because you are incapable of loving him.   You must be giving
your child an unhealthy love, what's wrong with you that you
smother him?"

An examination of parental roles in the U. S. reveals that

women have traditionally been the less moral sex, sym-
bolized by poor Eve, who, after all, was just a little
hungry, so to speak, and a trifle bit rebellious toward
authority. In the Puritan culture it was the father who
laid down the law and parents in the 1860s were concerned
that the baby might be fretful if the "mother's ill-governed
passions [were] transmitted through the milk."[26] But then,
mothers were not really very necessary, since wet nurses
were available.

By the 1890s, however, the mother had achieved a
status never reached before or since. The father, con-
taminated by the outside business world, was no longer fit
to guide his children, or so they said.[27] With a change
from an agricultural to a business economy, the father was
also away from the home more, and someone had to take
care of those children, and child-care publications are
very good at finding moral justifications for defining the
mother's role. Why tell mommy she's stuck home with the
kids because daddy is just too busy, when you tell her instead that she is fulfilling the highest human calling. As
one authority put it: "the roots of all pure love, of piety
and honor must spring from this home.... No honor can
be higher than to know that she has built such a home ...
to preside there with such skill that husband and children
will rise up and call her blessed is nobler than to rule an
empire...."[28] Pretty heady stuff, unless you really want
to rule an empire.

Having once established the mother role, and given
her a divine instinct for caring for her children, the experts were left in a quandary. If mother is divinely in-
stinctive, why does she need experts? Unfortunately it
didn't take the experts long to resolve that problem. Those
noble, loving mothers obviously needed help in curbing that
noble love, and help with the many mechanical things that
mom couldn't really keep tucked away in her tiny mind--
things like how to tell time so that she wouldn't vary five
minutes one way or another in the time she put the child
on the pot.

A couple of decades later, however, a new problem
arose. Through a superior educational system, mothers had
finally learned to tell time, and had learned to deny the
children their love. So what's a poor expert to do? That's
easy to figure out, if you're an expert. You look around
and discover that some children are unhappy, and that not

all adults are perfect, and you conclude that since it was
established without a doubt in 1890 that mothers are responsible for the raising and well being of their children,
whatever goes wrong with the children is mother's fault.
And thus began a thorough face slapping that continues to
the present time, leaving the poor ladies with rosy cheeks,
reeling heads, and quaking insecurities, stripped in public
of their divine instincts.

The period from the mid-1930s to the mid-1940s has
been characterized by Clark Vincent as the "baby's decade"
--a time when the authority and ideas of the mother "Become secondary to ... baby's demands ... [and] 'Momism'
and cherchez la mère become thematic. "29   During the
1950s the mother was obliged to "enjoy" her baby, and to
psychoanalyze herself if she didn't.   No longer was everyone
worried about what the baby did, and what could be done to
prevent him from doing it, but almost everyone was worried
about why it bothered the mother, and almost everyone worried the mother about it.   And she, having been raised by
the book to be inhibited by her mother, was left holding the
baby.

A curious underlying theme in many recent books on
child care is that the father's role is completed at the moment of conception.   Homan does not mean to suggest to us
that "fathers need be companions to their young, " but does
suggest that the "actual physical presence of the father is
not nearly so necessary as ... his strength and his backing
of the mother. "30   If this view is to be accepted, certainly
it can be advanced in the same way that the mother's role
is completed at the moment of delivery.   This logical connection is glossed over, however, for someone has to take
care of the infant, and the experts, most of them male, are
certain that that "someone" must be mother.

The experts, not usually overconcerned with scientific evidence, can back up their claims, in this case, with
scientific proof.   One of the most widely cited studies to
confirm without doubt that the mother's place is in the
home, is that of H. F. Harlow who studied the responses
of infant monkeys.   He placed newborn monkeys with surrogate mothers made of wire and pieces of rag, equipped
with feeding devices.   Never given access to a real mother,
these babies grew up to be weird adults, and their mating
and maternal reactions were unfavorably affected. 31   This
proves, ignoring studies on human beings which reach con-

trary conclusions, that mother's place is in the home, not in the factory. [32] In actual fact, fewer than fifty percent of the working mothers in America today place their newborn infants in rooms with wire and rag monkeys and leave them there until adulthood. This important statistic is generally overlooked by the experts, though.

Nevertheless, throwing their hands up in despair, some authorities are beginning to admit that some women may want to work and there's not much they can do about it, except saddle them with gigantic guilt complexes.

> It is unfortunate when mothers decide to leave their babies.... What the mother can give to her baby--and gain from him in pleasure--is hard to replace. The months of infancy go so fast, and can never be recaptured. If however, you decide that you must go out to work, make the best plans for the baby that you can. Perhaps the baby's grandmother can take over without any particular stress or upset to him, since, actually, he never leaves the home.

> Finding someone outside the home to take care of a baby isn't easy at all.... Finding the right person to look after your baby isn't all that is involved, however. Unless you have a great deal of energy, you are apt to find the care of the baby at night and weekends, plus the care of the household, too much.... So many things seem to take precedence over the welfare of the baby, and you may begin to feel worn out and ineffective in every sphere of life. Furthermore, you may find that you have very little money left over after you have paid for his care, your clothes, lunches, and transportation.

> Despite all this, some mothers are going to work outside their homes, and in all fairness it should be noted that some are considerably happier at a job than having the full-time care of a baby. A mother who finds that the unrelieved caring for her baby is too confining may be able to enjoy him more if she has the satisfactions of a job. [33]

This author, writing in the most recent edition of Infant Care, is charitable, though he slaps with a heavy

hand.   Ginott feels that some families may be able to handle
two careers, but cites the dangers in homes where traditional roles of women are not followed. [34]   Girls "may become competitive and feel compelled to outdo the boys, and
later the men, at their own game, " which isn't particularly
upsetting, since one has only to ask who defined whose game
to begin with, but he goes on to suggest that boys "may try
to overcompensate and to prove their masculinity by drinking,
promiscuity, delinquency, or cruelty to women. "

       It is accepted, in general, that women in the lower
class will work out of necessity, and that upper-class wom-
en will have nursemaids, and no one worries much about
the effect on their children.   One wonders why such apprehension is placed, therefore, on the specter of the working,
middle-class mother.   One would not presume to suggest
that authorities in the middle class fear the competition of
middle-class women for middle-class jobs, had not Ginott
said:

> While there should be sufficient flexibility for a
> person of either sex to find fulfillment in any
> occupational or political role, life is easier when
> most men and women are not engaged in mutual
> competition and rivalry. [35]

The current trend in child care reflects the sum of the historical vacillation.   Masturbation is still a casual activity,
and though some mention is made occasionally of the dangers
of habitual masturbation, there is also the implication that
a moderate amount may aid in normal sexual development.
Parents are encouraged to begin toilet training as late as
two years, rather than during the first month.   Emphasis
is put on the child's inability to be trained to do anything
until he is physically developed enough to do it.

       Where formerly critics of the literature traced many
practices to Freudian influence, they are now beginning to
doubt the effect of Freud, and Gordon suggests the "Maytag
Hypothesis":   later toilet training may be influenced by the
increasing numbers of homes having washing machines. [36]
If this is the case, the advent of disposable diapers may
further revolutionize toilet training.   Some critics find a
movement away from the permissive, developmental theories
of child raising, and there may be evidence to support this
hypothesis in the periodical literature, though an analysis of

recent editions of Spock's <u>Baby and Child Care</u>, and the
Children's Bureau's <u>Infant Care</u>, do not bear this out. [37]

The baby is now seen variously as a mechanism subject to developmental rules; as a lump with few inherited
characteristics to be molded eventually by his environment;
or, as a being complete at birth with everything but experience. The home, and especially the mother, though
society itself is not completely ignored, becomes the production line for turning the raw material into the finished
adult. How best to accomplish this manufacture of adults
depends, still, on the prejudices of the experts, but the emphasis is on good health care and the development of the
child's personality, emotions, intellect, imagination, and
psyche. Mothers are still threatened with dire consequences
should they depart from the paths of righteousness cleared
by the authorities, though Smith and Gersh seem notably
willing to let them off the hook, and the dreaded consequences now seem less that the child will end up constipated,
dull, or over-sexed, than that he will grow up unable to adapt
to his sexual role, in any or all of its aspects.

It is difficult to categorize the current child-care
books, because they tend to overlap so much in content.
For our purposes, however, we can break them down into
several classifications: those which offer general advice on
the several aspects of child care or "complete" child-care
books; those which put the main emphasis on the child's
psychological development, including his relations with his
parents; those which focus on the child's physical growth and
development; and a miscellaneous category of books which are
not actually child-care books, but which may be of interest
to parents who are too blasé to want to read child-care
books, but who have a guilty compunction to read <u>something</u>
about children.

It is fitting, in our consideration of the complete
child-care book, to begin with Newton I. Kugelmass' <u>Wis-
dom with Children: The Complete Guide to Your Child's
Development, Well Being and Care.</u> Dr. Kugelmass is the
author of many books on children, including <u>Growing Superior Children</u>, and <u>Superior Children Through Modern
Nutrition</u>, and seems to draw together, in <u>Wisdom with
Children</u>, philosophies from the past fifty years. The first
section of the work is devoted to general child care up to
adolescence, and is fairly standard in content. The second
section is more valuable in that it gives detailed information

on childhood diseases. In general, however, the book seems
to have been written in a time-wrinkle. He supplies some
of the most up-to-date advice on the role of the father,
stating flatly that there is nothing unmasculine about helping
with the baby, and that to do so is very rewarding, and then
turns about and recommends beginning toilet training at the
age of four months, repeating "the procedure in the same
room, on the same pot, at the same time every day."[38]
He recommends letting pre-school children see their parents
nude, which most authorities would find too potentially
"stimulating," but his section on masturbation is a nightmare.
In this section the author dreams that he believes the modern view that masturbation is harmless; he even says that
it will produce no ill effects, illness, or impotence. But
he cannot maintain this illusion. "When you find a child
indulging in the habit, treat the matter casually. Interrupt
the act by separating the legs or removing the hand from
that area of the body."[39] "The practice is contrary to
nature's plan."[40] Masturbation may prevent the child from
finding friends or engaging in normal heterosexual relationships; it may make women frigid; the expenditure of energy
is wasteful--but, all in all, it's perfectly normal and you
shouldn't make your child feel guilty about it. This peculiar dream-like quality makes this book recommended
reading.

        Dr. Willis J. Potts' Your Wonderful Baby: A
Practical Approach to Baby and Child Care (303 pp. Rand
McNally, 1966) is a practical approach to baby and child
care. Though he discusses parent-child relations, discipline, and the like, the treatment is brief and very general, unlike Spock's detailed instructions. Probably the
most valuable sections of the book are those dealing with
diseases, such as heart disease and cancer, which are not
usually covered in child-rearing literature.

        If one were consigned by some sadistic fate to
raising one's children on a desert isle with the assistance
of only one child-care book, he would do well to select
Marvin J. Gersh's How to Raise Children at Home in Your
Spare Time (223 pp. Stein and Day, 1966); he might even,
in his spare time, illuminate the title and change it to How
to Raise Children on a Desert Isle in Your Spare Time.
He would select the book on the basis of its humor and
readability, its sufficiency of practical medical and child-
care advice, and, every bit as much, on its relaxed tone,
for here is one book that tells its readers, "Don't feel

guilty, just relax and enjoy it, " a message just as relevant, even vital, on a desert island as in a suburban tract house. Gersh's work is certainly a candidate for the best child-care book since Soranus; it is perhaps even better, for he not only doesn't recommend rubbing the newborn with salt, he manages to see through most of the old experts' tales which have been used to frighten parents for lo these many years. It takes a lot of courage, though, for a parent to relax these days, so if you're a bit chicken you might sneak Spock, disguised perhaps as a Shakespearian folio, into your luggage before departing for that desert island.

Speaking of Shakespeare, Spock's Baby and Child Care (620 pp., Pocket Books Original, revised edition, 1968) is the number one non-fiction best seller of all time, next to Shakespeare and the Bible, which might indicate that child care is running third to drama and religion. It is popular to decry Spock's permissiveness, though he did not invent permissiveness and does not advocate any more extreme permissiveness than most other writers. Some claim that the revised edition is less permissive than previous issues, others claim that there is no change except that he is more strict about monitoring violent television programs. It doesn't really matter very much, since almost everyone who has children will be buying Spock anyway, for use as a reference tool if nothing else. He covers all phases of child care and development, and covers them thoroughly and in an easy-to-use format. Not having Spock in the home would seem almost as uncouth as leaving out the Bible and Shakespeare.

Ronald S. Illingworth starts right out in The Normal Child: Some Problems of the First Five Years and Their Treatment (380 pp., Little, Brown & Company, 4th ed., 1968) and within seconds is discussing statistics on breast feeding. He concludes immediately, in his sparse style, that any woman who really wants to can breast feed her baby. He goes on for almost four hundred pages, discussing medical and psychological problems in normal children, handling each problem with dispatch and conciseness. The book was written for health professionals, but may be easily understood by an educated layman with access to a medical dictionary, if he has never cultivated the ability to skip over the big words. The layman who has relied on Spock may find Illingworth refreshingly straightforward, and, since the book was written for doctors, may be relieved not to be constantly told to call his doctor when in doubt. And there

are some really bright moments. For instance, on page 6,
following a terse answer to the question "When should the
baby be put to the breast?", we are treated to a one-line
paragraph which puts everything in its proper perspective:
"Piglets start sucking before the last of the litter is born."

The United State Children's Bureau's Infant Care
(229 pp., Prentice-Hall, 1968, supplements and annotations
by Frederick W. Goodrich) has, as we have seen, been
coming out at irregular intervals since 1914, and provides
a kind of thermometer of the child-care climate. Since it
hopes to reach parents with a variety of educational backgrounds, it makes a special effort to be easily understood
and it also tries to avoid advocating any one particular
system. As quoted earlier, Infant Care, though it does
not really like the idea of women working, still is in the
avant garde among child-care books in its recognition that
women will work, and that some will receive great satisfaction from working.

Lendon H. Smith (The Children's Doctor, 226 pp.,
Prentice-Hall, 1969) emphasizes that all too often in the
past mothers have been encouraged to doubt themselves and
their handling of their children, and to treat a child's problems as emotional in origin while actually they are the result
of the child's genetic background, neurological damage, aller-
gies, or other actual physical defect. When this happens, and
he lambastes women's magazines for their hand in it, it is a
tragedy for the parents and the child. This is an exceptionally
witty and well-written book, covering all aspects of child
care. It includes "Yellow Pages," which cover in alphabetical order the headings "Emergencies," "Diseases," and
"Conditions and Definitions," a wide range of medical problems. He provides a "Developmental Map," and a chart entitled "Four Categories of Sick Children," in which he describes symptoms and then gives both possible physical
causes and the contributing factors, and finally suggests
treatment, including drugs which may control the problem.
You might do well to sneak this one onto that island, along
with Gersh and Spock.

A three-page foreword to Your Child From 1 to 12
(303pp., Signet, 1970) by Lee Salk, Ph.D., does not dis-
guise the fact that this book, copyright 1970, is actually an
apparent verbatim reprinting of three earlier United States
Children's Bureau publications, A Healthy Personality for
Your Child (1952), Your Child from 1 to 6 (1962), and

<u>Your Child from 6 to 12</u> (1966). These three publications
are available from the Superintendent of Documents for a
total of 65¢, thirty cents less than the Signet book. The
government publications acknowledge the contributors, authors,
and sources, which the Signet volume neglects to do, and
have illustrations, which are missing from the Signet volume. Other than that, the book is a fairly standard treatment of child care, physical and psychological development,
and illnesses.

One of the better books on psychological development,
now over ten years old, is Selma H. Fraiberg's <u>The Magic</u>
<u>Years</u> (305 pp. , Scribner's, 1959). It is still an excellent
book which goes far beyond merely providing case studies
and solutions; it goes into the child's own mind:

> The anxieties of the two-year-old are not the
> same as the anxieties of the five-year-old. Even
> if the same crocodile hides under the bed of one
> small boy between the ages of two and five, the
> crocodile of the two-year-old is not the same
> beast as the crocodile of the five-year-old--from
> the psychological point of view. He's had a chance
> to grow with the boy and is a lot more complex
> after three years under the bed than he was the
> day he first moved in. Furthermore, what you do
> about the crocodile when the boy is two is not
> the same as what you do about him when the boy
> is five. [41]

The book covers, in chronological order, the years
from one to six, and provides insights which are both provocative and helpful. By all means take it along to the
island.

Haim G. Ginott's <u>Between Parent and Child</u> (224 pp. ,
Macmillan, 1965) is variously praised for being simple and
clear, and condemned for being simplistic kitsch; the
kitsch side seems to have the preponderance of scientific
weight. His motivations are certainly good: to help the
parent see the child as a human being, to respond to the
child's feelings rather than to what he says, and to reflect
his emotions to the child, thereby improving communications.
But one must certainly have many reservations. Ginott
says, "The single most important rule is that praise deals
only with the child's efforts and accomplishments, not with
his character and personality. "[42] That sounds fine, but one

can hear other voices shouting, "You will make your child
believe that you love him only for his accomplishments, and
not for himself." Moreover, his "childrenese" takes the
form of countless sample dialogues between the parent and
the child, balancing Ginott's way, the good way, against the
usual way, the bad way. The bad way, when the child
enters the home upset, is to ask what happened. The good
way is to define the child's feelings for him, saying, usually,
"You are angry." Ginott does not approve of telling a child
that he is bad because it may make him define himself as
bad, and yet it would seem that constantly defining the child,
to the child, as angry, might well define the world to him
as a hostile place. If the child were not angry, but frustrated or anxious, or any number of other things, he might
easily come to the conclusion that his parents don't understand him. Perhaps Ginott can always define the child's
emotional state accurately, but it's doubtful that anyone else
can. And somehow, it seems an invasion of privacy to try.

Ginott's Between Parent and Teenager (256 pp.,
Macmillan, 1969) is a rehash of his previous book for an
older age level, and it suffers from the same problems,
and once below the surface, seems filled with platitudes
which ignore the intelligence and complexity of the children
with which it attempts to deal.

William E. Homan, in Child Sense: A Pediatrician's
Guide for Today's Families (305 pp., Bantam Books, 1969)
leaps on the bandwagon by promising to tell parents what
Spock and Ginott didn't tell about bringing up today's children. He fails to do that, unless his outpouring of prejudices fills the void. One cannot argue with the premise
that love, discipline, and independence form the tripod of
factors indispensable to the child's development, but this
is hardly new, and one must be skeptical of many of the
methods he urges. Unlike Ginott, he believes in praising
the child for what he is, rather than what he does; on the
other hand, you should disapprove of what he does, not of
who he is. The most unsettling aspect of the book is the
author's underlying urging to lie to the child. Tell each
child he is your favorite, and be assured that he will either
not catch on, or, if he does, will prefer the lie and fail to
acknowledge it. Tell the adopted child he was personally
chosen, though this is rarely the case. Tell the child of
divorced parents that the other parent was "different,
strange, atypical, sick, and not in any way representative
of parents in general." Homan sees no inconsistency in

"knocking a child across the room for misbehavior and then ... putting your arms around him, and telling him what a fine boy he is and how much you love him. " No inconsistency perhaps, but a fine training ground for masochism, as those other voices might say.

A short and simple guide on child growth and development is C. Anderson Aldrich and Mary M. Aldrich's Babies are Human Beings (112 pp. , Collier Books, 1954). It starts with the premise that children are born with certain characteristics that they retain through life.   Within hours after birth, one child is calm and quiet, another is active and noisy, and they stay that way.   The infant is controlled by reflexes originating in the lower levels of the mid-brain or in the spinal cord, and his first behavior is involuntary. As he grows his system develops and gradually his mind assumes control; this is a slow and orderly process which cannot be rushed.   Therefore, the child cannot, for instance, be toilet trained until he has gained control over those systems.   Developmental books in particular and child-care books in general, suffer from a quandary over developmental schedules.   Most such schedules are based on Arnold Gesell's early studies in child development, which do not seem particularly realistic in today's world of better nutrition and Sesame Street.   Nevertheless, child-care experts, and parents, are strongly attracted to developmental schedules on the one hand.   On the other hand, the authorities do not want to frighten their readers into believing that their children are retarded, nor encourage them to think their children are exceptionally bright.   Aldrich and Aldrich solve this problem by presenting a developmental schedule broken down into behavioral sets rather than time periods.

The Gesell Institute's Child Behavior (370 pp. , Perennial Library, 1955), by Frances L. Ilg and Louise Bates Ames, follows the same general philosophy as the Aldrich work, but in much greater depth.   Though it warns against taking time tables too seriously, it does break development down into "ages and stages, " defining cycles of behavior. In the first cycle behavior is in good equilibrium; each of these smooth and untroubled times is followed by periods where behavior is broken and troubled.   The authors appear to accept Sheldon's theories of the somatotypes, which have not been held in much scientific favor for many years. This book traces not only the child's general development, but goes into psychological aspects of sexual development,

familial relationships, discipline, and similar subjects.
Following Gesell, they recommend full development tests
before children are placed for adoption, a practice frowned
upon by most modern adoption agencies, since it keeps a
child from parental care until the tests, which are not always fool-proof, are completed.

The Gesell Institute's Parents Ask (510 pp., Dell,
1962) by the same authors is called the companion volume
to Child Behavior. It is a collection of letters divided by
subject, received over the years by the authors, with their
answers. Many of the questions relate to behavior so unusual as to be of little interest to the general reader,
though information may not be available on these problems
in other publications. The answers commonly reflect the
developmental bias, and the reader wonders that the authors
are so free with advice about children they've never seen.

While most child-care books concentrate on the early
childhood as the formative years, operating primarily on a
psychological basis, many other disciplines have contributed
important insights and data, and it is unfortunate these have
been generally ignored in the popular child-care publications.
The Growth and Development of the Young Child (528 pp.,
W. B. Saunders Company, eighth ed., 1969) by Marian E.
Breckenridge and Margaret Nesbitt Murphy, is a textbook
which draws together knowledge from the fields of biology,
psychology, sociology, education, anthropology, nutrition,
medicine, and psychiatry. It provides an in-depth approach
to child development, backed up with studies from these
disciplines presented without the usual biases. This book
should go along to the desert isle to bring the light of science to the dark ages of guesswork.

Though it might fit under any one of several categories, Where's Hannah? A Handbook for Parents and
Teachers of Children with Learning Disorders (272 pp.,
Hart, 1968), is included here because of its excellent and
painstaking description of Hannah's development. The book
tells of the ordeal undergone by Hannah's parents (Jane
Hart, one of the authors, is Hannah's mother) in trying
to obtain diagnosis and help for their child, and details,
often with illustrations, the methods they found for teaching
the child to locate herself, to learn the concepts of space,
and to develop tactual, kinesthetic, auditory, and visual
skills. The success wrought, over time, with Hannah, once
considered hopelessly retarded, should provide encouragement

to parents and teachers of children with learning problems, while offering insights on the learning patterns of normal children.

The following two books are provided here for the sake of parents who would like to read something about children, but would prefer to avoid child-care books, or who, having read child-care books, would like to read something else.

Joan Bel Geddes' Small World: A History of Baby Care from the Stone Age to the Spock Age (281 pp., Macmillan, 1964), is a collection of babylore, history, fact, and fiction about babies and how they have been handled. Considering the vacillation of child-care trends in recent history, one is hardly surprised that children once were given earthworms to eat, but may find the information comforting to reflect upon while watching his child eat earthworms. The book covers practices in various societies in various times related to bearing, naming, nursing and feeding, dressing, bathing, playing with, and bedding down the baby. The section on playtime includes a history of toys. If the fact that Leonardo da Vinci invented an alarm clock that awakened the sleeper by rubbing his feet seems to bear little relationship to child care, that's perfectly all right; who wants to read about child care anyway?

The World of the Child: Birth to Adolescence (457 pp., Doubleday Anchor, 1967), edited by Toby Talbot, is a well-chosen anthology of writings on childhood. Among the contributors are: Ariès, Ortega y Gasset, Rank, Sullivan, Jung, Balint, Piaget, Wolfenstein, Benedict, Anna Freud, Allport, Rousseau, and Shaw, and it is a candidate for an excellent addition to the smuggled desert isle collection.

In conclusion, much is said about child care, but there is little proof that any of it is valid. Were one to take all of the child-care books and separate all that is know to be factual from that which might be called supposition, the factual side of the ledger would be miniscule. Those who wrote popular child-care books rely heavily on their own clinical experience and their own intellectual orientations, ignoring other disciplines. This is unfortunate. Child-care practices generally reflect society as it was, not as it is coming to be. This is also unfortunate. Mothers, bless them, are damned if they do and damned if they don't. But

don't pity the poor mothers; they wanted children, didn't
they? And if they are not individuals enough to tread their
way through the trap wires, then perhaps a little frustration
at the vagaries of child-care books is small enough price to
pay for those children. On the other hand, they could get
good pediatricians and refuse to read child-care books at
all.

Works Cited

1. C. Anderson Aldrich and Mary M. Aldrich, Babies
        are Human Beings (Collier Books, 1954), p. 83.
2. Celia B. Stendler, "Sixty Years of Child Training
        Practices," Journal of Pediatrics, 36:1 (January
        1950), p. 122.
3. Martha Wolfenstein, "Trends in Infant Care," Ameri-
        can Journal of Orthopsychiatry, 23:1 (January
        1953), p. 121.
4. Michael Gordon, "Infant Care Revisited," Journal of
        Marriage and the Family, 30:4 (November 1968),
        p. 578.
5. Urie Bronfenbrenner, "Socialization and Social Class
        Through Time and Space," in Readings in Social
        Psychology, ed. Eleanor Maccoby, Theodore New-
        comb, and Eugene L. Hartley (New York: Holt,
        Rinehart, and Winston, rev. ed., 1958), p. 411.
6. Robert F. Winch, The Modern Family (New York:
        Holt, Rinehart, and Winston, rev. ed., 1963),
        p. 457.
7. Ibid., p. 458.
8. Ibid., p. 466.
9. Ibid., p. 451.
10. Ibid.
11. Stendler, pp. 125-26.
12. Winch, p. 452.
13. Stendler, p. 127.
14. Ibid.
15. Ibid., p. 128.
16. Wolfenstein, p. 121.
17. Stendler, p. 128.
18. Ibid.
19. Ibid., p. 129.
20. Ibid.
21. Winch, p. 543.
22. Stendler, p. 130.
23. Ibid., p. 131.

24. Wolfenstein, p. 121.
25. Stendler, p. 131.
26. Winch, p. 451.
27. Stendler, p. 126.
28. Ibid., p. 125.
29. Winch, p. 453.
30. William E. Homan, Child Sense: A Pediatrician's Guide for Today's Families (Bantam Books, 1969), p. 192.
31. United States Children's Bureau, Infant Care, supplements and annotations by Frederick W. Goodrich (Prentice-Hall, 1968), p. vii.
32. Lois Wladis Hoffman, "Effects of Maternal Employment of the Child," in Sourcebook in Marriage and the Family, ed. Marvin B. Sussman (Boston: Houghton Mifflin Company, second ed., 1963), p. 241.
33. Infant Care, pp. 130-33.
34. Haim G. Ginott, Between Parent and Child (Macmillan, 1965), pp. 175-76.
35. Ibid., p. 177.
36. Gordon, p. 580.
37. Ibid., p. 583.
38. Newton I. Kugelmass, Wisdom with Children: the Complete Guide to Your Child's Development, Well Being and Care (John Day, 1964), p. 29.
39. Ibid., p. 250.
40. Ibid., p. 251.
41. Selma H. Fraiberg, The Magic Years (Scribner's, 1959), p. xi.
42. Ginott, p. 39.

A DIRTY MIND NEVER SLEEPS
AND OTHER COMMENTS ON
THE ORAL HISTORY MOVEMENT

by Peter D. Olch

Reprinted by permission from the Bulletin of the Medical Library Association 59(3) July 1971, p. 438-443.

It is imperative that I begin with an explanation of this title as I am acutely aware of the copyright laws and do not wish to offend the W. W. Norton publishing company or Mr. Max Wilk, the author of a delightful book entitled, A Dirty Mind Never Sleeps. In his humorous work, Max Wilk presents one facet and some of the fervor behind the oral history movement, though one hopes in a purely fictitious manner. For this reason I will quote several passages from Mr. Wilk's book (1).

> Because history is a half truth. How can it be anything else? It's a pile of facts and dates, mixed together with dollops of hypothesis and conjecture. Compounds of legends and old-wives' tales, what archeologists dig up, or what's washed ashore; tomb stones, carvings, and let us not forget, great lacings of propaganda. (Of course the local monks were honest, but you can be damned sure they were not writing down and illuminating anything about Big Duke up in the castle that he might find irritating to himself and Big Duchess. Ah no, sire, those monks knew where their next pot of gold leaf was coming from).
> This is not to say history is fraud.
> (Why am I carrying on like this about history? Flunked it regularly.)
> But I'm beginning to understand why I flunked history.
> Couldn't relate. Read texts and studied maps and charts. Nothing. No essence.

No sense of smell, and frustration, no boils and
nightmares and bitching, sweat, the touch of skin,
the drives--

Began to get some of it out of Shakespeare. But
then began to question him, too.

For instance--what else did Julius Caesar say
when Brutus let him have it?

Et tu Brute?

Brief, poignant, dramatically right. A great
scene for an actor, obviously a crowd-pleaser at
the Mermaid and the Globe.

But--was that all he could think of to say?

To have been there and seen and heard it--not
like "See It Now," with all the actors reading
carefully scripted TV folksy-historic speeches in
response to questions from Mike Wallace and Bill
Leonard--no, I'm thinking and trying to feel
Caesar.

... he probably staggers back with his hand on
the hole in his toga, and gasps, "Why--you treach-
erous bum--after all I've done for you--aach--
and you give me the shaft right here in front of
the whole Senate--whoo, that hurts--like some
plebeian you caught in the sack with your uxor--"

... bang, he hits the floor.

Senators all shaken up--

"Hey, he stabbed Caesar!"

"... He's bleeding like a pig--"

"... What a mess!"

"The old man's dying--"

"Who do you think'll get the Number One spot?"
etc. etc.

That's my kind of history.

What do we really know about--say--Wilbur and
Orville Wright, that day at Kitty Hawk? (Went and
looked that one up. You can read Orville's diary
with its eyewitness description, but it's easy to
see he's holding back on all of the personal stuff.)

It's a chilly December day out on those windy
dunes, and the boys have decided to go for broke.
Orville lying flat on that rickety damned box kite
with a motor, and it rolls along the bumpy ground,
putt-putt-putt, and then all of a sudden, off she
sails, seven crazy miles an hour, up up, and
away! ...what do you think Wilbur said?

"Great Heavens, we are vindicated! All our

labors--our deepest dreams and ambitions and
hopes have come to glorious fruition--our gallant
little craft has conquered the mysterious kingdom
of the Air."

    I'm trying to <u>think</u> Wilbur.   Who wants to bet me
he said something <u>like</u> "Sonofabitch--the damn thing
works!"

    And then--"Dammit, how come my brother <u>al-
ways</u> gets to be first?"

    I'll never sell that version.   Why?

My generation has no Shakespeare.   But it does
have Darryl F. Zanuck and <u>his</u> history lessons.

We're brainwashed every <u>night</u> on the Late Show.

    Play Associations.

    Queen Elizabeth?   Bette Davis.

    Paul Gaugin?   George Sanders.   What did
Henry V look like?   Sir Laurence Olivier.   John
Brown--Raymond Massey.   Henry VIII--Laughton.

George M. Cohan--Cagney.   Abe Lincoln?   Why,
let's see--Henry Fonda the Young and ... Ray-
mond Massey the Old!

    --and the things they said.   Paul Muni and
Spencer Tracy, and the ever-popular Donald
Ameche, all face-haired up, acting out a storm.

"Ach, Sigmund, give opp zis madness of ze mind
and come to bed--tonight all Vienna is laughing at
you, but never mind, liebchen, I believe in you."

"I tell you, Mr. Disraeli, England will never
stand for your lunatic proposal to create a Suez
Canal!"   "...Son, y'see that hill over there?
Well, mebbe I'm jest a-dreamin' a dream, but
someday there's goin' to be a city there, with wide
streets and tall buildings, risin' right up to the
skies, 'n' I'm thinkin' folks'll call it ... <u>Denver.</u>"

"...Mummy, is that Queen Victoria in the <u>box</u> behind the black horses?"   "<u>Shh,</u> yes child."   "...
But Mummy, she was such <u>a little</u> woman..."

"...Rough Riders, we are <u>here at</u> the foot of San
Juan Hill--now I want you to carry our beloved
Stars and Stripes up to the top there--hit the line
hard--<u>bully--</u>charge!"

    That<u>'s</u> history?

. . . .

    I'd like to tune in on the truth.   What some of
those Rough Riders were saying under their breath,

while Teddy was giving them that Cuban pep talk
(the canned bully beef was rotten and how their
guts must have ached). And what about old George
W. at Valley Forge? Stone me, ladies of the
D. A. R. , but did our country's Father really spend
all his time giving out with those chin-up-men
readings? Isn't it possible there was one nasty
night when he blew his cool and yelled (through
his wooden teeth, which didn't fit properly), "All
ri, all ri--we are up the creek--but for God's sake
will one of you stop bitching and go out and chop
some firewood?"

Did Emile Zola ever have writer's block, and
if so, how did he handle it? When Byron quarreled
with Lady Caroline Lamb, were his epithets elegant,
or merely earthy? ... and Napoleon--and I don't
mean Charles Boyer with a spit curl and his hand
fingering his navel, I mean the man--what was he
really like? How did he behave, say, the night
before the retreat from Moscow? Is it possible
that he had a few shots of cognac (the good stuff,
out of his private trunk, not the Army-issue slop),
got slightly bombed, lapsed into maudlin self-pity,
sang, and then groaned, "Bon Dieu, why didn't I
listen to the little cabbage back at Malmaison?
She always told me to stay out of Russia--after
this she will be insufferable!"
... and the guard outside, on duty, freezing in
the Russian night, listening to his Little Cor-
poral belching and singing inside in the warm
tent? I'd like to hear what he said.

I'd like to hear a lot of things. What those
Zealots up on the top of Masada said to each
other when the Roman Legion showed up down below. How Michelangelo must have complained
about the arthritis in his back as he lay there
painting the Sistine Chapel ceiling, and what the
Viking crew was discussing on the seventy-fourth
night of their trip across the Atlantic. The dirty
jokes that must have been passed around the court
while Elizabeth played footsie with Essex, and dear
Adolf's last words (after you, liebchen?) in the
Berlin bunker. The arguments over whose wagon
went where in the line the day before the opening
of the Cherokee Strip, and G. B. S. arguing over

script changes with one of his early managers,
and the complaints of those poor lost kids on the
Children's Crusade....

"Where's all that? That's history--... gone,
all gone.
While it was happening, nobody was collecting
it. It didn't seem important enough, there were
no cassette portable tape recorders, and even if
there had been, everyone was too busy living it
to be bothered.
... the sound of music?
It's the sound of people that matters. People
talking--not for publication, or for an NBC News
mike, but completely off the record, unconsciously,
never suspecting anyone's listening....
It's exhausting to think about doing it.
But that would be history, courtesy of Sony and
Minnesota Mining.

Though amusing, there is in fact a message here.
Surreptitious recording is not a practice of the oral historian, but an important facet of the oral history movement
is to "tell it like it is," to delve beneath the surface of the
prepared and considered statement in order to obtain candid
commentary. Such a goal is quite worthy, if coupled with a
reasonable set of standards which will honor the respondents'
desires for restrictions on access.

I would like to present a brief historical review of
the movement, to discuss the present "state of the art,"
and to share my feeling about the future of oral history.

Dr. Louis M. Starr, the Director of the Columbia
University Oral History Research Office, and one of the
field's most enthusiastic supporters, traces the origin of
the term "oral history" to a certain Bowery character
named Joe Gould who set out on a life-long task of compiling what he called "An Oral History of Our Times."
This was to consist of an endless series of chance remarks,
fleeting bits of conversation as heard and overheard by
this denizen of the Bowery, on every subject under the sun.
(One finds an element of this in Wilk's chapter entitled "The
Old Piano Roll of Life or Sock the Sixties to Me.")   The
biographer of Joe Gould finally concluded that this monumental Oral History was a figment of Gould's fertile imagination, but there was the term recorded for posterity.   In

1948 when Allan Nevins established the first organization at
Columbia to obtain systematically from the lips and papers of
living Americans a fuller record of their participation in
the political, economic, and cultural life of their time, he
selected the name Oral History for the process and it has
remained.

Whatever the origin of the term, two things are
abundantly clear: (1) the term "oral history" is misleading;
and (2) the technique is here to stay. While it is true that
oral history begins with oral narration, usually in the presence of a tape recorder run by the interviewer, the end
product is generally a typewritten transcript, edited, indexed,
bound, and preserved--not as history, but as one man's
views and interpretations of a series of events or individuals
in his recent or distant past. The transcript is, therefore,
a historical resource which we hope will be useful to historians. That it is here to stay is unquestionable, not,
I fear, because of its proven value to scholars or historians,
but because it utilizes a "gimmick" and anyone can learn to
press the "ON" and "RECORD" buttons simultaneously.

From its inception in 1948, the Columbia program
has created the largest collection of oral history transcripts.
Dr. Starr and Elizabeth Mason, his assistant, have traveled
throughout the country as consultants and advisors to most of
the later programs to appear on the scene. In 1965 Columbia published a list of ninety-two oral history programs in
the United States (2). There probably are more than double
that number now.

In 1966, James V. Mink, the Archivist of the University of California, Los Angeles, and his colleagues in
the UCLA Oral History Program, put out a call nationally
for all parties involved or interested in oral history to
assemble at Lake Arrowhead, California, for the first
National Colloquium on Oral History. Seventy-seven individuals gathered representing academe, industry, government, and religious institutions. Any doubts as to the
existence of varied backgrounds, uses, or purposes of oral
history were confirmed in the session on Objectives and
Standards. Near chaos reigned as the arguments of the tape
savers vs. tape erasers; transcript editors vs. verbatim
transcribers; and concerned archivists and historians vs.
those who owed allegiance to a technique rather than a
discipline, split the cool mountain air in an ever rising
crescendo. The obvious multiplicity of backgrounds and

objectives represented in this group was to be responsible
for the major problems faced by the group while at the
same time greatly contributing to the charm, stimulation,
and unique nature of the membership. The multiplicity of
backgrounds, the lack of agreement on objectives and standards also quickly dampened the attempts of the UCLA con-
tingent to form a national association on the last day of this
meeting at Lake Arrowhead. However, there was no question that the groundwork and foundation had been laid. The
assembled participants agreed they should form an Oral
History Conference, an informal organization without constitution or bylaws, in order to have a confederation permitting oral historians to keep in contact with one another.

In the ensuing year the Steering Committee of the
Oral History Conference published the proceedings of the
Arrowhead meeting and the first of a series of newsletters.
They began to develop a series of "Goals and Guidelines"
for oral history programs and a bibliography of the literature on oral history. This Committee also prepared a constitution and the necessary Articles of Incorporation in the
hope that a permanent organization would be one result of
the second meeting schedules for the fall of 1967 at Arden
House in Harriman, N. Y.

The November meeting was again in a remote conference center where the natural beauty of the location, the
cuisine, and wine list challenged the stimulating presentations
by Henry Steele Commager, Luther H. Evans, Alfred Knopf,
Cornelius Ryan, and others for top billing. Those of the
146 participants who were members of the Oral History Conference reviewed and modified the proposed constitution,
approved the Articles of Incorporation, and selected a slate
of officers, and the entire package was submitted to the full
Conference membership by mail ballot. The prolonged labor
pains of the Oral History Association (OHA) were about to
end, as within a month the organization was voted into
being.

In 1968 eighty-nine participants gathered in Lincoln,
Nebraska, to hear a program featuring William Manchester,
Walter Lord, and James Rhoads, the Archivist of the United
States, and this past year, 165 gathered at Airlie House in
Warrenton, Virginia, to hear Elie Abel, Barbara Tuchman,
Frank Mankiewicz, Saul Benison, and Nathan Reingold.
Lest you believe that the Association meetings are merely
exposures to the interviewing experiences of leading authors

and journalists, I hasten to add that the bulk of each program has included such topics as "Oral History and the Law,"
"The Art of Interviewing," "Oral History in the Classroom,"
"Interdisciplinary Views on Oral History," to name but a
few. The membership of the Association at this time is
approximately 400, including institutional and individual members.

As one who has attended all four of these meetings,
I continue to marvel at the disparate make-up of the group,
with respected and recognized scholars participating side by
side with young, enthusiastic, bright-eyed (and frequently
miniskirted) practitioners of oral history whose limitless
enthusiasm and boundless inquisitiveness keep their ani-
mated discussions going until the wee small hours of the
morning, when, as often as not, they are interrupted for a
2:00 a. m. swim! Seriously though, the group as a whole
does share certain concerns for the practice of oral history.
The two major points on which most would agree are (1)
the need for adequate and serious preparation on the part of
the interviewer, and (2) the importance of adhering to an
ethical code whereby the respondent's request for confiden-
tiality or restricted access is honored. The numerous
points on which the group disagree are quite understandable,
as each has his own definition of oral history. To the
National Park Service it is "living history" or "interpretive
oral history" such as a mountaineer in the Great Smokies
describing his recipe for "white lightning" or an Indian in
Arizona describing ceremonial dances. To the National
Library of Medicine it is a technique to gather information
to supplement the written word, generally a man's personal
papers. To the Presidential Libraries it is a technique to
elucidate further the life and career of past presidents, and
to the Mormon Church it is a means for gathering genealogical data. With such diverse goals, the lack of unanimity
is to be expected.

As for oral history in the life sciences, there are
probably some twenty-five to fifty oral history programs
(depending on how you define this term). These vary from
a long term study of the development of biochemistry and
molecular biology being planned by the American Academy
of Arts and Sciences to a series of interviews with past
presidents of a variety of professional societies.

At the NLM we currently have about 290 interview
hours of oral history materials including those in process.

It is perhaps regrettable that we have not limited our area
of subject coverage. I say regrettable in the sense that the
limited man hours devoted to oral history could accomplish
more if each individual interview was a building block toward
the next interview. It is already becoming apparent that there
is a need for a "clearing house" or central listing of who is
doing what in oral history related to the life sciences. As
the American Academy of Arts and Sciences is preparing to
support a program on the development of biochemistry and
molecular biology, it finds that the NLM has already interviewed a number of leading figures in this field and the Salk
Institute for Biological Studies, in La Jolla, California, has
initiated an Archive of Contemporary Biology which includes
the preservation of manuscript material as well as tape recorded interviews with a number of members of the same
population within the scientific community.

Two steps have been taken to remedy this problem.
The National Union Catalogue of Manuscript Collections,
following a series of discussions between Mrs. Arlene
Custer and representatives of the OHA, will now accept and
publish listings of catalogued collections of oral history materials which either accompnay manuscript collections or
stand alone as collections of oral history transcripts. I
feel that this is a most important development and over the
long haul will make the scholarly community aware of those
oral history collections of substance which can be important
sources of historical information.

The OHA is developing a list of oral history programs which will include information on size, scope, and
availability of collections which should be published within the
year. It is hoped that this will be a complete list of oral
history programs or activities throughout the country. The
Association has also arranged for the revision and updating
of a publication entitled A Bibliography of Oral History.

As I try to visualize what the immediate and distant
future holds in store for the oral history movement, I am
reminded of a comment made by a speaker at the National
Academy of Sciences recently, namely, "A young lady's future seldom takes shape before she does." Nevertheless, as
the oral history movement enters the decade of the seventies, it is characterized by enthusiasm tempered by an increasing awareness of the pitfalls of the technique. The
loud voices which proclaimed the technique to be the salva-
tion of historians in the face of disappearing holographic

documents are now muted. The legion of recorder-bearing
individuals rushing to the doors of prominent Americans are
now walking and giving more attention to their preparation
and showing a concern for overlapping interests with other
programs, to say nothing of the ethical and legal considerations of importance to the oral historian. Increasing numbers of oral historians, or perhaps more accurately oral
history practitioners, are taking pause and wondering whether
they stand alone as "technicians" or whether in fact they
are members of more ancient guilds such as historians,
archivists, or journalists who have latched on to a "new"
technique which transiently at least sets them apart from
their brethren.

The "establishment historian" who scoffed at oral
history a few short years ago has at least loosened his
starched collar to admit publicly that oral history memoirs
can often be a source of interesting anecdotal material and
vivid expression. Some have even admitted that information
otherwise unavailable has been gleaned from oral history
materials.

I believe it is safe to say that oral history as a technique is beginning to gain a modest degree of respectability
even among the hard-core doubters who will swear by the
written word but immediately suspect the spoken word. The
burden rests upon the practitioners of oral history. If reasonable standards are followed and our products can with-
stand impartial review of content in the same sense as a
published work, I foresee a long and useful life for oral
history. The time has come, if you will, for oral historians
to actively seek out critical and penetrating analyses of their
products. This idea was vigorously put forth at the Fourth
National Colloquium by Dr. Saul Benison and I heartily agree.
It is not enough to keep a tally of how many individuals consult your collection or how many authors credit your oral
history collection as a reference. It is time for oral history products to stand or fall on the merit of their content
and not on the unique qualities of the technique.

In closing, I would like to quote from Allan Seager's
preface to his book, A Frieze of Girls: Memoirs as Fiction (3). Herein is a message to all who would make extravagant claims for oral history.

> I am old enough to know that time makes fiction
> out of our memories. Some people, some events

it pulls front and center. It stores others in the
attic until we find some use for them. It dis-
creetly buries a few forever. Can anyone remember his life accurately, objectively the way a
camera and a tape would have recorded it? I
doubt it. We all have to have a self we can live
with and the operation of memory is artistic--se-
lecting, suppressing, bending, touching up, turning
our actions inside out so that we can have not
necessarily a likable, merely a plausible identity.
In this sense we are always true to ourselves....

References

1. Wilk, Max. A Dirty Mind Never Sleeps. New York,
        1969. By permission of W. W. Norton & Company,
        Inc. Copyright (c) 1969 by Max Wilk.
2. Columbia University, Oral History Research Office.
        Oral History in the United States, New York, 1965.
3. Seager, Allan. A Frieze of Girls: Memoirs as Fiction.
        New York: McGraw Hill, 1964.

OF COPYRIGHT, MEN, AND A NATIONAL LIBRARY

by John Y. Cole

Reprinted by permission from The Quarterly Journal of the Library of Congress April 1971, p. 114-136.

> To the public, the importance ... of having a
> central depot, where all products of the American
> mind may be gathered, year by year, and pre-
> served for reference, is very great. The interest
> with which those in 1950 may consult this library
> ... can only be fully and rightly estimated by the
> historian and the bibliographer.
> --Charles Coffin Jewett
> "Annual Report of the Board of Regents
> of the Smithsonian Institution, 1849"

In the United States the practice of depositing, in a
single location, copies of items registered for copyright protection has served two purposes: deposit for record, whereby
it is kept for library use and the enrichment of library collections. The history of the national library is firmly
linked to the second purpose, as copyright deposit for use
was the method by which a national collection of books and
materials comprehensively reflecting the American national
life was accumulated.

The foundation of British and American copyright law
is the Statute of Anne (1710), which included a provision for
sending copyright deposits to several British libraries.
Copyright deposits were first received by the British Museum Library in 1814 and played an important role in that
institution's development into a national library during the
19th century. When Anthony Panizzi became Keeper of
Printed Books in 1837, the British Museum ranked seventh
in size among great European libraries. Because of his
strict enforcement of the copyright law, the size of the
Library had nearly doubled by 1852, and by 1859 the British
Museum had risen to second place among Europe's libraries. [1]

The establishment of copyright deposit as an effective method of building library collections was of greater
importance to the development of a national library in the
United States than it was in England.   The first U. S. law
providing for the enrichment of library collections through
copyright deposit was passed in 1846 but was largely in-
effective.   It was not until the copyright laws of 1865 and
1870[2] were put into effect that the concept of deposit for
use became a reality.   And the history of the development
of a national library in the United States followed the same
course.

Two American librarians, Charles Coffin Jewett,
Librarian of the Smithsonian Institution from 1847 to 1854,
and Ainsworth Rand Spofford, Librarian of Congress from
1865 to 1897, stood alone in recognizing the value of copyright deposits to their institutions and to the development of
a national library in the United States.   For a brief period
it appeared that Jewett's Smithsonian library might someday
be a national library, but at the close of the Civil War
the Library of Congress, under Spofford's direction, assumed the national role.   At the turn of the century the
Library of Congress was recognized as America's national
library.   When it occupied its magnificent new building in
1897, it was distinguished by the unsurpassed size and scope
of its collections relating to American national life, which
were overwhelmingly the result of the copyright law.

In the United States the concept of copyright deposit
for library use was enacted into State law at an early date.
A Massachusetts law of 1783 provided that one copy of every
book copyrighted in the State be forwarded "to the library
of the University of Cambridge [Harvard] for the use of
said University. "   However, the first Federal copyright law,
passed May 31, 1790, did not provide for deposit for library
use, even though the concept of deposit for record was implicit: as legal evidence of copyright, a single copy of the
registered book, map, or chart was to be forwarded directly
to the Secretary of State in Washington within six months of
publication.   The copyright amendment of April 29, 1802,
added designs, engravings, and etchings to the list of items
protected by copyright, but it did not affect the deposit requirements.

The act of February 3, 1831, the first general revision of U. S. copyright law, provided for the protection of
musical compositions for the first time and changed the

deposit procedure: copies were to be deposited with the
clerk of the U. S. district court, who would forward them to
the Secretary of State within a year, along with a "certified
list of all such records of copyright. "   The emphasis on
deposit as the legal record of copyright was further accen-
tuated in 1834 when, in Wheaton v. Peters (8 Peters 591),
the Supreme Court ruled that the deposit of a record copy
was essential for the validity of the copyright.

By 1837 there was a change in the intellectual climate in the United States which soon led to a renewed, if
passive, interest in copyright deposit for library use.   Considerable interest had developed among New England scholars
and literary men in the need for an American "national
literature, " and the need for a national library was frequently mentioned at the same time.   This new national
self-consciousness was stimulated by an increased interest
in national history, the desire to "free" American scholars
from dependence upon European literature and libraries,
and a growing awareness of the inadequacy of American libraries.   Many New England intellectuals, including Edward
Everett and George Ticknor, both instrumental in the founding of the Boston Public Library, linked the accumulation of
large libraries directly to the development of a national
literature.   Their views were echoed by a writer in The
American Almanac and Repository of Useful Knowledge for
the Year 1837, who also noted the desirability of government support, as the formation of several large libraries
"under the patronage and direction of the government ...
would afford the most important aliment to American literature, which might soon be expected to manifest a growth
more vigorous than hitherto witnessed. "[3]

The need for a large accumulation of books in an
American national library was frequently expressed in the
North American Review, the prestigious intellectual journal,
published in Boston.   In an extended article on libraries in
the July 1837 issue, historian George W. Greene, writing
from his position as U. S. consul in Rome, urged a concentrated effort to build a national library which would
"render the American student nearly independent of the vast
collections of European libraries. "   He advocated enlarging
the Library of Congress into the national library.

But the Library of Congress was a meager place in
1837.   The American Almanac, while listing it as the "National" library, ranked its collection of 24, 500 volumes in

fifth place among American libraries, behind the collections
of the Library Company of Philadelphia, Harvard, the Boston
Athenaeum, and the New York Society Library.   Congress
regarded the Library of Congress as only a small legislative library and by the late 1830's was turning its attention
toward the development of another Washington institution.

In 1838 the half million dollars bequeathed to the
United States by Englishman James Smithson for "an establishment for the increase and diffusion of knowledge among
men" was paid into the U. S. Treasury, and Congressional
debate on how best to spend the money intensified.
Smithson's gift had not been an easy one for the United
States to accept--John C. Calhoun felt, for example, it was
"beneath the dignity of the country to accept such gifts
from foreigners"--and it was even more difficult for Congress to agree on the type of "establishment" Smithson
had in mind.   An agricultural experiment station, a national
university, an institute for scientific research, a museum of
natural history, and a national library were among the
proposed establishments.   Rufus Choate, a book-loving
Whig lawyer from Massachusetts, elected to the Senate in
1841 to fill the vacancy created by the resignation of Daniel
Webster, led the national library advocates in the Smithsonian debate.   In a heroic Senate speech on January 8,
1845, a speech which a writer in the North American Review claimed would "render more memorable the day on
which it was delivered than that gallant military achievement
of which it is the anniversary" (the Battle of New Orleans),
Choate urged devoting the largest part of the Smithson bequest to the establishment of a national library:[4]

> does not the whole history of civilization concur
> to declare that a various and ample library is one
> of the surest, most constant, most permanent,
> and most economical instrumentalities to increase
> and diffuse knowledge?   There it would be--dur-
> able as liberty, durable as the Union; a vast
> store-house, a vast treasury.

Choate, chairman of the Joint Committee on the
Library, the governing committee for the Library of Congress, felt the small annual expenditure Congress allowed
for that Library could never "enable it to fulfill the functions of a truly great and general public library of science,
literature, and art. "

Representative George P. Marsh of Vermont, Choate's supporter in the House of Representatives during the Smithsonian debates and a fellow committee member, attacked those who felt a grand accumulation of knowledge in the form of a national library was not a noble purpose: "It is an error to suppose that the accumulations of the stores of existing learning, the amassing of the records of intellectual action, does not tend also to increase knowledge. What is there new in the material world, except by extraction or combination?" Marsh also insisted that the American national library, when established at the Smithsonian, be as comprehensive as possible, since it had to sustain "a people descended from men of every clime, and blood, and language."[5]

Choate, Marsh, and most advocates of a national library did not view copyright deposit as an important means of obtaining the necessary books, or "accumulations." Greene, in his 1837 North American Review article, had proposed that all American historical societies regularly transmit their published volumes to the Library of Congress but did not mention copyright deposit. Instead, immediate large annual appropriations appeared to these men to be the only way to acquire books on the scale intended, particularly if the United States were ever to rival the 700,000 volumes in the Bibliothèque Nationale or even the 300,000-volume library of the University of Göttingen, which Marsh claimed was "the most useful of all for the purposes of general scholarship."

Yet the act of August 10, 1846, which established the Smithsonian Institution, contained the first Federal provision for the use of copyright deposits to enrich American libraries. According to section 10, both the Smithsonian Institution and the Library of Congress were to receive one copy of each copyrighted article within three months of publication "for the use of said libraries." This provision was introduced by Senator Stephen A. Douglas of Illinois and was apparently accepted without debate.

Copyright deposit was clearly considered supplementary to the acquisition of books through purchase, for there were no enforcement provisions in section 10. As the deposit of copies at the Smithsonian and Library of Congress did not appear necessary for the validity of the copyright and the institutions had no legal power to claim delinquent deposits, the law was eventually ignored by most

publishers and authors.   The Library of Congress was probably included with the Smithsonian as a corecipient of the
deposits because Choate and Marsh, along with Senator
James A.   Pearce of Maryland and Representative Benjamin
Tappan of Ohio, other principals in the Smithsonian national
library debate, were all members of the Joint Committee on
the Library.   None of them, however, had any ambitions
for the Library of Congress as a national library. [6]

In spite of its obvious flaws, section 10 of the 1846
act was the first legislative recognition of the value of copyright deposits to American libraries since the Massachusetts
law of 1783 and was an important step in the development
of a national library in the United States.   Although the act
was a compromise among the various schemes proposed for
the Smithsonian, it helped keep the national library plan
alive through its stipulation that an appropriation "not exceeding an average of twenty-five thousand dollars annually"
should be made to develop a library "composed of valuable
works pertaining to all departments of human knowledge. "

At the Smithsonian,
Joseph Henry and Charles Coffin Jewett

The chances that the Smithsonian might grow into a
national library were enhanced by the appointment of Charles
Coffin Jewett, the prominent librarian of Brown University,
to the post of Assistant Secretary in Charge of the Library.
Professor Jewett was selected for the position by the national library proponents on the Smithsonian Board of Regents,
including Rufus Choate, Jewett's fellow New Englander and
strongest supporter.   The newly appointed Secretary of the
Smithsonian, Joseph Henry, professor of physics at Princeton, accepted the Regents' recommendation and Jewett was
appointed.   Although Henry had no objection to Jewett, ad-
mitting he could not think of any other possible candidates,
he recognized that agreement between himself and Jewett
concerning the Smithsonian was necessary and should be
achieved immediately.   Prophetically, on March 23, 1847,
Secretary Henry warned his new assistant, "we have em-
barked together on a perilous voyage and unless the ship
is managed with caution and the officers are of the same
mind and determined to pull together, we shall be in danger
of shipwreck. "[7]

As librarian and professor of modern languages and

literature at Brown, Jewett had spent over two years in
France, Italy, Germany, and England acquiring books,
visiting libraries and librarians, and studying languages.
In England he met and formed a strong friendship with
Anthony Panizzi, then Keeper of Printed Books at the British
Museum, and later Principal Librarian. Jewett spent
months observing the operations and admiring the collections
of the great foreign libraries and frequently contrasted their
riches to the poverty of American libraries. Once at the
Smithsonian, he set out to correct this deficiency by forging
that institution into a strong national library and bibliographic center, convinced that Congress shared his wish.

Secretary Henry, despite Congressional authorization
for a large Smithsonian library, definitely did not share
Jewett's national library views. The foremost American
scientist of his day, Henry insisted upon a limited library
designed solely to support what he, as Secretary, viewed as
the true purpose of the Smithsonian: the increase of knowledge by scientific research and the subsequent diffusion of
this knowledge through publication. In its first years, however, the ultimate direction which the Smithsonian would
take was not clear, and an uneasy peace prevailed between
the strong-willed Secretary and his ambitious librarian. 8

Late in the autumn of 1847 Jewett expressed his concern to Henry over the failure of the 1846 act to provide
for strict enforcement of the copyright deposit requirements.
The next spring, as most publishers were still not forward-
ing the required copies to the Smithsonian or the Library
of Congress, he reemphasized the need for enforcement
provisions:9

> if it be considered just & expedient to require three
> copies of every book, let the delivery of them be
> made obligatory & essential to the securing of a
> valid title. I have always thought that at least
> two copies should be required, because there is
> always danger of losing one by fire or otherwise.
> One of these copies should be kept in a safe de-
> pository, from which it should never be taken,
> except by order of a Court of Law.

Charles Coffin Jewett was the first American librarian to recognize and acclaim the potential value of
copyright deposits to the development of an American national library. In his 1849 annual report he explained why

a complete copyright collection was necessary:

> In coming years, the collection would form a docu-
> mentary history of American letters, science, and
> art.   It is greatly to be desired, however, that
> the collection should be complete, without a single
> omission.   We wish for every book, every pamphlet,
> every printed or engraved production, however ap-
> parently insignificant.   Who can tell what may be
> important in future centuries?

The keystone of Jewett's national library plan was to
be a centralized cataloging system for U. S. libraries, based
on the distribution of catalog entries produced at the Smithsonian from stereotype plates.   Other libraries could use
the plates in producing their own catalogs and would prepare
catalog entries and plates for items not in the Smithsonian
catalog.   To eliminate the duplication of cataloging effort
and to merge, in effect, the separate library catalogs,
Jewett proposed the use of uniform cataloging rules as a
necessary component in his national bibliographic system.
He also published a list of copyright deposits received at
the Smithsonian through 1850 in two appendixes to the 1850
annual report. [10]

The success of Jewett's national library plans depended on the accumulation of a comprehensive collection
at the Smithsonian, which was not possible without enforcement provisions in the copyright law.   Even though Jewett
claimed the ruling was not valid, he was disturbed by the
decision of the New York District Court in Jollie v. Jacques
(1 Blatchford 618) in 1850 that the deposit of copies at the
Smithsonian and the Library of Congress was not essential
to the validity of the copyright.

According to Jewett's statistics in his 1850 annual
report, only 15 percent of the books and pamphlets in the
Smithsonian library had been obtained through the copyright
law.   As an appendix to the report, the Smithsonian published Jewett's Notices of Public Libraries in the United
States of America, perhaps the best evidence of its librarian's national bibliographic activities.   A pioneering work,
the Notices contained historical and statistical information
concerning more than 900 libraries.   Jewett found that
Harvard, with its 84, 200 volumes, had the largest library
collection in the United States, followed by the Library Company of Philadelphia, Yale, and then the Boston Athenaeum

and the Library of Congress, both with approximately 50,000
volumes apiece. The copyright library in the State Department, recipient of deposits for record since 1790, numbered
only 10,000 volumes, and the Smithsonian library a mere
6,000. [11]

The first half of the decade of the 1850's witnessed
a surge of library activity in the United States; among other
events, the first national librarians' conference was held
in 1853, and New York's Astor Library and the Boston
Public Library opened in 1854. But Charles Coffin Jewett
and his plans for a national library at the Smithsonian
created the most excitement. The North American Review
proclaimed: "We must have a large national library ... the
Smithsonian Institution affords one of the most favorable opportunities that was ever offered in any country for the establishment of such a library." Norton's Literary Gazette,
leading publishing and literary journal of the day, took special note of the Smithsonian in a February 1852 issue and
expressed great hope for its future: "The Library has been
commenced; and although the funds have not been available
for its rapid growth, it is destined, we hope, to meet that
great want of American scholarship, a National Library for
reference and research."

In its only mention of the copyright law, Norton's
scolded publishers for not depositing copies but, like the
North American Review, it did not suggest copyright deposit
as a method of developing the national library which each
journal was promoting. Generally, the writers in the North
American Review were concerned only with the desired result, a grandiose national library which would put Europe to
shame, while Norton's viewed copyright deposit from the
standpoint of the publisher: deposit was the best possible
advertisement he could have. [12]

In his 1851 annual report, Jewett complained at
length about the copyright situation, estimating that the
Smithsonian received as deposits less than half of the works
annually copyrighted in the United States. Again pleading
for enforcement provisions, he suggested a reduction in the
number of copies required for deposit. While he could not
say "whether or not the deposit is desired by the guardians
of the Library of Congress," if the deposit requirement
were ever reduced to one copy, he felt it "could be most
properly placed in the library of the Smithsonian Institution."

By 1851, however, relations between Jewett and
Henry were deteriorating. Henry was becoming more ada-
ment in insisting that the Smithsonian library would not absorb more than a limited share of the annual budget, and the
outspoken Jewett was equally determined to gain greater
financial support in order to carry out his national library
plans; each stated his case in separate annual reports with
increasing determination, and each rallied his supporters
on the Board of Regents. Henry was never opposed to the
idea of a national library per se, viewing the idea, in fact,
with some favor; however, he was absolutely opposed to the
Smithsonian Institution's becoming that national library. He
felt the Government should establish and maintain a national
library in another institution and even looked to the Library of
Congress as a foundation "for a collection of books worthy of
a Government whose perpetuity principally depends upon the
intelligence of its people. " In the same 1851 report he
clearly warned Jewett, "The idea ought never to be enter-
tained that the portion of the limited income of the Smithsonian fund which can be devoted to the purchase of books
will ever be sufficient to meet the wants of the American
scholar. "

Jewett completely ignored Henry and increased his
own propaganda activities. In his 1853 report he reaffirmed
his goal: "There ought, therefore, to be in every country
one complete collection of everything published--one library
where everything printed should be garnered up, treated as
of some importance. "

In 1853 Jewett was the most eminent librarian in the
land, and it was only natural that he should play a central
role in the first librarians' conference in the United States,
held in New York City from September 15 to 17. The conference was conceived and organized by Charles B. Norton,
a New York bookseller and the publisher of Norton's Literary Gazette. Attended by over 80 delegates representing
47 different libraries in the United States, the conference
itself was proof of the growing national interest in library
matters. Jewett, elected conference president, held the
floor for half a day explaining at length his plans for the
development of the Smithsonian library. He began by
presenting statistics about copyright deposits received at the
Smithsonian, emphasizing, as always, the deficiencies in the
system and the need for enforcement provisions. In spite
of his difficulties with Henry, Jewett explicitly reaffirmed
his belief that "a large central library of reference and

research will be collected at the Smithsonian Institution, if
not by the expenditure of the funds of the Institution, then
by other means," and he warmed the hearts of supporters
of the national library cause by eloquently proclaiming a
great central library to be "an important national object;
as necessary to secure the literary independence of this
people as was the war of the Revolution to secure its political independence." The librarians responded enthusiastically and passed resolutions approving the idea of the
Smithsonian as the national library and endorsing Professor
Jewett's stereotype cataloging scheme. [13]

But time had run out for Jewett and his national
library plans at the Smithsonian. In 1854 newspaper and
magazine reports hostile to Secretary Henry and his plans
for the Smithsonian began to appear with increasing frequency; Henry correctly surmised that Jewett was responsible for the articles and resolved to take action. Assured
of the support of a majority of the Board of Regents, Secretary Henry fired Professor Jewett on July 10, 1854. Senator Choate angrily resigned from the Board of Regents,
Jewett strongly protested, dozens of outraged editorials
appeared, from Washington to Boston, and a Congressional
investigation reviewed the entire affair. But Henry had
gathered his evidence and built his case carefully, and
his victory was never seriously in doubt.

While Senator Choate and other national library supporters continued the battle in Congress, others conceded
defeat and mused that, after all, the Smithsonian might not
be the most suitable institution for the national library.
Norton's Literary Gazette took this position, stating that
Smithson's bequest "would not be more than sufficient to
lay the foundation of the library that our country should
now have." [14] Professor Jewett returned to New England,
became the successful Superintendent of the Boston Public
Library, and dropped his national library plans.

The value of the copyright deposits in the Smithsonian library was at the root of the disagreement between
Jewett and Henry, and once he was rid of Jewett, Secretary Henry turned his attention to securing the repeal of
the irksome deposit requirement. He had always been dismayed at the odd assortment of chromolithographs, maps,
and other objects brought into the Smithsonian by the copyright law and unhappy with the nonscientific contents of most
of the books. Henry felt most of the deposits were worth-

less and resented the administrative expense they represented, as well as the popular image and clientele they brought to his Institution.   On March 5, 1855, the Smithsonian was relieved of paying the additional postage due on deposits, as Congress finally passed an act allowing copyright deposits to be sent free through the mails, a reform long advocated by Jewett.

Henry favored the consolidation of copyright activities at the Patent Office, where the patent business was centralized, and felt that the deposit of a single copy would be sufficient.   On February 5, 1859, he was successful: the 1846 law requiring the deposit of copies in the Smithsonian Institution and the Library of Congress was repealed.   The copyright records and the 12,000-volume copyright library in the Department of State were transferred to the Patent Office, which was to receive the single copy forwarded by the district court clerks from that date hence.   After a 13-year trial the concept of deposit for use had suffered a severe setback, as the single copy now sent to the Patent Office was the deposit for record and not available for use. The lack of enforcement power in the 1846 law was the major reason for the failure of the first national effort in the United States to provide copyright deposits for the development of library collections.   Unable to establish an effective means of building a national collection, Jewett had failed to realize his national library plans for the Smithsonian.

Meanwhile, at the Library of Congress

The Librarian of Congress between 1846 and 1859, when the copyright law brought deposits to the two institutions, was John Silva Meehan, an appointee of Andrew Jackson.   Meehan supported Joseph Henry's efforts to have the deposit provision repealed; during the 13 years when it was in effect, the law brought only about 4,200 volumes into the Library of Congress, and it was never regarded as an important means of acquiring materials.   In December 1851 the Library had suffered a disastrous fire, in which 35,000 of its 55,000 volumes were destroyed, including many copyright deposits.   Congress generously appropriated $85,000 to rebuild the Library's collections, and Meehan devoted most of his time to preparing purchase lists for the Library's London bookdealer.   Between January 1852 and April 1856 more than 36,000 volumes were purchased, while only 2,000 were acquired through copyright. [15]

Meehan's assistant, E. B. Stelle, handled the copyright correspondence and viewed the whole copyright business
as a burden. The Library suffered the same problems in
relation to copyright deposits as did the Smithsonian: few
publishers bothered to deposit copies, and the issuing of
receipts and certificates was a troublesome administrative
duty. Publishers frequently forwarded the two deposit copies
in the same package, and Stelle continually requested them
to mail the deposits separately, one to each institution.

While he often pleaded ignorance of legal points related to copyright, Stelle did encourage publishers to deposit their volumes when in doubt. In 1854, apparently unaware of the Jollie v. Jacques decision, he wrote an Ohio
author:[16]

> Questions in relation to the perfection of copyright
> under this law have arisen among some of the pub-
> lishers of the north, but whether the question has
> been carried to the courts, I know not. I think
> you had better send your book, as required by
> law, and should the point arise with regard to the
> law being carried out, you will at least have shown
> your intention to have complied.

After the deposit requirement was repealed in 1859,
Meehan and Stelle dutifully notified major publishers that it
was no longer necessary to send copies to the Library. For
the next two years, until the trickle finally stopped, deposits
mistakenly sent to the Library were nonetheless usually absorbed into the collections. For example, Meehan informed
a Detroit author that the Library had kept his book, sent
four months after the law's repeal, "as it would be expensive to you to have it returned." Another author found his
errant deposit placed in the Library's collections "as a
'present' unless you send me directions to the contrary."
Not a collection-builder, Meehan simply found it more convenient to add the stray books to the collection than to return them.[17]

In 1859 the Manual of Public Libraries, Institutions,
and Societies in North America, originally intended as a
continuation of Jewett's Notices of Public Libraries (1849)
and compiled by William J. Rhees, Chief Clerk of the
Smithsonian, was published. By 1859 the American library
movement had blossomed, and Rhees' Manual was considerably larger than Jewett's slim survey; Secretary Henry, not

at all anxious to again associate the Smithsonian with a
"national" library survey, refused to publish the Manual under the auspices of the Institution, and Rhees published it
himself. According to his tabulation, Harvard was still the
largest American library, holding approximately 113,000
volumes, followed closely by the Astor Library, the Boston
Public Library, the Boston Athenaeum, Yale, and then the
Library of Congress and the Library Company of Philadelphia, each with 63,000 volumes. The Smithsonian library
contained only 25,000 volumes.

Ainsworth Rand Spofford

With the withdrawal of the Smithsonian Institution from
its position of leadership among American libraries, the repeal of the deposit-for-use provision in the copyright law,
and the widening of the sectional dispute between North and
South, Congressional and literary interest in the national
library cause subsided. Yet the Civil War proved to be an
indirect stimulus to the national library effort, for it brought
to Washington a Cincinnati bookseller and journalist who, as
Librarian of Congress from 1865 to 1897, successfully used
the concept of deposit for use to build the basis of a national
library.

Born in New Hampshire, Ainsworth Rand Spofford
moved to Cincinnati in 1844, where as a young bookseller
and editorial writer, he developed strong interests in literature and politics. In 1849, with the assistance of friends,
Spofford founded the Literary Club of Cincinnati, and under
his guidance the club became a western outpost of New
England culture and antislavery sentiment. His close friend
Reuben H. Stephenson, librarian of the Cincinnati Merchantile
Library, played an active role in the 1853 librarians' conference in New York and reported on proceedings to his fellow members of the Literary Club. While in Cincinnati,
Spofford developed his talents as an abolitionist pamphleteer
and literary essayist, publishing one of his first articles in
the North American Review in 1855.

In 1859 Spofford became associate editor of the Cincinnati Daily Commercial, a leading newspaper, and two of
his earliest articles were on the subject of copyright. As
with Jewett, the copyright deposits were of greatest interest,
and on February 10, 1859, Spofford wrote an article which
emphasized the variety of deposits received by the U.S.

district court clerk in Cincinnati, finding that "Twenty-six copyrights have been secured, of which one was for a cough label, one for a lithograph, three for maps, six for book-keeping and interest tables, and fifteen for books. Of the latter, five were revisions and new editions of old books, and ten were new books. "

Spofford was sent to Washington in 1861 as a correspondent for the Commercial. When not busy preparing dispatches for his newspaper, he visited Reuben H. Stephenson's brother, John G. Stephenson, who had recently been appointed Librarian of Congress by President Lincoln. Librarian Stephenson, impressed with the knowledge of books, enthusiasm, and Republican credentials of his brother's friend, offered Spofford the job as Assistant Librarian of Congress. Uncertain of his future with the Commercial, Spofford accepted.

While the Library of Congress tied for sixth place among U. S. libraries in the 1859 Rhees survey, Spofford never considered it anything but the national library. Like the national library advocates of the North American Review and the supporters of the cause in the Smithsonian debate, he felt the primary function of the American national library should be the accumulation of a comprehensive collection of American publications; his first official letter was therefore probably a poignant reminder of the potential role of copyright deposits in building a collection worthy of a national library. On September 23, 1861, he wrote a gentleman in St. Paul, Minn.:[18]

> In reply to your favor ... relating to your Map of Dakota, I would state that the Law requiring a copy of each publication issued to be deposited in this Library was repealed Feby 5, 1859, and all Books & Maps sent by mail to the Library of Congress are now deposited in the Department of Interior.

Spofford was the intellectual heir of Charles Coffin Jewett's views on the importance of copyright deposits to the development of an American national library, but his task was easier than Jewett's. For example, he could deal directly with Congress and was able to act effectively less than two months after his promotion to Librarian on December 31, 1864. By February the Joint Committee on the Library agreed to support an amendment which would return the copyright privilege of deposit to the Library of Congress.

Spofford originally proposed that the deposit copy sent to the Library be in place of the copy sent to the Patent Office, but it was instead agreed that an additional deposit copy be sent to the Library, designated by law for its use. Therefore, at the suggestion of the Librarian, Senator Jacob Collamer of Vermont, the chairman of the Joint Committee, added the desired deposit provision to a pending copyright amendment which extended protection to photographs. Collamer, however, was not telling the whole story when he explained to Senator Charles Sumner that the proposed change in the deposit system was "merely for carrying into effect what used to be the law formerly, that one copy of all these publications shall be sent to the library."[19]

For the 1865 deposit amendment was stronger than the 1846 law: it stipulated for the first time that failure to deposit a copy for use could result in the forfeiture of the copyright previously secured. But actual deposit within the Library was still not ensured, for the Librarian was responsible for detecting any violations and for claiming delinquent deposits. Nonetheless, the concept of deposit for use assumed a new importance when the amendment of March 3, 1865, passed, because the Library of Congress now had a legal right to claim for its collections and use "a single copy of every book, pamphlet, map, chart, musical composition, print, engraving, or photograph, for which copyright shall be secured."

In 1860 Joseph Henry sent a large accumulation of American newspapers to the American Antiquarian Society "in exchange for works more immediately in accordance with the design of the Institution." A fire in the Smithsonian Building in 1865 presented him with another opportunity to streamline the Smithsonian library. As Spofford had recently obtained Congressional authorization for the physical expansion of the Library of Congress into larger, fireproof rooms, Henry proposed the deposit of the 40,000-volume Smithsonian library in one of those rooms. His purpose was not to separate the collection from the Smithsonian, "for it must still bear its name and be subject to its control," but instead to place it "where its preservation will be more certain and its usefulness more extended."[20] Naturally Spofford was willing, if not eager, to receive the collection, and on April 5, 1866, Congress approved the transfer of the Smithsonian library, including its copyright deposits received between 1846 and 1859.

The transfer of the Smithsonian library to the Library of Congress, together with the Copyright Act of 1865, eliminated any possibility that the Smithsonian might someday become the national library. Nevertheless, as Jewett had hoped, the Smithsonian library formed the basis of a national library collection, but the national library was at the Library of Congress: the transfer of the Smithsonian library added 40,000 volumes to the Library's collection of 99,000 volumes, gave the Library of Congress the outstanding collection of publications of scientific societies in the Nation, and provided for its continued expansion. A few years later Joseph Henry fully recognized the importance, if not the irony, of the situation: "The collection of books owned by Congress would not be worthy of the name of a national library were it not for the Smithsonian deposit."[21]

In his 1866 annual report Spofford discussed the importance of enforcement power in the copyright deposit provisions, noting that "the benefits of the law to the Congressional Library will depend greatly on the means provided for its enforcement and the vigilance with which it is administered." Spofford himself tried to administer the law with utmost diligence, making periodic trips to the district courts in New York, Philadelphia, and Boston to obtain information from the copyright records so he could demand copies, as provided in the law. He also corresponded with more than 30 district court clerks throughout the country, asking them to forward transcripts from their copyright records from which he could claim deposits not received by the Library. In early 1867, tired of performing what he considered unnecessary labor to claim what legally belonged to the Library, Spofford, again acting through the Library Committee, proposed an amendment which imposed a $25 fine for noncompliance and clarified the postage-free status of deposits mailed to the Library. The amendment quickly became law, and the improved results were noticeably immediately.

In 1866, the first full year of the 1865 law's operation, only 1,996 items were deposited in the Library; but in 1867, with the enforcement amendment in effect for most of the year, 4,499 items were deposited, mostly books, pamphlets, and periodicals but also 1,256 pieces of music, 319 engravings and photographs, and 91 maps. By the end

of 1867, the Library's collection of over 165, 000 volumes
was the largest in the United States, [22] owing primarily to
the acquisition of the Smithsonian deposit and the collection
of Americana previously owned by Peter Force and purchased during the year. The Library's rooms had been expanded, and with the establishment of a more effective copyright law, Spofford admitted that the Library had experienced
a year "unexampled in its past history. "

But he was still troubled by the copyright law. While
the Library was now receiving over 75 percent of all U. S.
copyrighted publications, Spofford wanted all copyrighted
publications available in the Library, for it should represent,
as nearly as possible, "the complete product of the American
mind in every department of science and literature. " He
found that even with the "utmost diligence" it was impossible
to obtain all the copyrighted publications, since he was
forced to pursue delinquent publishers and authors through
the 44 U. S. district courts where the original copyright
registrations were still being made. [23]

The entire system needed changing, and Spofford proposed to eliminate the district courts and the Patent Office
from the copyright system altogether by centralizing all
registration and deposit activities at the Library of Congress.
According to his plan, both deposit copies--the copy for
legal record and the copy for library use--would be sent
directly to the Library of Congress. The Librarian would be
responsible for registration and for keeping the copies deposited as legal evidence separate from the general collection.

Early in 1870, Spofford presented his ideas for the
centralization of copyright activities to Representative Thomas
A. Jenckes of Rhode Island, whose Committee on Patents
was about to report out a bill for the revision and consolidation of the patent laws. Spofford previously had gained
the support of Samuel S. Fisher, a patent lawyer from
Cincinnati who had been appointed Commissioner of Patents
on April 26, 1869. Like Spofford, Fisher had been a member of the Literary Club of Cincinnati, and Fisher and
Jenckes had corresponded on the subject of patent law reform before Fisher came to Washington. Assured of the
support of the Patent Office, the copyright registration
agency and legal custodian of the deposit for record, Spofford wrote a 1, 600-word letter on April 9, 1870, to Representative Jenckes outlining seven arguments favoring the

First page of Spofford's letter to Representative Thomas A. Jenckes of Rhode Island, in which he argues that the Library of Congress should be the central agency for copyright registration and for custody of copyright deposits. Manuscript Division, Library of Congress.

centralization of all copyright activities at the Library:[24]

> Under the present system, although this National
> Library is entitled by law to a copy of every work
> for which a copyright is taken out, it does not re-
> ceive, in point of fact, more than four-fifths of
> such publications.
>
> The transfer of the Copyright business proposed
> would concentrate and simplify the business, and
> this is a cardinal point.... Let the whole busi-
> ness ... be placed in the charge of one single re-
> sponsible officer, and an infinitude of expense,
> trouble, and insecurity would be saved to the
> proprietors of Copyrights and to the legal pro-
> fession.
>
> The advantage of securing to our only National
> Library a complete collection of all American
> copyright entries can scarcely be over-estimated....
> We should have one comprehensive Library in the
> country, and that belonging to the nation, whose
> aim it should be to preserve the books which
> other libraries have not the room nor the means
> to procure.
>
> Having all American publications thoroughly cata-
> logued ... in an annual volume, carefully edited
> and authoritatively issued from the press of the
> Government ... would be an invaluable aid to
> thousands.
>
> The proposed reform of the present unsatisfactory
> methods of recording and perfecting copyright would
> take away all the objections now so freely brought
> against the law.
>
> The proposed change would be a great economy
> for the Government. It would save the Patent
> Office the trouble, expense, and room of providing
> for a great library of material which it cannot use
> and does not want.... A copyright is not an in-
> vention or a patent--it is a contribution to litera-
> ture.
>
> By requiring the Librarian to make an annual re-
> port to Congress, a highly important and interesting

class of facts would be added to our national
statistics.

Less than a week later, on April 14, 1870, Jenckes
skillfully condensed Spofford's eight pages of arguments into
a short, effective speech advocating the transfer of the copyright business to the Library, [25] and attached the proposal
to his bill revising the patent laws. Jenckes' bill passed
Congress easily, and when it was signed into law by President Ulysses S. Grant on July 8, 1870, the Library of
Congress became the first central agency for copyright
registration and for the custody of copyright deposits in the
United States.

While fully aware of the importance of copyright
centralization in establishing the Library of Congress as a
national library, Spofford never emphasized national library
arguments in his dealings with Congress on the subject.
Instead, as in his letter to Jenckes, he began with the
assumption that the Library was already recognized as the
national library and stressed the economies and efficiencies
which would result to the Government and the publishing
world through centralization. In his speech of April 14
Jenckes did not refer to the Library of Congress as the
national library or as a potential national library.

While Spofford's practical successes were his own,
his intellectual debt to Jewett, whose mantle and cause he
assumed, was great. Jewett and Spofford shared the same
view of five aspects of copyright deposit as a means of
developing a national library collection. Each was convinced
that: 1) deposit for library use protected the right of the
public, just as deposit for record protected the right of the
author; 2) his institution, as a Government-sponsored agency
open to the public, had an irrefutable claim to the deposit
copy intended for public use; 3) deposit for use was the
most practical channel through which a comprehensive collection of American publications could be accumulated; 4)
the centralized, permanent accumulation of the "products of
the American press" was a positive national benefit and the
natural basis of an American national library; and 5) the
collection of copyright deposits should be as complete as
possible, and completeness was ensured only by strong enforcement provisions in the law.

Spofford and Jewett each pursued the cause of a
national library zealously and enthusiastically. However,

before the Civil War, it was difficult for any national institution to succeed in the United States, and the Smithsonian
Institution presented special difficulties. Supported solely
by an endowment, the Institution had to limit its functions in
order to survive, a necessity recognized and skillfully used
by Joseph Henry to the dismay of Jewett and supporters of
the national library concept. At midcentury, in spite of increased library activity, a majority of Americans--including
most Congressmen and the press--were indifferent to the
subject of a national library, as they had been to a national
university and other proposals for national cultural or scientific institutions. And Washington, D. C., as a location
posed difficulties. Although the National Government was
situated there, the city was relatively isolated, and the
literary, commercial, and social centers of the country
were elsewhere; the Federal Government itself, rarely perceived beyond Washington, was weak and its very survival
becoming more questionable.

The Civil War changed the situation drastically. The
Federal Government not only survived, it established itself;
Washington emerged as a true political capital and an important Federal city. National pride, new wealth, and the
growth of new Federal agencies and institutions changed the
cultural climate and assisted Spofford's national library
cause. The Smithsonian Institution itself, through the efforts
of Joseph Henry, aided Spofford, not only through the Smithsonian deposit of 1866 but also by its example: an institution successfully promoting scholarly activity and contributing
to Washington's intellectual climate. Throughout the United
States scholarship achieved a new status and increased attention, with numerous professional associations created to
promote and sustain it. Intellectual activity was becoming
organized and institutionalized, and Congress, responding to
Spofford's pleas and proposals, began to recognize the need
for and the potential role of a national library in the United
States. [26]

The Library of Congress was exclusively a library,
and this was probably Spofford's greatest advantage over
Jewett. Unlike the Smithsonian Institution or the Patent
Office, the Library was intended solely as a library, and
Spofford faced no competing schemes for the development of
his institution. He was able to deal directly with members
of the Joint Committee on the Library and with all other
Congressmen, most of whom fully appreciated his talents
as a reference librarian, bibliographer, and speechwriter.

Spofford not only operated under more favorable conditions than Jewett; his personality was better suited to the task. Less mercurial and more tactful, Spofford deliberately maintained superb relations with all Congressmen; keeping his personal reputation above reproach, he did not hesitate to ask individual Congressmen for support when he felt it necessary. Put simply, Spofford was a skillful politician; Jewett was not.

At the same time Spofford's goals and efforts were more limited, for unlike Jewett he never viewed the national library as the center of a national system of libraries offering nationwide service. Instead, for Spofford the national library was essentially a centralized permanent accumulation of national literature to be used for the benefit of Congress and the American people. To attain his goal, he worked with a single-minded devotion, merging personal ambition with his ambitions for the Library, thereby making the cause of the Library of Congress as the national library a natural one for any Congressman to support and a difficult one to oppose. The copyright laws of 1865 and 1870 were striking successes in Spofford's campaign and crucial to his cause.

After passage of the 1870 law, the deposits began to arrive at an accelerated rate: over 11,500 articles in 1870, including 5,874 books and pamphlets, and almost double that number in the next year. The law required that all copyright records and deposits from the district courts and the Patent Office be turned over to the Library, and the Patent Office copyright library of 23,070 volumes was added to the collections in 1871, minus the law books retained at the Department of the Interior at the request of the Commissioner of Patents. Spofford was disappointed in the size of the Patent library and the quality of the collection, but he optimistically declared that "although consisting of schoolbooks and the minor literature of the last 40 years, (it) embraces many valuable additions to the store of American books, which it should be one object of the national library to render complete."[27]

In its 1876 survey of the libraries of the United States, the U.S. Bureau of Education listed the rapidly growing Library of Congress and Boston Public Library as the two largest libraries in the United States, with approximately 300,000 volumes apiece.[28] In one decade the Library of Congress had tripled in size and risen to the top rank of American libraries. Copyright deposits constituted over 40 percent of its collections.

By 1897, when it moved from its over-crowded rooms
in the Capitol across the east plaza into its spacious new
building, the collections of the Library of Congress easily
ranked first among American libraries, both in size and
scope. Over 40 percent of its 840,000 volumes and at least
90 percent of the map, music, and graphic arts collections
had been acquired through copyright deposit. [29]

After the monumental copyright law of 1870, one
other copyright law was enacted which added even further
luster to the Library's collections: the act of March 3,
1891, granted U. S. copyright protection to foreign authors
and brought deposits of foreign works into the Library for
the first time.

Between 1865 and 1897 the only major acquisitions
obtained directly from sources other than copyright deposit
were the Smithsonian library, Peter Force's Americana
library acquired for $100,000 in 1867, a collection of
English county histories purchased in 1875 for $5,000, the
gift of the library of Dr. Joseph M. Toner in 1882, and the
Rochambeau collection purchased in 1883 for $20,000. The
Library's annual appropriation for the purchase of books
averaged only $9,000, and while a system of international
exchange of public documents was successfully inaugurated,
the results had only a minor impact on the collections
during this period.

Between 1865 and 1897 unsurpassed "national collections" had been accumulated within each class of material
brought in by the copyright law. During these years copyright deposit added to the Library's collections approximately 350,000 books and pamphlets, 47,000 maps and charts,
250,000 musical compositions, 12,000 engravings, lithographs, and chromolithographs, 33,000 photographs, 3,000
etchings, and 6,000 dramatic compositions.

The centralization of copyright activities at the Library of Congress not only developed impressive collections
but also gave the Library an exclusive Government function
and the national prestige which naturally accompanied it.
For the first time the Library became part of the publishing
and, to a lesser extent, the literary world, as well as an
important Government institution rendering a service essential to the intellectual life of the Nation. As the collections
increased, so did the Library's reputation, and it came at
last to be generally recognized as a national institution.

As the sole copyright officer of the U. S. Government, Spofford corresponded with statesmen, scholars, and literary figures all over the United States, as well as with publishers and editors. In the process he succeeded in gaining new friends for the Library and new supporters in his long campaign for a separate library building. For example, in 1872 historian George Bancroft complimented Spofford: "Under your management the Congressional Library is attaining so high a character." After struggling with Spofford through copyright problems with The Gilded Age and A Tramp Abroad, Samuel Clemens gingerly asked permission for his nephew to "burrow a little" in Spofford's "grand literary storehouse." The influential Washington journalist Kate Field called Congressional neglect of Spofford's space needs "a disgrace" and strongly supported his efforts to secure a new building. [30]

In spite of the overcrowded condition in the Library, Spofford always placed great value on the comprehensiveness of the collection brought in by the copyright law, strongly believing that "what is pronounced trash today may have unexpected value hereafter, and the unconsidered trifles of the press of the nineteenth century may prove highly curious and interesting to the twentieth." He never ceased defending the Library against charges that it was filling up with "trash" brought in by the wide net of the copyright law, asserting that "every nation should have, at its capital city, all the books its authors have produced, in perpetual evidence of its literary history and progress--or retrogression, as the case may be." [31] He carefully ensured the complete representation in the Library of all editions of works from authors well known in his day, frequently querying established authors directly concerning the dates of new or revised editions of their works.

"Greatest Chaos in America"

Although essential to the growth and prestige of the Library, copyright deposit also created serious problems. Spofford was overwhelmed by the unceasing flow of deposits into his cramped Library. He cried to Congress for help almost immediately, and his 1871 annual report launched a 15-year struggle for an appropriation for a new building, which was not finally completed and occupied until 1897. In 1874, for the first time, the copyright law brought in more books than were obtained that year through purchase; in

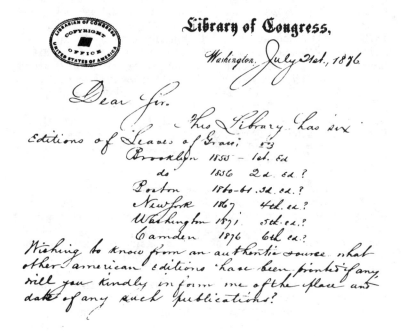

Library of Congress,

Washington, July 21st, 1876.

Dear Sir,

This Library has six Editions of Leaves of Grass;

Brooklyn 1855 – 1st. Ed
do   1856   2d. ed.?
Boston   1860-61. 3d. ed.?
New York 1867   4th. ed.?
Washington 1871. 5th. ed.?
Camden   1876   6th. ed.?

Wishing to know from an authentic source what other american editions have been printed, if any, will you kindly inform me of the place and date of any such publications?

Very respectfully,
A R Spofford

Mr. Walt. Whitman   *Librarian of Congress.*

Spofford's scrupulous attention to details about new or revised editions is illustrated in his letter to Walt Whitman, who in turn notes in his reply [opposite page]: "I write on the letter, & return it so, for greater definiteness." Manuscript Division, Library of Congress.

Camden N Jersey
July 22 '76

A R Spofford?
Dear Sir

The Editions of my "Leaves
of Grass," as within specified, are
the only ones I have published) —
(Two "Rivulets"
Vol. issued) & ne. I
& comprise all. the further Vol. just
& believe you have)

Walt Whitman

I write on the letter, & return it so,
for greater definiteness.

1880 the law would bring in twice as many. In 1875 Spofford warned Congress that its Librarian would soon be pre-
siding over the "greatest chaos in America," and by 1877
more than 70,000 books were "piled on the floor in all
directions."

As the mountains of books, maps, music, prints,
and photographs grew around him, Spofford was unable to
devote much effort to the other essential functions of the
Library: by 1896 the administration of the copyright law
required over 75 percent of his time and the full time efforts
of 26 of the Library's 42 employees. [32] Lack of space and
adequate staff to cope with the sharply increasing copyright
business contributed to another embarrassing situation for
the Librarian, as he was unable to keep the copyright accounts and records in presentable order. And finally Congress, while unwilling to take decisive action on Spofford's
annual pleas for more space and staff between 1872 and 1885,
used the congested condition of the Library and existence of
guaranteed acquisition through copyright as reasons for refusing larger appropriations for staff and the purchase of
materials.

The most serious problem was the chaotic condition
of the deposits themselves. Virtually inaccessible without
the aid of Librarian Spofford's remarkable memory, the
accumulated wealth of the collections was not fully appreciated
until they were transferred into the new building and cleaned,
sorted, examined, and counted. Unfortunately, numerous individual items stored in the Capitol had been damaged or
simply lost.

Of the copyright deposits, the map collection apparently suffered most from the crowded conditions in the old
Library. Many of the maps were stacked in damp and dusty
corners throughout the Capitol and emerged in a mangled
condition from the masses of material which were hauled
by one-horse wagons to the new building. But in 1897 the
superintendent of the new Hall of Maps and Charts reported
a collection of 26,500 maps--"perhaps the best collection in
the United States, unless precedence is given to Harvard."
The next year he was forced to admit that there were actually 46,605 maps; the sharp statistical increase was due,
not to the receipt of new material, but to the "discovery of
maps in the old Library, their rescue, mending, mounting,
and their final assignment."

The music collection suffered from the same crowded conditions as the maps, though it apparently suffered less physical damage. Stacked on the floor in ever-growing piles, where they could not be accessioned, classified, cataloged, nor made truly accessible, the pieces of music could not be sorted out and accurately counted until 1899. In 1898 Librarian John Russell Young asked for the first appropriated funds to purchase music. He was certain that Congress would comply, as the copyright law had already built a music collection of great value, and with an annual appropriation it "would soon be without a rival."

Most of the approximately 250,000 pieces of copyrighted music in the Library in 1897 were popular American compositions in sheet music form, vocal and instrumental, including music for the aeolian, pianola, and other special instruments. Of particular value were the 300 bound volumes of sheet music deposited in U.S. district courts between 1820 and 1859, originally collected and carefully tended in the State Department before they were transferred to the Library. The collection also included foreign musical compositions, mostly from England, Germany, and France, published and entered for copyright in the United States after the passage of the international copyright law of 1891.

The graphic arts materials in the Capitol building were in the same embarrassing state as the other collections. Spofford was unable to arrange them in the Capitol or even to make an accurate estimate of their number. Yet the accumulated copyright deposits of photographs, engravings, etchings, lithographs, and chromolithographs, once arranged and counted in the new building, provided the Library with a collection of pictorial Americana unrivaled by any other library. Even after its first enumeration in the new building, unexpected materials continued to be unearthed. Among discoveries noted in the 1897 annual report were 800 portraits of eminent Americans, several portfolios of photographs taken in Paris during the commune insurrection of 1871, and a portfolio of etchings made during the Civil War by Confederate artists.

The copyright law also provided the Library of Congress with a unique collection of early motion pictures. While the first public showing of a motion picture for a fee in the United States took place in 1894, the copyright law did not provide for the protection of motion pictures as such

until 1912. In the meantime pioneer motion picture producers registered their works as photographs, and 172
motion pictures were thus registered for copyright and deposited in the Library of Congress between 1894 and 1897.
All but nine of the films were registered by Thomas A.
Edison. [33]

The copyright privilege not only accelerated the growth
of the Library's collections; it determined the direction and,
ultimately, the quality of that growth. The very language of
the 1865 law, requiring the deposit of every copyrighted
"book, pamphlet, map, chart, musical composition, print,
engraving, or photograph, " not only ensured the future development of those collections but also the establishment of
separate Library departments for their cultivation and care.

The long-needed administrative reorganization came in
1897, when the Library was preparing for its move into the
new building, and separate map, music, graphic arts, and
copyright departments were established. Thorvald Solberg,
who had worked in the library from 1876 to 1889 and was by
then a nationally known copyright authority, was appointed
the first Register of Copyrights. The creation of a separate
copyright department officially recognized, for the first
time, the value of the copyright function to the national
library.

At the same time John Russell Young, a prominent
journalist and diplomat, replaced the 71-year-old Spofford
as Librarian. Established in its opulent new building, the
Library for the first time had ample space for the organization and storage of its copyright accumulations of 32 years.
Concurrently, in 1897 it was obvious that the Library must
go beyond its previous reliance on copyright as practically
the sole means of expanding its collections. In his first
annual report, Young succinctly described the situation
faced by the Library:

> We have a basis for a library of comprehensive
> research so broad that it only needs to be built
> upon with care, system, and liberality to become
> in a few years the most representative collection
> in the United States and one of the greatest li-
> braries of the world. While our own library has
> for twenty-five years lived so largely upon copy-
> right accretions, other libraries, aided by liberal
> appropriations and bequests, and fortified by lists

of desiderata by professional men and specialists
in every field, have strengthened their collections
until some of them far surpass us in important
branches of learning. Numerical strength does not
constitute the real force of a library.

A new era had arrived. In its 1855 editorial about
the demise of the Smithsonian's national library role, Norton's Literary Gazette accurately prophesized the eventual
need of sizable annual appropriations from Congress to
fully develop and adequately maintain a national library in
the United States. The New England scholars, intellectuals,
and Congressmen who fought for a national library wanted
such appropriations immediately, and the importance of large
appropriations was always acknowledged by Jewett and Spofford, even though they recognized copyright deposit as a
more immediate and practical method of achieving a national
library. In 1895 Spofford predicted that the new Library
building, "with the liberal fostering care of Congress will
yet be filled with the learning of all lands."[34]

In the United States annual appropriations adequate
to sustain a national library were not available until after
the basis for that library had already been established.
When the new Library of Congress Building opened in 1897,
sizable annual appropriations for the support and development of the national library and its collections were for the
first time not only feasible but imperative. Copyright deposit had provided Spofford with the means of accumulating
the necessary national collections and the argument for constructing the necessary building.

In 1899 Herbert Putnam, Superintendent of the Boston
Public Library, became Librarian of Congress, and in the
next four years the Library's national services--cataloging,
classification, reference, loan, and bibliographic--developed
spectacularly, and its place among the national libraries of
the world was assured. Putnam also extended the other
methods of increasing the collections, such as exchange,
gift, and transfer, and secured generous appropriations
from Congress to increase the collections; the 1902 appropriation for the purchase of materials was $70,000.

The national services and prestige of the Library
were based, as Putnam recognized, on the unparalleled
national collections already accumulated, the books, maps,
music, prints, and photographs acquired as copyright

deposits, mostly since 1865. By 1902 the Library of Congress was truly the national library, and Putnam paid homage to its collections and the ideals and efforts of Charles Coffin Jewett and Ainsworth Rand Spofford, while looking to the Library's challenging future: "The opportunities of the Library of Congress for rendering service properly to be expected of the National Library of the United States appear ample, and conditional only upon adequate development of the resources already at its disposal. "[35]

Today copyright deposit is still one of the Library's major acquisitions sources, [36] but between the years 1865 and 1897 it played a crucial role in the development of the national library.

Notes

1. Gertrude Burford Rawlings, The British Museum Library (New York, 1916), p. 78.
2. For copyright deposit from the legal standpoint, see Elizabeth K. Dunne, Deposit of Copyrighted Works (Washington, 1960. Copyright Law Revision Studies No. 20). See also Thomas G. Tanselle, "Copyright Records and the Bibliographer," in Studies in Bibliography (Charlottesville, 1969), vol. 22, p. 77-124; and Martin A. Roberts, Records in the Copyright Office Deposited by the United States District Courts Covering the Period 1790-1870 (Washington, 1939).
3. The American Almanac and Repository of Useful Knowledge for the Year 1837, edited by Charles Bowen (Boston, 1836), p. 82-83. On literary nationalism and library development, see Jesse H. Shera, Foundations of the Public Library (Chicago, 1949), p. 206-216; and Ray W. Frantz, Jr., "A Reexamination of the Influence of Literary Nationalism on the Public Library," Journal of Library History, 1:182-186 (July 1966).
4. Congressional Globe, January 8, 1845, p. 105.
5. The Smithsonian Institution: Documents Relative to Its Origins and History, 1835-1899, edited by William J. Rhees (Washington, 1902. Smithsonian Miscellaneous Collections 42), p. 381-382.
6. See discussion, William Dawson Johnston, History of the Library of Congress, 1800-1864 (Washington, 1904), p. 403-506.

7. Henry to Jewett, March 23, 1847, Smithsonian Institution archives.

8. See Joseph A. Borome, Charles Coffin Jewett (Chicago, 1951), p. 18-106; Wilcomb E. Washburn, "Joseph Henry's Conception of the Purpose of the Smithsonian Institution," in A Cabinet of Curiosities (Charlottesville, 1967), p. 106-129.

9. Jewett to Henry, April 26, 1848, quoted in Borome, p. 41-42.

10. For the cataloging scheme, see Annual Report of the Board of Regents of the Smithsonian Institution, 1850, p. 32-41; for the listing of copyright deposits, see Joseph W. Rogers, U. S. National Bibliography and the Copyright Law (New York, 1960), p. 21-29.

11. Charles C. Jewett, Notices of Public Libraries in the United States of America (Washington, 1851), p. 140-141, 190.

12. North American Review, 71:220 (July 1850); Norton's Literary Gazette, 2:23 (February 15, 1852) and 2:129 (July 15, 1852).

13. Norton's, 3:170-176 (October 15, 1853).

14. Ibid., n. s. 2:67 (February 15, 1855).

15. Deposit statistics compiled from 1849 Catalogue of the Library of Congress and its annual supplements, 1846-48, 1850-59, and from Meehan to Senator James A. Pearce, April 18, 1856, Librarian's Letterbook No. 4. This and other letterbooks of the Librarian are in the Library of Congress archives.

16. Librarian's Letterbook No. 3, February 28, 1854.

17. Copyright Letterbook, June 14, 1859, p. 474 and July 15, 1859, p. 476, Copyright Office archives.

18. Librarian's Letterbook No. 6.

19. Spofford to Messrs. Robert Clarke & Co., May 29, 1867, Librarian's Letterbook No. 7; Congressional Globe, February 22, 1865, p. 981.

20. Annual Report of the Board of Regents of the Smithsonian Institution, 1865, p. 70.

21. Ibid., 1873, p. 21.

22. City of Boston Annual Report of the Trustees of the Public Library, 1869, p. 39-40, appendix 23.

23. Annual Report of the Librarian of Congress, 1868, p. 4; and A. R. Spofford, "The Copyright System of the United States--Its Origin and Growth," in Celebration of the Beginning of the Second Century

of the American Patent System (Washington, 1892), p. 149-153.

24. Fisher to Jenckes, February 10, 1866, and Spofford to Jenckes, April 9, 1870, Jenckes papers, Manuscript Division.

25. Congressional Globe, April 14, 1870, p. 2683.

26. See A. Hunter Dupree, Science in the Federal Government (Cambridge, Mass. , 1957), p. 44-90; also Wilcomb E. Washburn, "The Influence of the Smithsonian Institution on Intellectual Life in Mid-Nineteenth-Century Washington," in Records of the Columbia Historical Society (Washington, 1966), p. 96-121.

27. Annual Report of the Librarian of Congress, 1871, p. 3.

28. U. S. Bureau of Education, Public Libraries in the United States of America (Washington, 1876), p. 1012-1142.

29. These statistics and the estimate that follows of the total number of copyright deposits received at the Library of Congress, 1865-97, are based on statistics in the Annual Report of the Librarian of Congress for the years 1866-1901; A. R. Spofford's A Book for All Readers (New York, 1900), p. 410-411; and a letter from Thorvald Solberg to John Russell Young, November 8, 1897, in Solberg's Copyright Letterbook No. 6, Copyright Office archives. The Librarian's 1901 Annual Report is especially useful.

30. Bancroft to Spofford, September 21, 1872; Clemens to Spofford, December 31, 1880; Field to Spofford, March 11, 1885, Spofford papers, Manuscript Division.

31. A. R. Spofford, "The Function of a National Library," in Herbert Small, Handbook of the Library of Congress (Boston, 1899), p. 125.

32. Joint Committee on the Library, Condition of the Library of Congress, March 3, 1897 (54th Cong., 2d sess. S. Rept. 1573), p. 33-127.

33. Compiled from Howard Lamarr Walls, Motion Pictures 1894-1912 (Washington, U. S. Copyright Office, 1953), p. v-ix, 71-90.

34. Norton's, n. s. 2:67; A. R. Spofford, Special Report of the Librarian of Congress (54th Cong. , 1st sess. , S. Doc. 7), p. 16.

35. Herbert Putnam, "A National Library for the United States," The Bookman, 15:52-57 (March 1902).

36. According to a table prepared by Joseph W. Rogers,
     15, 276, 183 copies of works were deposited in the
     Library between 1902 and 1957; see Dunne, De-
     posit of Copyrighted Works, p. 24.   The same
     study contains a discussion of the effect of de-
     posits on the Library's collections in this century.

SOME VERY TRENCHANT REMARKS
ON SELLING, BUYING & USING VTR

by Welby Smith

Reprinted by permission from Media & Methods March 1971, p. 19-21, 56-57.

In nearly two years of reading Media & Methods, I've been struck by the paucity of articles on videotape recording. Discourses, discussions and dissertations on film abound but, on VTR, mostly silence.

Why? Especially when VTR has so many apparent advantages over film--particularly as a medium for learning. To wit: There is little equipment-induced pressure when you are videotaping. If you don't get what you want the first time, you can simply back up and try again, right on the same tape. Nothing is wasted except time. Hour for hour, videotape is cheaper than film (if you include processing costs, much cheaper).

And, with the advent of the new half-inch EIAJ Standard VTRs, the cost of a single-camera videotape recording system is comparable to that of an adequate 16mm film setup. Color, of course, is very expensive in videotape (primarily because of the high cost of color cameras), but color in film is also an expensive proposition. Certainly, when you figure in the VTR's capacity for reprogramming, either on the spot (reshooting something that you're not satisfied with), or at a later date (updating a subject that time has made obsolete), then it becomes very attractive indeed.

Really? Then why isn't anyone doing anything with it? In my opinion, there are several reasons. Some of them are more or less valid, such as the instability and incompatibility of early VTRs and the doubt and confusion engendered by the huckstering sales approach of the VTR manufacturers. Other reasons have less validity. These include

the ideas that film is inherently a more "creative" (poor,
debased word) medium than videotape, and that so-called
audio-visual "specialists" should be allowed to monopolize
videotape recording equipment, quite literally keeping it away
from the kids and teachers who should be using it.

   Good or bad, justified or not, these and other "reasons" have stifled what should be a free, innovative and,
above all, enjoyable learning tool; have relegated it to dusty
closets, sterile "studios," or, worse yet, to the candy-
colored, tinsel-dripping, tomorrowland of the VTR manufacturer's latest promotional literature, replete with promises
of "Revolutionary" new developments. It occurs to me that
the VTR industry may be the first to reach that ultimate pin-
nacle of the American ad-man's dream--leaping from verbal
extravaganza to extravaganza with such monotonous regularity
that our jaded appetites are glutted by the very words and it
is no longer necessary even to produce, much less deliver,
the products (which, in any event, would have been outmoded in a week or so)!

   Where did we go wrong?

   I believe that the problem began some years back,
with our national knee-jerk reaction to Sputnik. With the
ensuing Total National Commitment To Education as a car-
rot, big business leaped into educational technology with both
feet and has remained firmly entroughed ever since.

   I don't know what things were like at educators' Conventions in the pre-Sputnik era. Rather drab, I suppose.
But, with all those Federal dollars floating around, things
began to liven up and the exhibit hall at Conventions today
looks like a cross between a County Fair midway and a Big
Three automobile commercial, complete with mini-skirted
lovelies, smooth-talking pitchmen, and convivial "hospitality
suites." The bedazzled educator, so recently cast into the
limelight to be assured, nay harangued, regarding his importance (after long years of lip service and neglect), can
perhaps be pardoned for carrying his consumer compulsions
into the educational marketplace. These were heady times!
His conditioned reflexes responded to the call of bright
promises and gleaming chrome, to the American tradition of
technological solutions to complex socio-cultural problems
(a tradition that still troubles us today). VTR WAS THE
ANSWER!

But, after the first flush of pride wore off, after
all the faculty and kids had "seen themselves on teevee,"
the honeymoon began to pall. Unnerving little facts that the
friendly salesman had "forgotten" or "overlooked" became
embarrassingly evident. Like, in order to make copies of
your videotapes, you had to buy a special VTR that cost considerably more than your original machine. And, even then,
good copies were a hit or miss affair. Or, maybe you found
that your rather expensive one-inch videotape recorder had no
provision for adding new sound over the existing picture
(audio dubbing), even though half-inch VTRs at half the cost
of your machine offered this feature as standard. Worst of
all, when you complained, the friendly salesman confided
that next year's models would offer all those special features,
at a small increase in price.

Then, if you wanted to send a copy of your prize
tape on the care and feeding of the bladderwort to a colleague in another District (or even another school), you had
to first ascertain that he possessed a VTR identical in
make and model to yours (and even this was no guarantee
that the tape would play back properly). If he didn't, you
had to get hold of this VTR, or another one just like it, and
providing that this machine was electronically compatible
with yours (and not all VTRs were electronically compatible),
you could then make a fair copy of your original tape which,
with luck, would play back on his VTR.

Sounds like a lot of work, right? Is it any wonder
that many educators simply wrote the whole thing off as a
dead loss? The real wonder is that any of them kept trying
(and, unfortunately, kept buying).

This brings us to another point--training (or lack of
it) in the basic operation and maintenance of VTR equipment. Since the only alternative requires that we take for
granted a total lack of responsibility on the part of the VTR
manufacturers, let's be charitable and assume that their
virtually unanimous disinclination to provide any kind of
comprehensible training material with their equipment simply
reflects that time-honored American merchandising ploy--
planned obsolescence. Nor are the Asian and European manufacturers any more forthcoming in this regard. Here, if
anyone cares to see it, is Twentieth Century man's basic
dilemma in microcosm--technologists spewing forth complex
and potentially revolutionary machines with neither a jot of
guidance as to their use, nor a tittle of responsibility for the
consequences thereof.

In the absence of responsible assistance from the
producers and suppliers of VTR equipment (though not because of that absence, since each new technological development breeds its own parasitic tribe of cognoscenti, eager to
corner the arcane knowledge of that particular machine and
exploit it to their own generally self-serving and obfuscating
uses), a new kind of educator appeared--the Audio-Visual
or Media Specialist.   In some cases, he simply evolved
from the position of custodian of the movie projector (a
disagreeable additional duty often foisted off on physical
education teachers or others equally ill-qualified), or more
or less by default, into the Media Coordinator.   In other
instances, he came equipped with a degree in Audio-Visual
Studies or Communication Sciences.   Now, neither of these
cases predicates a basic inability to realize the importance
of availability of equipment and advice in carrying out an
effective learning program.   And yet, after more than two
years of contact with a fair-sized sample of East Coast
educational media people (in various roles as trainer, consultant, program producer, system designer and equipment
sales representative), I must conclude that competent,
effective innovative audio-visual people are still a distinct
minority among those responsible for educational media.
Most so-called Educational Media Centers are nothing more
than parking lots for videotape recorders and other expensive a-v equipment, and appear to be run primarily for the
convenience of the people employed there.   The word facili-
tative is one which is evidently beyond their comprehension;
and, when the needs of classroom teachers and students do
impinge upon the manipulation of this equipment, it is more
likely to be coincidental than not.

It is tempting to speculate on the reasons for the
apparent widespread reticence of Audio-Visual Specialists
to initiate any but the most elementary training programs
for teachers in the application of VTR equipment, or (Hor-
rors!) to let kids get their hands on the gear.   It is my
experience that teachers and children, given a few hours of
intelligent guidance on the use of VTR, and the proper care
and operation of the components themselves, quickly outstrip
the usually structured and self-conscious efforts of the
"specialists."   (If you'll pardon another aside; isn't it interesting that, although the very development of helical scan
VTR represents an effort to break free of the bonds imposed
by the heavier and necessarily more precise and expensive
broadcast equipment, the "specialist's" first inclination is to
return to the warm, comforting womb of a "studio" and nail

all that beautiful, lightweight, portable equipment back down
to the floor.   Give the networks cheap, broadcast, portable
VTRs and see what would happen to those studios!)

So the teachers are taught to fear the videotape recorder, and the kids are deprived of the rare opportunity
to experiment in group and self-expression with no penalty
for failure.   So what else is new?

A final word about VTR vs film (although I really see
them as complementary media and enjoy working in both).
It requires little visual sophistication to observe that the
sharpest video image is less sharp than a good projected
film image.   On the other hand, as we've noted elsewhere,
VTR playback is instantaneous.   No gut-wrenching waits at
the lab to see if you really got what you wanted to get.
VTR sound, given reproduction equipment of equal quality,
is generally better than optical film sound.   16mm films,
while more expensive to produce, are easier and cheaper to
distribute (at least, as of now they are).   Videotape-to-film
transfers, which sounded like the best of all possible worlds
(i. e. , produce in VTR, and transfer to 16mm film for distribution) are simply not dependable as yet and, even when
they are as good as is technologically possible, people will
tend to reject the image quality, when projected, that they
raved about on the tube.   Perhaps with more dependable
processing equipment, and better audience appreciation of the
economies involved, this will become a more viable production method, but I doubt it.

We could go on all day, arguing the relative merits
of film vs VTR.   Suffice it to say that both have strengths
and weak points.   Why not maximize their strengths?   Why
not, for instance, use VTR to teach film-making, to demonstrate camera movement and technique, lens angles, points
of view?   Why not rehearse scenes in videotape, critique
actors and blocking, present proposals for films?   Take advantage of the VTR's instantaneous replay and re-program-
ming capabilities and, in the final version, where focus and
clarity and distribution potential are important, go to film.
Media aren't inherently antagonistic; that's a people problem.

Are things really as bad as I make them out to be?   Maybe
not.   A few recent developments, if properly exploited by
educators and other users of VTR, could bring some method
into this madness.   Chief among these are (1) the apparent

industry-wide agreement to standardize some half-inch
VTRs, (2) the trend toward reliable, (3) truly portable,
battery-powered VTRs, and (4) the evident shift away from
the heavier, relatively more expensive one-inch VTRs for
all but fairly serious production work.   Mind you, these are
not by any means unmixed blessings!   When the manufacturers heat up the hyperbole and prepare to do you a favor,
don't turn your back.

What is the EIAJ Standard, and what does it mean
to you?   Until early 1970, a tape recorded on one make of
VTR would not play back on VTRs made by other manufacturers; there was no interchangeability.   Of course,
some manufacturers sold their VTRs to other companies who
"private branded" them (e.g., Concord and Panasonic, both
produced by Matsushita; Sony and GE, both produced by
Sony, and the many and varied brand names that used the
"IVC Format," all of which were manufactured by the International Video Corporation).   There was also a lot of talk
about this or that format being the "standard of the industry."
In fact, as you've probably begun to suspect, there were
very few meaningful "standards" of any kind in this complex
and confusing situation.   From the manufacturer's point of
view, this was o.k., since the buyer who chose his VTR
initially was pretty well limited to that format for subsequent
VTR purchases.   Some manufacturers even went so far as
to design their whole systems, cameras and all, so that
they wouldn't work with other makers' equipment.   (At this
point, a word about the basic philosophy of the manufacturers
is in order.   Whatever their ad copy says, regardless of
their PR campaigns, the basic goal of all VTR manufacturers
is to sell as many machines as they can in as short a time
as possible.   That's how they make their money, and you
ignore that fact at your own peril.)

It was, in fact, the promise of more profit, rather
than any real concern for the needs of the VTR user, that
finally enticed the Electronics Industries Association of
Japan (EIAJ) to come up with the standardization that any
responsible industry would have introduced much earlier in
the game.   At least one major American manufacturer has
adopted the EIAJ format and, for now, this appears to be the
wave of the future in half-inch VTR.

Without indulging in the petty technicalities that so
often impede discussions of this sort, let me say that all
VTRs that subscribe to the EIAJ standard have the following

characteristics in common:

       * One hour playing time with a 2400 foot reel of
         videotape
       * Guaranteed interchangeability with all other EIAJ
         VTRs
       * Resolution of 300 lines or better
       * Light weight (around 33 lbs for most basic models)

     The EIAJ VTRs have lots of other characteristics in
common, but these are the important ones that standardization has brought about.   Prices hover around the $700.00
mark for most basic VTRs.   However, there are some very
important differences among EIAJ VTRs.   Standardization,
fortunately, left some room for differentiation, mostly in
production capabilities; but more about that in a later article.

     Back to EIAJ Standardization's effect on you; whether
you already have EIAJ equipment, have non- or pre-EIAJ
gear, or are just in the market for VTR.

     To begin with, if you already have an EIAJ machine,
you can interchange tapes with all other EIAJ VTR owners
(if you have any tapes worth exchanging, that is).   And,
surprisingly, this is not just a manufacturer's claim--it
really works.   Your effort expended in lugging around heavy
equipment has been cut dramatically (anywhere from 20 to
50 pounds below the weight of older non-EIAJ VTRs).   The
one-hour record/playback time panders to our broadcast-
attuned compulsions (or, if you prefer, gives you more time
for your money), and the increased resolution does provide
more picture detail.

     But--dramatic reductions in weight have been achieved,
in many respects, at the expense of durability and general
reliability; increased resolution has brought with it picture
instability that at least one major manufacture claims is
"unavoidable"; and increased programming time just means,
in many cases, longer bad programs.

     The manufacturers, while they titillate us with their
new hardware, studiously ignore desperately-needed software
and training that might help to make this jumble of gadgets
more comprehensible.

     The message for the prospective purchaser of VTR
equipment is loud and clear--<u>Caveat</u> <u>Emptor</u>!

What about the poor soul with non-EIAJ equipment?
Are you totally out of it? Shamefully outmoded? Should
you just junk the old stuff and shell out for new, as the
manufacturers suggest?

Probably not. It depends primarily on what you do
with your equipment. If you are producing duplicate copies
of your tapes for playback in satellite locations (e. g., a
media center/local school situation), then interchangeability
is important to you. However, if you've already purchased
pre- or non-EIAJ VTRs for the whole system, they're working well, and your need to exchange with or use videotapes
in other formats is limited, there's certainly no need to
junk perfectly good equipment. You might consider adding
one or more EIAJ VTRs as you need new equipment, or as
the older machines wear out. This would give you the
ability to "translate" your tapes into a "standard language, "
and also to play back commercial or other pre-recorded
materials not produced by your system. By the way, I
wouldn't hold my breath until more pre-recorded material
is available. I've heard the predictions about a veritable
flood of tapes on every conceivable subject but it hasn't
happened yet and shows no signs of happening. Indeed, the
few pre-recorded materials I have seen are miserably produced and incredibly boring.

On the other hand, if your application of VTR is
primarily concerned with immediate feedback (such as role-
playing, micro-teaching, self-concept development, etc.),
then your VTR, whatever its format, is good for as long
as it will record and play back decent picture and sound.
A lighter machine and a longer playing time might be nice
but, that's a budgetary, not a production consideration.

While EIAJ standardization might initially make the
idea of producing and distributing program material in videotape more feasible, unless frequent updating or re-program-
ming is necessary, the higher cost of tape vs film and the
still sparse scattering of EIAJ VTRs militates against it.
It may be that the VTR's unique capacity for instantaneous
reprogramming and replay will remain its most significant
feature, and the business of distributing pre-recorded materials will be left to film, EVR, etc. If so, it will be a
big joke on the manufacturers, who are currently spawning
a whole new crop of emasculated VTRs that (poor things)
only play back. It is, I think, characteristic of the manufacturers' general lack of imagination that, in the desperate

race for the dollar, they would strip the VTR of its one
unique competitive advantage over other media. As play-
back-only systems go, EVR, 16mm film and even Super-
Eight with sound are far superior to videotape in cost, in
convenience, and in durability.

A word about portables--the shoulder-carried, battery-powered types. They look great in the ads, right?
And, for some applications, they are irreplaceable. But,
most videotaping situations with which I am familiar can
either (1) be accomplished with a standard, AC line or
automobile inverter powered VTR and extension cables for
mike and camera, or (2) are not important enough to the
subject of the tape to warrant the additional expense of a
portable. (For about $100.00 you can have an inverter in-
stalled in your car that will deliver power stable enough to
drive any half-inch VTR single-camera system I know of.
And, with a long impedence mike and a long camera cable,
there aren't many places you can't go. Imagination, not
money, is the prime mover behind excellence, in VTR programs and elsewhere.)

If you must have a portable, insist that it (1) play
back through the viewfinder on location, (2) have convenient
and inexpensive AC and DC adapters for external power,
and (3) produce tapes that are totally interchangable with
those made on your basic VTR. If you settle for less in
any category, you're going to be very disappointed.

These and other areas of videotape recording urgently
need informed explication. I hope to cover many more in
future articles, and I trust that your questions and opinions
will be a springboard for mutually informative exchanges.
As you may have gathered, I am a practioner, not a tech-
nologist or engineer, and my opinions are strongly held and
the product of experience. But don't be put off--like Mon-
taigne, "I would not say all these things if it were my due to
be believed. "

Remember, despite all the medium and message jargon, videotape is only another learning tool--nothing more,
nothing less. It can be remarkably effective in a variety of
learning situations, but only when teachers and children have
the training that engenders confidence in the medium and
themselves, and the latitude to employ it in new and different ways.

And now, a word for the Media Specialists. If you think I've been a little tough on your group, ask yourself what you've done lately to foster that aforementioned spirit of self-confidence and innovation among kids and teachers. If your conscience is clear, hooray! Let us share in your ideas. But if the shoe fits....

There may be some who think I've been less than generous with the manufacturers and suppliers of videotape recording equipment. That's correct. As long as these guys insist on taking as their model the flatulent absurdities and flashy gimmicks of Detroit, they deserve criticism. We cannot continue to tolerate and even reward planned obsolesence and conspicuous consumption in our educational systems without diverting funds from more important areas of learning to the uninformed, impulse-buying of next year's model (when this year's isn't even being used properly). The day of accountability is coming. Unfortunately, when the crunch comes, it will be as always the kids who suffer.

Perhaps these are hard words, but they need saying --here, and in every school system in America.

OSTRICHES AND ADOLESCENTS

by Mary Kingsbury

Reprinted by permission from Journal of Education for Librarianship 11(4) Spring 1971, p. 325-331.

Ostriches do not hide their heads in the sand when confronted by danger.   Contrary to that popular belief, they run away.   Today, many librarians are acting like frightened ostriches.   Faced by adolescent demands for relevant books and the possibility of parental or administrative censure if they provide them, librarians flee.   Fear makes the ostrich a great running bird; the librarian a mockery.

In an effort to halt the flight, concerned writers call for greater relevance in the choice of books for adolescents. John Igo complained, "We take kids off 1966 streets and give them 1916 answers."[1]   "The time is overdue for much more realistic literature, " wrote Frank Bonham.   "These kids live in a real world, not in a fiction world."[2]   And the perennial pleader for greater relevance in literature for young adults, Nat Hentoff, protested that "the real disservice you do kids is to pretend that everything is cool when they know damn well it isn't."[3]   Reiterating the same point in "Baby Dolls Are Gone, " Nancy Larrick discussed the need for books reflecting our social and economic crisis. "This is what youngsters are living with.   It is what many of them want to read about."[4]

After pointing out that there are books which face the realities of today's world, Linda Lapides queried, "Where are the librarians who read these books, grasp their meaning for teenagers, and use them?"[5]   Margaret Edwards suggested that they may have little genuine interest in their young patrons.   "Why do so many librarians seemingly dislike teenagers. . . .   [A]re they afraid of adolescents?"[6]

Thus, from within and without the profession, involved individuals sound the alarm.   How many more articles

must librarians read before they take action? Is it too late?
Have libraries lost the present generation of young adults?
In Books for the Teenage Reader, G. R. Carlsen wrote,
"Studies seem to indicate that adolescence is the crucial
period in developing the habit of reading."[7]   His statement
points up the critical need for supplying relevant books to
this age group.   Yet, in her article, Miss Lapides noted
the discrepancy between the books professionals judge will
appeal to young people and the books teens actually read.[8]

     This incongruity between adult selection and adoles-
cent expectations is not a problem peculiar to the seventies.
The classic example of mismatch occurred with the reception accorded Catcher in the Rye.   The book appeared in
1951.   Twelve years later, librarians admitted it to the
pristine pages of the 1963 Supplement to the Standard Catalogue for High School Libraries.   By the time this "controversial" book made the Standard Catalogue, it had been read
by the young people for whom librarians evidently considered
it unsuitable and was losing its relevance for contemporary
readers.   The Standard Catalogue is a safe guide for librarians afraid to rock the boat of adult complacency.   It
is not an adequate guide for librarians attempting to select
books that will appeal to today's teenagers.   Librarians
may never span the generation gap, but by sensitive book
selection they can demonstrate an awareness of the particular hang-ups being lived through by young people.

     The challenge may prove impossible.   Librarians may
be unwilling to risk the confrontations required to sensitize
their perceptions of young adults.   Yet, inadequate insight
results in irrelevant book selection.   Students told a Fortune
editor, "To understand us you have to do what we do:
smoke pot."[9]   Must adults responsible for adolescent book
selection "trip out" in order to tune in to their prospective
patrons?   Librarians would give short shrift to the proponents of such a course.   Tripping out is not the sine qua
non for coming to terms with youth.   Those entrusted with
the responsibility for selecting books for adolescent readers
cannot escape that trust by claiming that few adults understand today's young people.   The biggest obstacle to adult
understanding of the adolescent sub-culture is refusal by
adults to remove their blinders.

     Removing blinders means running the risk of pain.
Adolescents threaten adults by reminding them of experiences
they have successfully repressed.   The presence of the

adolescent threatens this repression and recalls painful
memories.   Understandably, few of us welcome painful
encounters--especially with ourselves.   And yet, such encounters are essential for re-awakening the realization of
what it means to be young.

More than anything today, young people seek relevancy.   They are the exponents of candor and spontaneity.
However, in the realm of literature for adolescents, candor
commands little clout.   High schools teem with more sex
than one of Hugh Hefner's Bunny Clubs or a North Beach
topless a go-go.   The young Portnoy's complaint is far
more typical of the male high school population than most
adults care to recognize or remember.   As a former coun-
selor, this writer knows that Nabokov's Lolita escaped the
pages of his novel and lives lustily in the high schools.   If
labeled accurately, the dating games people play in high
school would read "Making It vs. Not Being Made."   But
where is the novel "suitable for young people" which honestly
depicts the adolescent sexual scene?   Perhaps it is now making
the rounds seeking a publisher.   Perhaps it is still in the
mind of an author who is waiting for the climate which will
nurture such a book.

Telling of his difficulties in finding a publisher for
Durango Street, Frank Bonham noted that it "went through
three publishers before it was finally published."[10]   Publishers are cautious about accepting a book which might be
rejected by librarians who feel their job security threatened
by the local guardians of teenage virtue.   If publishers
were certain that the so-called "controversial" books would
find a favorable reception among librarians, they would publish them.

Maia Wojciechowska in "An End to Nostalgia" placed
the responsibility for closing the gap between adult selection
and reader expectations on the librarians.   "The gulf between
the real child of today and his fictional counterpart must
be bridged.   And that is the responsibility of authors, publishers, and librarians.   In that order.   For the last of the
three have the power to build the bridge or dynamite it.
They can buy the books that are meaningless or they can
boycott them."[11]

Considering the chain involved in making relevant
books available to young people, Wojciechowska correctly
labeled librarians the most important link.   Books originate

with authors, but they end up with librarians. Until librarians demand books that do speak to youth, authors will continue to have difficulty locating publishers for them.   Publishers are the connecting link, but the selectors control
the chain.

    We must add a fourth link to the chair of responsi-
bility if the problem of relevant book selection is to be
solved.   The librarian-selector is the crucial link.   However, if those who select materials for young people have
been dynamiting more bridges than they have been building,
those who forge the links in library schools must assume
much of the responsibility.

    The majority of library school courses which empha-
size materials for young people fail to produce librarians
equipped to work effectively with young adults and to select
books meaningful to them.   If this were not true, why the
articles reflecting concern for the state of book selection
for young adults?   An adage from vocational literature applies.
Jobs that are attractive today may not exist tomorrow.
Books and materials that are relevant today may be outdated tomorrow.

    Two examples from the past reflect this.   Seventeenth
Summer has greater relevancy for junior high readers than
for the "with it" generation.   Only an over protective adult
could consider it meaningful to most senior high school students.   The problems facing today's Angies and Jacks are
not whether to drink beer on a picnic or to kiss on the first
date but whether to smoke marijuana at a party or to "go
all the way" on a subsequent date.   Even the still controversial classic of the fifties, Catcher in the Rye, is a bland
book by today's standards.   What does it have to say to a
young adult population whose mores are being shaped by
movies such as The Graduate, A Man and A Woman, and
Easy Rider?   The author recalls waiting in line for admission to The Graduate and talking with a high school sophomore who assured us we were about to see a great movie.
Although it had been playing only a month, he was seeing
it for the third time.

    The course for young adult literature and materials
has become the "love child" of the library school curriculum.
We would feel guilty abandoning it, but we do not know how
to raise it.   The Library Bill of Rights provides one out.
Because it condemns discrimination on the basis of age,

library schools could eliminate the course in materials for
adolescents.   When 80 per cent of the Bowker Annual's list
of "Books Suitable for Young Adults" are adult titles, are
we justified in spending time on the 20 per cent written
specifically for a teen audience?   The pablum of the adolescent novel will not attract the "non-readers."   The "readers"
select adult books.   A recent example is Valley of the Dolls.
The paperback edition became the book of the 1967-68 academic year in high school reading circles.

To date, the majority of library schools have opted to
retain the course.   To make it more effective, instructors
should stop wasting time on the objects of the selection process which quickly become dated and begin investing time in
the selectors themselves.   If the library schools graduate
librarians who understand the adolescent sub-culture and
who are open to change and unthreatened by it, the problem
of book selection will resolve itself.   Authors will not hesitate to write relevant books and publishers will not hesitate
to accept them.   These "now" librarians will be demanding
them for the "now" generation who will be reading them.

Library schools can produce such paragons by placing
emphasis on the development of attitudes.   The graduate of
a successful "attitudinal" course would be non-censorial,
non-shockable, and non-authoritarian.   Strongly authoritarian
personalities experience constant threat from today's challenging youth.   The teen population declare off-limits a library dominated by an authoritarian figure.   A fourth quality
the graduate should possess is a well developed sense of
humor to help him keep his cool.   In fact, so essential is
a sense of humor in working effectively with young people
that a candidate who lacks one should be counseled into
some other avenue of library work.

Careful screening of candidates for library service to
young adults is one of the responsibilities which the library
school must assume.   Future young adult librarians should
spend time observing in a high school library and in the
public libraries where teens gather in the evenings to further
their social lives under the guise of studying.   If this initiation is not enough to discourage those who should not work
with adolescents, the course instructor or library school
administrator should encourage the student to re-evaluate
his potential for working with young people.

In addition to first hand observation, several psy-

chology books are helpful in developing an awareness of
what patterns of behavior to expect before adolescents acquire mature behavior styles.   Goodenough's Developmental
Psychology, Blos's The Adolescent, and Erikson's Childhood
and Society offer valuable insights.   Incorporating such
readings into the course serves two purposes.   First, they
provide standards of behavior to be anticipated from adolescents.   If a future librarian feels unable to cope with such
behavior, he can turn to other library work rather than
burden young people with his lack of understanding.   Second, such books supply the theory needed to understand
other reading assignments.

For the course reading will concentrate on books
about adolescents rather books for them.   Students will
read books which describe the adolescence of the characters.
Hesse's Demian, Bellow's Adventures of Augie March,
Braithwaite's To Sir, With Love, Brown's Manchild in the
Promised Land, Salinger's Catcher in the Rye, Miller's
Cool World, and Goldman's gem, Temple of Gold all help
foster understanding.   In selecting books for the course,
the criterion should not be "Is this a book suitable for
young adults?" but rather "Is this a book suitable for adults
seeking greater understanding of young people?"

Today's youth are mad about movies.   Films as
disparate as Bonnie and Clyde and The Graduate speak to
the young so eloquently that multiple viewings are a commonplace.   Adults who want to communicate with this age
group cannot ignore the films that are shaping or at least
reflecting the attitudes of the young.   Assignments to see
movies such as Goodbye, Columbus and Last Summer should
be an integral part of a course directed at developing openness to young adults.   High school students who have paid
to see The Graduate eight and nine times have evidently
found something they value in the film.   Few books judged
"suitable for young adults" command that degree of devotion
from adolescent readers.   Librarians need to view the
movies being seen by students so they will know what degree of relevance to demand in the books they select for
them.

Underground newspapers are another source of insight into the interests of today's youth.

Music, on the other hand, turns on nearly all members of the adolescent world.   More than any other medium,

music carries the message to young people.   And if adults
are willing to listen, it can carry the message to them.

College students are another non-book source for
developing an awareness of the thinking of the adolescent
mind.   The enterprising professor should invite college
freshmen to participate as resource people in the courses
for young adult materials.   To paraphrase Wordsworth,
freshmen can provide "Intimations of Adolescence from Recol-
lections of High School."   Adolescents themselves, freshmen students are available on any campus and are eminently
qualified to interpret the high school scene to future librarians.

The foregoing is not to suggest that librarians totally
ignore the "suitable for" books.   They should introduce
Seventeenth Summer and Catcher in the Rye as historical
examples of books that were once particularly relevant to
young people.   Students should read Donovan's I'll Get
There. It Better be Worth the Trip and Wojciechowska's
Tuned Out for a picture of contemporary attempts at relevancy for junior and senior high school readers.   However,
the greater part of the course reading should be those books
and articles which will help the librarian to better understand young adults, their interests, needs, and behavior.
The course emphasis would change from the traditional
"Selection of Materials Suitable for Young Adults" to "Selection of Librarians Suitable for Young Adults."   The focus
of the course would become the development of young adult
librarians who are committed to youth, relevance, and confrontation.

Like the ostrich, such librarians will become great
runners.   However, they will run toward, not away from
danger.   For the librarian who demands relevant books
from publishers and who supplies them to young readers
may risk his job.   The question is whether the risk of confrontation with threatened (and threatening) parents and
principals is offset by the reward of winning a generation
of readers.   The history of printing demonstrates the
dangers of working with books.   Commitment to relevant
book selection for young people requires more courage than
any other activity in modern library service.   Library
schools must train young adult librarians with such commitment.

References

1. Igo, John: "Books for the New Breed." Library Journal, 92:1705, April 15, 1967.
2. Bonham, Frank and Duggins, James: "Are We for Real with Kids?" Top of the News, 24:252, April 1967.
3. Nat Hentoff quoted in Haskel Frankel's "On the Fringe." Saturday Review, 51:34, Sept. 7, 1968.
4. Larrick, Nancy: "Baby Dolls Are Gone." Library Journal, 92:3817, Oct 15, 1967.
5. Lapides, Linda: "Question of Relevance." Top of the News, 24:57, Nov. 1967.
6. Edwards, Margaret: "The Urban Library and the Adolescent." Library Quarterly, 38:71, Jan., 1968.
7. Carlsen, G. R.: Books and the Teen-age Reader. Bantam Books, 1967, p. 5.
8. See entire article by Lapides cited above.
9. Ways, Max: "The Faculty Is the Heart of the Trouble." Fortune, 79:97, Jan., 1969.
10. Ref. 2, p. 252.
11. Wojciechowska, Maia: "An End to Nostalgia." Library Journal, 93:4691, Dec., 15, 1968.

"I'M GONNA KILL YA"

by Caroline J. Feller

Reprinted by permission from **PNLA Quarterly** Winter 1970, p. 4-14.

The above title may seem unorthodox and ungenteel for an article in a library publication. It was meant to be just that! The title quote was one answer to the question, "What do you say when you hate somebody?", asked of third graders in Basalt, Colorado, and Leaburg, Oregon. Most of the answers contained violent expressions. The child may not means what he says, but it worries adults.

Parents are concerned about the effect of a violent environment on their children's behavior, and rightly so. After all, a majority of arrests for major crimes against property and a substantial minority of arrests for major crimes against the person involve people under the age of twenty-one. [1]

Perhaps librarians should examine some of the folk-lore of children, including their rhymes, songs and games, and listen to the verbal violence of childhood. Let's begin with nursery rhymes. Surely "Mary Had a Little Lamb" is a passive enough rhyme, but the children have new words:

> Mary had a little lamb
> Her father shot it dead
> And now it goes to school with her
> Between two chunks of bread. [2]

Then there is:

> Hickory dickory dock
> Three mice ran up the clock
> The clock struck one
> And the other two escaped with
> minor injuries. [3]

                                     or

> Little Miss Muffet
> Sat on a tuffet
> Eating her curds and whey
> Along came a spider
> And sat down beside her
> And she picked up a spoon and beat
>   the hell out of it. [4]

Patriotic songs also have been given new words by children.
Voicing their dislike of authority, children have been found
singing this song on either coast of our nation--in Oregon
and in New York.   Some sing only the chorus, others the
entire song!

> (To the tune of "Battle Hymn of the Republic")

> Mine eyes have seen the glory
> Of the burning of the school
> We have tortured all the teachers
> And we've broken every rule

> We have burned all the books
> And we've hung the principal
> Us brats go marching on! [5]

> Glory, glory hallelujah
> Teacher hit me with a ruler
> The ruler turned red
> And teacher dropped dead
> And that was the end of school.

                                     or

> Glory, glory hallelujah
> Teacher hit me with a ruler
> Met her at the door
> With a trusty .44
> And I ain't seen the old bat since!

                                     or

> Glory, glory hallelujah
> Teacher hit me with a ruler
> I hit her in the bean
> With a rotten tangerine
> And the juice came running out. [6]

Teachers are always a popular subject for parody:

> Row, row, row your boat
> Gently down the stream
> Throw your teacher overboard
> And listen to her scream. [7]

On a sign in Lake Oswego, Oregon saying "Drive slowly--
you may kill a child," someone had penciled in: "Wait for
a teacher."[8] Pop folk songs, too, are translated into
"childrenese" with violent overtones:

> (To the tune of "This Land Is My Land")
>
> This land is my land
> It is not your land
> I've got a shot gun
> And you ain't got one. [9]

Popular songs have always been parodied, but the children
even take a mild, gentle Christmas song and turn it into a
tale of violence, perhaps inspired by television westerns:

> (To the tune of "Rudolph, the Red-nosed Reindeer")
>
> Rudolph the red-nosed cowpoke
> Had a very shiny gun
> And if you ever saw it
> You would turn around and run.
>
> All of us other cowpokes
> Used to laugh and call him names
> They never let poor Rudolph
> Join in any poker games.
>
> Then one foggy Christmas Eve
> Sheriff came to say
> Cowpoke with your gun so bright
> Won't you kill my wife tonight.
>
> Then how the cowpokes loved him
> As they shouted out with glee
> Rudolph the red-nosed cowpoke
> You'll go down in history. [10]

Children sometimes construct their own rhymes to tease
their peers:

> Tell tale tit
> Your tongue shall be slit
> And all the dogs in the town
> Shall have a little bit. [11]

Morbid jokes are also part of children's folklore.   Many of
the "Moron" jokes take a cavalier attitude toward death:

> Why did the moron jump off the
>   Empire State Building?
> To show his girlfriend he had guts.

A variant on the "guts theme" is the remark that one bug
made to the other bug when they were splattered against
the windshield, "Bet you don't have the guts to do that
again. "[12]

Songs or rhymes may accompany games.   A common jump-
rope rhyme is:

> I had a little brother
> His name was Tiny Tim
> I put him in the bath tub
> To teach him how to swim
>
> He drank up all the water
> He ate up all the soap
> He died last night
> With a bubble in his throat. [13]

>   or

> Yankee Doodle went to town
> Riding on a stage coach
> Hit a bump and skinned his rump
> And landed in the city dump. [14]

Many children's games also have a measure of violence in them.   Sometimes the name of the game changes
according to locale or national climate, but the rules remain the same.   An example is the chase and capture of
the variously named cops and robbers, cowboys and Indians,
spacemen and Martians and the recently reported cops and
demonstrators. [15]   Follow the leader has often had a violent
aspect to it.   In New York City, it is played walking on
window ledges high above the ground. [16]   In the country the
same game often ends up with the leader crossing angry

little streams on thin planks.   The object seems to be to
injure the less agile followers.

Sometimes activities that are first played by children
end up as real violence.   "Territory," played in Brooklyn,
N. Y. , by fifth graders using two teams and a circle of
chalk that cannot be violated, evolved into a more deadly
version as "territory" becomes a game of guns and knives
exemplified in West Side Story.

Spectator sports which could be interpreted as exalting
violence, are brought into the home via television.   Young
and old alike flock to car races and demolition derbies to
see a crash.   The body contact sports, such as professional,
scholastic or "little league" football, boxing and wrestling,
maintain complicated rules in order to regulate the physical
violence.   Children make up their own rules to regulate violence, imitating the adults.   These accepted codes of conduct
usually include the following taboos: do not hit another who
wears glasses, two are not to gang up on someone alone,
and do not gang up on anyone from behind. [17]

Where do children get such ideas?   Parents or other
adults, both directly and indirectly, expose children to violent influences.   One example is parental pleasure when
their child physically fights back against the school bully.
This is called manliness.   Pillow fights and wrestling
matches are often instigated by parents.   The popular doll,
"Bobo," a large rubber top, was purchased in large quantities by parents a few years ago so that children could take
out their natural aggressions by hitting it instead of each
other. [18]

Children learn semi-violent games like dodge-ball
from adults.   The object of the game is to hit the person
who is "It" with a ball.   The children then adapt this game
to a sort of "dodge-stone" and hurl rocks at a disliked fellow student.   At the John Eaton School in Washington, D. C.
some years ago, the children threw stones at a third grade
girl because she was "a Jew and had killed Christ. "

Thus it might seem that parents and teachers teach
children the "how to" of being violent and further sanction
it by prescribing rules for carrying out the actions.   Adults
also invent rhymes that influence children to do the same.
In a recently circulated handbill entitled "Riot Rhymes," this
appeared:

> We got segregated in the looting
> Integrated in the shooting.

Sick jokes can be collected from both children and adults.
A sixth grader unabashedly chanted this one:

> Willie with a thirst for gore
> Nailed his sister to the door
> Mother said with humor quaint
> Now Willie dear, don't scratch the
>   paint. [19]

or

> Into the family drinking well
> Willie pushed his sister Nell
> She's there yet, because it kilt her
> Now we have to buy a filter. [20]

Children frequently get the ideas on which to base stories
or rhymes such as the above from similarly violent tales
told to them by adults.

At the library story hour, the children beg the adult
storyteller for a scary story told with the lights out. When
the story is over and the lights come on and they feel secure and safe once more, the children rush out to the play-
ground to tell others their own version. Invariably, the gory
parts are enlarged and overshadow the rest of the story in
the retelling.

Currently several versions of Little Red Riding Hood
share the booksellers' shelf. The parent is able to choose
between two editions illustrated by Caldecott Award winners
--Nonny Hogrogian and Helen Orton Jones. The first and
older text portrays Little Red Riding Hood as being eaten
by the wolf because she "talked to strangers." In the Jones
version, Little Red Riding Hood, swallowed whole by the
wolf, is rescued by a passing woodman. It is the older,
child-eating version which seems to persist, resurrected
periodically to overshadow the bowdlerized re-writings.

Adults who award prizes in children's literature seem
to be aware of the attractiveness of violence to children.
The 1963 Caldecott Award-winning children's book came in
for attack because it was alleged to be too frightening for
children, but despite the parents' fears the children laughed

at the monster's claws and sharp teeth in Maurice Sendak's
Where the Wild Things Are.   A possible contender for the
1968 Caldecott Award was Mercer Mayer's There's a Nightmare in My Closet.   The book is intended to take a humorous view of a child's fear of the dark, but some parents
resist showing it to their children for fear of frightening
them.

Violence in children's literature has a long history:

A more puritanical book than the New England Primer is difficult to imagine.   Published in over three hundred
editions beginning around 1687, [21] it was filled with lessons
and prayers for righteousness.   Yet almost every edition
used, as a frontispiece, a vivid depiction of John Rogers
being burned at the stake with his wife and nine children
watching!

Heinrich Hoffman's Struwwelpeter was first published
in 1844 and has periodically come under attack for its violent rhymes and stories, but it has been cherished by generations of German children.   Many Americans are familiar
with the English translation in which Conrad's thumbs are
cut from his hands because he insisted on sucking them;
Augustus starves to death because he wouldn't eat his soup
and Harriet burns herself playing with matches:

> So she was burnt, with all her
>   clothes,
> And arms, and hands, and eyes and
>   nose;
> Till she had nothing more to lose
> Except her little scarlet shoes;
> And nothing else but these was
>   found
> Among her ashes on the ground. [22]

While adults purposely cater to the child's desire for
violence in rhymes and stories, they try to avoid exposing
them to real-life violence.   Television is under the most
stringent attack.   This most popular product of our culture
brings the violence of the adult world to children.

Never before have we been able to view war so
graphically as in the live action films of the horror of the
Vietnam war.   The murder of a Presidential assassin and
the shooting of a Senator had on-the-spot coverage.   Surely,

it should surprise no one that children imitate the riots and war on television in their own games and songs.   However, there has been research done on the effects of television on the children who view it.   The results may be surprising to some.

The Task Force on Juvenile Delinquency of the President's Commission on Law Enforcement and Administration of Justice asked the question, "Do mass media increase delinquency?"   They said in part: "Studies have been generated by the popular belief that crime depicted in newspapers or comic books or on the television or cinema screen produces criminal behavior.   The seriousness of the allegation cannot be denied, since mass media overwhelm any possible impact of organized leisure time.... While there is no contesting the importance of these influences, it is very difficult to assess their nature....   The most extensive study of the influence of television on children was made in England and involved 4, 500 youngsters in five different cities.   There it was found that violence on television did not influence non-delinquent viewers to delinquency. It was only in instances wherein a young person was predisposed that a television show might be seen as triggering delinquency. "[23]   Whereas mass media may bring violence to the attention of the children, they cannot be blamed for creating it.

It has been stated by a number of writers, such as Robert Ardrey in African Genesis, that man is essentially a violent creature. [24]   In the controversy over our involvement in Vietnam some have characterized America as the most "violent nation in the world. "   If this is true, it would be unnatural if children were not as interested in violence as their parents are.   Karl Menninger recognizes that "we love violence, all of us, and we all feel secretly guilty for it.... "[25]

Today's problems are often considered to be unique, but the tradition of violence in children's folklore is certainly not of recent origin.   Iona and Peter Opie claim that some of the parodies of "Mary Had a Little Lamb" were first quoted at least as early as 1886. [26]   Tuer's History of the Horn Book indicates that the first children's schoolbook was not only useful for learning one's letters, but was also a useful weapon for paddling one's fellow students and for the teacher to use against the student. [27]   Scattered throughout W. W. Newell's 1883 book, Games and Songs of American

<u>Children,</u> are little ditties collected from children such as:

> Tit for tat,
> Butter for fat,
> If you kill my dog,
> I'll kill your cat. [28]

In Peter Breughel's 1560 painting, "Children's Games," we see many games that are being played with equal violence by American children today.

We can identify trends, too, in the concern of adults over violence in children's literature. For example, in the 1930's a wave of criticism resulted in the toning down or excluding of violence in books for children. Munro Leaf's <u>The Story of Ferdinand,</u> illustrated by Robert Lawson, might be thought of as an example of this "anti-violence" reaction. A bull who would rather smell flowers than fight is certainly one of the first leaders of a resistance movement.

During World War II many children's books began to feature the defeating of the enemy and children reacted accordingly:

> In nineteen forty-three
> Old Hitler climbed a tree
> Down he fell
> And went to hell
> In nineteen forty-three. [29]

In the 1950's, during comparative world peace, the Grimm brothers' fairy tales came under attack for "too much violence" and consequently went out of fashion.

Now as the 1960's draw to a close, we see an ambivalence in the criticism of violence in children's books. For instance, the Grimm brothers' tales and the <u>Arabian Nights</u> are still being attacked. A recent editorial reported that some Australians are criticizing the violence in old folktales and advocating that they be kept from children. [30]

Television and toys are also under attack. Months before the shocking King-Kennedy murders appeared on home screens, a group of California mothers had complained that the violence in television cartoons would lead to the creation of a violent generation. [31] One result of the King-

Kennedy murders was that Sears Roebuck and Co. and Montgomery Ward & Co., the nation's two largest mail order
houses, announced in June, 1968 that there would be no toy
guns or fire arms in their Christmas catalogues.[32]

On the other hand, there are those in our society
who agree with Anne Eaton that in order to work effectively
with children and fully understand them, "we must have retained or we must recapture for ourselves something of the
child's own attitude toward life and the world."[33]   Adults
who remember their actual childhood feelings understand
that some of the children's seeming pre-occupation with
death and violence is a reaction to something they don't
fully understand.   Most of those reading this article could
contribute a few rhymes to the collection--usually chants
learned from older children.   The reader probably remem-
bers the rhymes with which he taunted his peers or teachers
as being very funny, but has never considered them as violent literature.   Children may be attempting to cover their
fear, confusion and frustration with humor.

Let's think twice before climbing on the "Let's stamp
out childhood violence" bandwagon.   This folklore has existed
and been handed down from generation to generation for a
very long time and there is no evidence that its influence
has been detrimental.

An editorial in the University of Oregon student newspaper concluded, "Someday pretended violence may no longer
be a staple of every American boy's childhood, and someday
real violence may no longer haunt this country with such
great intensity."[34]   Yes--someday that might be the case,
but it might help make us dull and humorless.   Those average, normal children who invent and chant this vicious nonsense are the same imaginative youngsters who become creative chemists, writers or classical scholars later in life.
They pretend, imagine, create this nonsense as children,
and as adults they are able to create useful elements for
our society.   If we stamp out imagination we will also stamp
out creativity.

Children are primarily attracted by the humor in
this folklore.   If one examines the child's violent articula-
tions closely, it is apparent that the majority of them are
silly nonsense, not truly violent at all.   A very nice, little
nine year old boy recited this jump-rope rhyme:

Last night and the night before
21 robbers came knocking at my door
As I ran out they ran in
They knocked me on the head with
    a rolling pin.

The rolling pin was made out of metal
They knocked me flat right on the kettle
One of those robbers turned it up
And my rump started burning up. [35]

This is too fantastic to be thought of as really violent. It
is cartoon-type violence, humorous nonsense only. It is a
rhyming of words without concern for the actual meaning.

There is another aspect of this "violent folklore" of
children. Perhaps it is cathartic in nature in the same way
that old Punch and Judy shows or modern cartoons are said
to be. Children are restrained by society from physical release of tensions. The younger the child, the more likely
he is to take out his aggressions by physically hitting his
parents and other children. It may be that the verbal violence of childhood is a transition from frustration expressed
physically to frustration spoken and argued genteely at din-
ner parties. Verbalization by highly volatile, lively and
emotional children is a more acceptable form of release
than fighting.

Furthermore, this verbal violence of childhood is a
link between generations. The modern parent looks for communication between himself and his child. To wipe out these
little ditties is to lose one link of communication between
the generations. Further, if these gory parodies are suppressed, adults may no longer hear them, but the child's
playmates will. In fact, one of the delicious aspects of
violent rhymes for children is that they are naughty, forbidden. If they are no longer forbidden, maybe they won't
seem too prevalent, but they will continue to exist.

In conclusion, please realize that the author is not
advocating excessive violence in books, on television and
in our lives, nor suggesting an overindulgence in blood and
gore. Undoubtedly, the networks do need to tone down their
program offerings--violence for its own sake is not art.

A closing thought from Walter de la Mare is appropriate, "I know well that the rarest kind of best in anything

can be good enough for the young. "[36]   Is violence included
in this rarest kind of best?

References

1. U. S. President's Commission on Law Enforcement
    and Administration of Justice, The Challenge of
    Crime in a Free Society: A Report (Washington:
    U. S. Government Printing Office, 1967).
2. Iona Opie and Peter Opie.   The Lore and Language of
    Schoolchildren (Oxford: Clarendon Press, 1959),
    p. 90.
3. Remembered by Ed Whitlaw, age 27, from his child-
    hood in Wichita, Kansas.
4. Collected from student, children's literature class,
    University of Oregon, 1968.
5. Collected by Janet Bohlool, librarian, Cottage Grove
    (Oregon) Junior High School.
6. Chorus variants collected by Johanna Hurwitz, Librar-
    ian, Calhoun School, New York City.
7. Collected from Matilda Burian, age 6, Long Beach,
    New York.
8. Seen by the author, North State Street, Lake Oswego,
    Oregon.
9. Collected from Sandra Robinson's family, Eugene,
    Oregon.
10. Robert M. Atkinson, "Songs Little Girls Sing: An
    Orderly Invitation to Violence, " Northwest Folk-
    lore, I, No. 1 (1965), p. 7.   Other examples of
    popular song parodies may be found in Opie and
    Opie, pp. 91-92.
11. Opie and Opie, p. 189.
12. Remembered by Everett Johnston, age 30, from his
    childhood.
13. New York Times Book Review, Sept. 22, 1968, p. 27.
14. Collected from Marjorie Toelken, age 10, Eugene,
    Oregon.
15. As seen on television coverage of the Democratic
    National Convention in Chicago, August, 1968.
16. Ralph Schoenstein, The Block (New York: Random
    House, 1960), p. 20.
17. Jean Piaget, "The Rules of the Game, " quoted in
    Toby Talbot, The World of the Child (New York:
    Doubleday, 1967), pp. 230-254.
18. Albert Bandura and Richard H. Walters, Social Learn-
    ing and Personality Development (New York: Holt,
    Rinehart & Winston, 1963), pp. 62-63.

19-20.   Collected from a student in children's literature at
         the University of Oregon from her student teaching
         experience.
21.   The exact date of publication of The New England
         Primer is unknown.   See Paul Leicester Ford, ed. ,
         The New England Primer (New York: Columbia
         University Press, 1962), pp. 16-23.
22.   Heinrich Hoffman, Struwwelpeter (New York: Fred-
         erick Warne), p. 7.
23.   Commission on Law Enforcement, p. 334.
24.   Robert Ardrey, African Genesis (New York: Atheneum,
         1966), p. 336.   In a recent newspaper article
         (Henry Raymont, "Scientists Oppose Man-Is-Bad
         View: Montagu in Group Criticizing Lorenz-
         Ardrey Pessimism," New York Times, Sept. 15,
         1968, p. 60) it was reported that a group of
         American and British behavioral scientists "have
         warned that the spread of the theory that man is
         inherently aggressive could increase the chances
         of war. "
25.   Saturday Review, Sept. 7, 1968, p. 22.
26.   Opie and Opie, p. 90.
27.   Andrew Tuer, History of the Horn Book (New York:
         Charles Scribner's, 1897), p. 20.
28.   William Well Newell, Games and Songs of American
         Children [Republication of 2nd (1903) ed.] (New
         York: Dover, 1963).   This rhyme also appears
         in Carol Withers, Rocket in my Pocket (New York:
         Holt, 1948), a popular book with children.
29.   Opie and Opie, p. 103.
30.   Eugene Register-Guard, Sept. 19, 1968, p. 10 A.
31.   Jerry Buck, "T.V. Superviolence Causing Concern, "
         Eugene Register-Guard, Oct. 1, 1967, p. 10 B.
32.   Eugene Register-Guard, Oct. 2, 1968, p. 3 C.   David
         R. Boldt of the Wall Street Journal (Nov. 5, 1967,
         p. 11) reported that the Stuntmen's Association
         is complaining about a lack of violent stunts to
         perform on television.
33.   Anne Eaton, Reading with Children (New York: Viking,
         1940), p. 38.
34.   Oregon Daily Emerald, Nov. 15, 1968, p. 6.
35.   Collected from Kenji Toelken, age 9, Eugene, Oregon.
36.   Walter de la Mare, Bells and Grass (New York:
         Viking, 1942), p. 11.

Part IV:

THE SOCIAL PREROGATIVE

LET IT ALL HANG OUT

by Sanford Berman

Reprinted by permission from Library Journal June 15, 1971, p. 2054-2058, published by R. R. Bowker (a Xerox company), and copyright (c) 1971 by the Xerox Corporation.

If anybody really loves libraries today, it must be the power companies and electronics industry, for we gleefully purchase, so it seems, almost anything that plugs in, flashes, bleeps, or hums. There are the giant computers, some of which occasionally spew out--at enormous cost-- cumbersome, promptly outdated lists of serial holdings, or the siren-activating, turnstile-locking detection systems to encourage pilferers to reach new levels of sophistication.

Bright young circuitry-men and information-retrievers speak enchantedly about their programs and machines as if these were inestimable ends in themselves. Research, teaching, and development money appears increasingly directed to mechanical gimmickry. Despite all the lofty talk about "social responsibility," the electric socket seems to enjoy progressively more dollars-and-cents attention than the flesh-and-blood reader. Librarianship, of course, is not unique in this. In the nation itself (let alone the world), about a third of the populace, including 5,000,000 aged, the "old folks" who safely and devotedly squired many of us through wars and depression, is under-fed and under-housed. Yet national resources are overwhelmingly channeled into either an expensive, circus-like, ego-tripping space-race or to pacify the uppity, ungrateful "natives" of Southeast Asia, Africa, and Latin America. Experts acknowledge that the delivery system for medical care verges on a breakdown, that only the fortunate fraction of our citzenry who can pay for it receive full medical attention. Yet "medical" funding for esoteric research and gadgetry, together with frenzied "empire building"--both unrelated to immediate human needs --escalate, while federal grants for cancer study have de-

clined.   Unemployment is chronic, presently exceeding six
percent of the employable.   (Sweden, as a comparative
example, proclaims a national crisis when this figure approaches two percent.)   Yet job-killing automation continues
unabated, and necessary, job-generating social projects remain unbegun.   Our environment nears catastrophe.   Yet
the very corporate interests who profit from junk production,
blissfully pollute the atmosphere, and haphazardly alienate
the land suffer only polite knuckle-rappings--for they bulwark the whole politico-economic structure.

A classical Luddite might indiscriminately damn all
the multiplying soft- and hardware.   But that would be fool-
ishly naive, sentimental, Utopian.   The age of cottage industry and idyllic agriculture is past.   And that many
library-related machines perform essential, service-improv-
ing tasks cannot be challenged.   (Indeed, the warmly welcome Alternative Press Index owes its existence to a computer.   So does the annual Periodicals in East African Libraries, which vastly facilitates interlibrary borrowing
among a number of otherwise isolated, "developing" institutions.)   Still, the suspicion grows that an untouchable elite
is developing within the profession: a coalition of technocrats and bureaucrats dedicated--even if somewhat un-
wittingly--to making themselves indispensable by virtue of
their ability to manipulate and expand the "new technology"
plus the more complicated administrative-budgetary apparatus
associated with it.   If many colleagues share this suspicion,
it might be well to profoundly re-assess our fundamental
attitudes and priorities before things get totally out of hand.

To what extent, for instance, may super-mechaniza-
tion of libraries--and its all too likely depersonalization of
services--actually "turn off" current and potential users,
many of whom want little more than access to the books,
magazines, and nonprint items that will satisfy their personal interests and curiosity, and who "dig" the opportunity
to rap at leisure with another sensitive, literate, helpful
person?   (Should this sound preposterously old-fashioned,
undertake a simple experiment: Try rapping with a teaching
machine or microfilm reader.   It's a frustrating experience,
certainly less pleasurable than discourse with a live, albeit
imperfect, human.   One fellow's encounter with a talking
cigarette-automat a few years ago in Germany proved completely lopsided.   The contraption never stopped its own
guttural rumbling long enough to understand that, since no
weed packet had been ejected, the would-be smoker only
wanted his Deutsch-Mark back.)

To what extent might library automation contribute to
worsening unemployment? Or has already done so? Is it
considered as a factor in deciding whether to install new
machinery or systems that such "innovations" may permanently displace or eliminate some of the library labor force?
Even acknowledging "efficiency" and cost reduction per se as
cardinal elements in our Western, industrial mythology, may
it not be socially irresponsible to heartily embrace labor-
saving devices that will unconscionably dump people into an
economy ill-prepared to ensure them a decent livelihood (not
to mention soul satisfying work)? Or, on the positive side,
have we sufficiently explored the possibility, for instance,
of hiring capable, unemployed youths and senior citizens to
perform exit-checks instead of relying upon magnetic fields
that don't have to pay rent or buy bread?

To what extent may the mounting emphasis on technology impose inflexibility on many of our operations and,
further, permit or dictate certain regressive policies? To
illustrate: Reform of obsolete or offensive subject headings
has been opposed in some places not because such reform
is itself unwarranted, but rather due to a fear that local
alterations will not mesh or harmonize with, say, the computerized LC scheme upon which individual institutions may
have become dependent. In other words, a library might
reluctantly choose to retain the slaver-derived, black-de-
nounced, ambiguously-assigned head, "Negroes," rather
than replace it with the more accurate and patently acceptable terms, "Afro-Americans," "Afro-Brazilians," etc.,
solely out of an anxiety that to deviate from the computer
standard would wreak havoc in its catalog or, correlatively,
invite heavy expenditures in changing the centrally provided
data on tapes and cards. LC's recently developed music
headings have already alarmed several catalogers, who
allege that they were constructed not with music and users
as the primary foci, but rather to placate the computer.
And an ostensibly admirable project like Bell & Howell's
micro-package of UPS titles, while a thoughtful and requisite gift to future generations of scholars, could equally
function as a ready-made alibi for subscribing libraries not
to stock the inky, perishable--but immensely more enticing
and readable--"underground" originals for the benefit of
right-now patrons. The unhurried researcher may be content to scan a six-month-old run of Kaleidoscope in a quiet,
secluded micro-cubicle. Others, however, for whom tabloids
like Kaleidoscope express vital aspects of their daily life
and furnish instantly usable information, want the latest

edition as quickly as the library can get it--and are sure to "groove" on it all the more when they can relax with it, perhaps even share it with nearby brethren. The danger, in short, is that of sacrificing immediate reader needs and satisfactions to what is essentially an archival, elitist, long-term objective. (The solution, clearly, is to take both media forms, yet the temptation will undoubtedly be to buy the micro-package and then argue that this fulfills the two distinct obligations. The same argument, of course, could be applied to the New York Times and London Times. But won't be.)

Returning to priorities, to attitudes: Given that any library--and the profession as a whole--has resource limits in labor and funds, how are these resources to be distributed? What projects more urgently demand our money and creative energy than others? It may be--as much of the recent professional literature and agitation suggest--that we have reached a philosophical, if not also spiritual, watershed. Which way do we go? Which side are we on?

Now that gadgetry apostles, administrative autarchs, and those whom Phillip Berrigan has termed "passive robots in the technological waxworks" have probably dismissed most of the foregoing as retrograde nonsense or Leftist cant, let's get to the nitty-gritty: The libraries we work in, where we get our kicks, where we think we're doing something worthwhile and socially productive, the libraries in which we've invested our training, imagination, adrenalin, and lives, could soon become magnificently irrelevant to ourselves, our society, our world. This is not to predict a sudden apocalypse, only to note a discernible drift.

Much verbiage has been expended on how to become "relevant." Much doubt, however, surrounds the question of whether that verbiage has in fact transformed many attitudes or notably redirected our available resources. All of us suppose that libraries do something valuable, that they have some impact, some effect. (Otherwise, why willfully make a career of librarianship?) Okay. Is that effect in reality benign or malignant? Are we retreating to "safe," static conventionality or moving toward a dynamic involvement with our fast-changing human and physical milieu? Sure, the answers depend on your values, your Weltanschauung. A value judgment can't be escaped, except at the price of outright surrender to external pressures (like Government and its military-industrial puppeteers) or strong, self-

propelled internal elements (call them, collectively, the
Techno-Bureaucratic Library Establishment). While admittedly an over-simplification, the value problem seems
to resolve itself into polar choices: people vs. things,
participation vs. pyramidal authority, compassion vs. convenience, engagement vs. neutrality. Were our profession
magically transmuted in time and space to Germany of the
1930s, would it be "neutral" about Yellow Stars, Blitz-
kriegs, KZs, book-burning, forced labor, organization-
banning, Gypsy guinea pigs, etc. ? Would these events and
practices not be regarded as anathema to humane values,
to uninhibited scholarship, learning, and dialogue, to the
very well-being of our clientele and colleagues?

　　　If we rejected "neutrality" under those circumstances,
how can we be "neutral" or dispassionate about the American onslaught in Asia (replete with torture, massacre, and
charred infants), widespread repression of dissent at home
(by means of gun, gavel, computer-bank, and publicly-paid
spies), continued subjugation of racial and ethnic minorities
(who require no brightly colored, sew-on symbols to identify
them), and "criminalization" of our long-haired young
(achieved through pot-busts, police-induced "riots, " rigid
appearance-codes, etc.) ? Are these events no less anathema to humane values, to a climate of trust and unfettered
dialogue, to a rational distribution of resources? Will the
"good Germans" claim that they are not our concern, that
war and racism--as outstanding examples--don't affect libraries, or--more cogently--that libraries can exert no influence on them? If we opt for people, participation, compassion, and engagement, there are things to talk about and
do. Some, already well-stated--like heightened recruitment
and promotion of minority group members; swift, concrete
support for the censor's victims; the professional imperative to declare for peace; sanctions against segregated
libraries; urging publishers to midwife prejudice-free, inter-
racial books for children; and opposition to governmental
prying into patrons' reading habits--need no repeating here.
Still others, though, have hardly--if ever--been raised (and
fellow "Luddites" can undoubtedly refine these, as well as
citing many more):

　　　1.　Outreach. On the Association level, the one
serial publication devoted to servicing outside groups--in
this case, labor--has been discontinued. The tragedy in
this is not entirely that a useful, horizon stretching newsletter has folded, but that it was the only such publication

to begin with. Not only should the labor vehicle be rein-
stated, but sister publications are manifestly needed to
chronicle, analyze, and assist library services to many
more specific groups whose needs are at once pressing and
distinctive: Indians, Mexican-Americans, blacks, GIs and
draft-age men, women, and the poor. Also, providing it
doesn't restrict the mag's independence, money might be
allocated to enlarge Sipapu's format and circulation so that
it becomes an effective catalyst/clearinghouse in the slightly
chaotic realm of radical and "underground" literature.

The ALA suspension is perhaps ominously sympto-
matic of the profession's attitude toward innovative "outreach" programs themselves. How many public libraries,
for instance, have established (in easy-to-reach locations;
e.g., storefronts) special collections of material on welfare
rights, the draft, child care, community organizing, and the
like--perhaps staffed by local people, with qualified coun-
selors appearing at regularly-scheduled times? Some, to
be sure. Indeed, some--like the Free Library of Phila-
delphia--appear to have wisely harnessed the computer to
meet the unmistakable, wide-ranging information requirements of the urban "underprivileged." Some, then.

But enough to make a difference, to redress the ter-
rific imbalance between services hesitatingly supplied to
low-income ghetto or migrant peoples and those unstintingly
offered to Beverly Hills-variety affluents or some far from
underprivileged multiversity students now pampered with
phone-requested, direct-to-dorm book delivery? Are even
the existing programs funded securely enough to guarantee
their continuation, or likely to collapse--like so many other
highly-touted, "pilot" enterprises--when the voracious mili-
tary-space moguls decree more rockets and bombs? Has
a lobby been mounted to press the Bureau of Indian Affairs
to supply pertinent, identity-bolstering library collections,
together with wanted bookmobile, oral-history, and other
services to the wonderfully neglected "reservations"? Have
hitherto submerged elements like street "gangs," junkie
communities, and welfare mothers been asked what kind of
library service they want? Have well-endowed universities
which so painlessly maintain Colleges of Business Administration been pushed to create legal aid and other Goliath-
dismembering literature that libraries might then promul-
gate throughout the inner city? Have library school students been encouraged, perhaps in lieu of theses, to develop
reading and media programs for slum-dwellers, farm-worker
families, etc.? And has...?

2. Subject and classification schemes. Our fundamental "tools of the trade"--Dewey, LC, Sears--in many
respects embody the conceits and wrongheadedness of another
era.   Far from being the disinterested, universally applicable, and fair-minded schema that an enlightened profession
could employ--and disseminate abroad--with pride, they are
appallingly marred by pro-Christian bias, Western chauvin-
ism, misogyny, prudery, and WASPish racism; often denigrate the young; defame the sexually unorthodox; and largely
underwrite a magisterial, laissez-faire view of economic
and social life.   In short, they subtly reinforce pernicious
stereotypes and questionable, if not untenable, notions concerning humankind.   If this judgment seems rash, only
examine the Dewey "Religion" schedules; note the DDC equa-
tion of "premarital relations" and "homosexuality" with "perversion"; compare the disparate treatment of "Capitalism"
and "Socialism" in both Dewey and LC; and then consider--
merely as examples--these active LC subject heads, many
of which Sears echoes:

> LITERATURE, IMMORAL
> ART, IMMORAL
> CHILDREN--MANAGEMENT
> DISCIPLINE OF CHILDREN
> NATIVE RACES (as both a primary and subhead)
> MAMMIES
> JEWISH QUESTION
> RACE QUESTION (as a subhead)
> JEWS AS FARMERS [SCIENTISTS, etc.]
> INDIANS OF NORTH AMERICA, CIVILIZATION OF
>   (i.e., Anglo-Saxon efforts to "civilize" the Indians)
> NEGROES AS BUSINESSMEN [COWBOYS, etc.]
> JAPANESE [CHINESE, MEXICANS, etc.] IN THE
>   U.S. (but never Americans)
> WOMEN AS AUTOMOBILE DRIVERS [LIBRARIANS,
>   etc.]
> MANAGEMENT RIGHTS (but no "LABOR RIGHTS")
> YELLOW PERIL
> HOMOSEXUALITY
>   XX Sexual Perversion
> LESBIANISM
>   XX Sexual Perversion
> CATHOLIC [JEWISH, NEGRO] CRIMINALS (uniquely)
> SABOTAGE
>   XX Socialism
> SOCIETY, PRIMITIVE

    ANARCHISM AND ANARCHISTS
      XX Terrorism
    NAPALM
      XX Metallic Soaps (!)
    HEROES (but no "HEROINES")
    PAGANISM
    DISCOVERY AND EXPLORATION (subdivision under
      names of continents and countries "discovered"
      and "explored" by Europeans)
    KAFIRS (i. e. , in South African parlance, "niggers")

The situation seems sufficiently alarming to warrant thoroughgoing, critical studies of all the major cataloging tools and then their urgent revision to accord with modern knowledge, as well as elementary canons of human decency and dignity.

      3. Selection. If a single keyword or rubric encompasses the multitude of overlapping movements and ideas that within the past decade have forcefully emerged among blacks, students, Jews, teachers, Chicanos, women, the young, Asian-Americans, servicemen, Indians, ecophiliacs, still-colonized peoples, workers, the impoverished, homosexuals, and even some psychiatrists, athletes, retirees, sociologists, and librarians, it is "liberation." The library press and SRRT have suitably reported aspects of this many-faceted "liberation" scene, as well as engendering extensive booklists, bibliographies, and other selection-aids (e. g. , Alternative Books in Print). The hangup, evidently, lies not with the library press nor SRRT, but rather with libraries. The "liberation" materials have been identified. They can easily be acquired. It is now incumbent upon collection developers to get them--in order, naturally, to document the whole phenomenon for posterity--but even more compellingly to satisfy the contemporary informational needs of "liberation" activists and spectators alike. The multi-pronged "movement" has obviously assumed such proportions that it can no longer be regarded as a temporary fad. (Its roots, in any event, reach deep into the past, and many of its organs have attained a "respectable" longevity.) A library that cannot furnish at least a few appropriate books and magazines, together with knowledgeable advice, to patrons who want material on Gay Liberation, Workers' Control, senior citizen's campaigns for lower transportation rates and higher Social Security benefits, or Third World revolutionary struggles risks becoming utterly useless and pointless to those patrons.

If it's not thought unbecoming nor unusual to lavishly provide directories, newsletters, magazines, and special information services like Barron's, Moody's, The Wall Street Transcript, Advertising Age, and Fortune for businessmen, investors, and stock market speculators, why flinch at providing even a modest amount of material to "liberationists" who, as equally bona fide members of the community, have no less right to library resources? Further, LJ, the Booklist, and Choice could much enhance the ongoing identification-selection process by more frequently reviewing the books and pamphlets generated by offbeat, "liberationist" presses such as the powerful graphic statements by L. A. Free Press cartoonists Ron Cobb and Ed Badajos published respectively by Sawyer and Olympia, War Incorporated: The Complete Picture of the Congressional-Military-Industrial-University Complex, and Autopsy of the A. M. A. , an Analysis of American Health Care Delivery Systems, both confected by Berkeley Student Research Facility, or the Africa Research Group's explosive tract, The Extended Family. Also, we need to abandon our condescending, curator-like, rubber-gloves-and-forceps mentality with regard to "alternative" publications. They belong on open shelves, not in glass cases nor padlocked vaults. Students of social problems and current Radical America, Women, and Tricontinental Magazine are just as fitting and citable for term papers and dissertations as material culled from Foreign Affairs, Time, and Business Week. The oft-enunciated dictum that such matter should only be collected as fodder for the historian, much as intriguing cadavers are gathered and then pickled or frozen for later study by anatomists, must be rejected as wholly repugnant species of in-group arrogance.

4.   Participation. If the boards and committees upon which we increasingly sit have no decision-making power, why sit on them? Without authority to actually enact change or create policy, the activity qualifies as a dreary, spirit-killing charade, a successful management device for co-optation, spawning the illusion that our views and desires really figure in the decision-making calculus. It is altogether too much to expect that libraries will shortly undergo complete democratization, that all employee-strata will soon participate effectively in the decision-making process. But we can sure as hell begin discussing the subject, begin exposing the present shams that pass for "participation, " begin devising participative models, and--when sufficient strength and solidarity develop--begin demands for real power-sharing.

5. <u>Publishing</u>.   Judging from its recent output, ALA appears to regard itself as a scholarly publisher.   Some colleagues could certainly produce manuscripts that, while not conforming to a stiff, conventional definition of "scholarship," nonetheless dealt in depth with clearly significant topics and honestly represented dissident, "heretical" opinions not yet accorded book-length treatment.   Remarkably few such titles, though, have ever appeared under the ALA imprint.   This is not to gainsay the bibliographic and historical value of works, for instance, on Carnegie libraries or German exile publishing in the U.S.   It is only to observe that such works seem to constitute the norm, while possible tomes of much greater immediacy--and intellect-stimulating controversiality--go unprinted.   If ALA Publishing Services haven't so far done so, why not speedily commission:

--a Frommian-Goodmanesque critique of traditionally hierarchic, authoritarian library administration?

--a pro-and-con symposium on library unionism, perhaps including case studies of unions-in-operation and appending a few representative contracts?

--an anthology in which <u>Synergy</u>-type "Young Turks" forthrightly rap about the numerous skeletons in our professional closets?

--a collection of all major documents and reports relating to the abolition of "pornography" censorship in Denmark, indicating why and how it came about, together with its results?

--an exploratory study on how libraries--like schools--might become subject to genuine community control, with evidence (if any) from wherever it has actually occurred?

--a women-authored volume--perhaps comparable to E. J. Josey's recent opus dealing with black librarianship--on the historic and current status of women within the profession?

--a survey and discussion of current professional priorities which, among other things, assembles comprehensive budgetary and manpower statistics so we can determine less intuitively in what directions--electronic, "outreach," etc. --we're now travelling?

--a levity-laden tome composed of parodies, satires, graf-
fitti, caricatures, and cartoons--however irreverent--that
booby-traps professional pomposity and reveals the frolic-
some, funny dimension of librarianship?

--a compendium of historical, evaluative, and bibliographic
writings on the Underground Press, "counter-culture,"
and "liberation" publishing, plus a cross-section of views
on what the library attitude should be toward such materials and some objective data on how libraries have actually
responded to them thus far in terms of selection, display,
publicity, access, and censorial encounters?

      6. Watchdogging. If any group has the competence
and wherewithal to first identify and then exercise pressure
to correct malpractice or delinquencies in tax-supported,
federally operated libraries, it's ALA. The same holds for
state and municipal associations with respect to state, county,
and city institutions.

      Prison libraries are notoriously understocked and
poorly staffed. Moreover, prison officials often deliberately
and arbitrarily restrict the reading opportunities of inmates
according to their own, private beliefs or whims about
"what's good for the cons." At minimum, ALA could spon-
sor a survey of prison library facilities and practices (which
should include interviews with convicts, penologists, and
warders), prepare basic guidelines, and--where necessary--
intercede with authorities to improve conditions.

      USIS. Library and general periodicals have abundantly
disclosed that the globe-spanning U. S. Information Service
library system practices a "mainstream," Babbitt-like censorship which largely excludes material by radicals, paci-
fists, black militants, avant-garde literati, counter-culturists,
and even extreme rightists. The agency, for example, will
apparently not even consider buying a book issued by International Publishers in New York, whose list includes major
works by W. E. B. DuBois, John Reed, Herbert Aptheker,
Clarence Major, Phillip S. Foner, and "Big Bill" Haywood.
In all likelihood, a similar ban obtains for the Pathfinder
Press, formerly Merit Publishers, whose catalog features
a half dozen titles by and about Malcolm X, a collection of
Eugene Debs' speeches, the stenographic record of the IWW's
founding convention, and a pamphlet on Chicano studies--all
important pieces of Americana. The "image" these collections project to overseas readers is a distortion. It is not

the everyday America we know, at once hopeful and floundering, imaginative and mediocre, violent and gentle, hate-ridden and loving. The thoroughly sanitized, plastic-packaged "America" marketed by USIS libraries insults us and affronts literate prople abroad, many of whom surely recognize the put-on and can hardly think well of a nation that by perpetrating such deceit plainly thinks so little of them. Our national reputation would indisputably suffer less from candor than from bullshit. A possible ALA role might be to initially investigage USIS selection policy, not merely examining official statements and other documentary evidence, but also conducting first-hand checks at random facilities, and then-- if the data so indicate--simultaneously make these findings public and demand change, perhaps with an explicit threat of sanctions.

Military libraries have long ignored the Library Bill of Rights' injunction to represent all possible political and other viewpoints. It is doubtful that any presently receive and openly display GI anti-war papers, scores of which have blossomed in the States, Europe, and Asia, although their relevance to servicemen is perfectly obvious. And one Special Services librarian in Europe not so long ago encountered truly incredible static when he attempted to add the "Wolfenden Report," several outspoken volumes on the Afro-American experience, and some modern literary classics--by Henry Miller, William Burroughs, Allen Ginsberg, Lawrence Ferlinghetti, Jean Genet, and others--to a local collection. Of these works it was said either that "We have enough of that sort of thing already" or "No one will read them," both contentions being equally absurd. The system had, in fact, bought Sartre's treatise on Genet, but balked at stocking anything by the celebrated playwright-novelist. Additionally, the operative myth regarding homosexuals in uniform is that there are none. Later, when that same librarian protested against the official distribution and endorsement of palpably right-wing material produced by the Freedoms Foundation, he was advised by superiors that he might be happier working someplace else.

Moreover, the implicitly sanctioned role of military librarians--almost exclusively women--has been as much that of high-caste sex-ornament and morality-maid as book-jockey and mind-vibrator. And, at least a few years ago, off-duty social liaisons with enlisted men were definitely taboo, a sure-fire way to dis-ingratiate oneself with the higher ups. If military libraries remain oblivious to many soldiers',

sailors', and airmen's authentic interests and needs (even
when these conflict with brass-pronounced orthodoxy) and
continue to thrust degrading, sexist roles upon our sisters
who staff them, the situation merits attention by the whole
profession.   A first step might be for present and former
military librarians to openly document the matter from their
own experience.   The Wilson Library Bulletin, for example,
could profitably devote a full issue to the topic, possibly
including contributions from GI library users, as well.
Were such a symposium to demolish the above allegations:
Beautiful! If not, the necessity would persist to "shape up."

Finally, given an honest commitment to "social responsibility," to tackling, library-wise, the manifold problems
of poverty, imperialism, discrimination, and public waste,
ALA cannot in the future hold its meetings in plush hotels
and racist atmospheres, nor charge impecunious colleagues
and even ordinary (but concerned) folk what may be a pro-
hibitive fee to simply watch the Association at work.

UNLIMITED PUSHBUTTONS
AND PARAPHERNALIA TO
THE TECHNO-BUREAUCRATS!

DYNAMIC, RESPONSIVE,
SANELY-EQUIPPED LIBRAR-
IES TO THE PEOPLE!

Under which banner do we proceed?

POLITICS OF PORNOGRAPHY

by Paul Good

Reprinted by permission from Evergreen, September 1971, p. 21-23, 54-63.

You may have picked up this Evergreen from a news-dealer, in the Library of Congress, or in the flossy waiting room of a literate dentist. But one place I know you didn't get it is from the open shelf of the public library in Groton, Connecticut.

In March, the library board there voted to banish the February issue of Evergreen from the building, and to keep all past and subsequent issues off the open shelves. The February issue contained a story entitled "The Fine Art of Lovemaking" by Mary Phillips, which examined the paintings and philosophies of a New York artist named Betty Dodson. Her philosophies favor eroticism and her paintings depict men and women having sex--heterosexually, homosexually, and autosexually. Autosexually, in this case, does not mean in the back seat of a car, which is a generally popular position in Groton and other localities with car dealerships.

Now, if your first inclination is to condemn the entire library board as a bunch of repressed Yahoos, don't. On the night of March 8th, with an anti-pornography injunction handing over their heads, they were told by Groton Town Attorney Joseph Moukawsher that they might be promptly fined and imprisoned if they did not remove Evergreen, and that he might not defend them. The board voted six to three to submit. In the defiant minority were a housewife, a black high school teacher, and board chairman Paul Richardson, a sixty-nine-year-old Methodist who looks and sounds like a man whose life was laid out with a plumb line, scrupulously squared. He emerged from the meeting visibly shaken and told newsmen: "There's been a lot of attorney's advice tonight that I don't understand. In fact, the man in the street could call it blackmail. "

The March 10th <u>New York Times</u> told the Groton
story in three economical paragraphs under the neat headline:

Groton Library Unit Bows
To Court's Magazine Ban

But to explain what made a man like Richardson use
a word like blackmail requires the telling of a long, complex
story, a story as American as apple pie or a helicopter gun-
ship.   It's a story from the New England heartland where
hypocrisy and honor vie over those few square--or round--
inches of the human body for centuries a battleground where
lunatics and lovers, the passionless and the passionate, have
contended.   The story embraces small-town politics and the
military-industrial complex.   It includes flinty Yankees defending the rights of sensualists, public officials who
threaten library funds when their sexual tastes are offended,
Kiwanians and Rotarians both noble and ignoble.   And if
there are some elements that make America grate on the
nerves of civil libertarians, there are others that reveal
an American character crafted by New England conscience
to thrust, despite impediments, as truly, stoutly, and beautifully as a Connecticut stone fence.

At the outset, let me file a disclaimer to objectivity.
I approached the story conditioned against censorship and
pornography-hunting in general.   I did not pretend otherwise
in conversations with those favoring the ban, those very few
that is, who would talk.   I promised them a fair rendering
of their position and accurate quotations.   For those, like
the town attorney, who refused to be interviewed, I have
tried wherever possible to use their own written words
supplemented by newspaper reports verified by observers
on the scene.   To the best ability of a writer trying to
make sense out of our random and conflicting sexual laws
and mores, this is a true account of why <u>Evergreen</u> for
February 1971 was banned in Groton and other issues were
circumscribed.

What happened to <u>Evergreen</u> in March begins in October with
the library the locus.   It is a sixty-year-old building of
fading brick, an abandoned schoolhouse sitting above Route 1
by a bridge over the Poquonnock River.   The front door is
scabrous, white paint peeling, in such disrepair that a sug-

gestion to cut a slot in the door for book returns was rejected for fear cutting the slot might cave in the door.   The
interior is bright but overcrowded.   In a community of forty
thousand, two dozen patrons using the library at the same
time puts a premium on chairs and browsing space.   A new
library is obviously needed.   The town building inspector
has already condemned the basement for human habitation
although the thirty-year-old librarian, John Carey, is permitted to keep his office down there according to some
Grotian law of expendability.

From the library, on a clear day, you can see the
Thames River separating Groton from New London.   You
are literally overlooking history that links America past to
America present, a history colored by a military-industrial
complexion that today insures Groton and New London top
priority on any list of U. S. cities to be scorched by an
enemy in the event of nuclear war.   The General Dynamics-
Electric Boat Co. , which in 1954 launched the world's first
atomic-powered sub, the Nautilus, is on the Groton bank
of the Thames, and across the river is the U. S. Navy sub
base.   During the American Revolution, Yankee shipbuilders
and privateers on the river plagued the British.   An English
force under Benedict Arnold landed and a Colonial garrison
in Groton commanded by Col. William Ledyard was massa-
cred.   The victorious British officer demanded of Ledyard
who commanded the fort.

"I did, sir, " Col. Ledyard replied.   "But you do
now. "

The Briton rammed his sword through Ledyard,
demonstrating one response to unpopular free speech.

Two hundred-odd years later, Ledyard's name is
commemorated on a street sign and the area remains
some kind of epitome of the military-industrial complex.
Ten thousand Navy men and dependents live in Groton, and
Electric Boat, with fourteen thousand employees, is a vital
paycheck machine.   Rear Admiral Hyman Rickover occasionally surfaces there to fire verbal torpedoes at anybody
to the left of Ayn Rand and, in April, the New London
NAACP charged the company with racial discrimination.
The other big Groton employer--Pfizer Chemical--was also
accused in April.   The charge made before the Federal
Environmental Protection Agency was that Pfizer had been
dumping solid waste into Long Island Sound for fifteen years.

Pfizer responded by threatening to close its Groton facility
unless it was permitted to dump. Ah to be in April, now
that Electric Boat and Pfizer are here!

From its Puritan past to Pentagonian present, Groton
and the southeastern corner of Connecticut in general have
maintained a provincialism strongly reminiscent of certain
Deep South areas. It is marked by political conservatism,
distrust of outsiders from New York or Hartford, and a
highly subjective interpretation of law enforcement. The
town of Groton itself is a civic state of mind only possible
where municipal individualism--reflecting the area's political
lifestyle--runs rampant. It occupies a chunky peninsula
from the Thames over to the pretty Mystic seaport, and includes eight or so partially autonomous subdivisions like the
City of Groton and the Noank Fire District. Their individual
distinctions are something a writer masters only to find out
that his readers don't give a damn. But the government of
Groton is important to the story.

It combines a town council, a town manager, and
a representative town meeting, or RTM. The RTM is a
relic of the old New England town meeting which has acquired in history a mythic character of pure democracy it
rarely displayed in practice. Hippies like Thoreau got short
shrift when they spoke, but the town banker holding mortgages was commonly deemed oracular. Anyhow, the Groton
forty-member RTM has to approve budgets set by the council
and technically can force reconsiderations of budgets and other
legislation. But the clout rests with the nine-member council, which appoints the town manager, controls appointments
to commissions like the library board, and decides whether
things like new libraries will be built. This governmental
primer is admittedly tedious, but our society, for good or
ill, thrives or declines through decisions of councils, and
freedom either finds a way down the gray corridors of
municipal buildings or is waylaid en route.

Last October 14, Robert Secor--an Electric Boat
employee, former councilor and Baptist church deacon--
went to the library with his twelve-year-old son. The son,
whose name I don't know because Secor refuses to talk,
chose from the forty thousand books and two hundred periodicals in stock a copy of a now-defunct underground magazine called Broadside which lay on the open shelf in the
adult section. It contained a comic strip called "Little
Orphan Anphetamine" which chronicled the misadventures of

a girl who lives in a big house with a rich Daddy.   The
Katzenjammer Kids it was not.   The reader learns that the
Little Orphan is unhappy with Daddy's conservative lifestyle
when she tells him, "Oh, fuck you, Daddy."   She runs
away to California and the trip is a bummer.   A hardhat
attacks her on the roadside, she crashes badly with a hippie,
and finally limps home with a drug hangover.   Although
Daddy takes her in, the final panel leaves nothing resolved
because the Little Orphan is again telling him, "Oh, fuck
you, Daddy."

Some might have read the strip as a crude morality
play about the perils of youthful freelancing.   But Secor's
sensibilities seem to have been genuinely outraged.   He
later expressed his feelings in a letter to the New London
Day:

> I was not taking issue with either the politics or
> philosophy expressed in the publication, but rather
> I was disturbed that obscene material was avail-
> able for the perusal of children.   The first line
> of defense to brand someone as a book burner is
> as shallow and as void of virtue as the lack of
> professional and ethical standards that allowed it
> to be in the public library in the first place....
> Five years in the U.S. Marine Corps and traveling
> through the Orient exposed me to people completely
> devoid of human dignity.   As for my children and
> their future, I still have hope and absolutely can-
> not see the intent or purpose of exposing them to
> material which is completely unredeeming.

Secor said nothing to Librarian Carey, a slender,
neatly bearded, and mild-mannered Marine Corps veteran
who had attended St. Bonaventure's (Roman Catholic) College and was the new father of an infant son.   Instead,
Secor took Broadside to Groton Mayor John Small.   Last
year, when the Democratic party swept the town elections
for the first time in history, Councillor Small was elected
to the largely honorary but still coveted post of mayor by
his fellow councillors.   A veteran of World War II and
Korea, he is built on the lines of Burl Ives and was a
musician before becoming business manager of a New
London radio station.   Small is a Kiwanian who wears a
Nautilus tieclasp given out by Electric Boat, a bluff, hard-
working man who boasts he spent eleven cents on his political campaign for council: "I bought one cigar and

smoked it myself." Mayor Small goes out of his way to
stress, with a gargantuan air of sincerity, that the only
black member of the library board, Marion Greene, is both
his next door neighbor and a "helluva nice guy."

"I have seven kids and I found Broadside repulsive,"
he says. "It struck me as a helluva thing to find in the
library. I think that kind of rubbish said something about
Carey's judgment. The only principle I had was the children.
You worry a lot today about what's wrong and I think the
kids are getting a lot of new values."

The next day, library board chairman Paul Richardson was summoned to a Town Hall meeting where he found
Small, Secor, Police Chief Robert Falvey, Town Attorney
Moukawsher, and Councillor Andrew Ciminera. Ciminera,
who also works at Electric Boat, had lost out to Small in
the council vote for mayor. The councillors had reappointment power over Richardson, a clothing store owner who had
taught high school in Sandusky, Ohio, and worked for years
with the New York State Department of Education.

"I was amazed at the reception committee because I
had no idea why they wanted me at Town Hall," says Richardson, a Republican and Rotarian. "For all I knew the
library had burned down, a distinct possibility. I was kind
of flabbergasted myself at the cartoon. I was raised in a
strict Methodist family, no smoking, no dancing on Sundays,
so I think my background was more Puritanical than theirs.
For an elderly square like me, the cartoon represented a
nihilistic philosophy, gang rape in the drug cult, that sort
of stuff. I didn't see any value and they all wanted me to
take it off the shelf. Then Ciminera said that I should go
through the library weeding out everything like that and I
said, whoa, that's censorship."

Richardson snickers in remembrance. That's the
only word to describe it, a guileless whinny that brings a
boy back into the ascetic face of a sixty-nine-year-old who
has taken good care of himself.

"I had a hunch some of those fellows might want to
make something of it, so I saw Carey and discovered we
hadn't even subscribed; Broadside just mailed it in. I
said it was creating a big fuss, why not take it off the
shelf? He just refused. Said it was up to the board to
decide policy. So I called a board meeting and we all

decided as a matter of principle we weren't going to take
anything off the shelf because somebody said we should."

Their reasons were rooted in longstanding library
practice, and that practice should be understood because most
of the members stuck to it--with one small slip--until the
night of March 8th.

For a decade, the Groton Public Library had supported an "open-shelf" policy. The policy held that no material should be restricted in circulation or removed from
open shelves "because it is more suitable for one age level
than another, or because its subject matter, viewpoint, or
treatment may be distasteful to certain individuals or groups."
This policy was in keeping with the American Library
Association's "Library Bill of Rights" and the 1953 "Freedom
to Read" statement endorsed by the ALA, the American Book
Publishers' Council, the American Booksellers' Association,
the Book Manufacturers' Institute, and the National Education
Association. The statement said in part:

> The censors, public and private, assume that they
> should determine what is good and what is bad for
> their fellow citizens. We trust Americans to recog-
> nize propaganda, and to reject obscenity. We do
> not believe they need the help of censors to assist
> them in this task.

So the Groton shelves containing Broadside--and
Evergreen--also offered a journal of the Libyan-Arab Re-
public with a story headlined: "First Woman Cosmonaut
Denounces Tel Aviv." There were copies of American
Opinion with an article on "Gay Libb [sic]," with lines like,
"We were out there demanding our Constitutional rights to
be as sweet as we want." A browsing child or adult, black
or white, could read in H. L. Hunt's Life Line "Freedom
Talk" an attack on present history-book descriptions of
slavery as compared to earlier versions preferred by H. L.
Hunt.

> Had our students lived in the days of slavery,
> they would have been taught, as were their an-
> cestors, that Africans were brought to this country
> out of savagery, disease, and poor diet. Young
> Americans of those days were taught that Chris-
> tianity was introduced to the slaves, and Africans
> were encouraged to think of themselves as human

beings of great value to God and Jesus Christ.
Far from the gloom, filth, and dirt which some
historians paint as the general condition for slaves
throughout this early country, the great plantations
and even many of the industries provided solid and
adequate housing, ample and balanced diets, clothing,
medical care, transportation, and education.

Filth and dirt unrelated to slavery were preoccupying
a number of councillors and, on November 24th, the council
summoned the library board to a secret meeting. Again the
demand was made to remove Broadside and again it was rejected. Liberation magazine was denounced and one councillor seriously suggested that Playboy's subscription be
canceled and two or three subscriptions to National Geo-
graphic bought in its stead. Participants who will be quoted
later say that Mayor Small threatened to cut off funds for
the new library, and Councillor Ciminera assumed a leading
role in trying to force the board to clean out the shelves.
He is a stocky, jut-jawed man in his mid-forties whose longstanding obsession to be mayor of Groton is acknowledged
by friend and foe alike. He was also a strong political
supporter and friend of the late Conn. Sen. Thomas Dodd.
According to some observers, his political relationship with
Dodd, who lived nearby in Old Lyme, was a factor in
Ciminera's burgeoning interest in the censorship controversy.

Word of the "secret" meeting was leaked to local
newspapers and this set the stage for the first public performance of the Groton Pornography Case, a farce, morality
play, or American tragedy, depending on your point of view.

On November 27th, Secor and Ciminera arrived at
the library. They soon were joined by a library board
member, Mrs. Mary Virginia Goodman, a grande dame of
Groton who once ran a private school and was noted for her
large floral hats and florid opinions on diverse matters.
Another anti-Broadside councillor, Francis Hagerty, drifted
in, as did Councillor Everett Brustolon, who had leaked
the whole business to Ted Irvine, a political reporter for the
New London Day.

A pawing over the open shelves began with Broadside
pulled out, along with Evergreen, the Los Angeles Free
Press, the Village Voice, and Liberation. No one kept a
completely accurate scorecard on who said what, but voices
were raised denouncing sex ads in the Freep, and radical

articles in general.   Cries of "smut" and "Commie crap"
startled library patrons and Mrs. Goodman declared she
would recommend the board "throw out this scurrilous material. "   When Councillor Hagerty seconded that motion,
Councillor Brustolon shouted: "Goddamn it, you won't tell
me what to read. "

It remained for Councillor Ciminera to focus the
angry rhetoric.   Reliable observers say that the councillor
loomed over Carey, waved a finger in his face, and reminded him that the council could do something about his
$12,000 salary.

"I want this crap out of here, " he said.   "Unless
something's done you won't get any library funds or a new
building. "

"It was like bad opera, " Carey recalls.   "I was a
little bit in the middle because Richardson had been leaning
on me somewhat about Broadside.   Although later he really
got lead in his pencil.   But those people storming around
were worried about four-letter words that are part and
parcel of the New Left style.   If somebody wants to use
the library to understand the New Left, the material should
be there for them.   It was curious that nobody ripped out
Playboy with its creamy, unreal girls in the centerfold.
That's a sexually dishonest fantasy that really exploits
women.   But that was OK. "

Ironically, Broadside had gone out of business.   But
Little Orphan Anphetamine lived on in Groton, her notoriety
assured as area newspapers began coverage generally sym-
pathetic to the "open-shelf" concept.   In the Mystic weekly,
Compass-Comment, published by Richard and Hazel Ross,
Rev. Carl Daley wrote:

> The picture of the town's elected officials creating
> a scene in the public library on Friday is not a
> pretty one.   With Ciminera voicing threats against
> the library's future and Hagerty in a trembling
> rage, it must have been quite a sight. ...   What
> is this, anyway?   Why do we have to engage,
> periodically, in an act of purgation?   Is it be-
> cause our community guilt over our own lifestyle
> is so great that we have to find something or
> somebody to put it all on so we can get rid of it?

The New London Day questioned twenty-four persons
at the library and found virtually all opposing any banning.
The Rev. Edward A. Winter, pastor of the Groton Methodist
Church and father of a twelve-year-old daughter, had a
typical reaction: "It's ridiculous.   There's worse stuff
down the street at [a local supermarket] and three times as
many kids down there."

On the other hand, Pastor Rudolf Keyl Jr. of the
Faith Lutheran Church in Groton wrote that his governing
body was against both Broadside and Evergreen being accessible to children, and that they should be removed or placed
in an Adult Section.

> When publications degrade sex or marriage, or
> home, or the human body, and these publications
> are offered openly in a library supported by fami-
> lies of our congregation, then we must make our
> feelings known publicly.   To remain mute would
> be against our principles as a Christian Church.

Pastor Keyl made no specific complaint against
Evergreen and his tone was temperate if the charges vague.
Other letter-writers came on stronger.   A library member
requesting anonymity told the Compass:

> If this communistic propaganda is allowed in our
> libraries, then poor old Benedict Arnold got the
> shaft.   He was tried for treason for less.   I'm
> all for picketing.

A father was quoted thusly:

> This fr-- stuff certainly does not belong in a li-
> brary.   Our kids are too impressionable.   They
> read these leftist papers and blame us the parents
> on the world's problems.   As far as these leftist
> views of change go, I say if a bullfrog had wings
> he wouldn't bump his ass every time he hopped,
> too.

Despite a flickering coherence level, a message was
coming through loudly and clearly that more than sexual psyches were being pinched in Groton.   That the words and
deeds of the Little Orphan were an affront to some morali-
ties is undeniable.   But political opportunism had its eye to
the peephole and forces were in motion pointing inevitably

to the March 8th showdown on Evergreen. A brief examination of Groton politics is necessary before we can return to
artist Dodson and more syrupy sexual considerations.

The Democratic party throughout Connecticut and
particularly in the southeastern corner has been in disarray
since Thomas Dodd went into decline following a scandal
about his personal use of funds raised for political cam-
paigning. He lost his power base, and a minister named
Joseph Duffy, who headed Americans for Democratic Action,
won the party senatorial nomination in 1970. But many conservative Democrats like Ciminera could not stomach Duffy,
who was against the Vietnam War and for certain progressive ideas associated with the 20th century. At Electric
Boat, Duffy's stock was lower than an eel's belly since
peace was inimical to proper functioning of the paycheck
machine. Old Tom Dodd, however, always stood tall with
military industrialists, and people in the Groton-New London
area paying off mortgages, eating, and engaged in other such
homely pursuits appreciated Dodd's Washington efforts to
protect defense spending. The late Mendel Rivers was
similarly appreciated in Charleston as Lyndon Johnson was
in Houston; it's an old political story going back beyond
Nebuchadnezzar and the most distant pharaos to some slope-
skulled human progenitor who discovered that power came
to him who could insure a rising heap of kitchen midden
through encouraging battle-ax production. What this says
about human moral evolution is a long, lugubrious story in
itself, but there is also a link to the Nevergreening of
Groton.

Dodd ran independently against Duffy and the eventual
winner, Republican Lowell Weicker. Democratic town committees everywhere were wracked with dissension and, in
Groton, DTC mailings for Duffy sometimes bore Dodd material. Duffy finished behind Weicker and an inch ahead of
Dodd in Groton, and much bad feeling was engendered within the party. So much that it appeared doubtful, because of
the election and other reasons, whether the DTC would re-
endorse Ciminera for council in 1971. Old politicians
never die, they just run again, and it is understood that
Ciminera's friend Dodd hoped for a ticket back to Washington via a run for Congress in 1972 from Connecticut's 2nd
Congressional District. Democratic town committees
nominate candidates and so a prerequisite for Dodd's renas-
cence would have been the backing of a town committee
like Groton's.

If you've followed this far, come a little further
where supposition mixes with fact. Ciminera, anxious to
establish authority within the DTC on his own behalf and
Dodd's, needed an issue, and sexual morality has always
been a hot item in American politics. Ogden Nash summed
it up in a salutory poem to the late Senator Smoot, a big
antipornography man in the early 1900s:

> Smite, Smoot, be rough and tough,
> For smut when smitten is front page stuff.

On December 1st, the Democratic town committee
held its annual vote on endorsements for Democratic members of the library board whose terms were about to ex-
pire. It was a rubber-stamp procedure, and in the history
of Groton every such endorsement had been honored by the
town council. Up for reappointment were Mrs. Goodman,
who wanted to remove "scurrilous material," and two members who didn't want to remove anything--Mrs. Jessie Kohl,
for ten years library board secretary, and Paul Plasse.
Councillor Ciminera nominated Peter Connolly, another
Electric Boatman, who worked in the public relations department. All incumbents won over Connolly, amounting to
a vote of confidence in the library board's position and an
attendant slap in the puss to Ciminera.

Undaunted, Ciminera enlivened a December 8th
council meeting by trying to hang Xeroxes of Little Orphan
Anphetamine on the walls of the council chamber. He
was dissuaded, but carried them to a meeting next night of
the representative town committee where he did not get to
speak. But every other speaker, except Mayor Small, de-
cried efforts at library censorship. Mayor Small suggested
that "bad stuff" be placed behind the librarian's desk, at
what risk to her morals from orgonic emanations none could
predict. Former Groton Mayor John Hunter, Board of Education Chairman Dr. Stanley E. Kilty, State Rep. Lillian E.
Erb, former Mayor Thomas Hagerty and his wife, Martha,
who had been library director for eight years before re-
tiring, all argued against council interference with the library board. As a group, they were mostly middle-aged
and, whatever their private proclivities, they resembled the
people our children are warning us against. But they held
some old-fangled views on individual liberty that predated
the Berkeley Free Speech Movement, and they applauded a
statement by Librarian Carey that summed up some of them:

A public library is established as a hunting
ground for the seeker of truth. The seeker relishes the clash of ideas, of moral stands, and of
philosophies to be found in any good library, for
it is this very conflict that gives his search meaning. As a librarian then, what I propose to give
this seeker is a library as a mirror of the universe, a reflector of things that may appear true
or false, pious or blasphemous, beautiful or ugly,
depending on who is looking in the mirror.

Many of us are familiar with the ideas of American historian Frederick Turner Jackson, who interpreted the history and character of America in
terms of the frontier. He warned us of the tensions that our society would endure as the frontier
was closed. You see, for well over two hundred
years whenever a man felt his community was intolerant of his ideals, he could always strike west
to establish his own community.

Today, the frontier is closed. But hopefully an
American who finds his society closing down on
him can still strike out for the public library,
with expectations of finding there, if not anywhere
else, an open intellectual society, a frontier of
thought and feeling with boundaries wide enough to
permit perfect freedom of thought and spirit, to
give full scope to the varieties of dissent necessary to keep alive our imperiled experiment in
human freedom.

The Christmas holidays brought an interlude of calm
to Groton. Wreaths decorated the town hall, snow hissed
in the Thames and Mystic, and the charm of a small-town
New England Christmas created the transient illusion that
people in Groton and elsewhere were really motivated by
good will for their neighbors. On the periodical front, the
Village Voice, whose name had somehow gotten mixed up in
the smut outcries, sent a craven letter to the council
pleading its acceptability. The ongoing issue was library
freedom, but the Voice seemed to miss the point. Sounding like an old tart gone respectable, it described the
journalistic prizes it had won, the fact that John F. Kennedy
read it, and, in its rush for a suitable Groton image, the
paper said it had been included by Xerox Corp. and Bell &
Howell for sale nationally to libraries on microfilm. Its

protests were unnecessary.   Within a few weeks, Ciminera's
right-hand smut hunter, Connolly, would declare:

"The Village Voice is all right.   It's probably the
best of the underground papers. "

Liberation's Dave Dellinger, Staughton Lynd, and the
other whiteys over on Lafayette St.   did not protest because
the magazine had been described by one alarmed councillor
as a "black militant" publication.   And Evergreen, which
had published some 19th-century erotic art in its January
issue, was unwittingly on the verge of becoming a cause
célèbre.   February would contain a dozen articles, stories,
and poems of which four were primarily concerned with sex.
The lead article was from Mike Royko's book on Chicago's
Mayor Daley, and it was accompanied by a full-page drawing
of the mayor's face which some find obscene, but which does
not come under existing pornography statutes.   There was a
Nat Hentoff piece on politics, an asexual story of LeRoi
Jones, John Lahr on Orlando Furioso, etc.

But the eye-grabber and mind-blower was the illustrated article by Mary Phillips about the artistic and sexual
liberation of artist Betty Dodson.   Sixteen of Miss Dodson's
large canvases were reproduced, reduced to about three
square inches each or about the size of half a theater
ticket.   One of a man and woman making love with the man
over the woman and between her legs filled a two-page
spread.   Six of the small reproductions depicted that general arrangement.   Two showed cunnilingus, one showed a
woman making love to another woman, four had men and
women masturbating alone, two with vibrators, etc., etc.
Some of the scenes were racially mixed, painted with a
warm, sympathetic brush, and showing people doing what
they have done for as long as I or anyone else can remember.   Miss Dodson's comments were as explicit as her
brush.   Asked if people looking at her pictures became
sexually aroused, she said:

> I think sexual arousal is very desirable and posi-
> tive.   I would like to draw pictures that would con-
> sistently turn everyone on--but that's probably not
> possible.

Before her sentiments ever reached Groton, two
events occurred that would affect Evergreen's fate.   On
January 3rd, the library board decided to compromise with

its critics and relocate "offensive" material out of the reach
of children.

"No titles were mentioned so I asked Mr. Richardson
which ones, Freep and Evergreen?" Carey says.   "He said,
well, I guess that's it.   I didn't want to lock them in a
drawer, so I put them on top of the six-foot periodical shelf.
Later I realized there was a stool in that corner so I removed the stool.   It was all pretty absurd."

The positioning meant that a tall teenager still could
see Evergreen where a short adult--say about the size of
Lieut. Calley--might miss it. Compass-Comment was warning
editorially about the dangers of appeasement.

> What is now happening is the inevitable result of
> compromise.   The library board has compromised
> its original position which was an unequivocable
> statement in support of free access to all material
> in the library....   We suggest the library board
> reread and reaffirm that.   In the battle against
> censorship by politicians, there is no common
> meeting ground, no minor compromise which can
> be safely made, no fixed point at which compro-
> mise can be ended.   There is only the certain
> knowledge that principle alone can be the guiding
> rule.

Richardson says:

> I thought it was sort of throwing out bait to the
> council so they wouldn't appoint somebody in place
> of Mrs. Kohl and Paul Plasse.   You see, in
> eleven years on the board we never had this kind
> of controversy, and it was something new to
> handle.   Six months before if somebody had asked
> me about Evergreen, I would have said it was
> some kind of Christmas tree.   Put it up six feet
> --well, it seemed a small thing to bend our open-
> shelf policy a bit for the larger good.

But the Compass-Comment warning on compromise
proved right.   The day after Evergreen and Freep assumed
their lofty perch, the town council voted five to four to replace Mrs. Kohl and Plasse with Ciminera's original candidate, Connolly, and with Pastor Keyl, who had written the
letter condemning an earlier Evergreen and Broadside.

It was a combination of censorship, politics, and
unmitigated ego on the part of people like Small
and Ciminera [Mrs. Kohl says]. Somebody like
Small devotes an enormous amount of time to the
town, takes a lot of abuse, goes to meetings long
into the night after his own work ends. But unfortunately, he thinks that makes him God with all
the answers to civic and moral problems. He
may deny it, but at the 'secret' meeting between
the council and board back in November, when he
saw we weren't going along on Broadside, he
yelled at the top of his lungs: 'you can kiss your
new library goodbye.'

When we came up for reappointment with Mrs.
Goodman, they accepted her because she had voted
the way they wanted it. We hadn't so they got
rid of us. The fact it was a library with all that
connotes meant nothing. They can't be swayed by
appeals to reason because they're operating out of
mixed political motives that really aren't concerned
with the issue of pornography. Ciminera, for
example, never wanted a new library built. So
this controversy erupted at the worst possible
time for us, when we were ready to move on a
new building. I don't think the timing was coincidental. But I can't prove it.

Connolly's first action as a board member was to
take out a library card. His next, in tandem with Ciminera,
was to go after Evergreen. The public occasion on February 8th was the best-attended library board meeting in
Groton history with townspeople crowding into the children's
reading room to discuss smut under a large home-drawn
mural of the land of Oz. Ciminera and Connolly had been
busy at a Xerox machine (an Electric Boat Xeroxer, by
most opposition accounts). Ciminera waved copies of the
comic strip he loved to hate, "Little Orphan Anphetamine."
It had already brought him a small measure of fame. The
Wilson Library Bulletin, a leading librarians' journal, had
named him Vigilante of the Month for threatening the library's funds. Connolly showed Xeroxes of Evergreen,
shoving one under the nose of the elderly former librarian
Mrs. Hagerty, who had formed a citizens' group opposing
censorship.

With a combative tone quickly established, it is no

wonder the meeting never really considered the content of
Evergreen as a whole or the sexual questions it raised in
particular.   If it was wrong to show a man and woman lovemaking, why was it wrong?   If it was wrong for art to be
designed frankly to trigger prurient emotions, was it equally
wrong for advertisers to picture half-clad girls with their
products, since their only function was a sexually provocative one?   Why do high school cheerleaders kick their legs
in the air?   Is it more, or less, healthy for a child entering puberty to see a painting of a man or woman masturbating, thus establishing that the practice is a fit subject for
viewing, or should the child learn orgasm in sexual solitary
confinement?   What were the implications for Groton in the
1969 survey of psychologists and psychiatrists by the Chicago
University Medical School, which found eighty-three percent
agreeing that most persons who actively fought "pornography"
were themselves victims of severe sexual repressions?

These questions were never raised, and a visitor
coming late onto the Groton scene suddenly wonders: in the
long history of American town meetings where sewers and
mill rates have been so freely discussed, has there ever
been a meeting anywhere when citizens stood up and spoke
to the issue of their common sexuality?

The board placed in record a letter from Grove
Press, Evergreen's publisher, objecting to any action which
would "deprive Grove of its constitutional rights and also
involve the library in a violation of the freedom to read of
its patrons."   Phrasing things better was Cassandra Burnett,
a member of the Connecticut Civil Liberties Union, which
was backing the board.   Addressing Ciminera and his faction,
she said: "If you get hung up on censorship, it's your loss.
But I would hate for your narrow-mindedness and hangups to
be passed on to the beautiful children."

Mrs. William Caird, president of the Fitch Senior
High School Home/School Association, delivered an im-
promptu Evergreen commercial.   She said her high school
senior daughter "used Evergreen for four or five term
papers and has gotten an 'A' on every one of them."

Ciminera responded with an attack against "a lot of
crap on the library shelves.   I'm for sex all the way," he
said, "but don't tell me about filth."   He flourished his
Xerox of the defunct Broadside's comic strip which by this
time he may have committed to memory.   "This stuff is
garbage," he said.

Councillor Henry Haley was milder. "Please put
this out of the way of small children," he said. "Who can
tell me that such graphic illustrations are necessary to the
moral upbringing of a child?"

Councillor Ann Graham, who voted with the Ciminera
majority on the town council and whose forte was protecting
Groton from X- and R-rated movies, said she was asking the
state library board if it couldn't amend the Library Bill of
Rights. (The state board replied eventually that it could
not.)

Finally, Connolly introduced a motion which fore-
shadowed the eventual legal action:

> Enforcement of criminal obscenity laws should
> never be construed as censorship. In the event
> of a legalized formal complaint against the publi-
> cations in question ... we are willing, as pre-
> scribed by law, to let contemporary community
> standards determine the obscenity of these publi-
> cations.

Richardson replied that the motion was redundant
since the board already had a regulation stating that obscenity laws should be enforced. "Where do you draw the
line?" he asked. "We are not a law enforcement body."

Connolly's motion failed and the meeting ended with
Evergreen still standing six feet tall and Grandfather Richardson displaying the cool eye and set mouth of a man who
once had taken a step back but now would not budge a centi-
meter if the Prince of Darkness himself tried to move him.
And what of Ciminera and Connolly, who have not been
characterized kindly so far, how did they answer the charge
of politics, the assertions that they were trying to act as
censors for a community of forty thousand, the suspicion in
some quarters that their sexual behavior as much as Miss
Dodson's was pertinent to the controversy? I tried to talk
by phone to both of them, explaining that I was a freelance
writer preparing an article for Evergreen.

"How much will they pay me?" Connolly said. "I'll
talk for five hundred dollars."
"Are you serious?" I said.
"That's right," he replied. "I got nothing to say to
them."

"But you would talk for five hundred dollars.   Where's
the morality in that?"

"They got to pay for my time," he said.   "And you
can tell Barney Rosset that."

Ciminera came on with the high-pitched, rapid-fire
delivery of a man who had sat through too many screenings
of Joe.   He told me an interview would "cost me," but
there was no price, his time was "negotiable."   He was,
for a noninterviewee, fairly loquacious.

> I've been quoted on what I say and what I read
> [he said].   It's like the Vietnam War, what you
> read and what you hear are two different things.
> The word Evergreen has never come out of my
> mouth, OK?   I never bought it, right?   I
> wouldn't read it and my two children wouldn't
> read it.   I've been called a vigilante.   It's my
> fifth term as councillor, OK?   Everything I do is
> for the town, right?   It costs me maybe one
> hundred fifty dollars a year, OK?   But I'm not
> a hero and I'm not aspiring to be president.   But
> I tell you one thing.   If you don't live in this town
> and you start preaching to me, I could tell you
> something.

Ten days after the February 8th board meeting,
Groton Police Chief Falvey (a fine police officer, from all
accounts) received a formal complaint from Connolly.   He
could not buy the "evidence" in any store since all the publicity had sold out Evergreen for miles around.   So Librarian Carey let him take the library copy.   Chief Falvey
was processing Connolly's complaint under Section 53 of
Connecticut's General Statutes, which, in common with most
states, follows language of a 1957 Supreme Court decision
sketching the outlines of the pornographic--"Whether to the
average person, applying contemporary standards, the
dominant theme of the mailable matter ... taken as a whole
... appeals to prurient interest."

It was clear that under prevailing statutes anomalies
abounded as Chief Falvey carried the offending Evergreen
to the New London office of Harold Dean, chief prosecutor
for the 10th Judicial District.   A bookstore five minutes
from Dean's office was doing a brisk front-room trade in
girl-and-guy magazines while dildoes were moving well in
the back room.   Area candy stores sold a paperback called

First Hump and boxed parlor games in the manner of
Monopoly and Parchesi called Adultery and Strip Tac Toe.
Barbra Streisand in The Owl and the Pussycat was making
a clean breast of her talent to anyone with the admission
price at a local drive-in.   Noncommercially, every nomin-
ally desirable girl in southeastern Connecticut--some even
defended in divorce cases by Dean, who practiced privately
while prosecutor--wearing miniskirts or hot pants was deliberately appealing to the prurient interest of every male
with a modicum of vision and a still-warm body.

        Dean's problem, however, was Evergreen, and he
faced it squarely:

            I looked at it and thought it was pornographic.
            From the standpoint of the children.   The worst
            thing to me was the lesbians making love.   I
            thought that was repulsive.   Now understand, I
            don't tell the world that Harold Dean is right.   I
            received a complaint and I go by the law.   And to
            make certain, I asked my five assistant prose-
            cutors what they thought.   Four out of five agreed
            it was pornographic.

            [The lone dissenter, Gilbert Shasha:]   I think the
            question to a prosecutor, 'Do you think this is ob-
            scene?', is a marvelously irrelevant question.
            My basic feeling is this is something where you
            just don't invoke criminal law.   It's political in the
            old Greek sense of the word and it should be left
            to the community, to the library board appointed
            by the community, to make the decision.

        Dean has been in the prosecutor's office for ten
years as assistant and chief, appointed by the judges of the
court he works in.   A lawyer who has known him closely
over the years describes him as "a very likable guy socially,
highly volatile, often acts out of emotion, egocentric, and
dotes on the power his job has given him to act like a
knight on a white charger protecting everybody's morals."
Dean agrees that he loves his job.   Sitting in his private
office, where Time is the only magazine displayed, he
exudes an attractive middle-aged dynamism.   His pepper-
and-salt hair is ample, eyes electric, manner robust.   He
says:

            I frankly love the prestige of being prosecutor.

And the chance for service. In this case, each
person has a different interpretation of what's
pornographic.   Now I think '69' is unnatural.   I
don't think there's anything wrong between the
normal act of sex done between husband and wife.
Of course not.   But sex between unmarried people
can lead to hurt.   Look, I'm no kid, I've been
around.   I have a twenty-year-old son and I
would want him to be chaste before his marriage.
I wouldn't want him to hurt a girl.   But I realize
there's a double standard.   You know, I was in
Amsterdam last year and they have a, you know,
a certain area there.   Maybe that's the answer.

I ask Dean about the reference in the law to "prevailing community standards." He said:

If this case had come up ten years ago, I wouldn't
have hesitated a minute to prosecute, but today it's
different.   Ten years ago you couldn't get a girl
to admit she wasn't a virgin.   I had one in my
office the other day admit she was a lesbian.   But
that doesn't mean what was pornographic ten years
ago isn't pornographic today.   It is but you can't
get a conviction.

Now in this case, I took no legal action at the
start.   I tried to convince the board it should
get rid of the offensive material.   Do they believe
in my integrity or not?   If they believe in it,
then if I indicate to them that it shouldn't be exposed to children, they should accede to my request.

Shouldn't an entire community rather than one prosecutor make the judgment on something as subjective as sex?

As far as asking the community, the process is
so slow that not days but years would go by.
Then you have the fact that the majority of people
opposed to pornography are not so vehemently
opposed as to take action.   The people who will
take action are the extreme left.   They would vote
whereas the other group would not.   Look, you
see a fight down the street, how many people
would become involved to stop it or report it?
Nobody.   But the extreme left would become involved.   Particularly if blacks were in it.

What about the local bookstore catering to varied
sexual tastes?   He never went after it directly, but it was
rumored he tried to pressure the owner of the building to
get rid of the store's tenants.

"It's true they are selling magazines far worse then
Evergreen," he says, "but I've received no official complaint.
So I'm not going to stick my neck out, I'm not looking to
prosecute people.   Anybody says I pressured the owner is
a liar.   The leaseholder talked to me.   I told him the type
of store it was.   He said chances were he wouldn't have
rented it to them if he had known.   But I didn't call him
to talk.   I ran into him on the street.   I had no way of
knowing he was the owner."   Dean pauses.   "I couldn't
tell you exactly how it happened I talked to him.   But I
didn't threaten any landlord."

The shop in question removed some books on besti-
ality and still operates.   This was the testimony of Prosecutor Dean, who was empowered by the State of Connecticut
to proceed with criminal action against the Groton Library
Board.   But aware of the difficulty in getting pornography
convictions, Dean tried to settle the complaint out of court
and according to his own ethical lights.   He began a series
of conversations with Groton Town Attorney Moukawsher
which resulted in mounting pressure on the board members
to capitulate.   Dean arranged to attend a March 2nd board
meeting in the hope it would believe in his integrity and
accede to his request.   An interesting matchup was in the
offing when somebody suggested artist Dodson should attend
the meeting, too.   She agreed:

> People up there had so many fantasies about me.
> We thought it would be good for them to see I was
> a live woman without fangs.   So I went up and
> had dinner with Carey and his wife, very sweet
> people with a new baby.   I thought he was a little
> flakey from all the pressure, but very courageous.
> This kid was really putting his ass on the line.
> I can say to smut-chasers, 'Fuck off if you don't
> like it.'   But he has to stay and take it.   I also
> thought Richardson was a very together old man,
> cool, groovy, and nice.

It probably was the first time in his life anyone
described Richardson as "groovy."   Miss Dodson says she
asked him whether he found her paintings terribly upsetting,

and Richardson said he didn't personally but he understood
that others might be upset.

> I saw a lot of fear at that meeting [she says].
> I think Dean picked up on the fear and used it.
> But those goddamned smut-chasers are frightened
> themselves and they have every right to be.
> Erotic art done by a woman is going to put heavy
> demands on people, make them think about how
> much freedom they really have over their own
> bodies and souls. They're going to realize that
> freedom is the toughest trip of all and you can't
> go halfway.

Miss Dodson might just as well have remained in
Manhattan; she never spoke to Dean or the spectators, and
most of the board was unaware of her presence.   The
meeting itself had a Kafkaesque quality about it with Dean
and Richardson talking directly at each other but in accents
that neither understood.   The prosecutor was angry to find
a dozen spectators in attendance, although board meetings
are always open to the public.

Dean: I felt we could discuss this in gentlemanly
fashion.   I didn't expect to appear before a large audience.   I thought we could have a little private meeting
to reach some sort of settlement, so to speak. ...   If
we can't meet on that basis, then I say you leave it
to me to take whatever steps I deem are necessary,
feasible, and advisable.   May I say to you respectfully
and to members of the board that I make no threats
because that isn't my job to threaten anybody. ...   So   ,
if, sir, you care to meet with me and your board I
would be happy to meet with you.
Richardson: Well, we are gathered here right for that
purpose.   Let's proceed.

Dean: But we're gathered with this group to make a
display.   I don't want to make a display. ...   I personally feel this is a very delicate situation.   The
language I would be compelled to use, the pictures I
would be compelled to show from this magazine.
Richardson: [The temptation here is to write Welch in
the margin because his replies stir a strong echo of
the Joseph Welch of the McCarthy hearings. -- P. G.]   I
would like to reply that our present "open-shelf" policy
doesn't permit removal of material, even if it is porno-

graphic. But if you get a court order, we'll certainly abide by it.

Dean: That's what I was trying to eliminate. There's been enough furor.
Richardson: Too much.

Dean: I think the material in this particular magazine I wouldn't want to show my children, and my children are over twenty-one.
Richardson: A library is an open window on the world. I don't agree with everything in it either.

Dean: I think if a page was displayed to a child between ten and sixteen, it would create a risk of injury to his morals. I don't think you'd want to exhibit some of the magazines that are exhibited in New York City. New York City tolerates them.

At this point, Pastor Keyl asked what proved to be a pertinent question and received what proved to be a misleading answer.

Pastor Keyl: Will the library have a chance to remove it before prosecution?
Dean: Well, yes. Once it's adjudicated it becomes pornographic. It's adjudicated pornographic by the court, you either remove it or I use a warrant.... An injunction is commenced. And if the injunction is brought to the circuit in New London, if at that time it's adjudged pornographic, you are enjoined from exhibiting it, you see.

But the penalty phase of the Connecticut pornography statute does not say this. It says,

> Any person having knowledge that mailable matter, films, or records have been adjudged obscene or who has knowledge that an order to show cause why such matter should not be adjudged obscene has been issued, who sells, exhibits, offers, or gives away the material shall be fined not more than $1000 and imprisoned for not more than two years.

Evidence suggests that Dean really did not understand this provision, which judged by American legal standards, is incomprehensible. It means that in the interim

period between a judge summoning a defendant to court for
a hearing on the alleged pornographic content of a magazine
and the hearing itself, the defendant may be sent to jail
without speaking a word in his own defense. Applying the
law to a more familiar injunctive proceeding underlines its
apparent unconstitutionality. Suppose a union is striking and
the city tries to stop it with an injunction. On a Monday,
it obtains a show cause order from the judge ordering union
leaders into court on Friday to answer why they should not
be enjoined from striking. But on Wednesday, before they
can appear, the judge throws the leaders into jail. The
customary course of the law is for the judge to issue a temporary injunction pending a full court hearing or a jury trial.
This is what the library board members understood would
happen when Dean left them, and a majority of the board,
by actual head count, stood behind Richardson in the belief
that a court test was the only way to resolve the dispute.

Dean left angry. The board had not trusted to his
"integrity," had not acceded to his "request." He prepared
an injunction application against Evergreen, making defendants of the magazine corporation, editor Barney Rosset,
and every member of the library board, including Connolly.
"I wasn't taking any chances," he said. "I felt they were
all equally responsible, so I brought them all in."

How the smut-chasing Connolly could be equated with
Barney Rosset is hard to understand until you discover the
absence of clear legal distinctions in Dean's application.
It is a farrago of sex charges, steaming with words like
"lust ... perversion ... lewd ... lascivious."

The mailable matter [it says] is calculated to
deprave and corrupt the minds of those into whose
hands it might come, including and especially
minor children.... The dominant theme of the
material, taken as a whole, appeals to prurient
interest.

Dean would later deny to me that he meant the magazine as a whole, only the Dodson article. "But how," he
asked, "can you cut out the heart of a person and not kill
the body? You must bring in the entire magazine."

But that isn't what the statute says, holding that the
entire publication must be judged. Since no more than
twenty percent of the February Evergreen's pages had any-

thing to do with sex, licit or otherwise, illicit sex could
hardly qualify as the dominant theme. As a matter of fact,
Dean's contention that he meant only the Dodson article (in
which case the application's legality is questionable) is con-
tradicted by much of the language in it, and is flatly belied
by the fourth charge: "The advertising matter contained
therein is designed to appeal to and stimulate prurient interest. "

        Since the advertising matter was not within the Dod-
son article, Dean must have been charging the entire issue.
And what, in any event, was being advertised?   Well, there
was a stereo sale featuring Henry Mancini on "Moon River. "
There was a World-of-Cheese Club display with adjectives
like "creamy, semi-soft, and zesty. "   There was an ad
for some Evergreen Book Club sex novels and a half-assed
(bare) ad for blue jeans.   But the vast majority concerned
things like Tarot cards, draft-resistance books, and African
education films.   Could Dean have been referring to the
Simon and Schuster Marriage Manual?   And did the complaint turn on accessibility to children or not?   If the prosecutor, judged by his application, was not clear on what
he was trying to prosecute, his case could have a difficult
time in the courts.   However, Circuit Court Judge John M.
Alexander did take the first judicial step by issuing a show
cause order calling all defendants into court eight days later
on March 16th.

        The court action was barely instituted before Dean
was agreeing with Town Attorney Moukawsher to drop it if
the library board would give in and get rid of Evergreen.
Was this, as Dean says, the considerate action of a prosecutor who did not really want to subject persons to criminal
proceedings if it could be avoided?   Or was it an effort to
pressure the board to act without bringing a shaky case into
court?   Moukawsher began an intensive round of phone calls
to board members, stressing the gravity of their position
and urging a meeting with him.   Richardson felt it would
serve no purpose but reluctantly agreed after talking to
alarmed members.   Just hours before the March 8th meeting,
Moukawsher sent him a five-page letter, mustering many
arguments against the board's determination to see the case
decided in court.   It reviews at length Moukawsher's movement in the case, almost as if he were building a case for
himself should some possible legal action arise involving
him.

> When I was unable to reach you by telephone at
> your place of business (March 5), I visited you
> personally and spent approximately one and one-
> half hours explaining to you the various ramifica-
> tions of this action. I certainly hope that I made
> it clear to you at that time that it was my opinion
> as town attorney that the library board should not
> become involved in these proceedings, that it was
> inappropriate and perhaps improper for members
> of a public body holding public office under a
> charter granted by the State of Connecticut to re-
> sist or oppose the state prosecutor in these par-
> ticular circumstances.

The letter goes on to review the legal developments,
and then says:

> This situation leaves the library board in an ex-
> tremely difficult and embarrassing position. It
> compels me as town attorney if the town council
> so directs to appear on behalf of the library board
> members in a matter about which I feel the li-
> brary board is acting improperly. If the town
> council refuses to permit me to appear on behalf
> of the library board members, the situation would
> be more complicated. It would be, in my opinion,
> a determination that the library board members
> are acting beyond their authority in this matter
> and will not be afforded legal counsel at the ex-
> pense of the Town of Groton and could be subject
> to liabilities of varying kinds as a result of their
> action.

What was Moukawsher saying in these paragraphs?
In the first, did he mean that a prosecutor's charge against
public-office holders was a law unto itself and should not be
opposed? In the second, was he suggesting there was something wrong in a town attorney defending a position by public officials that was personally unpopular with him? Was
he threatening to leave the board undefended because some
council members did not like its policies? I was unable to
clear up these points with Moukawsher, who made eighteen
thousand dollars last year as a Groton public official. "I
refuse to answer any questions or make any statements,"
he said to me. "As attorney for the town, I refuse to talk
to the press."

Moukawsher talked at length and often angrily to the board members the night of March 8th. He explained, for the first time, the bizarre penalty provision in the pornography law although he did not point out that there was little chance the judge would invoke it without a final injunction trial or that it might never survive appeal if he did. To members shocked at the prospect of jail, he added the specter of the town refusing to defend them, throwing them back on their own resources. Was it worth it over the copy of one magazine? Richardson, housewife Dorothy Miller, and Marion Greene, a grandfather teaching at New London Junior High School, thought it was. But they were outvoted six to three, and Richardson emerged to say, "The man in the street could call it blackmail."

The reactions of two members who cast opposite votes say a good deal about the caliber of the men and the essence of the issue joined in that meeting. Greene, Mayor Small's black neighbor, says:

> I think the vote might have gone the other way ex-
> cept that people were pushed into it by the threat
> the town wouldn't help us. Nobody wants to spend
> his own money for a lawyer or go to jail. True,
> I took the chance. I believe in something, I just
> believe in it, and it's not worth anything if you
> don't back it. As far as that Evergreen went, I
> wouldn't have purposely put it where my child
> could get at it. But if he saw it I would have had
> a natural answer for it. Some, like the mayor,
> don't think that way, and we're as far apart as a
> grapevine and an apple bush, though we get along
> fine as neighbors. I think the whole affair did a
> great injustice to Carey, who's doing a wonderful
> job. But they couldn't get him on anything else
> so they got him on that. It was wrong, absolutely
> wrong, not to let this thing get heard in court, and
> tomorrow I'd vote the same way on it.

Pastor Keyl, appointed to the board on the strength of his letter assailing Broadside and Evergreen, says:

> For me, personally, the Evergreen article was
> morally offensive. But I still feel that the board,
> myself included, should not make a judgment on a
> publication's obscenity. The courts are in a posi-
> tion to make that judgment and since we hire a

library director we should abide by his decisions
unless the courts rule otherwise. So I wanted to
vote we wouldn't remove anything, even a file card,
unless a court said so. But we were pressured
into it because we really didn't understand what
Mr. Moukawsher was talking about. I feel bad
about it, but I got to the point where I said to
myself, you don't have one thousand dollars to pay
a fine, you have a wife and three children to support.

Pastor Keyl is also troubled by some developments
that followed after the vote was taken and Prosecutor Dean
dropped the case:

At the next board meeting, Mr. Connolly was
raising the question of phone calls Mr. Carey
made during the crisis to different people throughout the country--to the artist, I think, and some
library associations. I understand that in some
way he got hold of the numbers and had them
checked out. Mr. Connolly didn't think he had the
right to make those calls with taxpayers' money.
Well, he didn't like it very much but I didn't
agree. I support Mr. Carey and feel he's doing
a fine job, although what's morally right for him
may not be morally right for me. I know that I
get into crisis situations sometimes and start
using the telephone, and it's wrong to damn a man
for that. But now, nothing has been resolved and
I don't know when the whole thing will stop.

The lack of any real resolution was spelled out in a
long story in the New London Day by Steve Scott, a young
reporter who had been in the Navy and was released as a
conscientious objector. He wrote:

... the issue never got a full court hearing that
would have permitted both sides to present their
positions. The board, at the urging of Town Atty.
Joseph E. Moukawsher, short-circuited the procedure.
    Whatever interpretation is placed on what
Moukawsher told the board, there is little doubt
that some board members felt themselves intimidated.

Scott pointed out that Connolly had said that the only
way to test Evergreen's obscenity "is to get it to a law
test." "Yet," Scott notes, "when the situation had evolved
to the point where the library board could take the issue to
a law test, Connolly was among the six voting against this
procedure."

After this story appeared, Connolly remarked at a
library board meeting that Scott was "running a draft-dodging
service in New London." The reporter concedes that he had
privately helped three Navymen to process their CO applications. How did Connolly know this? The Day shortly
began receiving a spate of letters calling attention to Scott's
CO discharge and calling for his removal on the grounds he
was a "Commie ... a pinko slacker." The newspaper management stood firmly behind its reporter while it tried to
get at the root of the anonymous complaints. But what was
the source of the information that Scott had been CO'd from
the Navy? Did it lie in the intimate intelligence association between Electric Boat and the Navy?

All the months of controversy left only questions in
its wake. February Evergreen was out of the library although the board did not physically remove it. In a final
ironic touch that you could either laugh or cry over, on the
afternoon of the climactic meeting, a thirteen-year-old boy
was caught trying to steal the issue hidden inside a copy of
Jaguar, and the police picked it up as evidence. The
April Evergreen was behind the desk, available on request,
although there was no official limitation on the age of those
who could successfully request it. Sixteen? Eighteen?
Should it be given to a known adult sex offender? A magazine on the open shelf carried an ad for a book, The Delinquent Girl.

> Esther's story [ran the promo] progresses through
> foster homes, a return to her mother who was re-
> leased from prison when Esther was 10, sexual
> experiences (heterosexual and homosexual), running
> away, flunking in school, shoplifting, arson, and
> contacts with pushers, pimps and prostitutes.

Should that magazine join Evergreen behind the librarian's desk? The magazine was called Police--The
Journal Covering the Professional Interests of All Law Enforcement Personnel. One of Carey's own workers had
taken out a book called Studies in Erotic Art. It was being

passed around in certain circles and Connolly had indicated
he wanted the board to examine it.   The book was a by-
product of the Kinsey Institute.   Would it be up for pro-
scription next month along with some new Evergreen issue?
Should Carey go through the shelves anticipating future
challenges?   Already he was preparing compilations of reviews of possibly controversial books to offer as evidence
of respectability should they be challenged.   Richardson felt
that the controversy might prove beneficial in the long run
because it had at least put the library on the map.   But the
new budget (in an admittedly tight time for tax dollars)
was cutting new acquisition funds in half.   Did this presage
defeat for badly needed library construction?

"I don't think so," Richardson says.   "But now you
can't be sure.   In retrospect, I guess we as a board fudged
the issue with that vote and I feel bad about it.   I never
should have called that special meeting with Moukawsher.
Let the courts be the censor, not us.   But there was so
much pressure that principle was hard to maintain."

CLU attorney Hyman Wilensky, who was prepared to
enter the case, is bothered by the lack of real resolution.
"As it stands," he says, "The only place in Connecticut that
Evergreen is obscene is on the shelf of the Groton Library.
The outcome means that any one individual can set himself
up as a one-man censoring committee, and, if he can get
the prosecuting attorney to agree with him and the judge to
issue a show cause order, you've got your censorship."

Some citizens, including liberal Compass-Comment
editor Ross, want to get the case back into the courts,
fight it out, get a ruling.   But there is a general inclination to let things stand.   Connolly and the prosecutor have
won a victory without a real legal fight; the losers have other
life problems preoccupying them.

So, by default, steps to clarify the issue would not
be taken, and the rationale behind the Evergreen ban would
remain fuzzy.   I drove out to station WNLC where Mayor
Small worked to see if he could throw it into a clearer
perspective.   While generally siding with the Ciminera-Con-
nolly faction, his public involvement had been reserved and,
by all accounts, he was a keen political animal, expert at
sniffing out public opinion in his town.   At fifty-seven, he
has the kinetic energy of a big, middle-aged man who has
fought successfully all his life to stay alive, built a minor

but solid niche in business and raised a large family without
begging.   On the street they would say, Small takes care of
himself.

> Look, Paul [he said], we're not a bunch of trog-
> lodytes on the council.   We're a pretty good cross
> section of America.   A lot of union people--I hold
> a card in Musician's Local 285--and we care about
> our community.   Hell, I've always been for the
> underdog.   My father raised me that way.   He
> was an assistant U. S. Commissioner of Education,
> dean of the College of Education at the University
> of Maryland, and he voted for Teddy Roosevelt in
> 1912.   I was practically raised in the Library of
> Congress and I respect books.

> I supported Eugene McCarthy.   I hate this war in
> Vietnam.   What the hell are we sending our boys
> ten thousand miles to die for people over there.
> I also backed Ribicoff, a damned good guy.   Dodd?
> Well, I've got mixed feelings.   He's a courteous,
> gentlemanly man, always attentive when you write
> to him.   When I ran for state representative in
> '58 and lost--he won, of course--he sent me a
> letter saying, 'it's people like you who help people
> like me win elections. '   I never forgot that.   But
> as far as politics being involved in this, that's
> ridiculous.

It is difficult to keep Mayor Small talking on the issue
of the Groton Pornography Case.   An ecologist, he continually slides off to talk about the gypsy moth, a legiti-
mately dirty word in Connecticut.   A doer in the nitty-gritty
of town administration, he switches from Evergreen to the
sewage plan the council has pioneered for Groton, the need
for a central alarm fire system, a possible taxpayers' revolt over a fourteen-mill rate increase.   He says that these
are major concerns in Groton.   And, of course, he is absolutely right.   It's easy to deride his kind of municipal concern for sewers, but you feel no derision when you flush a
Groton toilet and it works.   It is understandable that a man
of action like Small has little patience with men of ideas,
understandable if not acceptable why he feels that a bearded
young librarian like Carey, who thinks differently from some
town councillors, should have no standing before the court
of community opinion.   It is in this area of abstract principles that the mayor's mask of democratic reasonableness

slips and a less attractive face appears.   His first comment
is that liberal editor Ross is late in paying his bills to the
station.   He says that "bearded beatniks" complain about
society without working to change it.   And he claims that the
library board had been operating like a "country club."

> First of all, if they had just put that Broadside
> thing away when we asked them, all this wouldn't
> have happened.   Mr. Carey is not a policy maker.
> We on the council make policy the same as we
> make it for the sewer commission, and we tried
> to give the board the same consideration we give
> the commission.   No, the library board doesn't
> have to follow our policy, but members of the
> board should agree with it.

Was that why he voted to get rid of Mrs. Kohl?
First, he replies, the vote to replace her had nothing to do
with the Broadside issue.   Then he says the board was in a
rut and had to be revitalized.   Finally, he admits she was
replaced because he thinks "we have to have board members
who are like-minded as the council."

> But I never threatened library funds, like she says.
> I don't think she understood what I said in that
> November meeting.   I said it was unfortunate that
> the controversy came up and that I questioned
> whether people would pass a referendum for a new
> building under the circumstances.   I never threat-
> ened the new building.   I think we need it.   I
> think our kids need it.   But you see, a lot of out-
> side influences got into the act.

What outside influences?

> Oh, people writing letters to the editor from
> Waterford and places like that, stirring things up.
> Actually, I never read that Evergreen at all.
> Somebody tried to pass it to me at a meeting but
> I didn't have my glasses and I couldn't see it.
> I was too busy to read it, working sixty, seventy
> hours a week.   But I don't think that type of maga-
> zine is in too many libraries in Connecticut and
> I don't like Groton being the guinea pig.   Perhaps
> I belong to another generation.

Was the issue resolved by putting Evergreen behind
the desk?

It is if Mr. Carey will let it be. If he's looking
for a fight, he'll get it. I understand he made a
speech the other day to the League of Women
Voters, using four-letter words. If he thinks that
makes friends for the library, OK. But I think
all we need there is some judgment. See, they
try to draw you into a corner about the age of
people who should see it. I'd say maybe a junior
or a senior in high school. Or maybe a mature
sophomore.

The questions could continue but we are discussing
two different ball games, conflicting sets of rules, varying
goals. A majority of the mayor's non-troglodytic council
believes it knows what the sexual score is in Groton and,
since a library board is equatable with a sewer commission,
the majority members feel the library board should play
along with them. The council's private sex lives are at
once their own business and community business too; so a
sewer, individual sexual psyches, ultimate sexual standards,
and a library shelf merge into a Groton status quo supported
by the mayor. Mayor Small and I are about to part amic-
ably, if wary about our respective positions. He suggests
an ecologically approved spray called Biotrol for my apple
trees, and I thank him. His handshake is firm and I appreciate the fact that he has spoken at length when those like
Moukawsher and Ciminera and Connolly ducked.

"One thing that burns my tail," he says. "Some of
those people on the other side have been saying things about
our sex lives. I don't think that's right." I agree that
there has probably been unfairness on both sides. For example, people were spreading rumors that a reporter named
Steve Scott who covered the controversy was a Commie.

"Who's Steve Scott?" he says. "Scott? I never
heard of him." I explain that he is a New London journalist
and add that there has been malicious letter-writing about
his conscientious-objector discharge from the Navy.

"I never knew he was in the Navy," says Mayor
Small.
"But I thought you never heard of him?" I say.
"Well, I mean, if there were four or five reporters
in this room now, I wouldn't know him."

There is nothing left to say to Mayor Small but

goodbye.   I recall the words that Little Orphan Anphetamine
said to Daddy.   But what would be the point, I decide, of
piling obscenity on obscenity?   Still, a few minutes later,
driving out of Groton and thinking of Carey and Richardson
and the young kid who stole Evergreen tucked inside Jaguar,
I do say it to myself.   But it doesn't do much good for me
and it doesn't change a think back there in Groton.   Not one
f-----g think.

CENSORSHIP--REEVALUATED

by Dorothy Broderick

Reprinted by permission from School Library Journal,
November 1971, p. 3816-3818, published by R. R. Bow-
ker (a Xerox company) and copyright (c) 1971 by the
Xerox Corporation.

What follows is what I like to think of as reflecting
middle-aged maturity, although I recognize that for others
it will be seen as postdoctoral senility. I like to think I
would have eventually reevaluated my thoughts about censorship just as a matter of course. But I had a great deal of
help and would like to acknowledge it.

You are all familiar with the domino theory. I never
believed in it until it happened to me. My first mistake was
to pay my ALA dues. This led to the arrival of American
Libraries, which I insist upon calling ALA Bulletin despite
my newfound mental flexibility. It is essential to keep in
mind that we all carry within us the seeds of our own down-
fall. My weakness is that I am a compulsive reader and
thus, month after month I continued to read the column on
Intellectual Freedom, knowing full well it was driving me
into the enemy camp, but unable to stop myself.

It took me months to figure out what bothered me.
At first I thought it was the absence of phrases like "the
selection process" and "weeding the collection." Only gradually did it dawn on me that anyone who can write about
intellectual freedom as ex cathedra dicta cannot possibly be
understanding the concept. Now, I fully recognize that
Judith Krug of the Intellectual Freedom Office could answer
this charge with one of my favorite quotations, namely, "It
is the misfortune of the purist to be considered arrogant
when all he is doing is being right." That reply would get
right to the heart of my objections. It is bordering on sui-
cide to be a purist about so complex a question as censorship.

Besides, has something happened behind my back?
Did librarians suddenly and magically become infallible?
Has everyone learned never to make a mistake in adding a
book or magazine to the collection? Has everyone found the
time to ruthlessly weed out the hundreds and thousands of
books that are no longer worthy of shelf space (if they ever
were)? Is the complainant always and automatically wrong?
Is there no occasion when we might be wrong? Somehow,
to be self-righteous under the banner of intellectual freedom
strikes me as the ultimate in absurdity.

Moreover, the dogma coming from the Office of Intellectual Freedom shows no signs of understanding either
the history of the public library or recognition of concepts
being developed in other fields concerning the question of
freedom. Having decided once and for all to be in favor
of intellectual freedom, a segment of our profession has
then closed its mind to all consideration of the opposing
point of view. Again, this rigidity does not meet any
definition of an intellectually free person.

In On Becoming a Person, Carl Rogers discusses why
he chose not to become a minister. Rogers says:

> My beliefs had already changed tremendously, and
> might continue to change. It seemed to me it
> would be a horrible thing to have to profess a set
> beliefs, in order to remain in one's profession.
> I wanted to find a field in which I could be sure
> my freedom of thought would not be limited. [1]

That is how I thought of the library profession--a
place where change and growth were possible. Now I discover that the only freedom being expounded is the freedom
to believe in absolute freedom. Despite my reputation as
some kind of weird radical, I would suggest to you that I
have never accepted this premise. Everything I have written
has been within the framework of the selection process and
if, on occasion, I have seemed radical, it was in the cause
of opening up that process--but not to do away with it.

This belief was reinforced during the process of
writing my dissertation. Few people can probably claim
that doing a dissertation changed their lives for the better,
but mind did. And in the process, I came to feel strongly
that if freedom meant the right to warp children's minds,
to put our stamp of approval on bigotry, then I would do
with a little less of it.

Before we return to the here and now, I want to
take you on an historical excursion. The purpose of taking
the historical route is to point out: 1) the public library
was not founded as a bastion of intellectual freedom; 2) the
early librarians understood and accepted this premise, and
3) librarians of our time have unilaterally broken the cove-
nant that existed between the community and the library.

Libraries were founded originally to offer a growing
literate populace approved alternatives to the wares of the
newsstands. Dime novels, the girly magazines, and The
Police Gazette had to be counteracted. While rarely men-
tioning libraries, Paul Boyer's Purity in Print[2] offers a
fascinating account of the social forces that gave rise to
Anthony Comstock and his compatriots and makes quite
reasonable the need for anti-vice societies without making
Comstock himself any more acceptable. The book ranks
high on my reading list for the insights it offers into the
relationship between social conditions and intellectual climate. And I strongly suspect that it is not accidental that
the two major cities to give rise to Comstock and the
Watch and Ward Society, New York and Boston, were also
forerunners in the public library movement.

In 1895 the American Library Association conference
concerned itself with the topic, "Improper Books: Methods
Employed to Discover and Exclude Them. "[3] Here are some
of the choice quotes from that symposium.

From Theresa H. West, Librarian, Milwaukee Public
Library:

> The underlying principle of my own selection of
> books, for a library which is essentially for the
> people, is that books which speak truth concerning
> normal, wholesome conditions may be safely
> bought, however plain-spoken. While on the other
> hand, books which treat of morbid, diseased con-
> ditions of the individual man, or of society at large,
> are intended for the student of special subjects.
> Such are bought only after due consideration of the
> just relation of the comparative rights of students
> and general readers. [4]

From the librarian of the San Francisco Public Library, George T. Clark:

> What, then, shall be the standard for a public li-
> brary maintained by revenues derived from taxa-
> tion?   To determine this, we must arrive at some
> definite idea as to the proper functions of public
> libraries.   Why has the State enacted laws under
> which holders of property are compelled to pay
> taxes for the support of such institutions?   It is
> expected that a public library will contribute to
> the general welfare of the people, and be an in-
> fluence on the community.   In fact, that it shall
> assist in the education of the people and the making
> of good citizens.   Unless it does exercise these
> functions, what justice is there in making it a
> burden on the taxpayers?   What right has it to
> exist?[5]

Since the beginning of libraries, there has always
been the problem of how to respond to public pressure for
a book the library would rather not buy, or having bought,
would prefer to control its circulation.   J. N. Larned of the
Buffalo Public Library came up with this solution.

> In the case of one recent book for which many
> applications were made in our library, I have
> been trying the experiment of sending a circular
> note to each applicant, briefly describing its char-
> acter and saying that I am not willing the book
> should go into the hands of any reader without
> clear knowledge of what it is.   The result has
> been to cancel a large part of the requests for
> the book, while those who read it take on them-
> selves the whole responsibility in doing so.   It
> seems to me that a general policy of dealing with
> such books may be framed on the principle indi-
> cated in this experiment. [6]

Before moving on to the next writer, I would like to
suggest that we could have a nationwide contest sponsored
by one of our periodicals to see who can write the best
letter telling patrons that they are dirty old men without
offending them.   The prize would be an ex officio seat on
the Intellectual Freedom Committee, which isn't any more
ridiculous than Gaines serving on the Board of Trustees of
the Freedom to Read Foundation.

The last of the contributors to the ALA conference
was William H. Brett of the Cleveland Public Library.

Brett makes a point I want to stress, so let me quote him at some length.

> There are, as we all know, many books published every year on economics, politics, and other important subjects which, adjudged by opinions that are now accepted, are utterly worthless. But, at the same time, there is in those fields such a diversity, such a contrariety of opinions that we may well be very careful about excluding books because they differ from the opinions which are accepted now. We must remember that the cranky idea of today may possibly be the accepted belief tomorrow; so that there are none of these books that we, perhaps, should absolutely exclude.
>
> It is only when we come to books which affect the question of morals, the question of conduct, that we feel that we have the right to draw the line of exclusion; that we will have therein the support of right-thinking people, no matter what their religious opinions may be, no matter what their belief or lack of belief. We are all practically united on what constitutes right living. Matthew Arnold says that conduct is three-fourths of life; yet, conduct is but the working out into life of what a man thinks, and what he believes, and this moulded largely by that he reads. Among the books which influence opinion and mould belief, are many which are classed as fiction, and it is largely in that class that the line of exclusion will be drawn ... I believe that we have a perfect right to exclude from our shelves books which seem likely to prove harmful, no matter with what reputation as classics they come to us. I think we have a right to judge these books and exclude them, just exactly as we do books of the day. [7]

What Brett makes clear is that there is a difference between diversity and licentiousness, just as there is a difference between freedom and anarchy. But the major point is that the old timers were not frightened by the idea of making value judgments. They understood they had a charge from the community to act as professionals and make decisions.

In my opinion, the only thing that has changed from

those days is the concept of "the good life." Despite the
innumerable and seemingly insurmountable problems of our
society, I am encouraged by the movement toward openness
and the acceptance of cultural and racial diversity and a
beginning awareness that all men are entitled to respect and
dignity.

The role of libraries under these conditions is to
support life-affirming materials. One Corrine Bacon, writing
in a 1909 issue of New York Libraries on "What Makes a
Book Immoral," put it this way:

> What does it matter of what he writes so that his
> heart be true to the finer possibilities in human
> nature? The book which degrades our intellect,
> vulgarizes our emotions, kills our faith in our
> kind, is an immoral book; the book which stimu-
> lates thought, quickens our sense of humor, gives
> us a deeper insight into men and women and a
> finer sympathy for them, is a moral book, let its
> subject-matter have as wide a range as life itself. [8]

Were this a book instead of a talk, we could pursue
this value judgment argument by further quotes from such
LJ symposia as the one in 1908 entitled "What Shall Libraries Do About Bad Books?"[9] and its repeat in 1922 on
the subject "Questionable Books in Public Libraries."[10]

Because time is short, we are going to jump to the
early 1950s. For 100 years the public library religiously
fulfilled its charge from the public that supported it. Then
came the grand days of Senator Joe. Suddenly, it was not
a question of whether men like Lawrence, Joyce, and
Hemingway had a right to literary freedom; it was not even
just a question of political diversity--this time it was libraries themselves under attack. And we fought back, much
as the scribes in England fought against the importation of
the printing press. It was our world that was being
challenged. Make no mistake: we fought for self-preserva-
tion, not for the abstract concept of intellectual freedom.

We can learn a valuable lesson from those days that
has great application to our present situation in relationship
to the turmoil within ALA. The profession took a stand
against McCarthy's attacks. But, quietly, as Fiske and
others have shown us, librarians were engaged in self-
censorship that was often far more restrictive than the

communities would have imposed. And there was that never-to-be-forgotten occasion when the big, brave librarians told Ed Murrow that it was all a lot of nonsense while refusing to have their faces photographed.

Even so, what the elder statesmen of ALA do not understand is that during those years of fighting McCarthy, they created an illusion that led many socially concerned young people--myself included--to think that being a librarian might be an honorable profession. Yet at rock-bottom, they resembled nothing quite so much as Brother Librarian in Miller's A Canticle for Leibowitz: "To Brother Librarian, whose task in life was the preservation of books, the principal reason for the existence of books was that they might be preserved perpetually. Usage was secondary, and to be avoided if it threatened longevity. "[11] Miller might well have added, "or if it threatened the established social order. "

The leadership had no intention of broadening the fight from the preservation of libraries to the idea that librarians --as librarians--might also feel compelled to fight for the preservation of the world in which we live. You may recall that as recently as the June 15, 1970 issue of LJ one Ervin Gaines took us to task for indulging in a faddist relationship with Vietnam and pollution. We were told to chant daily: "I believe that it is my duty as a public librarian to collection information to the maximum extent possible, to make it freely available to everyone, and to assist people to find and use that information to the best of my ability. "[12] Eleven months later, May 15, 1971, Gaines, his faddist relationship with intellectual freedom relegated to the past, explains to us that "everyone" only meant adults and not young people and that restricted shelves aren't such a bad idea after all. [13]

Buried as a news item in the same issue of LJ is the information that the San Jose Public Library had won a grand fight for intellectual freedom by keeping the racist Epaminondas and His Auntie on the open shelves. And here, after all these words, we come to the crux of the matter.

In the name of intellectual freedom we defend materials that perpetuate attitudes that hinder the growth of individuals who are intellectually free. No racist is intellectually free. Try as I may, I can see no issue of intellectual freedom involved in a request to remove Epaminondas and His Auntie from library shelves. Except for re-

search libraries, the process known as weeding the collection should have eliminated the book years ago.   But the
library remains what it was when founded: a reflection of
white ruling class values.   As long as it is black people
being offended we invoke intellectual freedom and tell blacks
that bigots have rights, too.

In the case of the Minneapolis Public Library's fight
over the alternate press periodicals, it was the establishment being attacked.   That is not good.   In the name of
intellectual freedom we will let young minds be warped by
racism, but let us keep youth from thinking that the American corporate structure needs revamping--or even elimination.

To quote my favorite public figure, let me make it
perfectly clear: I do not believe in an abstract concept of
intellectual freedom.   If some men are more free than
others, it is because they exist in environments that make
such freedom possible.   One does not have to accept Skinner's "technology of human behavior" theory to recognize
the validity of his emphasis upon environment as a controlling feature of man's behavior.   After all, that is precisely what goes on in a classroom if real learning takes
place: the environment makes it possible for the person to
change.   That is what happens in therapy and sensitivity
training and that is what happens to us if we join a reasonably homogeneous group whether it be the Black Panthers,
Gay Lib, NOW, or a political party.

We also know that when we find ourselves in an alien
environment we have but two choices: change our attitudes
or find a new environment.

What does all this have to do with libraries and self-
censorship and the overwhelming problems we are faced
with?   For me, everything.   Libraries are in themselves
"an environment," but they are also a microcosm of the
larger unit we call society.

The fight we are experiencing within the profession
at the moment would seem to be built around two alternatives.   The first is to go right on doing what we've been
doing, namely, reflecting attitudes rather than affecting them.
The second is to fight to make the library an instrument of
social change.   Should we opt for the latter, and frankly I
cannot conceive of that happening,   there are two steps

necessary. First, we must have a public debate with our
communities, asking that the traditional role of the library
be redefined. We need a mandate from the public, for
whatever our private convictions, we must keep in mind
that we are talking about a public institution and if we don't
like what the public wants, we can always find something
else to work at.

Secondly, we have to recognize that such a fight cannot be carried out under the banner of intellectual freedom,
unless that phrase is redefined to mean that we will do all
in our power to offer individuals experiences through materials that will broaden, not limit, their possibilities for
growth. That means making value judgments. That means
we have to be brave enough to say that love is a better
emotion than hate, that fear and distrust of others are
destructive to the person holding such emotions.

Actually, there is only one question that need be
asked about books in this relationship: how does this book
reflect the sanctity of life? In these terms we can look
at Down These Mean Streets, the book under discussion at
the moment. The obscenity of the book is that our society
has relegated segments of the population to lead the kind of
life Piri Thomas describes. It is attacked, and censored,
by those who, were they to admit its validity, would then be
forced to feel they should do something about the conditions
the book describes. How much easier it is to label the book
obscene than to face the fact that the real obscenities are
racism and poverty.

It is right and proper that librarians fight for the
right of youth to read Down These Mean Streets or Soul on
Ice or To Kill a Mockingbird--they are all life affirming
books. But we cannot say that "intellectual freedom" justifies pornography, nor should we confuse political and social
diversity with pornography. Few librarians ever see any
pornography; if more did, we might rephrase our intellectual
freedom concerns more realistically and in the process
make them more defensible.

For me, racist materials are simply another form of
pornography. They are anti-human. And just as Laura
Hobson in her New York Times article, "As I Listened to
Archie Say Hebe,"[14] says it is cruel to subject children to
the idea that bigotry is fun, so I object to the library stocking materials that say bigotry is just another point of view.

I fail to understand how the people who are concerned with social responsibilities can also be gung-ho for the current stance being offered by the Office of Intellectual Freedom. The whole concept of social responsibility implies value judgments--some things are right and some things are wrong and it is that simple. In modern jargon, that is known as an elitist point of view, and elitist is a very dirty word, indeed. But here I stand and until my next great change of life, here I remain.

References

1. Rogers, Carl. On Becoming a Person. Boston: Houghton, 1970, p. 8.
2. Boyer, Paul. Purity in Print. New York: Scribners, 1968.
3. "Improper Books: Methods Employed to Discover and Exclude Them." Symposium. Library Journal, December, 1895.
4. Ibid., p. 32.
5. Ibid., p. 33.
6. Ibid., p. 35.
7. Ibid., p. 36.
8. Bacon, Corrine. "What Makes a Book Immoral," New York Libraries, 1909.
9. "What Shall Libraries Do About Bad Books?" Symposium. Library Journal, September, 1908, p. 349-54.
10. "Questionable Books in Public Libraries." Symposium. Library Journal, October 15, 1922, p. 857-61. Continued in the November 1 issue.
11. Miller, Walter. A Canticle for Leibowitz. New York: Lippincott, 1969.
12. Gaines, Ervin. "Viewpoint." Library Journal, June 15, 1970, p. 2235.
13. Gaines, Ervin. "Viewpoint." Library Journal, May 15, 1971, p. 1687.
14. Hobson, Laura. "As I Listened to Archie Say Hebe." New York Times, September 12, 1971.

THE SIOUX ARE SILENT,
BOY GENERAL WITH THE GOLDEN LOCKS

by James G. Igoe

Reprinted by permission from North Country Libraries,
March-April 1971, p. 2-10.

In January of 1971, 160 public libraries in Vermont, New Hampshire, and Maine filled out and returned a questionnaire. The answers to this survey of service to the French-Canadian community were fascinating, albeit bleak, with many indications of amazing attitudes among the public librarians of this area.

I accepted all answers as true because they are, in all probability, true to the librarian's perceptions, if not to the ethnic cultural reality in which the library functions. The picture produced is obviously distorted but the distortion is toward conservatism. Few humans exaggerate the poor job they are doing; the sinful tendency is rather to pretence to a higher quality than we actually possess. In other words, the error is toward inflation of service and toward depression of unmet need and unanswered patron, not vice-versa.

A. Let's look carefully at the tabular summation of answers to a few of the basic questions from the 26 libraries reporting the largest French-speaking community in their service area:

% French-Speaking (% French Background)		Vols. in Public Library	% in French (% with French or Fr.-Canadian Orientation)		Maga-zines	% in French or with French-Canadian Orientation
20%	(40%)	40,000	0%	(0%)	100	0
50	(80)	28,893	1	(-)	57	0
22	(22)	10,932	0	(0)	30	0

% French-Speaking (% French Background)	Vols. in Public Library	% French (% with French or Fr.-Canadian Orientation)		Magazines	% in French or with French-Canadian Orientation
50% (50%)	200,000	1%	(2%)	850	1
35 (50)	5,000	0	(0)	20	0
80 (80)	9,143	0	(10)	25	0
12 (33)	18,000	0	(0)	45	0
40 (50)	6,816	2	(0)	-	0
17 (33)	22,000	0	(0)	18	0
65 (80)	3,123	0	(0)	10	0
13 (15)	54,555	0	(0)	218	0
33 (--)	24,000	-	(-)	40	-
60 (75)	11,650	0	(0)	25	0
65 (80)	48,000	2	(1)	100	1
20 (50)	25,132	0	(0)	101	1
25 (50)	31,529	1	(0)	105	0
15 (20)	76,000	0	(0)	90	0
95 (95)	14,614	3	(0)	2	0
40 (50)	--	0	(0)	0	0
30 (35)	8,000	-	(4)	28	0
30 (35)	1,200	1	(0)	41	0
10 (60)	61,000	0	(-)	100	0
90 (90)	7,000	0	(0)	20	0
33 (50)	10,000	1	(1)	25	0
22 (30)	33,572	1	(1)	91	5
25 (25)	8,000	0	(0)	20	0

B. Only two of the 160 public libraries replied yes to the question "Do you conduct any programs aimed especially at the French-Canadian community? Such as: story hours, discussion clubs, films, adult education, others? In French? In English? Mixed?

C. The most fascinating insights into the relationships between the public library of Northern New England and the French-Canadian community come from the spontaneous comments made by the librarians to an open-ended question at the end of the survey. Analyze these statements; many are stunning in their assumptions and implications.

A frequent, almost self-defensive response was:
1. "This questionnaire does not apply to our area."
2. "What is behind this questionnaire?"

3. "This survey does not concern us because this is an old New England town with very few French or French-Canadians. "
4. "There may be some French names but there are no French or French-Canadians in town. "
5. And several librarians had asked their board and the board said it was not pertinent to their town and to send it back without figures.

D. There and not:

"Do you consider the French-Canadian community in your service area to be numerically large enough to justify special services, programs, or materials aimed at them?"

1. "We see no such need. " (In a community with 25% French background.)
2. "No. We have no requests for French material. Most people in our area read and write in English. Few speak French." (In a community 13% French-speaking and 33% with French background.)
3. "No. " (French-speaking 33%; French background 50%.)
4. "No. The French-Canadian element is nearly non-existent in our white collar community. " (Librarian estimate: less than 1%; U. S. Census 1960 shows Canadian foreign stock of 20-29%.)
5. "We do not have French-Canadian or French-speaking people in our town. " (U. S. 1960 Census: 10-19%.)
6. "No. Most are second generation and speak and read English. " (Librarian's estimate: 10-20%; U. S. Census: 20-29%.)
7. "Would not think there is a need. " (20% French-speaking or background.)

E. Difficulty of community concept:

1. "No such community noticeable. " (25% French-background.)
2. "There is a large number of French-Canadians. But they seem well mixed into the general population. The few who do want to read French materials are the well-educated families trying to preserve a French heritage, or the few (8 or 10) new families from Quebec. "

3. "We do not have a French-Canadian community.
We do have people with a French background. "
(80% French-speaking and 80% French background.)

4. "In spite of the low percentage of Poles (4%), they
have more clubs, activities, and civic involvement
than any other ethnic group. " (French-Canadians
22%.)

5. "While the number of French background persons
is large, they no longer speak French at home, are
no longer taught Canadian history in schools; young
people do not join the various French-Canadian societies. "

6. "Integrated. No real F. C. Community. " (Just
before complaint that large number never learn to
speak English.)

7. "The French-Canadians here are losing their cultural solidity through inter-marriage in the community. Most are third-generation. They are not
unified, except, possibly, politically. "

8. "The community seems quite contented to be U. S.
citizens and the U. S. is their main interest. "

9. "One whole community not separated into different
nationalities. " (11% French-speaking; 21% French
background.)

10. "They don't seem to function as a community. I
don't think they have real leaders.... I find these
questions hard to answer. There is no special
French-Canadian community. The French are active
in our town. Many are leaders in PTA and 4H
work. They join other organizations and use the
library, reading English books. In the past there
were some who didn't speak English, but I don't
think that is true now. "

11. "There is no French-Canadian community here.
There are a few with a F-C background but I doubt
if they can even speak French any more. Should
any ethnic minorities materialize, we would attempt
to have something for them--should they request it. "

12. "The French-Canadian community ... is quite well
integrated with the community as a whole. There
are, I suspect, many French-oriented and French
organized activities in the city which are not known
to me. "

13. "French-Canadians thoroughly integrated into community. "

F. But everybody gets poor service:

    1. "Our library is open one hour per week. Only $25 given me to spend on books yearly."

    2. "The whole community is so tiny that one can not separate various groups. The library is not very well attended. We are trying to improve this." (1964 volumes; 5 magazines.)

G. Where do you get materials to meet this slight demand?

    1. "Have obtained French books from bookmobile."

    2. "We have Canadian materials supplied by the Canadian embassy."

    3. "If the French speaking patrons want books we try to borrow them from the State Library for them. We have considered subscribing to magazines in French but find that not too many of them would be borrowed."

    4. "We borrow from the State Library."

    5. "Whenever I hear of a prospective journey or interest (re Canada) I obtain a good supply of pertinent material from the State Library; this is used and appreciated."

H. How does the French-Canadian community obtain info and material "other than through the library"?

    1. "... these few take in the French program on TV as well as radio."

    2. "Adult education in the school system."

    3. "... our neighboring community has a large French community and therefore handles their needs. French people in our community go there for any organized groups or services other than the library. At our library we have had no requests for any French material other than one class in school."

I. What you want is wrong!

    1. "An approach to the typical working man would do more to help the French-Canadians than a program with an ethnic appeal."

    2. "The French-Canadian people in our community have been here just as long as any of the other people, and to separate them and treat them differently from everyone else would seem very strange

to members of other minority groups. " (French-
surnamed librarian.)

3. "Why is it necessary to distinguish people of this
background, to separate them? Why should there
be any group working with the French-Canadians?
Unless there is a specific language problem, why
invite a differentiation of various ethnic groups?
We don't have special programs for the Germans,
Britains, Italians, etc. "

4. "They are far enough removed from being French-
Canadians so that they are doing very nicely being
northern New Hampshire citizens using the English
language. They need trade books rather than French
language books, how to fix and make things, ways
to make a living. "

5. "There are about a dozen families with French-
Canadian background but not to my knowledge looking
for special treatment because of their background.
They patronize the library on equal footing with all
other ethnic groups. "

6. "This town is not large enough to have any groups
distinguished by racial background or language. "

7. "Most people are second or third generation and
would not want to be singled out as they consider
themselves Americans. "

J. And a pecking order:

1. "He said though he is Canadian born of French
descent, he considers himself Franco-American as
distinguished from unnaturalized residents whom he
would call French-Canadians. I think this indicates
the reason for my feeling that this community,
though largely represented by people of French
descent, would not be interested in special materials or programs with French-Canadian orientation. "

2. and e contra "... [T]hese people are proud of
their French-Canadian background. We are within
5-20 minutes drive of the Canadian border; many
were born in Canada; some of the present school
children do not speak the language of their parents,
while others learn that as a first language. I have
had many children come to the first grade unable
to speak a single word in English. "

3. "Most of the laborers are not interested in learning
English. Many who have lived here for some time
do not speak English!"

4. "The people who are bi-lingual read books in English. Most of the people who can speak only French cannot read in any language. I doubt if they would come if I had a program for them."

5. "I am not French and I think the only way the poor, uneducated French people can be reached is by someone who is also French and who is also not too well educated or well off. The extension service had poor luck until they used such people."

6. "Some of our French background friends use the library. The majority are woodsmen who keep to themselves."

7. "The persons of French-Canadian background in this community will not be coming to the library as they are in their 70's, do not go out; many cannot read anyway."

8. "Only a very few French-Canadian pulp cutters in our area. They do not make their homes here but are transient workers."

9. "No special program needed, only a very small number of elderly would be termed illiterate, everyone speaks English, takes a share in all community activities." (25% of people speak French as well.)

10. "According to a French-Canadian, the group here 40 years or below are all for the American ways and the older ones are learning that way; some prefer to speak English rather than French."

11. "I know of only one woman who has difficulty with English.... All the others are bi-lingual." (Service and programs are thus reduced to facility in English.)

12. "No call for French-Canadian materials. Most Canadians are from other provinces. Have had requests for materials on other areas of Canada. Never for Quebec in 16 years I have been librarian here."

13. One form was returned with all reference in the questions changed from French-Canadians to French-Acadians.

14. "The (second) generation ... were ashamed to speak French and broken English. Many conquered the English language, but without help from school teachers, who had no time to give any additional help. These grew up to read only a little French. The French newspaper ceased publication. The French books at the library gathered dust on the shelves, while the language barrier diminished...."

Now these people have discovered that being bi-
lingual is a credit to make possible better employment. Again the city library has more readers of
French books. " (French-surnamed librarian.)

K. Recognition of the need:

1. "There is a need to develop a program to encourage
cultural attitudes among the parents of the young
French-Canadians in the community. From the point
of view of the library it might be well to buy current French-Canadian magazines to encourage the
people to keep up on current issues. "

L. And a reward for the surveyor:

1. "Is this something you want me to cultivate?"
2. "I would have to look into this. The French-
Canadian population has greatly diminished here-
abouts in recent years. We are about to make a
survey, which may scare up some F. C. "
3. "Thank you for stimulating our thoughts on this
matter; in the past we have been neglectful of this
group and we will try to make some changes. "

M. What then are the probable conclusions which seem indicated by this mass of data?

First, there is precious little being done by the public
library for the French-Canadian community of Northern
New England. And one or two admirable exceptions do not
change the fact that 99% of the libraries replying said they
were not doing anything.

Second, there is a larger context into which service to
this minority must be placed and that context is one of generalized, impoverished library service to the entire Northern
New England community.

Third, New England self-defensiveness emerges at a
number of points.

Fourth, Anglo-Saxon snobbery does also; there are
shadings of strong and weak self-image within the "French-
Canadian" community.

Fifth, there is great evidence of the lack of awareness
as to what constitutes "community. " To many it seems to
mean a ghetto, a Gallic "Little Italy. "

Sixth, service to the French-Canadian community is
shrunk, very frequently, in the mind of the local librarian

to the question of verbal or literal difficulty with the English language.

Seventh, the responses are out of phase with general U. S. thought by about 45 years (i. e. , the ideal is to "make them Americans just like us"). There is almost no appreciation of the richness of the contribution which the French-Canadians can make to the whole.

Eighth, the numerical reality of ethnic math is frequently not that perceived by the local librarian.

Ninth, there is a good deal of evidence in their eagerness to be accepted the French-Canadians failed to appreciate, even tended to denigrate, the value of their difference. There is some evidence that slight reversal is occurring among the more secure third generation.

Tenth, there is evidence that the problem varies greatly from community to community with the degree of integration and that a mere totaling up of the percent of French-Canadian backgrounds would not be adequate to generate a cluster of effective programs.

Epilogue

THE CATALOGING ON THE WALL

by David Peele

Reprinted by permission from Wilson Library Bulletin, April 1971, copyright (c) 1971 by the H. W. Wilson Company.

> Athletes usually have good physiques, they're all male, well-proportioned, they don't look like a librarian.
> --Nancy Seaver, as quoted in McCall's

In spite of years of talking to ourselves in the pages of our journals, Nancy's view remains the image of men in library work. New measures are called for to reach today's young men to encourage them to become librarians. When the citizens of East Orange, New Jersey, were awakened at midnight by the police because their books were long overdue--even though Harold Roth expected the call to come at 2 p. m. --the image of a new librarian had its beginning. In what follows we show the end. Fiction here not only follows truth; it catches up with and surpasses it.

Quellery Een, librarian, sat in his office. Slinki Porter, cataloger, sat on her reputation. In his left hand the famed detective-now-librarian held his treasured first edition of the Viking Portable Mickey Spillane. With his right hand he was scanning Slinki to the measured cadences of the Old Master's prose:

> ... She leaned forward to kiss me, her arms out to encircle my neck. The roar of the .45 shook the room ...

Quellery regarded Slinki's slumping form mournfully. "I always read that part too rapidly," he said to his father,

as the chief of the D. O. M. Division of the library entered
the office. "And since I've been studying at the Actor's
Studio, I must live the part and so . . . . " The famed actor-
detective-now-librarian was looking down at Slinki's corpse.

"You're carrying The Method to madness, Son, " said
his father. As the famed compiler-actor-detective-now-
librarian quickly wrote down that phrase for submission to
the Reader's Digest, the older man added, "Now if you
would read a different book. . . . "

"A different book, " repeated Quellery slowly. "But--
what else is there?" His cheeks began to redden, and his
father, knowing how sensitive Quellery was on this point,
quickly changed the subject. "Here, let's bury Slinki, " he
said. Quellery brightened with quick appreciation of his
father's tact.

He had always been grateful to his dad for pointing
out one large segment of the public completely neglected in
book and periodical acquisition policies--the dirty old men.
Quellery had responded to that need by setting up a D. O. M.
room right next to the children's corner and making his
father the chief. As a direct result the library now had
back files of Peer, Leer, Wink, See, Saw, Margery Daw,
and Squint, many from volume one number one to date.
Interlibrary loan business had, of course, quadrupled immediately, and Quellery was now chairman (and only member) of a committee whose purpose it was to get these
titles covered in the Applied Science and Technology Index.

Father and son dumped the body in a bed of quick-
lime, where the famed author-compiler-actor-detective-
now-librarian kept most of his plots. As they completed
the happy task, caretaker Whaley broke down the door.
"Dames to see you, sir, " he snorted. "Fifteen of 'em--for
the cataloging vacancy. "

Quellery shook his head in wonder. Slinki's body not
yet cold and already there were that many candidates applying for the position. It was even more remarkable because
working conditions in the Cataloging Division were not too
good. A mix-up with the supplier had delayed the delivery
of desks, so all work had to be done either standing up or
sitting on Quellery's knee. "This certainly is a work of
fiction, " he thought to himself. "Fifteen candidates!" But
even Quellery did not realize how his reputation had spread

through the American Library Association.   The erect figure, lean and sensuous hips, muscular shoulders, insolent
eyes, handsome, arrogant face--this was a man to make a
woman forget the Dewey rules.

The famed rakehell-author-compiler-actor-detective-
now-librarian looked the group over.   There was one in the
back row who, for some reason not immediately discernible
to Quellery, seemed to be a bit different.   Perhaps it was
the flimsy bikini.   Or it might have been the message the
violent poppy eyes were sending as they impudently stared
at Quellery; a message the famed interpreter-rakehell-au-
thor-compiler-actor-detective-now-librarian instantly translated.   Seizing the girl, he locked her lips in a clinging
kiss.

"Mene, mene, tekel, upharsin," she said five minutes later.   "They didn't teach you to kiss like that in the
Library of Congress."

Quickly whisking the girl into a separate room,
Quellery locked the door before his father and Whaley could
follow.
"Now, my dear," he said, "what is your name?"
"Elsie Dinsmore," said the girl.
"Mmmmm," murmured Quellery, "certainly not the
Elsie I remember.   Tell me a little about, and show me all
of, yourself.   Did you go to an accredited library school?"

"No, Mr. Een," sobbed the girl.   "And my papa
says he can't spare me.   All he lets me do is classify
books he likes to read--Memoirs of a Woman of Pleasure,
Moll Flanders, The 100 Dollar Misunderstanding, and the
like.   But Mr. Een," she added quickly, for the librarian's
face was a mask of rage at such treatment, "I still love
my papa.   I can't leave him."

"There, there, child," said Quellery.   "Why just
from hearing you talk about your father I know he'd be
happy to work here with my dad in our special room.   And
as for classifying those books, there's no real problem.
Just give them a call-girl number."

"Oh, Mr. Een," breathed Elsie.   And suddenly she
burst forth and tried to shed her state of unemployment.
"Kiss me, my fool," she moaned, as she squtched her
heaving bosom against Quellery's chest.

"That sex dialogue is terrible, Son," said his father, stepping through the door Caretaker Whaley had just broken down. "If a girl has shed her pride, her next line is not likely to be, 'Kiss me, my fool'--unless she is Groucho Marx! And what's this word 'squtched' you used? That sounds like something you do to a wasp against a pane of glass, which is not an image that will overwhelm your male readers with lust and your female readers with longing for passionate fulfillment. Worst of all, there's no clinical detail. I think you'd better leave that kind of writing to people who know how to handle it."

"I suppose it was sloppy," apologized Quellery. "I can do better; it's just that I haven't had my fix this week." Quickly thrusting Elsie into the kitchen sink with the other dirty dishes, the junkie-interpreter-rakehell ... librarian plunged a needle into his vein. As he pushed in the plunger of the syringe he thought with contentment that nowadays he needed only one of these a week. In former times, when he had merely been a junkie-interpreter-rakehell-author-compiler-detective, his daily struggle with the world had consisted only of inadequate supplies of heroin, inadequate supplies of women, irregular verbs, deadlines, up-staging, and getting sapped, slugged, and kicked in the stomach. This routine existence palled on a man who craved excitement, and he found himself mainlining it once a day. But now he was a librarian, and his days were so full of challenges and responses that he had become Toynbee's thesis personified. There was the fight against the league to Keep Our Children Undefiled when they wanted to remove The Catcher in the Rye from the shelves. There was the problem of the mayor's brother, and his failure to understand why the librarian did not want to accept his gift of twenty years' back issues of Sewage and Industrial Wastes. Then he had to cope with the information retrieval boys. The effort it took just to understand their language provided enough stimulation to set his teeth on edge for weeks--and in that position he sometimes wished he could bite them all.

"Hey," rumbled Whaley, who had just returned from breaking down all the doors still left standing in the building, "Aren't you going to see the other candidates?"

"I'll talk to them, Son," said his father. "You seem to have your hands full with--of--the first one." He had had to change the preposition because Quellery, having finished his shot, was now patting dry the somewhat damp

Elsie. With a sigh, the younger man dropped the towel.
"I'd better go with you," he said, "or you'll spend all the
time pinching them."

The three men strolled back to the office, but Quellery, rather than interviewing, did several things that would
have baffled the layman. He stood on a stepladder and
sniffed the ceiling. He feverishly enlarged a mouse hole
and stared intently into it for several minutes. He went to
the windows in front of the library and broke the third pane
of glass from the left.

"Those things you're doing would baffle the layman,
Quellery," said his father. "I must confess I'm mystified
too. I trust you'll reveal the purpose of it all when you tell
us the name of the person you've chosen as cataloger."

"Oh, all that was just for my story, Dad," said
Quellery. "Actions such as those puzzle the reader and
throw him off the scent. They have no bearing on the facts
whatsoever. You see, I've already made my choice."
With his finger he pointed to Miss Dinsmore.

> CHALLENGE TO THE READER: You now have all
> the clues I had when I made my choice of a new
> cataloger. By the exercise of strict logic and
> deductions from the given data you should be
> able to prove Miss Dinsmore the ideally qualified
> person.
>
> --Quellery Een

The two other men and the fourteen other candidates
stared at Quellery. "But, Son," said his father, giving
voice to the horror felt by all, "she didn't graduate from
an accredited library school!"
"Nevertheless, Dad, she has everything she needs
to work here. Remember what she said when I kissed her?"
"Why yes--it was, 'Mene, mene, tekel....'"
"The handwriting on the wall," interrupted Quellery.
"Clearly a person who can handwrite on walls is ideally
suited to affix call numbers in a Cataloging Division with
no desks."
As his father gasped at this brilliant piece of reasoning, Quellery pressed on: "What is Miss Dinsmore's
first name?"
"Elsie."
"Say it rapidly."

"Elsie, Elsie, Elsie ... L. C. !" exploded his father. "My stars, the Library of Congress--built right into her!"

"And finally, when I took her out of the sink how was she?"

"How was she?" repeated his father. "How was she? ... You were drying her off afterwards; she must have been wet."

"Not 'wet,' Dad," said the librarian. "Reread the passage. She was just 'somewhat damp.' In other words, Dewey."

There was a silence. In fact, the rest is silence.

CONTRIBUTORS

Z. P. BARYSHNIKOVA works in the Department of Book Hygiene and Restoration at the State V. I. Lenin Library of the USSR in Moscow.

SANFORD BERMAN is librarian of the Institute of Social Research Library, Makere University, Kampala, Uganda, and a well known contributor to the counter-culture movement in libraries.

DR. RALPH BLASINGAME is associate dean and professor at Rutgers Graduate School of Library Service.

DOROTHY BRODERICK, a well known commentator on the passing scene of library science, and more particularly on intellectual freedom, is on the faculty of the School of Librarianship at Dalhousie University, Halifax, Nova Scotia, Canada.

HERBERT COBLANS has written on and about English libraries and the world of library science for many years and is a well known commentator and lecturer.

JOHN Y. COLE is the technical officer in the Reference Department of the Library of Congress.

RICHARD EMERY is social sciences librarian at University College, Cardiff, England.

RENEE FEINBERG is school librarian, I. S. 55, Ocean Hill-Brownsville, Brooklyn, New York.

CAROLINE J. FELLER is assistant professor of librarianship at the University of Oregon, Eugene, specializing in children's literature.

FEMINISTS ON CHILDREN'S LITERATURE is "a collective of women who are preparing a list of non-sexist children's books." The collective includes mothers, high school students, librarians, and other professionals in writing, publishing, and education.

466

D. J. FOSKETT is librarian of the Institute of Education at the University of London.

LEONARD H. FREISER is deputy director of the Chicago Public Library.

PAUL GOOD is the author of two books, Once to Every Man and The American Serfs, as well as articles in various magazines.

DANIEL GORE is director of the Macalester College Library in St. Paul, Minnesota.

JAMES G. IGOE is director of the Vermont Department of Libraries.

MARY KINGSBURY, formerly assistant professor of library science at the University of Portland, is now a doctoral student at the University of Oregon.

F. W. LANCASTER is a professor in the School of Library Science, University of Illinois.

ELLSWORTH MASON is director of library services at Hofstra University in Hempstead, New York.

VIRGIL F. MASSMAN is director of libraries at the University of South Dakota.

CAROL A. NEMEYER is senior associate, Education and Library Services of the Association of American Publishers, in New York City.

PETER D. OLCH, M. D. is deputy chief, History of Medicine Division, National Library of Medicine, in Bethesda, Maryland.

SHIRLEY OLOFSON, before her untimely death in late 1971, was a well known contributor to the library literature and a beloved Kentucky librarian.

DAVID R. OLSON is head of public services at the University of South Dakota Library.

DAVID PEELE is librarian, Staten Island Community College.

ANTHONY RALSTON is chairman of the Department of Computer Science at the State University of New York at Buffalo.

JACK SHADBOLT, one of Canada's best known artists for many years, has published a book on the creative process in the work cycle of art entitled, In Search of Form.

WELBY SMITH is currently a partner in Smith-Mattingly Corporation, a Washington, D. C. media production firm. He has worked in film, commercial broadcasting and telecasting and audio production.

I. A. WARHEIT is presently program administrator of Information Systems Marketing, Data Processing Division, IBM, in San Jose, California. In the past he was chief librarian for the AFC and was the chairman of SLA's documentation division.

CELESTE WEST is editor of Synergy, the San Francisco-based magazine which is an answer to the dullness in library literature.

CARL WHITE is the coordinator of collection development at the University of California, San Diego.

PATSY WILLEY, originally a New York State librarian, is now director of a library in Fairbanks, Alaska.